CLARENDON LAW SERIES

Edited by

TONY HONORÉ AND JOSEPH RAZ

CLARENDON LAW SERIES

The Concept of Law
By H. L. A. HART

Introduction to Roman Law
By BARRY NICHOLAS

Legal Reasoning and Legal Theory
By NEIL MacCORMICK

Natural Law and Natural Rights
By JOHN G. FINNIS

The Foundations of European Community Law (2nd edition)
By T. C. HARTLEY

The Law of Property (2nd edition)
By F. H. LAWSON AND BERNARD RUDDEN

An Introduction to the Law of Torts (2nd edition)
By JOHN G. FLEMING

An Introduction to Administrative Law
By PETER CANE

Conflicts of Law and Morality
By KENT GREENAWALT

Bentham and the Common Law Tradition
By GERALD J. POSTEMA

An Introduction to the Law of Contract (4th edition)
By P. S. ATIYAH

The Principles of Criminal Evidence
By A. A. S. ZUCKERMAN

An Introduction to the Law of Trusts
By SIMON GARDNER

Public Law and Democracy in the United Kingdom and the United States of America
By P. P. CRAIG

Principles of Criminal Law
By ANDREW ASHWORTH

Precedent in English Law (4th edition)
By SIR RUPERT CROSS and J. W. HARRIS

Playing by the Rules
By FREDERICK SCHAUER

The Philosophical Origins of Modern Contract Doctrine

BY

JAMES GORDLEY

CLARENDON PRESS · OXFORD

1991

Oxford University Press, Walton Street, Oxford OX2 6DP
Oxford New York Toronto
Delhi Bombay Calcutta Madras Karachi
Petaling Jaya Singapore Hong Kong Tokyo
Nairobi Dar es Salaam Cape Town
Melbourne Auckland
and associated companies in
Berlin Ibadan

Oxford is a trade mark of Oxford University Press

Published in the United States
by Oxford University Press, New York

British Library Cataloguing in Publication Data
Gordley, James
The philosophical origins of modern contract doctrine. —
(Clarendon law series).
1. Law. Theories
I. Title
340.1
ISBN 0–19–825664–7

Library of Congress Cataloging in Publication Data
Gordley, James.
The philosophical origins of modern contract doctrine /
James Gordley.
(Clarendon law series)
Includes bibliographical references and index.
1. Contracts—History. I. Title. II. Series.
K840.G67 1991 346.'02–dc20 [342.62] 90–21224
ISBN 0–19–825664–7

Set by Hope Services (Abingdon) Ltd.
Printed in Great Britain by
Biddles Ltd, Guildford and King's Lynn

ACKNOWLEDGEMENTS

I WOULD like to thank for their suggestions and encouragement John Barton, Robert Cooter, Robert Feenstra, Scott FitzGibbon, Phillip Johnson, Stephan Kuttner, Blanche Lutz, Hilary Martin, Walter Pakter, Michael Sherwin, Michael Smith, and Peter Stern. I owe special thanks to Harry Davidow, Augustine Thompson, and my wife Barbara for their careful reading of my manuscript. I am also grateful to those who first interested me in comparative legal history, and particularly to Harold Berman, John Dawson, and Arthur von Mehren.

J.G.

CONTENTS

1
INTRODUCTION

WITH the enactment of the Chinese Civil Code, systems of private law modelled on those of the West will govern nearly the entire world. Western legal systems, moreover, are much alike. Both 'common law' systems such as those of England and the United States and 'civil law' systems such as those of France, Italy and Germany have a similar doctrinal structure based on similar legal concepts. They divide private law into certain large fields such as property, tort, and contract, and analyse these fields in a similar way. Problems of property law are approached by distinguishing ownership from possession. Tort liability is discussed by distinguishing fault from strict liability and by requiring that the defendant's conduct be the proximate or adequate cause of the plaintiff's harm. The formation of a contract is analysed by applying doctrines of mistake, fraud, duress, and offer and acceptance. The obligations of the contracting parties are determined by using general canons of interpretation and by holding the parties to a set of 'implied terms' to be found in the law of sale, lease, or whatever other type of contract they have entered into. The enforceability of a contract is determined, *inter alia*, by a distinction between gift and exchange. The organization of the law and its larger concepts are alike even if particular rules are not. Accordingly, though answers may differ, the problem of whether a boy is liable for injuring a playfellow or a seller is liable for defects in his merchandise is analysed in much the same way in Hamburg, Montpellier, Manchester, and Tucson, or for that matter in New Delhi, Tel Aviv, Tokyo, and Jakarta.

The origin of this common doctrinal structure is, at present, something of a mystery. Supposedly, the common law developed through the decisions of English courts. The civil law was based on the Roman texts of the *Corpus iuris civilis* of the Emperor Justinian, which was in force in most parts of continental Europe before civil codes were enacted nearly everywhere in the late eighteenth and nineteenth centuries. Nevertheless, one cannot find the doctrinal structure just described in either the English court decisions before the nineteenth century or in the Roman texts. Before the nineteenth century, English law was organized not by general concepts of property, tort, and contract, but by 'forms of action' such as trespass and assumpsit. The Roman law of the *Corpus iuris* contains many particular rules, a few general maxims, but hardly any systematic doctrine.

It is true that, when one already has the modern doctrinal structure in mind, one can describe the law of the pre-nineteenth-century English courts or the ancient Romans in its terms. Nevertheless, the English courts and the Roman jurists themselves did not do so. For example, today, the world over, lawyers organize much of their discussion of contract law around the principle that contracts are formed by consent. It often mattered to the English judges and Roman jurists, of course, whether a party had consented. In English law, a person who broke a promise was liable in an action of assumpsit. In Roman law, consent to an object and price constituted a contract of sale. One can therefore regard English rules about assumpsit and Roman rules about sale as instances of the principle that the parties must consent to be bound to a contract. The English and the Romans themselves, however, did not state their law in such general terms. Similarly, when a contracting party is in error or has been defrauded or coerced, courts today grant him relief by applying general doctrines of mistake, fraud, and duress. Pre-nineteenth-century English judges and Roman jurists gave relief in similar situations. But they formulated no general doctrines.

The gap that lies between these larger doctrines and concepts and the Roman texts or English case law has been recognized only in this century. Among continental legal historians the recognition came only after 1900, when, with the enactment of the German Civil Code, the Roman texts ceased to be in force. Before that time, scholars tended to miss the difference between saying that a Roman text could be cited to illustrate a particular doctrine and saying that the ancient Romans themselves had formulated that doctrine. The English legal historian Maitland did see this difference. He knew that the judges who created the English forms of action did not have 'the great elementary conceptions, ownership, possession, contract, tort and the like', distinctly in mind. He concluded that these conceptions had somehow evolved from the English forms of action, although he acknowledged that the history of how they evolved had yet to be written.[1] As Charles Donahue has observed, 'we know a considerable amount more today than we did when Maitland wrote. . . . What we have learned, however, is puzzling.

[1] F. W. Maitland, 'Why the History of English Law is Not Written', in *The Collected Papers of Frederic William Maitland*, ed. H. A. L. Fisher (1911; repr. Buffalo, 1981), i. 480 at 484.

Relatively little of the history of the forms of action seems to deal with "the great elementary conceptions," like ownership, possession, tort and contract.'[2] A question therefore arises:

> [T]here can be little doubt that there are great elementary conceptions, both in our law and, with some modifications, in the law of the Continent, and if their evolution is to be found only in part, perhaps in rather small part, in the history of the forms of action, where is the story of their evolution to be found?[3]

This study will provide an answer, although not one that fits easily with many popular notions about legal history. In the sixteenth and early seventeenth centuries, a fairly small group of theologians and jurists centred in Spain self-consciously attempted to synthesize the Roman legal texts with the moral theology of Thomas Aquinas. The fundamental concepts and doctrines of private law with which we are familiar are a simplification of the synthesis they achieved. This book will show that this is the origin of present-day contract doctrine, and I believe a similar story can be told of the emergence of the modern law of property and tort.

Thomas Aquinas was a thirteenth-century Dominican friar. Shortly before his birth, Aristotle's works on metaphysics, physics, politics, and ethics first became available in the West. They touched off the sort of storm we associate with the work of Newton or Darwin. Thomas, it is commonly said, baptized Aristotle. He achieved a synthesis between the Greek philosophical tradition that Aristotle represented and the religious tradition of Christianity.

The *Corpus iuris civilis* of Justinian had been rediscovered and had become the object of academic study about two hundred years before Thomas was born. This revival of Roman law affected almost every aspect of medieval religious and political life. Intellectually, it contributed to a preoccupation with law that is apparent in the work of Thomas. Nevertheless, no genuine synthesis between Roman law and Thomistic or Aristotelian philosophy took place until the end of the Middle Ages.

In the sixteenth and early seventeenth centuries, a synthesis finally was achieved by a group of theologians and jurists known to historians as the 'late scholastics' or the 'Spanish natural law school'. The greatest representatives of this school were Francesco de Vitoria, Diego de Covarruvias, Domingo de Soto, Luis de Molina,

[2] Charles Donahue, 'Why the History of Canon Law is Not Written', Selden Society Lecture delivered in the Old Hall of Lincoln's Inn, 3 July 1984, London, 1986, 6.

[3] Ibid. 6.

and Leonard Lessius. They built a system of doctrines Thomistic and Aristotelian in ground plan and Roman in much of its detail. They thus gave Roman law a systematic doctrinal organization which it had previously lacked. In the works of Molina and Lessius, the synthesis became so complete that these works can be described with equal accuracy as treatises on Aristotelian and Thomistic moral philosophy annotated to Roman law, or as treatises on Roman law in which the particular rules are organized and presented as illustrations of Thomistic and Aristotelian principles.[4]

In the seventeenth and eighteenth centuries, the doctrines of the late scholastics were taken over and popularized by members of the northern natural law school such as Hugo Grotius, Samuel Pufendorf, and Jean Barbeyrac. From the works of these authors, or of those they influenced such as Jean Domat and Robert Pothier, these doctrines made their way into the modern common and civil law. In the nineteenth century, for the first time, common lawyers wanted a doctrinal system. They created one by borrowing extensively from Grotius, Pufendorf, Barbeyrac, Domat, and Pothier. They then cited English cases to illustrate the doctrines they had borrowed—doctrines which the courts surely did not have in mind when these cases were decided. The drafters of the French Civil Code borrowed almost two-thirds of that document and nearly all the provisions on contracts from Pothier and Domat. These provisions were then declared to be 'the will of the legislator', and almost all the efforts of nineteenth-century French jurists were devoted to interpreting them. Nineteenth-century German jurists devoted their energy to building as perfect a doctrinal system as they could. They did so by refashioning the doctrinal system they had inherited from the previous century. The doctrines of the nineteenth-century common and civil lawyers, with various modifications, endured into the twentieth century and have now been disseminated throughout the world.

This account of the origins of modern legal doctrine will seem odd to those who are used to economic explanations of legal change. None of the changes we shall consider had much economic significance. What did change was the way contract law was understood.

This account will also seem odd to those who have read a good deal of legal history without ever encountering Aristotle or Thomas Aquinas or the late scholastics. Nevertheless, it is an account

[4] Thus, as Molina said on the flyleaf of his book, perhaps at the instance of his publishers, it was an 'Opus non solum Studiosis, Theologis, Canonistis; verum etiam Legum Latarum Doctoribus in utroque foro, tam Ecclesiastico, quam Seculari versantibus, apprime utile et necessarium'.

towards which the work of various modern scholars has been moving. English scholars have a traditional bias in favour of gradual change and against foreign influence. They have long recognized, however, that a marked change did occur in the nineteenth century. Few of the modern doctrines of contract or tort law existed before then in anything like their present form. In 1975, in his article 'Innovation in Nineteenth Century Contract Law',[5] Simpson showed that the nineteenth-century common lawyers were borrowing extensively from seventeenth- and eighteenth-century natural lawyers and from those they influenced: from Grotius, Pufendorf, Barbeyrac, Domat, and Pothier.

Continental legal historians have long recognized that nineteenth-century French and German jurists also borrowed from the seventeenth- and eighteenth-century natural lawyers. They are finally recognizing the debt that the natural lawyers owed to the late scholastics. It was once thought that the systematic doctrine began with the founder of the northern natural law school, Hugo Grotius. Few paid attention when Josef Kohler discussed the importance of the late scholastics in 1917.[6] More attention was paid to an article by Hans Thieme in 1953 that made the same point.[7] It inspired Malte Diesselhorst to investigate the sources of Grotius's ideas about promises,[8] and Robert Feenstra the sources of his ideas about mistake and unjust enrichment.[9] In 1967 the German historian Franz Wieacker acknowledged the seminal role of the late scholastics in the second edition of his leading treatise on legal history, *Privatrechtsgeschichte der Neuzeit*.[10] In 1973 Paolo Grossi organized a conference in Florence to consider the work of the late scholastics. It began with an address by Hans Thieme. There are instances in legal history, Thieme said, when an achievement is not

[5] Simpson, 'Innovation in Nineteenth Century Contract Law', *Law Quarterly Review*, 91 (1975), 247.

[6] Kohler, 'Die spanischen Naturrechtslehrer des 16. un 17. Jahrhunderts', *Archiv für Rechts- und Wirtschaftsphilosophie*, 10 (1916/17), 235.

[7] Thieme, 'Natürliches Privatrecht und Spätscholastik', *Zeitschrift der Savigny-Stiftung für Rechtsgeschichte Romanistische Abteilung*, 70 (1953), 230.

[8] M. Diesselhorst, *Die Lehre des Hugo Grotius vom Versprechen*, Forschungen zur neueren Privatrechtsgeschichte, 6 (Cologne, 1959).

[9] Feenstra, 'L'Influence de la scolastique espagnole sur Grotius en droit privé: quelques expériences dans des questions de fond et de forme, concernant notamment les doctrines de l'erreur et de l'enrichissement sans cause', in *La seconda scolastica nella formazione del diritto privato moderno* (Florence, 16–19 October 1972), ed. P. Grossi (Milan, 1973), 377.

[10] F. Wieacker, *Privatrechtsgeschichte der Neuzeit under besonderer Berücksichtigung der deutschen Entwicklung*, 2nd edn. (Göttingen, 1967), 266, 270–1, 291, 293–7.

recognized for decades or even centuries. One such instance is the work of the late scholastics.[11]

Certainly, it is a long road from the *Summa theologica* of Saint Thomas to the *Jus Naturae et Gentium* of Hugo Grotius, and we do not wish to deny the differences between the one and the other. But there are also many points of convergence between the original scholasticism [of Thomas] and the natural law of rationalism, and the mediator between them was Spanish scholasticism.[12]

A careful study of late scholastic concepts of contract and promise and their relationship to those of Grotius has since been done in a thesis by Paolo Cappellini.[13] Writers who still disregard the work of the late scholastics are drawing criticism.[14]

It is not fanciful, then, to identify the late scholastics as the builders of a doctrinal system that, after various modifications, is still with us. That is precisely what one would expect if there are large and fundamental concepts shared by modern common and civil law; if Donahue and others are right that they did not emerge from the common law forms of action; if modern Roman law scholars are right that they were not found in the *Corpus iuris*; if Simpson is right that the nineteenth-century common lawyers borrowed many of these concepts from the northern natural lawyers; if continental historians are right that nineteenth-century civil lawyers did the same; and if Thieme, Feenstra, Wieacker, and many others are right that the northern natural lawyers borrowed from the late scholastics.

It is, however, a surprising story. Its most surprising feature is that doctrines which, in modified form, now govern most of the world were founded on philosophical ideas that fell from favour centuries ago. Indeed, in their original form these doctrines depended directly on Aristotelian and Thomistic moral conceptions about

[11] Thieme, 'Qu'est-ce que nous, les juristes, devons à la seconde scolastique espagnole?' in *La seconda scolastica nella formazione del diritto privato moderno* (Florence, 16–19 October 1972), ed. P. Grossi (Milan, 1973), 7 at 20.

[12] Ibid. 7, n. 11.

[13] P. Cappellini, *Scemi contrattuali e cultura theologico-giuridica nella seconda scolastica: verso una teoria generale*. Thesis, University of Florence, 1978/9.

[14] e.g. K. Nanz, *Die Entstehung des allgemeinen Vertragsbegriff im 16. bis 18. Jahrhundert*, Beiträge zur neueren Privatrechtsgeschichte, 9 (Munich, 1985); criticized in I. Birocchi, *Saggi sulla formazione storica della categoria generale del contratto* (Cagliari, 1988), 25. As Birocchi notes, Nanz is not oblivious to the role of the late scholastics. After explaining that 'the essential elements of the modern concept of contract law can be traced to Grotius' (p. 139), Nanz observes that 'Grotius supported himself—as Diesselhorst has shown—on the doctrine of the late Spanish scholastics, and in particular, on that of Molina and the Dutchman Lessius' (pp. 142–3). One wonders, then, why a fuller account of this doctrine is not given in his book.

virtue and metaphysical conceptions about the nature or essence of things. Making a contract, for example, was an exercise of the virtue of liberality by which one enriched another, or of the virtue of commutative justice by which one exchanged things of equal value. Each type of contract had a certain 'nature' or 'essence' from which certain obligations followed. In the seventeenth century, even as these doctrines were being disseminated in northern Europe, the moral and metaphysical ideas on which they were based were called into question by Descartes, Hobbes, Locke, and others. This attack ultimately broke the authority of Aristotle. In the mid-seventeenth century, Hobbes complained that 'the Philosophy-schooles, through all the Universities of Christendome', followed Aristotle.[15] Pufendorf complained that most educated people regarded Aristotelian philosophy as a summit beyond which the human mind could scarcely advance.[16] By the mid-eighteenth century that philosophy had lost its hold on the schools and on educated people alike. By the nineteenth century it was all but unintelligible.

One would have expected the legal doctrines founded on this philosophy to fall along with it or else to be reformulated under the influence of more modern philosophical ideas. But that is not what happened. As we will see, throughout the seventeenth and eighteenth centuries the doctrines remained much as the late scholastics had left them. Jurists such as Pufendorf and Barbeyrac jettisoned Aristotle's metaphysics and moral philosophy, adopted various principles from the philosophies of their own day, but made only minor changes in the doctrines themselves. The doctrines drifted, cut off from their old philosophical moorings and left without any real tie to the professed philosophical beliefs of the jurists who were now disseminating them.

These doctrines were finally reformulated in the nineteenth century, but with little relation to the philosophy of Bentham, Kant, or any other thinker then popular. English, American, French, and German jurists eliminated concepts that had meaning in the context of Thomistic and Aristotelian philosophy but, in the nineteenth century, seemed wrong or unintelligible. They then bent and stretched the concepts they retained to make them do the work of those they had rejected.

In the field of contract law, with which we shall be concerned, the result was what have been called 'will theories' of contract. The will of the parties became, in Simpson's words, a sort of *Grundnorm* from which as many rules of contract law as possible were to be

[15] T. Hobbes, *Leviathan* (Cambridge, 1935), I. i. 2.

[16] S. Pufendorf, *De iure naturae et gentium libri octo* (Amsterdam, 1688), I. ii. I.

inferred.[17] The late scholastics and the natural lawyers had recognized as fundamental the principle that contracts are entered into by the will or consent of the parties. They had formulated general doctrines of mistake, fraud, and duress by considering how these influences affect the will. The nineteenth-century innovation was not to pay attention to the will but to reject other concepts of Aristotelian origin that had previously figured in contract doctrine. Making a contract was regarded simply as an act of will, not as the exercise of a moral virtue. The parties were bound simply to what they willed, not to obligations that followed from the essence or nature of their contract.

No doubt, modern philosophy created an intellectual environment in which the concept of will seemed perfectly acceptable whereas these other concepts did not. That, however, seems to be the limit of what modern philosophy has contributed to the reformulation of doctrine in the nineteenth century. No school of jurists formulated doctrine by applying the principles of Kant or Bentham as late scholastics had applied the principles of Thomas, and the attempts of Kant and Bentham themselves to do so were generally ignored. Indeed, in the absence of consensus among philosophers, jurists became wary: They tried to do their job without commitment to any philosophy. They claimed they were not asking philosophical questions but were simply interpreting their own positive law: the law of the Anglo-American cases, of the French Civil Code, of the Roman texts that remained in force in Germany.

In the twentieth century, a doctrinal crisis began that is still with us. Even as Western law spread throughout the world, Western legal scholars wondered if it was possible to have coherent legal doctrine. In the field of contract law, as we shall see, the problem was that the nineteenth-century jurists had borrowed part of the earlier doctrinal system and had not managed to make that part work by itself. They claimed to be interpreting positive law. But the positive law did not simply enforce whatever the parties willed and only what they willed—nor could it. The positive law distinguished gift from exchange and one type of exchange from another. It held the parties to obligations that depended on the type of contract they had made even if they had not willed these obligations expressly. It sometimes released the victims of unequal bargains from obligations they had willed expressly. Twentieth-century critics pointed out that the will theories could not explain these aspects of contract law. In fact, they were the very aspects that the late

[17] Simpson, *supra* n. 5, p. 266.

scholastics had explained with the Aristotelian notions of essence and virtue that the nineteenth-century jurists had discarded.

The crisis has continued because the critics found themselves unable to rebuild the edifice they had razed. Grant Gilmore summed up the current state of contract law by saying: 'The systems have come unstuck and we see, presently, no way of glueing them back together again.'[18] Yet the nineteenth-century doctrines drift on, riddled with twentieth-century qualifications and exceptions.

It is indeed surprising that our modern legal doctrines were founded originally on philosophical ideas discarded long ago. It is also surprising that in all these years no adequate substitute for these ideas has been found. Nevertheless, we can understand the history of Western legal doctrine only when we recognize that this is so. The absence of these ideas has made itself felt like the loss of an organ removed from some living creature. Jurists have responded in different ways: in the seventeenth and eighteenth centuries by repeating doctrines framed in Aristotelian terms while repudiating the principles that had given these terms meaning; in the nineteenth century by purging the Aristotelian terms; in the twentieth century by acknowledging the incoherence that the nineteenth-century purge created. For three and a half centuries, however, one of the most important facts about Western legal history has been that something is missing.

The importance of this fact appears most clearly when we consider the law of contract, and that is the reason this field has been chosen as the subject of this study. Aristotelian and Thomistic philosophy stressed intellectual order and moral virtue. When this philosophy was abandoned one might have expected trouble in fields such as criminal or tort law. But contract law deals with agreements freely entered into. If modern jurists cannot deal even with this field of law without the systems coming unstuck, then something is seriously wrong.

By understanding what is wrong, we may be able not only to understand our history, but also to shape it. If we lost something long ago which we have been unable to do without, we should try to remember what it was like. We should consider why it was so important.

[18] G. Gilmore, *The Death of Contract* (Columbus, Ohio, 1974), 102.

2
ARISTOTLE AND THOMAS AQUINAS

GREEK philosophy and Roman law contributed in different ways to the synthesis the late scholastics achieved in the sixteenth century. Roman law provided a wealth of legal detail and also gave the late scholastics an agenda. They wished to solve the problems the Romans addressed by applying larger philosophical ideas. They took the ideas themselves, however, from the philosophy of Aristotle as it had been interpreted by Thomas Aquinas.

Aristotle had discussed virtue. The late scholastics built their contract doctrines around three of the virtues he described: promise-keeping, commutative justice, and liberality. In doing so, they drew on Thomas, who had taken the first steps towards synthesis by showing how Aristotle's principles could be used to consider not only virtue, but moral law. Thomas discussed the requirements for a promise to be binding. He observed that, by promising, a party could perform either an act of liberality or an act of commutative justice. He explained how a contract could violate the equality that commutative justice requires. He showed how particular contracts, such as sale and lease, could be defined by classifying them as acts of commutative justice or liberality, and by identifying an end that each contract serves. He suggested a method for inferring from this definition the various obligations of the contracting parties.

These ideas gave the late scholastics the ground plan on which they built. We shall examine them and then their relation to some more general principles of Aristotelian and Thomistic philosophy.

Aristotle described promise-keeping when he discussed the virtue of telling the truth:

> Let us discuss . . . the truthful man. We are not speaking of the man who keeps faith in his agreements, i.e., in the things that pertain to justice or injustice (for this would pertain to another virtue), but the man who in matters in which nothing of this sort is at stake is true both in word and in life because his character is such. But such a man would seem to be as a matter of fact equitable. For the man who loves the truth, and is truthful

where nothing is at stake, will still more be truthful where something is at stake.[1]

Thus, a person who breaks his word is not truthful. If he breaks his word in matters that pertain to justice and injustice, then he is lacking in 'another virtue' as well, a virtue Aristotle later identified as commutative justice.

Similarly, Thomas Aquinas explained that promises are binding as a matter of fidelity and honesty.[2] Promise-breaking is like lying although with a distinction:

> One who promises something does not lie if he has the intention to do what he promises because he does not speak contrary to what he has in mind. If, however, he does not do what he promises, then he appears to act unfaithfully because his intention changes.[3]

Thomas, however, explained not only why it was virtuous to keep promises, but when they ought to be kept. By so doing, he went beyond Aristotle's discussion of virtue and described a moral law, a 'natural law', that governs the keeping of promises. By natural law, Thomas said, all promises are binding. Roman law did not enforce them all because 'other conditions are necessary for a man to be under a civil obligation through a promise he has made',[4] conditions that Thomas left unspecified.

To determine when a promise is binding by natural law, Thomas first explained what a promise is. He did so by identifying an end that promises serve. They permit an order to be established in which one person's actions are directed to the benefit of another. In that respect, they are like commands. By commanding, however, a person directs what another is to do for him, while by promising he directs in advance what he is to do for another.[5] A promise is thus like a law he makes for himself.[6]

The requirements for a promise to be binding follow from this description of its end. Thomas explained them in his discussions of vows, oaths, and betrothals.[7] By promising, the promisor directs his

[1] *Nicomachean Ethics*, IV. vii. 1127[a]–1127[b].

[2] Thomas Aquinas, *Summa theologica*, II–II, q. 88, a. 3; a. 3, ad 1; q. 110, a. 3, ad 5. The similarity is remarkable, since Thomas was using a revision of Robert Grosseteste's translation of the *Ethics*: J. Weisheipl, *Friar Thomas d'Aquino: His Life, Thought and Work* (New York, 1974), 380. In this translation, the reference to keeping faith in agreements was replaced by a reference to telling the truth in court. *Ethica Nicomachea*, trans. Roberti Grossetesti Lincolniensis, ed. R. Gauthier (Leiden, 1973), IV. vii, no. 13, p. 448, in *Aristoteles latinus*, ed. L. Minio-Paluello, xxvi. 1–3, fasc. 4. See Thomas Aquinas, *In decem libros Ethicorum Aristotelis ad Nicomachum expositio* (Turin, 1934), lib. 4, lec. 15.

[3] *Summa theologica*, II–II, q. 110, a. 3, ad 5.

[4] Ibid. q. 88, a. 3, ad 1.

[5] Ibid. q. 88, a. 1.

[6] Ibid. q. 88, a. 10.

[7] Ibid. q. 88 (vows); q. 89 (oaths); Suppl. q. 43 (betrothal).

relations with another. The direction of one's actions, in Aristotelian philosophy, pertains to human reason and will. Therefore, a promisor must understand the promise and consent to it. Thomas worked out the implications of this rule by applying Aristotelian ideas about understanding and choice.[8] Moreover, since promises order the relations of the promisor and the promisee, the promisor must do more than understand and consent. Unless the promisee is God, who knows human thoughts, the promisor must communicate the promise by words or other outward signs.[9] Again, since promises proceed from the reason and will of the promisor, they bind the promisor only under the circumstances in which he intended to be committed. Thomas explained this principle by drawing on Aristotle's theory of equity in the application of laws. According to Aristotle, since laws are framed in general terms but must apply under particular circumstances, cases can always arise in which a literal application would go beyond the intention of the law-giver. In such cases, Thomas explained, neither laws nor promises are binding.[10]

The late scholastics elaborated Thomas's natural law of promise-keeping to explain when a contract was binding. To explain the obligations of the contracting parties, they drew on another idea of Thomas's. By promising, a party could exercise one of two other Aristotelian virtues: commutative justice or liberality. The party's obligations depended on which virtue he was exercising.

Justice, according to Aristotle, was distributive or commutative:

> Of particular justice and that which is just in the corresponding sense, (A) one kind is that which is manifested in distributions of honour or money or the other things that fall to be divided among those who have a share in the constitution (for in these it is possible for one man to have a share either unequal or equal to that of another), and (B) one is that which plays a rectifying part in transactions between man and man. Of this there are two divisions; of transactions (1) some are voluntary and (2) others involuntary—voluntary such transactions as sale, purchase, loan for consumption, pledging, loan for use, depositing, letting (they are called voluntary because the origin of these transactions is voluntary), while of the involuntary (a) some are clandestine, such as theft, adultery, poisoning, procuring, enticement of slaves, assassination, false witness, and (b) others are violent, such as assault, imprisonment, murder, robbery with violence, mutilation, abuse, insult.[11]

[8] See Ch. 4 above, pp. 82–3, 85–7.

[9] *Summa theologica*, II–II, q. 88, a. 1.

[10] Ibid. q. 88, a. 10; q. 89, a. 9 (on when promises are binding); q. 120, a. 1 (on when laws are binding).

[11] *Nicomachean Ethics*, V. ii. 1130^{b}–1131^{a}.

According to Aristotle, distributive justice, the justice 'manifested in distributions', follows a geometrical proportion. Each citizen receives in proportion to merit. Political regimes differ, however, on what constitutes merit: 'democrats identify it with the status of freeman, supporters of oligarchy with wealth (or with noble birth), and supporters of aristocracy with excellence'.[12] In contrast, commutative or rectificatory justice follows an arithmetic proportion. One person has too much and another too little. He has too much in involuntary transactions because he has taken something from the other, in voluntary transactions because things of unequal value have been exchanged. Justice is done by taking the amount necessary to restore equality from one party and giving to the other.[13]

According to Thomas, when a person promises to transfer property to another in the future, or consents to do so in the present,[14] he exercises either the virtue of commutative justice or that of liberality:

Voluntary commutations are when a man voluntarily transfers his thing to another. And if he transfer it simply so that the recipient incurs no

[12] Ibid. v. iii. 1131^{a}.

[13] Ibid. v. iv. 1131^{b}–1132^{b}. Thomas's discussion is similar: *Summa theologica*, II–II, q. 61, a. 2. He gives a more general reason for the distinction between distributive and commutative justice. The individual is a part of the community, and so one can distinguish an order of the whole community to each part, which is directed by distributive justice, and an order of one part to another, which is directed by commutative justice. (Ibid., q. 61, a. 1.)

[14] As already noted, Thomas thought that some of the contracts that Roman law enforced were entered into by making promises. He distinguished a promise to transfer a thing from the transfer of a thing when he discussed the difference between simple and solemn vows to enter a religious order. 'A thing ceases to be in one man's power from the fact that it passes into the power of another. Now the promise of a thing does not transfer it into the power of the person to whom it is promised, wherefore a thing does not cease to be in a person's power for the reason that he has promised it': *Summa theologica*, Suppl., q. 53, a. 1. Similarly, a simple vow is 'merely a simple promise', unlike a solemn vow, which is an actual surrender of power over oneself: ibid. There is the same distinction between betrothal, which is a promise of marriage, and marriage itself, in which 'a man surrenders himself actually to the power of his wife': ibid., ad. 1. Thus, a person who has taken a simple vow is still capable of marrying, and a person who is betrothed is still capable of taking a solemn vow, because he has not yet surrendered power over himself, although if he does so he will be guilty of breaking a promise: ibid., a. 1; a. 2. Thomas also drew this analogy between simple and solemn vows and the promise of a thing and the actual transfer of it in his Commentary on the Sentences of Peter Lombard: *Scriptum super libris Magistri Sententiarum* (Parma, 1868), lib. 4, dist. 38, q. 1, art. 3. Aubert claims there is a difference between the views Thomas expressed in the Commentary and in the *Summa theologica* (J.-M. Aubert, *Le Droit romain dans l'oeuvre de saint Thomas* (Paris, 1955), 53–7). I do not see this difference, since in the passage he cites (*Summa theologica*, II–II, q. 88, a. 7) solemn vows are also described as a surrender of oneself like marriage. The matter need not be discussed here, however, since Aubert claims that Thomas changed his mind about simple and solemn vows, not about promises to transfer things and the actual transfer of them.

debt, as in the case of gift (*donatio*), it is an act, not of justice but of liberality.[15]

Liberality, according to Aristotle, is a virtue manifested 'in the giving and taking of wealth, and especially in respect of giving'. '[T]he liberal man . . . will give for the sake of the noble and rightly; for he will give to the right people, the right amounts, and at the right time, with all the other qualifications that accompany right giving.'[16]

The obligations of the parties depended on which virtue they were exercising. Unlike acts of liberality, acts of commutative justice require equality. According to Thomas, it is a violation of this equality to sell a thing at an unjust price or with a fault in it or with undisclosed defects, and to lend at usury.[17] Thus, Thomas again moved from Aristotle's account of a virtue to a description of a moral law that a person observes when exercising this virtue. In doing so, he referred repeatedly to Roman law. In discussing the just price, he cited a Roman text that gives a remedy to those who sell land at half its value.[18] In discussing faults in an object sold, he used the Roman example of sick animals.[19] He drew a Roman distinction between concealed and manifest defects.[20] In discussing usury, he tried to explain why, although lending at interest is evil, Roman law permits it.[21]

When the late scholastics analysed the contractual obligations of the parties, they started from Thomas's discussion of commutative justice and liberality, and particularly from his observations about equality. In doing so, they relied upon a method that they also borrowed from Thomas. The method proceeded by defining an object of study and then extracting consequences from the definition. Particularly contracts such as sale or gift were defined by classifying them as acts of commutative justice or liberality and by identifying an end that the contract serves. The obligations of the parties could be determined when the definition was known.

Thomas defined a number of contracts familiar from Roman law:

A voluntary transfer belongs to justice insofar as it includes the notion of a debt. This may occur in three ways. First, one may simply transfer his thing to another in exchange for another thing, as happens in sale and purchase

[15] *Summa theologica*, II–II, q. 61, a. 3.

[16] *Nicomachean Ethics*, IV. i, 1119^b–1120^a. Thomas discusses liberality in a similar way: *Summa theologica*, II–II, q. 117, aa. 2–4.

[17] Ibid. q. 77, aa. 1–3; q. 78, a. 1.

[18] C. 4.44.2; cited in *Summa theologica*, II–II, q. 77, a. 1, obj. 1 & ad 1.

[19] *Summa theologica*, II–II, q. 77, a. 2. Sick animals were discussed in D. 21.1.38.

[20] *Summa theologica*, II–II, q. 77, a. 3. The distinction is drawn in D. 21.1.14.10.

[21] *Summa theologica*, II–II, q. 78, a. 1.

(*venditio et emptio*). Second, one may transfer his thing to another so that the latter may have the use of it with the obligation of returning it to its owner. If one grants the use of the thing gratuitously, the transaction is called usufruct (*ususfructus*) in things that bear fruit, and simply loan for consumption (*mutuum*) in things that do not bear fruit such as money, pottery, and so forth. If, however, not even the use is granted gratis, the transaction is called lease and hire (*locatio et conductio*). Third, one may transfer his thing to receive it back again, not so that it can be used, but so that it can be kept safe, as in a deposit (*depositum*), or because of an obligation, as when one obligates his thing by a pledge (*pignus*), or stands surety for another (*pro alio fideiubet*).[22]

Thomas must have written this passage with Roman law in mind. All of the transactions he mentions were familiar from Roman law, and though most of them were also mentioned by Aristotle in the paragraph quoted earlier, *ususfructus* and *fideiussio* were not.[23]

The most significant difference between this paragraph and Aristotle's, however, is that, while Aristotle illustrates by naming specific transactions, Thomas defines these transactions. He does so by identifying an end that each transaction serves and a larger type to which it belongs: it is an act of commutative justice or an act of liberality.

Although Thomas never wrote a treatise on the law governing these contracts, the late scholastics found it easy to imagine how he would have proceeded. He would have started from these definitions. He would have tried to show that each contract carries with it a set of obligations that follow from its definition. Either these obligations are included in the concepts used to formulate the definitions, or they are means to the end in terms of which the contract has been defined.

Aristotle had developed this method of analysis. Thomas used it to examine the moral lawfulness of human actions. We have already seen an instance in his discussion of promises. He formulated a definition of promises and then used it to determine when a promise was binding. One can also see this method at work in Thomas's discussion of marriage, which is the only contract he treated in detail. He defined marriage in terms of its ends, and then explained the rules governing marriage as following from these ends. Thomas said, relying on Aristotle,[24] that marriage has two ends: a principal

[22] Ibid. q. 61, a. 3.

[23] Thus this 'liste des contrats' is not, as Aubert says, a 'simple transcription du texte de L'Ethique, v, 2, 13'. (Aubert, *supra* n. 14, p. 127, n. 1.)

[24] 'Between man and wife friendship seems to exist by nature; for man is naturally inclined to form couples—even more than to form cities, inasmuch as the household is earlier and more necessary than the city, and reproduction is more common to man

end, which is the good of the offspring, and a secondary end, which is an association of a man and woman in which each sex makes a different contribution.[25] Thomas defined marriage in terms of these ends: it is a 'joining' by which 'certain persons are directed to one begetting and upbringing of children, and again to one family life. . . .'[26] This 'joining together' is the 'essence' of matrimony.[27] An action is contrary to natural law if it 'wholly hinders' these ends or 'renders the attainment [of them] difficult or less satisfactory'.[28] For example, according to Thomas, marriage to a close relative,[29] marriage to an impotent person,[30] and dissolution of a marriage by divorce[31] are contrary to the principal end of marriage, the begetting and rearing of children. Polygamy and adultery are contrary to the secondary end, the association of the married persons.[32] These are only examples. By the time Thomas finished, he had explained much of the Canon law of marriage.

Moreover, by defining an action such as marriage in terms of its end, Thomas was able to distinguish the minimum a person must know to perform an action such as marrying from the many consequences the action might have. To be married, the spouses need to understand the essence of marriage,[33] defined by the ends for which marriage is entered into. The couple need not know all of the consequences of marriage according to Canon law. According to Thomas, however, these consequences describe what is necessary or advisable to attain the ends by which marriage is defined. The parties would normally want these consequences if they want these ends to be achieved.

As we will see, the late scholastics discussed particular contracts such as sale and lease in the same way that Thomas discussed marriage. They defined each contract in terms of its end and tried to show that a set of obligations followed from its definition. In order to contract, the parties had to understand the essence of the sale, lease, or other particular contract they entered into. If they did, however, they were then bound by all the consequences specified in the law of sales, of leases, and so forth.

with the animals. With the other animals the union extends only to this point, but human beings live together not only for the sake of reproduction but also for the various purposes of life; for from the start the functions are divided, and those of man and woman are different; so they help each other by throwing their peculiar gifts into the common stock.' (*Nicomachean Ethics*, VIII. xii. 1162^{a}.)

[25] *Summa theologica*, Suppl., q. 41, a. 1.
[26] Ibid., q. 44, a. 1.
[27] Ibid., q. 44, a. 2.
[28] Ibid., q. 65, a. 1.
[29] Ibid., q. 54, a. 3.
[30] Ibid., q. 58, a. 1.
[31] Ibid., q. 67, a. 1.
[32] Ibid., q. 65, a. 1.
[33] Ibid., q. 51, a. 2.

The late scholastic synthesis thus depended on these Aristotelian virtues and this Thomistic method. The virtues and the method were meaningful, however, only in the larger context of Aristotelian and Thomistic philosophy. Indeed, as we shall see, the late scholastic synthesis began to break down when modern philosophers called the central principles of that philosophy into question. To understand the synthesis and its breakdown, it is important to see how it depended on the Aristotelian and Thomistic picture of the world.

The world according to Aristotle and Thomas is made up of individual things technically referred to as 'substances'. People, animals, and plants are substances, as are the elements of the inorganic world which they believed to be earth, air, fire, and water.

Each of these things tends to behave in a definite way; for example, pear trees have a tendency to produce pears and no tendency at all to chase cats. Indeed, if something had no tendency to behave in any definite fashion, it would not be an individual thing. The way in which a thing tends to behave is its 'final cause' or 'end'. The 'end' of a thing, in this sense, is not a conscious purpose but simply the characteristic way the thing behaves. The pear tree has no conscious purposes, and its end is a distinctive manner of growth and reproduction, not the production of pears for people to eat.

Each thing, moreover, behaves as it does because of something within it. If it behaved as it did because of something outside it, the behaviour in question would be that not of the individual thing itself but of the something outside it. That within a thing which is responsible for how it behaves is called its 'nature'. Things with the same nature are the same kind of thing. Pear trees are one kind of thing and dogs another. Those properties that a thing must have to be a thing of a certain nature are said to belong to its 'substantial form'. It cannot lose these properties and remain the same thing. Characteristics that it can gain and lose while remaining a dog or a pear tree are 'accidents'.

When a tree burns to ashes, it loses its substantial form and becomes a different thing; and yet something remains that was present in the tree. Otherwise, one could not say the tree turns to ashes. One would have to say that the tree completely disappears and ashes appear. That which was present in the tree and remains present in the ashes is its 'material cause' or 'matter'. This 'matter' is not a form but is defined as that which can assume different forms such as that of a tree or that of ashes.

Final cause, substantial form, and matter are three of the four 'causes' that every substance must have. The remaining one is the 'efficient cause', which brings a thing into being by uniting its matter with its substantial form. The efficient cause of an animal or plant is its parents.

A thing may have many parts and many activities, and yet, to be a single thing, it must have a single substantial form and a single end. It can do so because of the way its parts and their activities are related. Each part has an 'end' or activity of its own which contributes to the activity that is the end of the whole. Each part of the pear tree contributes to the characteristic manner of growth and reproduction that is the end of the pear tree. Anything attached to the tree that did not contribute to this end, such as a pebble embedded in the bark, would not, properly speaking, be part of the pear tree. As Thomas said in one of his commentaries on Aristotle, there are two kinds of order, the order of part to whole and the order of means to ends, and the first of these is based upon the second.[34]

To know what a thing is, one must know its substantial form. One does so by forming a concept of the thing in one's mind. This concept in the mind that corresponds to the 'substantial form' is the 'essence' of a thing. When the essence is fully understood, it can be captured in a definition. A definition states the genus or general class to which a thing belongs and the specific difference that constitutes a species or distinct kind within that general class. The specific difference, Thomas explained, describes a way in which the potentialities present in the genus are realized.

By knowing the definition of a thing, one can understand why the thing has the parts and other characteristics that it does. They are included in the concepts that form the definition, or they are means to the end that such a thing must have. Thus, Aristotle said in the *Parts of Animals*:

> The fittest mode, then, of treatment is to say, a man has such and such parts, because the conception of a man includes their presence, and because they are necessary conditions of this existence, or, if we cannot quite say this, which would be best of all, then the next thing to it, namely, that it is either quite impossible for him to exist without them, or, at any rate, that it is better for him that they should be there. . . .[35]

[34] Thomas, *supra* n. 2, lib. 1, lec. 1.

[35] *Parts of Animals*, 1, i. 640^a–640^b. Aristotle speaks of the way these characteristics are related to the whole as 'hypothetical necessity'. 'For there is absolute necessity, manifested in eternal phenomena; and there is hypothetical necessity, manifested in everything that is generated by nature as in everything that is produced by art, be it a house or what it may. For if a house or other such final object is to be realized it is necessary that such and such material shall exist; and it is necessary that first this and then that shall be produced, and first this and then that set in motion, and so on in continuous succession, until the end and final result is reached, for the sake of which each prior thing is produced and exists. As with these productions of art, so also it is with the productions of nature.' (Ibid. 1. i. 639^b.)

Thus,

> the true method is to state what the definitive characters are that distinguish the animal as a whole; to explain what it is both in substance and in form, and to deal after the same fashion with its several organs; in fact, to proceed exactly the same way as we should do, were we giving a complete description of a couch.[36]

Aristotle applied this method to every subject he investigated. In the *Politics*, he called it 'the method that has hitherto guided us',[37] and 'our usual method'.[38] 'As in other departments of science, so in politics, the compound should always be resolved into the simple elements or least parts of the whole.'[39] Similarly, in the *Physics* he said, 'we do not think we know a thing until we are acquainted with its primary conditions or first principles, and have carried our analysis as far as its simplest elements'.[40] By the simplest elements, he meant, on the one hand, the concepts by which a thing is defined, and, on the other, the parts of which it is composed.[41] When he discussed virtues such as promise-keeping, commutative justice, and liberality, he was applying this method to the study of human beings. When Thomas discussed moral law by defining actions such as promising or marrying and by drawing consequences from these definitions, he was giving Aristotle's method a new application.

For Aristotle, virtues are parts of man. To understand them one must first understand what man is. The essence of man is that he is a rational animal. He acts through reason and will, unlike the pear tree, which acts without awareness, or the dog, which acts through sensation and desire. Reason is the capacity to understand the world through concepts. It enables man to understand the ends of his actions and the contribution they make to his ultimate end. Will is the capacity to choose for the sake of this ultimate end. Man's ultimate end or final cause is the life proper to such a being, a life in which his capacity for understanding and rational action is fully realized.[42]

[36] Ibid. I. i. 641^{a}.

[37] *Politics*, I. i. 1252^{a}.

[38] Ibid. I. viii. 1256^{a}.

[39] Ibid. I. i. 1252^{a}.

[40] *Physics*, I. i. 184^{a}.

[41] 'Thus we must advance from generalities to particulars; for it is a whole that is best known to sense-perception, and a generality is a kind of whole, comprehending many things within it, like parts. Much the same thing happens in the relation of the name to the formula. A name, e.g. "round," means vaguely a sort of whole: its definition analyses this into its particular senses. Similarly a child begins by calling all men "father", and all women "mother", but later on distinguishes each of them.' (*Physics*, I. i. 184^{a}–184^{b}.)

[42] *Nicomachean Ethics*, I. vii. 1097^{b}–1098^{a}.

Virtues are states of character, acquired through training, that enable man to perform the actions that contribute to his end.[43] 'Intellectual virtues' such as 'philosophic wisdom and understanding and practical wisdom' perfect his capacity to understand and to choose on the basis of what he understands. 'Moral virtues' such as temperance perfect the capacities that man shares with other animals by making them obedient to reason.[44] Each virtue, being part of man, contributes something to the fully human life that is man's end. In the *Nicomachean Ethics*, Aristotle examined the contribution of each virtue as though he were studying the organs of an animal or the parts of a couch.

Thomas discussed virtue in much the same way as Aristotle. As has often been observed, his innovation was to concern himself far more than Aristotle with moral law. As we have seen, for example, he discussed not only the virtue of keeping promises but when they ought to be kept; he discussed not only the virtue of commutative justice but when a transaction violated equality. By so doing, he elaborated the requirements of a 'natural law'.

This concern about moral law was one aspect of Thomas's Christianization of Aristotle. As Alasdair MacIntyre has said, '[w]hat Christianity requires is a conception not merely of defects of character, or vices, but of breaches of divine law, of sins'.[45] Thomas discussed moral law, however, by applying Aristotle's own method to the study of particular actions. He formulated definitions of actions such as promising or marrying. He then tried to show that the rules governing promise-keeping or marriage follow from these definitions.

To do so, he had to treat acts such as promising or marrying the way Aristotle had treated things. Aristotle had explained the features of a thing such as a couch or a man by its essence and end. According to Thomas, one could also speak of the essence and end of a human action. It seemed odd, he acknowledged, to say that an action, which is an accident of a human being, has an essence and accidents of its own. But, he said, the difficulty is merely apparent. One can speak of colour as the accident of a surface which itself is the accident of a body.[46]

[43] *Nicomachean Ethics*, I. vii. 1098^{a}; I. v. vi. 1106^{a}.

[44] Ibid. I. xiii. 1102^{b}–1103^{a}.

[45] A. MacIntyre, *After Virtue: A Study in Moral Theory* (Notre Dame, 1981), 157.

[46] Thomas explained that whenever two accidents are together in the same subject, one can be said to be an accident of the other. Sometimes they have no relation to each other. Sometimes, as in the case of colour and surface, the subject receives one accident by means of the other: *Summa theologica*, I–II, q. 7, a. 1, ad 3.

A further problem arose out of a list Aristotle had made of the 'circumstances' of a

According to Thomas, the essence of an action is defined by the end for which it is performed.[47] In that respect, an action is like a man-made thing such as a couch or a house. Such things are defined by the ends for which they are made.

To speak of the 'end' or 'final cause' of a natural thing such as a pear tree is not to speak of anyone's conscious purpose for the pear tree. It is to identify an end—as we might say now, a function—which makes it the kind of thing it is and which its parts co-operate to bring about. Similarly, an action such as swimming or a man-made thing such as a house is defined by an 'end' that makes it the kind of action or thing it is: moving through the water, or giving shelter. As in the case of the pear tree, all the parts of the swimming stroke or the house co-operate to bring about this end. In the case of an action or a man-made thing, however, this end exactly corresponds to a conscious purpose—the immediate end of proximate final cause—of the person who performs that action or makes the thing. The swimmer intends to move through the water, the architect to build something that will give shelter. He may have had many other purposes or remote ends to which this purpose was a means—he may swim for exercise or to win a race; he may build for

person's action. They were 'who he is, what he is doing, what or whom he is acting on, and sometimes also what (e.g. what instrument) he is doing it with, and to what end (e.g. he may think his act will conduce to someone's safety), and how he is doing it (e.g. whether gently or violently)'. (*Nicomachean Ethics*, III. i. 1111^a.) According to Thomas, these circumstances were the 'accidents' of an action. The problem was that 'what' seemed to refer to the essence of the action and 'to what end' to the end in terms of which the act was defined. These could not be accidents. Thomas answered that the circumstance 'what' is something beyond the essence of the act. For example, that a person should wash another by pouring water on him is not a circumstance of the action of washing. That he should chill him by doing so is a circumstance. Similarly, 'the end that specifies the act is not a circumstance, but some additional end . . .'. Thus, the end of fighting valiantly for the sake of the good is not a circumstance of an act of fortitude but the end that defines such an act. To fight valiantly for a particular cause such as to deliver the state is such an end. (*Summa theologica*, I–II, q. 7, a. 3, ad 3.) Yet another problem is described in the following note.

[47] The end of an action is the object that the powers of the actor are directed to bringing about. (*Summa theologica*, I–II, q. 18, a. 5.) It followed, as Thomas noted, that if more than one human power were directed to producing an action, the action would have more than one essence depending on how it was considered. From the standpoint of the faculties man shares with the other animals, 'sexual intercourse' is the end that defines one species of action. Considered from the standpoint of reason directing man to his ultimate end, sexual intercourse with one's own spouse is essentially different from sexual intercourse with the spouse of another person. (*Summa theologica*, I–II, q. 18, a. 5, ad 3.) Thomas found no difficulty with the idea that a thing or an action could have more than one essence. A fruit can belong to only one species in so far as its substantial form is concerned; considered as to its colour, it can belong to another species, 'white things'; and considered as to its smell to still another, 'sweet-smelling things'. (*Summa theologica*, I–II, q. 18, a. 7, ad 1.)

money or fame. Nevertheless, in order to swim or build a house, he must have had an immediate purpose corresponding to the end of the action or thing.

When a person acts rightly, the end for which he acts is always a means to his ultimate end as a human being. Some actions, however, are defined without reference to this ultimate end, for example 'swimming', or, to use Thomas's examples, 'walking in the field' and 'picking up a straw'. Other actions are defined by characteristics that indicate their compatibility with that ultimate end, for example marrying, using one's own property or giving one's property away to meet the needs of another. A person who performs such actions might still not be acting rightly since he might not be performing them as a means to his ultimate end; as Thomas said, he might be giving away property out of vainglory.[48] Nevertheless, to explain marriage, property, or liberality one must describe a relationship to the ultimate end of man. Still other actions are defined by characteristics that indicate their incompatibility with that ultimate end, for example adultery and theft.[49]

Thus, for Thomas, to define actions such as marriage or adultery, one had to determine their relation to man's ultimate end. Conceptual reasoning, by which one moved from a definition to its consequences, was therefore inseparable from teleological reasoning, by which one moved from a desired end to a conclusion about the appropriate means. For example, one can see from the definition of marriage and property that intercourse with one's own spouse or the use of one's own property are lawful actions and that adultery and theft are not. These definitions, however, are themselves based on independent arguments about the ends of marriage and property. As we have seen, Thomas defined marriage by the ends of raising offspring and forming an association between a man and a woman. He explained property by the end of enabling people to obtain the goods they need with fewer quarrels and, greater incentive to produce and care for them than if everything were held in common. He concluded that to take another's property in order to preserve one's own life is not a theft because it does not interfere with the ultimate end of property, which is to meet people's needs.[50] Had he concluded—and he did not—that one could sometimes have intercourse with another's spouse, he would have said such an action is not adultery: it would not violate the obligations of marital fidelity.

[48] *Summa theologica*, I–II, q. 20, a. 1.
[49] Ibid. I–II, q. 18, aa. 5–8.
[50] Ibid. II–II, q. 66, a. 7, ad. 2.

Thus, in Thomas's philosophical account, essences are linked to ends, and the essences of moral actions are defined by ends that are themselves means to the ultimate end of man. Consequently, for Thomas and the late scholastics, contract, like marriage, is defined by an end that is at once the immediate end of the parties and a means to their ultimate end. Since contract is defined by the immediate end of the parties, the definition expresses the minimum the parties must know in order to contract. It also identifies an end to be served by other obligations that belong to the contract although the parties may not have had them consciously in mind. Moreover, since this end is itself a means to the parties' ultimate end, contract can be analysed in accordance with an ultimate standard that goes beyond the conflicting interests of the parties.

The basic features of this account of contract consequently depend on a metaphysics of essences linked to ends. The account was mortally threatened, as we shall see, when modern philosophers challenged the legitimacy of speaking either about essences or about an ultimate end of man. More generally, however, it is threatened by any philosophy that divorces essences from ends and so makes it impossible to reason in a manner that is at once teleological and conceptual. Such a threat was posed, within half a century of Thomas's death, by the philosophies of John Duns Scotus (*c.*1265–1308) and William of Ockham (*c.*1280–1349).

It is sometimes thought that Scotus and Ockham undermined the Aristotelian and Thomistic view of natural law by making morality depend on divine will rather than human reason. Scotus did say that every good action is good because it has been commanded by God.[51] Ockham claimed that, because God is perfectly free, He can command any action He wishes, and such an action will then be good.[52] Nevertheless, Scotus and Ockham also believed that an action can be good naturally[53] or 'according to the dictates of right reason'.[54] They did not think that this belief contradicted their

[51] This seems to be meaning of his famous statement, 'the divine will is the cause of good, and so by the fact that He wills something it is good'. (J. Duns Scotus, *Reportata Parisiensia* lib. 1, dist. 48, q. 1, in *Opera* (Paris, 1893/4), xxii. 512.) See F. Copleston, *A History of Philosophy*, ii, *Medieval Philosophy*, pt. ii: *Albert the Great to Duns Scotus* (New York, 1962), 270–1. Scotus did not believe that morality has no foundation except an arbitrary divine will. (E. Bettoni, *Duns Scotus: The Basic Principles of His Philosophy* (Washington, 1961), 160–82; C. R. S. Harris, *Duns Scotus* (New York, 1959), 331–3; A. Wolter, *Duns Scotus on the Will and Morality* (Washington, 1986), 56–7.)

[52] *Reportatio*, lib. 2, q. 15, in *Opera theologica*, v. 353. See *Ordinatio*, lib. 1, dist. 47, q. 1, in *Opera theologica*, iv. 680–5.

[53] J. Duns Scotus, *Opus oxoniense*, lib. 2, dist. 40, q. 1, no. 3, in *Opera*, xiii. 426. See ibid., lib. 1, dist. 17, q. 3, no. 14, in *Opera* x. 76.

[54] William of Ockham, *Quodlibeta*, ii, q. 14, in *Opera theologica*, ix. 177.

claims about the ultimate source of morality or the freedom of God. In their metaphysical worlds, however, right reason could not work as it had for Aristotle and Thomas. In their worlds, a single entity did not need to have a single form linked to a single end. Therefore, moral philosophy need not, and possibly could not, analyse virtues and moral actions by asking what they contribute to that end.

According to Scotus, man possesses not a single form, but a number of distinct 'formalities' which are united in a way that he never clearly explained. Matter is a formality. It is not, as Thomas and Aristotle said, that within a thing which potentially can receive other forms.[55] Indeed, 'it is contradictory to affirm that anything has a purely potential being and that it exists in act'.[56] For that same reason, life, animality, and rationality are distinct formalities in man.[57] For Thomas, they are united in a single form because 'rational' is a certain realization of the potentialities of being an 'animal', and 'animal' a certain realization of the potentialities of being alive. For Scotus, that explanation again had the vice of describing purely in terms of potentiality something that is supposed really to exist.[58] For similar reasons, Scotus also claimed that the intellect and will are formalities rather than powers distinct from the essence of man, as they were for Thomas.[59] He claimed that things are individual because they have an individuating formality—a 'thisness' or 'haeccitas'—and not, as Aristotle and Thomas thought, because their forms are present in different matter.[60]

So conceived, an entity is like a series of transparencies overlaid to form a picture. Each transparency is incomplete without the others. Nevertheless, the transparencies are not parts with separate functions. One cannot study them as one would the parts of a couch or the organs of the body, which was the method of Aristotle and Thomas.

One can see the difference when Scotus discusses contract. Unlike Thomas, he does not analyse a transaction in terms of a virtue exercised or an end served. He decomposes it into a cluster of conceptually distinct elements. These elements are like the formalities of his metaphysics. They are not defined or explained in

[55] Scotus, *Opus Oxoniense*, lib. 2, dist. 12, q. 1, in *Opera*, xii. 546–74.

[56] Ibid., lib. 2, dist. 12, q. 2, no. 2, in *Opera*, xii. 575.

[57] Ibid., lib. 4, dist. 11, q. 3, nos. 46–9, in *Opera*, xvii. 429–31.

[58] Specifically, he argued that if the differentia marking off a species included that which was already expressed in the genus, the genus would be superfluous, and the same thing would have been said twice. (Scotus, *supra* n. 55, lib. 4, dist. 11, q. 3, no. 48, in *Opera*, xvii. 430.)

[59] Ibid., lib. 2, dist. 16, q. 1, nos. 3–10, in *Opera*, xiii. 24–8.

[60] Ibid., lib. 2, dist. 3, q. 6, no. 12, in *Opera*, xii. 134–5.

terms of their end or function. An example is his account of why 'the owner of a thing . . . may donate it to another person who is willing to receive it':

The proof is that, since the owner was an owner by an act of his own will, he is able to cease to be the owner voluntarily. The other party wills to receive the thing, and therefore is able to begin to be its owner. No higher cause prohibits the one person from ceasing to be the owner and the other from beginning to be the owner. Therefore, by such a donation there is a true and just transfer of ownership.[61]

Thus Scotus analysed donation in terms of the concepts of owning and willing, not in terms of the end of a liberal act. He then explained the rules that govern donations, not as means to an end, but as consequences of the conceptual elements he had identified:

From these considerations, it can be seen that there are three requirements for a just donation: transfer by the donor for the benefit of another, willingness to receive on the part of the party to whom the donation is made, and freedom on the part of the one to give and on the part of the other to receive, that is, that neither the one nor the other be prohibited from doing so by any higher law. . . .[62]

Similarly, he did not explain contracts of exchange by identifying a distinct end served by such contracts. He added to his definition of donation further conceptual elements which then entailed further rules. Whereas in transactions such as donation the transfer of property is 'solely for another's benefit' (*mere liberalem*), in an exchange the transfer is 'for another's benefit according to a consideration' (*secundum quid liberalem*);[63] such a transfer 'is not simply for another's benefit', but 'the transferor expects something equivalent to what he transfers'.[64] Consequently, 'the conditions which were mentioned earlier in regard to donations' must be satisfied and also 'other conditions that pertain to just exchange', such as the absence of fraud and the preservation of equality.[65] The analysis is conceptual but no longer teleological.

The metaphysics of William of Ockham was quite different. Individual things have neither formalities nor substantial forms. Men resemble each other more than they resemble donkeys, but that is not because of a form all men possess.[66] Consequently, a

[61] Ibid., lib. 4, dist. 15, q. 2, no. 11, in *Opera*, xviii. 277.
[62] Ibid., lib. 4, dist. 15, q. 2, no. 11, in *Opera*, xviii. 277.
[63] Ibid., lib. 4, dist. 15, q. 2, no. 11, in *Opera*, xviii. 277.
[64] Ibid., lib. 4, dist. 15, q. 2, no. 12, in *Opera*, xviii. 282.
[65] Ibid., lib. 4, dist. 15, q. 2, no. 13, in *Opera*, xviii. 282–3.
[66] E. Gilson, *History of Christian Philosophy in the Middle Ages* (London, 1972), 492.

concept such as 'man' is not the abstraction of such a form. It is 'a common or confused intellection' through which 'singular things outside the mind are known'.[67]

> For instance, to have a confused intellection of man is merely to have a cognition by which we do not understand one man rather than another, but by such a cognition we do know or understand a man rather than a donkey. And this means that such a cognition, by some kind of assimilation, bears a greater resemblance to a man than to a donkey, but does not resemble one man rather than another.[68]

Such concepts or cognitions are signs that 'by their nature stand for actual things outside the mind or for other things in the mind, just as the spoken words stand for them by convention. . . .'[69]

Ockham said little about contract, and, indeed, it is hard to imagine how contract could be approached from this metaphysical standpoint. While the metaphysics of Scotus divorced concepts from ends, the concepts were supposed to correspond to those intelligible aspects of things that he called formalities. One could discuss contract by identifying the intelligible aspects of contract. In the world of Ockham, however, concepts are mere signs, and they can only designate individual things and resemblances or relationships among these things. It is difficult to see how one could discuss contract if that is all one's concepts can designate.

Ockham claimed, nevertheless, that a 'demonstrative moral science' presumably encompassing such matters as contract could 'deduce conclusions syllogistically' from principles known either 'of themselves' (*per se*) or 'through experience' (*per experientiam*).[70] By 'experience', he presumably meant direct observation of singular things and the ways they are related. His example of a principle known through experience is that 'angry people are to be appeased by soft words'.[71] While one can observe the effect of soft words on angry people, however, it is hard to see how one could observe the definition of a contract, the binding force of a promise, the content of a contractual obligation, or the knowledge the parties must have to contract. Presumably, these matters are governed by the other sort of principles, those known 'of themselves'. Such principles, according to Ockham, are evident as soon as their terms are

[67] William of Ockham, *Expositio super primum librum Perihermenias*, cap. 1, in *Traditio* 4 (1946), 324.

[68] Ibid.

[69] Ibid. 323. See *Summa logicae*, pars 1, cap. 14, in *Opera philosophica*, i. 47–9.

[70] Ockham, *supra* n. 54, ii, q. 14, in *Opera theologica*, ix. 177.

[71] William of Ockham, *Quaestiones variae*, q. 6, a. 10, in *Opera theologica*, viii. 281–2.

understood.[72] His examples are that 'the will should conform to right reason', 'blameworthy evil is to be avoided',[73] and 'good is to be done to a benefactor'.[74] Presumably, Ockham would have counted as further examples such principles as 'promises are to be kept' or 'exchange requires an equivalent'. An approach to contract along these lines might have looked more conceptual than that of Scotus. One wonders what such principles can rest on, however, if the real world consists of singular things, and these principles do not rest on observation of these singular things or relationships among them. They would seem to tell us nothing except how the person framing the principle has chosen to define his terms.[75] Ockham's metaphysics thus seems to lead towards the conclusion reached by David Hume, whose work will be discussed at a later point: that moral science is impossible because empirical observations are devoid of moral content, and definitions are arbitrary.

Although Ockham would have denied this conclusion, he did not suggest how a distinctively Ockhamite approach to contract could be developed. Neither did Jean Gerson (1363–1429) or Gabriel Biel (1410–95), who were regarded in the fifteenth century as the foremost representatives of the nominalist philosophical movement that Ockham had founded.[76] Significantly, their brief discussions of contract owe almost nothing to Ockham or his metaphysics. They both drew heavily on Scotus. Biel added some ideas taken from Thomas and some reflections of his own on the value of money and

[72] William of Ockham, *Scriptum in librum primum sententiarum ordinatio*, lib. 1, prolog., q. 1, in *Opera theologica*, i. 5–6.

[73] Ockham, *supra* n. 54, q. 14.

[74] William of Ockham, *Quaestiones variae*, q. 6, a. 10, in *Opera theologica*, viii. 281–2.

[75] Ockham did not think these definitions were arbitrary. Although concepts were signs standing for individuals, they were natural signs, and so there could be a natural rather than an arbitrary order among them. In this sense, Ockham did not give, as Leff says, 'a purely psychological explanation of universals'. (G. Leff, *Medieval Thought: St Augustine to Ockham* (Baltimore 1958), 284.) Certainly it is wrong to conclude, as some scholars have done, that for Ockham the moral order could have no philosophical foundation. (e.g A. Ghisalberti, *Guglielmo di Ockham* (Milàn, 1972), 226.) On the other hand, one cannot say with Freppert that Ockham left intact a natural ethics resting on right reason and natural reward on which he superimposed a higher Christian morality based on love. (L. Freppert, *The Basis of Morality According to William Ockham* (Chicago, 1988), 171–81.) Natural ethics is hardly left intact when concepts are said to be mere signs, and the relationship between moral principles and reality becomes so mysterious.

[76] While questioning whether Gerson was truly a nominalist, Gilson acknowledges that 'the nominalists of the fourteenth and fifteenth centuries were constantly claiming him as one of them'. (Gilson, *supra* n. 66, pp. 528–9.) Nor does he doubt that nominalism deeply influenced Gerson's outlook. On Gerson's nominalism, see H. Oberman, *The Harvest of Medieval Theology: Gabriel Biel and Late Medieval Nominalism* (Cambridge, Mass., 1963), 332–3.

the right of princes to alter it.[77] Gerson added some observations on the ability of a legislator to remedy abuses in contracting.[78] Ockham's ideas had little effect on the approach to contract, even of men so deeply influenced by his work.

The reason may have been not merely that Ockham's ideas were difficult to apply to contract, but that the fourteenth- and fifteenth-century partisans of Thomas, Scotus, and Ockham did not compete by showing how their larger philosophical ideas could be applied to concrete problems of moral philosophy. They fought their battles at the upper reaches of theology and metaphysics. When they displayed more than a passing interest in such matters as contract, that interest was practical, and their work lacked theoretical significance.

The Dominican Antoninus of Florence (1389–1459), for example, had a lively practical interest in the ethical problems raised by business transactions. He was bishop of a great commercial city and confessor to the richest banker in Europe, Cosimo de' Medici. His theoretical contributions to the study of contract were modest. He followed Scotus in classifying contracts[79] and Thomas in discussing the just price and the effect of fraud.[80] He referred to Roman law but did not integrate it with the positions of Thomas and Scotus. He made some perceptive remarks on how prices are determined and why one cannot sell at an unjust price even though one can refuse to sell altogether.[81]

A practical interest also motivated those theologians who wrote handbooks to help priests deal with moral problems, particularly in the confessional. One of the most influential was the *Summa poenitentia* of Raymond of Penafort (d. 1275), a great canonist and a contemporary of Thomas Aquinas. Since moral problems were thought of in legal terms, this work drew heavily on both Roman

[77] Biel followed Scotus's definitions as well as his account of the owner's power to donate and of the rules governing donations. Like Thomas, he then described exchange as an act of commutative justice, and said that commutative justice is violated by defects in the substance, quantity, or quality of the goods sold. (G. Biel, *Collectorium circa quattuor sententiarum libros*, lib. 4, dist. 15, q. 2.) He drew on Scotus and Thomas in his account of the just price. (Ibid., q. 10.) For his observations on the value of money see ibid., q. 9.

[78] In his short treatise on contracts, Gerson defined contracts in much the same way as Duns Scotus. (J. Gerson, *De contractibus*, nos. 1–4, in *Oeuvres complètes* (Paris, 1973), ix. 386–8). These remarks are followed by a long discussion of usury. In contrast, the discussion of injustices committed in contracting in the *Summa theologica et canonica* attributed to Gerson considered the same problems Thomas dealt within his *Summa theologica* in the same order as Thomas and arrived at the same conclusions ('de sacramento poenitentiae', qq. 9–11). For his remarks on the legislator's ability to correct abuses, see *De contractibus*, nos. 9–12, in *Oeuvres*, ix. 390–2.

[79] Antoninus of Florence, *Summa theologica* (Verona, 1740), pars 3, tit. 8, cap. 2.

[80] Ibid., pars 2, tit. 1, caps. 16–17.

[81] Ibid., pars 2, tit. 1, cap. 16.

and Canon law. The Dominican John of Freiburg (d. 1314) then wrote a *Summa confessorum*, which drew on both Raymond and Thomas. Similar works appeared over the next two centuries, each modelled on its predecessors: the *Summa Pisana* of the Dominican Bartolommeo Pisano (d. 1347), the *Summa Angelica* of the Franciscan Angelo Carletti (d. 1495), the *Summa Roselle* of the Franciscan Baptiste de Sale (d. 1496), and the *Summa Sylvestrina* of the Dominican Sylvestro da Prierio (d. 1523). These works were written not to explore theoretical problems but to present moral theology and law in a simplified form to meet a practical need. Their authors place the opinions of Thomas (or, in the case of Carletti, those of Scotus) side by side with Roman and Canon law without attempting a synthesis. For example, they discuss sale by giving a technical legal definition, dealing with some technical legal problems, then paraphrasing Thomas (or Scotus) on equality in exchange, defects in goods sold, and duties of disclosure, and finally turning to more technical legal problems.[82] Philosophers and theologians did not make a serious attempt at a synthesis until late scholastics launched a Thomistic revival in the sixteenth century.

[82] John of Freiburg, *Summa confessorum*, tit. 8, qq. 7–20; Bartholomaeus de Pisis, *Summa pisana*, 'emptio', fos. 92^{v}–94^{v}; Angelus Clavasius, *Summa angelica*, 'emptio', fos. 255^{v}–265^{v}; Baptista Trovamala de Salis, *Summa roselle*, 'emptio', fos. 74^{r}–76^{r}; Sylvester Prierias, *Summa sylvestrina*, fos. 246^{v}–251^{v}. The entries for 'contractus', 'donatio', and 'pactum' are drawn from Roman and Canon law in the *Summa pisana* (fos. 45^{v}; 78^{v}–80^{r}; 234^{v}), and the *Summa roselle* (fos. 47^{r}; 58^{v}–62^{v}; 179^{v}), as are those for 'contractus' and 'donatio' in the *Summa angelica* (fos. 169^{v}–170^{v}; 215^{v}–226^{r}). In treating 'pactum', however, the *Summa angelica* places a discussion of when an agreement is binding in Roman and Canon law alongside the opinions of theologians, including Thomas, as to when it is binding in conscience (fos. 613^{r}–616^{v}). So does the *Summa sylvestrina* (fos. 207^{r}–209^{v}), which also places side by side the Roman classifications of contract and more philosophical definitions ('contract', fos. 159^{r}–159^{v}) and the opinions of theologians and jurists concerning gifts ('donatio', fos. 207^{r}–216^{r}). Again, however, opinions are placed alongside each other without any real attempt at synthesis.

3
ROMAN LAW AND THE MEDIEVAL JURISTS

ALTHOUGH Aristotelian philosophy and Roman law were studied intensively in medieval universities, the medieval jurists also failed to synthesize these intellectual traditions. They nevertheless interpreted certain Roman texts in ways that fit easily into the synthesis that the late scholastics eventually achieved. Often, as we will see, they did so because they were familiar with Aristotle and Thomas and read the opinions of these philosophers into their texts.

ARISTOTLE AND THE MEDIEVAL JURISTS

The Organization of Roman Law

The study of Roman law in medieval Europe was based on the *Corpus iuris civilis*, a collection of Roman legal texts made by the Emperor Justinian in the sixth century. As modern scholars recognize, these texts were shaped by different minds responding to different needs, different philosophical currents, and different social and political circumstances over a long period of time. These historical influences will not concern us here, however, because the medieval jurists were blind to them. For them, the texts were a simultaneously valid whole. The meaning of each text was to be found by interpreting it in the light of every other.

The texts themselves evidenced a method and a set of concerns different from those we have seen in Aristotle and Thomas. Doubtless, Greek philosophy influenced the development of Roman law in a variety of ways. Nevertheless, the Roman jurists did not write like Greek philosophers. The jurists were interested more in the particular, less in ferreting out ultimate principles. As has often been said, the Romans had no theory or general law of contract.[1] They had a law of particular contracts such as sale, lease, pledge, and partnership, each with particular rules which they had worked

[1] e.g. A. Watson, *The Law of the Ancient Romans* (Dallas, 1970), 58; W. W. Buckland, A. D. McNair, and F. H. Lawson, *Roman Law and Common Law*, 2nd edn. (Cambridge, 1952), 265; H. Coing, *Europäisches Privatrecht*, i, *Älteres Gemeines Recht (1500 bis 1800)* (Munich, 1985), 398.

out *ad hoc*. They had not tried to explain in any general or systematic way why these contracts had the rules they did or what features all contracts had in common.

Their organization of contract law, to the extent that they organized it, was similar in only one respect to the approach of Aristotle and Thomas. The Roman jurist Gaius distinguished between contract and delict much as these philosophers distinguished between voluntary and involuntary commutative justice. According to Gaius, obligations arise by contract (*ex contractu*), by delict (*ex delictu*), or on the analogy of contract and delict (*quasi ex contractu* and *quasi ex delictu*).[2] The reason, according to some modern scholars, is that Gaius borrowed directly or indirectly from Aristotle.[3] He was the first Roman to speak of contracts and delicts in general rather than about what we would call particular contracts and delicts. As he is known to have borrowed other ideas from Aristotle, he may have borrowed this distinction as well.

In any event, the resemblance went no further. Gaius immediately turned to the particular Roman contracts which he classified according to Roman rules as to when they become binding. Sale, lease, partnership, and *mandatum* (a kind of gratuitous agency) all became binding upon consent of the parties, and for that reason he classed them as contracts *consensu* or consensual contracts. Gratuitous loans and bailments as well as pledges became binding upon delivery of the thing (*res*) loaned, bailed, or pledged, and so he classed them as contracts *re* or real contracts. Other contracts became binding on completion of a prescribed formality and were classified by Gaius as contracts by words (*verbis*) or by writing (*literis*) according to the nature of the formality.[4] A contract by words was made through a formality called *stipulatio* in which one party asked the other, 'Do you promise such and such?' and was answered 'I do promise such and such.' A contract by writing was made by entry into an account book. Contractual arrangements that belonged to none of these recognized types were called 'innominate' and had no legal effect until one party had performed. An example was barter.[5]

[2] I. 3.13.2.

[3] Coing, 'Zum Einfluß der Philosophie des Aristoteles auf die Entwicklung des römischen Rechts', *Zeitschrift der Savigny-Stiftung für Rechtsgeschichte, Rom. Abt.* 69 (1952), 24 at 37–8; M. Kaser, *Das Römische Privatrecht*, 2nd edn. (Munich, 1971), i. 522.

[4] I. 3.13.2. See Kaser, *supra* n. 3, i. 524–7.

[5] Ibid. i. 522–83. For a general discussion of Roman contract law, see Watson, *supra* n. 1, 58–75; W. W. Buckland, *A Manual of Roman Private Law* (Cambridge, 1953), 247–71; M. Kaser, *Roman Private Law*, trans. R. Dannenbring (Durban, 1965), 162–208.

In these general observations about contract, Gaius did not mention promise at all, let alone a virtue of fidelity. He mentioned consent only as the way in which one special class of contracts becomes binding. His classification of contracts cut across the distinction Aristotle and Thomas drew between liberality and commutative justice. Barter was, in Aristotle's terms, an act of commutative justice, and yet it was an innominate contract that was not binding until one party had performed. *Mandatum* was gratuitous but was binding on consent. A *stipulatio* could be used to make any contract binding, gratuitous or not.

The difference is not that Aristotle and Thomas used concepts that were wholly alien to the Romans. It is rather that these philosophers paid attention to concepts that were helpful in building theories. The Romans were interested not in building such theories but in analysing particular legal problems. Often, principles so universal as to draw the attention of an Aristotle or a Thomas are not stated by the Romans in any general form just because they are obvious. On the occasions when the Roman texts state these principles, they offer them as interesting observations, not as starting points for analysis.

The Romans knew, for example, that parties could commit themselves contractually by making promises and giving consent. They enforced a promise called a *pollicitatio*, in which a person undertook to support public works or to do something for the city in gratitude for an honour he had received.[6] One Roman text observed that a *pollicitatio* was the consent of one party only, as distinguished from a *pactus* or agreement, which was the consent of both.[7] Another text said that a *pactus* was the consent of two or more parties to one thing.[8] Another text said that every contract requires agreement including contracts *re* and *verbis*.[9] Although the Romans referred to consent, promise, and agreement, however, they did not use these concepts to explain when, in principle, a contract is binding. Similarly, they recognized mistake, fraud, and duress as defences but did not explain them in terms of any larger notion of what constitutes consent. In the *Corpus iuris*, mistake is discussed in some confused remarks that appear as a special topic of the law of sales, fraud is discussed in the context of the *actio de dolo*, and duress in the context of the *actio metus causa*.

Similarly, the Romans distinguished between gratuitous and onerous contracts, between gift and exchange. They had special

[6] See Kaser, *supra* n. 3, i. 604.
[7] D. 50.12.3.
[8] D. 2.14.1.
[9] D. 2.14.1.3.

rules to govern when a promise to make a gift was binding. For example, in later Roman law such a promise could be made binding by a special formality, *insinuatio*, in which the promise was formally registered.[10] But they did not explain these special rules by discussing the virtue of liberality or in any other way. Again, later Roman law gave a remedy in one instance of unequal exchange. A person who sold land at less than half its just price could demand that the buyer either rescind the sale or pay the rest of the just price.[11] But the Romans did not explain the remedy in terms of a virtue of commutative justice or a principle of equality in exchange.

The Initial Encounter with Aristotle

The medieval study of Roman law began about the year 1100, when a man named Irnerius began to lecture on the *Corpus iuris* at Bologna. Legal historians refer to Irnerius and his successors as the 'Glossators' on account of the marginal notes or glosses they wrote to Roman texts. The last and perhaps the greatest of the Glossators were Azo and his pupil Accursius, who wrote in the early thirteenth century. Accursius wrote the standard gloss or *glossa ordinaria* to the *Corpus iuris*, which was a vast compilation of over one hundred thousand individual glosses. Partly because of the enormous influence of the Accursian gloss on later jurists, the age of the Glossators is generally said to end with Accursius. The jurists who wrote from the mid-thirteenth century onward are said to belong to a new school, the 'Post-Glossators' or 'Commentators'.

Although Aristotle's works on logic had long been known in the West and were used extensively by the Glossators,[12] his works on metaphysics, physics, politics, and ethics became available only in the late twelfth and early thirteenth centuries.[13] Fragments of the *Nicomachean Ethics* were translated into Latin before 1200, and a full translation was made in the 1240s.[14] The newly available works of Aristotle touched off firestorms in theological circles. Nevertheless, the jurists did not immediately make use of them. There are a few citations to the *Ethics* in early thirteenth-century Canon law

[10] See Kaser, *supra* n. 3, ii. 81; Buckland, *supra* n. 5, p. 52.

[11] C. 4.44.2.

[12] On the Glossators' use of logic and dialectic, see Genzmer, 'Die iustinianische Kodifikation und die Glossatoren', *Atti del Congresso Internationale di Diritto Romano*, Bologna and Rome, 17–27 April 1933 (Pavia, 1934), i. 345 at 380–8, 397–403; Brugi, 'Il Metodo dei Glossatori Bolognesi', *Studi in Onore di Salvatore Riccobono nel XL Anno del suo Insegnamento* (Palermo, 1936; repr. Aalen, 1974), i. 21.

[13] F. Van Steenberghen, *Aristotle in the West* (Louvain, 1955), 62–3, 93–4.

[14] Ibid. 93–4.

manuscripts.[15] But none of the Glossators, even Accursius, seem to be acquainted with the new Aristotelian learning.[16] A citation to the *Physics* appears in some manuscripts of the Accursian Gloss but it was almost certainly a later addition.[17] The Aristotelian principles that the Glossators occasionally mention were gleaned from his logical works or taken second-hand from Boethius. Azo and Accursius knew, for example, that a thing could remain the same while changing its 'accidents' but could not do so while changing its 'substance'. They knew that according to Aristotle there were ten 'categories' of predicates: 'substance' and nine types of accidents. As Kantorowicz has said, they knew of Aristotle's formal, final, efficient, and material causes only as 'trivialized' by Boethius, and the use they made of them was loose and confused.[18] We shall soon see examples of just how confused.

The influence of the newly available Aristotelian works can first be seen clearly in the writings of the 'ultramontane' jurists Jacobus de Ravanis (d. 1296) and Petrus de Bellapertica (d. 1308), who taught at Orléans and were noted for their brilliance and iconoclasm. At the time they wrote, the new Aristotelian learning was being carried outward from its centre in Paris by students of the arts, theologians, and especially members of the Dominican order which had produced the two great pioneers of Aristotelian studies, Albert the Great and Thomas Aquinas. It is not surprising that the new learning reached Orléans before it reached the centre of legal studies in Bologna. Not only was Orléans closer to Paris, but, unlike Bologna, the professors, including Iacobus and Petrus, were

[15] S. Kuttner, *Repertorium der Kanonistik (1140–1234)* (Vatican City, 1937), 36 (in an early 13th-c. French manuscript), and S. Kuttner, *Kanonistische Schuldlehre von Gratian bis auf die Dekretalen Gregors IX* (Vatican City, 1935), 49 (by Laurentius in an early 13th-c. manuscript).

[16] See Otte, 'Die Aristoteleszitate in der Glosse', *Zeitschrift der Savigny-Stiftung für Rechtsgeschichte, Rom. Abt.* 85 (1968), 368; Horn, 'Philosophie in der Jurisprudenz der Kommentatoren: Baldus philosophus', *Ius Commune*, 1 (1967), 104 at 131; Brugi, 'Della interpretatione della legge al sistema del diritto', in *Per la storia della giurisprudenza e delle università italiane: Nuovi saggi* (Turin, 1921), 15 at 26–7.

[17] The citation, which is to book VIII of the *Physics*, is in the gloss to I. 2.1.28 to *in sua substantia*. Landsberg had assumed it was genuine although he believed the new Aristotelian corpus had little influence on Accursius. (E. Landsberg, *Die Glosse des Accursius und ihre Lehre vom Eigenthum* (Leipzig, 1883), 34.) Neither Brugi (*supra* n. 16, p. 26) nor Otte (*supra* n. 16, p. 373) thought that Accursius actually wrote it, nor did the editor of an early printed edition of Accursius, who noted in the margin: 'Istam glossam non credo esse Accursii quia non reperitur in antiquis originalibus nec de ea doctores aliquam faciunt mentionem.' I checked some of the manuscripts in the Vatican library and found the citation to the *Physics* in Vat. Lat. 1433 (14rb). It was missing from Barb. 1441 (10rb), Barb. 1463 (10ra), Ross. 584 (13vb), Vat. Lat. 1431 (17va), Vat. Lat. 1432 (17rb), Vat. Lat. 1434 (12va), Vat. Lat. 1436 (17va).

[18] H. Kantorowicz and W. W. Buckland, *Studies in the Glossators of the Roman Law* (Cambridge, 1938), 41.

churchmen.[19] Theology was taught there by Dominicans. Iacobus had debates with them and sometimes cited their opinions.[20] In Orléans, moreover, unlike Bologna, the students took a degree in arts before commencing their legal studies.[21]

Nevertheless, it would be a mistake to think the ultramontanes pioneered a new legal method based on Aristotelian philosophy or even seriously applied that philosophy to specific legal problems. The complaints of some Bolognese jurists might lead one to think they had done so. The fourteenth-century jurist Albericus de Rosate began his own commentary on the *Digest* by recording the complaints made by another jurist, Richardus Malumbra, early in the century:

[Richardus] made fun of certain Doctors who were his contemporaries who tried to treat our science in a syllogistic, sophistic, and dialectical manner. . . . [This manner] had its origin with the ultramontane Doctors of whom some, in many things, the majority, were more subtle than useful though some were of great excellence and knowledge. In our science, when it is a question of chopping someone's head off, to argue about formed and form, substance and accident, and in similar ways and by syllogistic arguments is not, I believe, well founded. Nor was this style followed by our older fathers and Doctors: Iohannes [Bassianus] who was sufficiently subtle, Azo, Bulgarus, Martinus, Odofredus or others. They argued from the witness of our laws which were close to the matter in question. I do not say that one cannot argue from the lesser to the greater or from the contrary meaning and in other ways we find approved in our law and which we urge upon all whoever applies himself to our law. But they followed in the footsteps of our older jurists and fathers and doctors, sticking to the text and the gloss and the opinions of the most respected doctors. They did not turn to fables or make arguments so logistic and sophistic that they have no truth but only its appearance. Nor is this only a vice of our modern Doctors and advocates. This disease, indeed, has crept into the science of theology for the modern preachers forsake sacred scripture for figures, philosophers, poets, and fables. . . .[22]

[19] E. M. Meijers, *Études d'histoire du droit*, iii, *Le Droit romain au moyen âge* (Leiden, 1959), 113.

[20] Ibid. 25, n. 93; 59, n. 223.

[21] Ibid. 114.

[22] 'Ipse enim irridebat aliquos Doctores contemporaneous suos, qui studebant tradere scientiam nostram silogistico, sophistico, et dialectico modo: et dicebat considerari debere, quod scientia nostra tradi non debet hoc modo. . . . [Hoc modo] originem habuit a Doctoribus ultramontanis, qui in multis plus eorum aliqui fuerunt subtiles, quam utiles, et aliqui magnae excellentiae, et scientiae. Arguere enim in scientia nostra ad decapitationem alicuius de formato, et forma, de substantia, et accidenti, et similibus modis et argumentis silogisticis non crederem bene tutum, nec hunc stilum secuti sunt patres, et Doctores nostri antiqui Iohannes qui satis fuit subtilis. Azo. Bulgarus. Martinus. Odofredus. nec alii, sed arguerunt ex testibus legum nostrarum vicinis ad materiam, de qua agabatur: non dico, quod non possit

Thus Richardus criticized the ultramontanes for abandoning traditional legal methods and arguing over specifically Aristotelian philosophical terms—'formed' and 'form', 'substance' and 'accident'. One might at first imagine he was complaining about an enthusiasm for the new Aristotelian learning, an enthusiasm reflected in a new method. Indeed, after describing one of Iacobus' debates with the Dominicans, the fourteenth-century jurist Cinus called him not merely a 'philosopher', which was a term jurists sometime applied to themselves,[23] but a 'great master of all philosophy'.[24]

In fact, however, though the ultramontanes seemed philosophical to the Bolognese, to the students in Orléans who were acquainted with the new learning they must have seemed prickly defenders of traditional legal studies. The debate with the Dominicans probably made a different impression on them than on Cinus. It concerned the sort of hypothetical question that perenially occupies moral philosophers: if one's father and one's son were both starving, and one had a single loaf of bread that could save either of their lives but not both, to whom should one give it? The Dominicans said, to the son, because 'love does not ascend but descends'. Iacobus answered that the Roman law allowed a starving father to sell his son into slavery to save his own life, that therefore the father had the legal right to take the loaf of bread away from his son's son, and that consequently to give the loaf to the son would be pointless.[25] Iacobus seems not to be embracing philosophy but to be asserting the importance of law.

There is a similar defensiveness in a comment he made when discussing definitions of justice in the Accursian Gloss that were taken from non-legal sources such as Cicero. 'In the gloss we have many definitions of justice. You can take another if you want to be a

argui a minori ad maius a contrario sensu et modis aliis, qui in iure nostro approbati reperiuntur, ex quo hortor quoscunque studiosus iuris nostri, quod sequantur vestigia iurisconsultorum, et patrum, et Doctorum nostrorum antiquorum, inherendo text[um] et gloss[am] et opinionibus Doctorum magis approbatis, et se non convertant ad fabulas nec argumenta si logistica, et sophistica, ex quibus veritas non habetur, sed sola apparentia. Nec istud est solum vitium nostrorum doctorum et advocatorum modernorum. Imo etiam iste morbus irrepsit in scientia theologiae quia predicatores moderni relictis sacris scripturis ad figuras, philosophos, poetas, et fabulas se convertunt. . . .' Albericus de Rosate, *Commentaria*, Proemium.

[23] D. 50.5.8.4, said: 'Etenim vere philosophantes pecuniam contemnunt.' The jurists applied the text to themselves; e.g. Accursius, Gloss to D. 1.1.1.1, who added 'nam civilis sapientia vera philosophia dicitur, id est, amor sapientiae . . .'; Post, 'Philosophantes and Philosophi in Roman and Canon Law', *Archives d'histoire doctrinale et littéraire du moyen âge*, 29 (1954), 135.

[24] Cinus de Pistoia, *In Codicem Commentaria* to C. 4.43.2, no. 6.

[25] The story is told by Iacobus de Ravanis, *Lectura super Codice* to C. 4.43.2, and by Cinus, *In Codicem Commentaria* to C. 4.43.2, no. 6.

preacher.'[26] Apparently, it is fine for preachers to collect opinions about justice from poets and philosophers, but jurists should stick to their legal texts.

Petrus was similarly unenthusiastic about the learning of the *artistas*, persons who had studied the liberal arts and then came to Orléans to study law.

> [They] come from Paris and make themselves out to be smart. One of them said to me last year that this science [law] is making him stupid. I said that this science does not make anybody stupid if he were smart to begin with. But when these people first come they do not believe that there is anything to understand beyond what is encapsulated in their literary studies. I say that their little bit of what-not makes them stupid. So they ought not to come to this science with their fists clenched. It would be better to listen to something first.[27]

Moreover, as Meijers has observed, their method differed from that of the Glossators primarily by being more subtle, filled with fine distinctions and remote analogies to legal texts.[28] As Stein says of the Post-Glossators in general, 'Their commentaries abounded in acute distinctions which they built up into vast Gothic edifices of exposition.'[29] If they were sculptors one would call their style Hellenistic. The texts have become plastic and the display of technical skill almost distracting. Most likely, Richardus was irritated by the increase in subtlety and skill, and objected to the Aristotelian vocabulary not because it was philosophical, but because it was another display of erudition by people who he thought were too clever by half. Thus, he objects that their chains of logic are taking them too far from their texts. His comparison with the preaching of his day is revealing. It reminds one of Dante's complaint about preachers who are overly inventive in order to be

[26] 'multas diffinitiones iustitiae habemus in glossa. potes aliam ponere, si vis esse predicator': Iacobus de Ravanis, *Super Institutionibus commentaria* to I. 1.1.1.

[27] '[Artistae] veniunt de parisius et faciunt se subtiles. Quidam dixit mihi anno praeterito quod ista scientia reddiderat ipsum rudem. Dico ista scientia non facit aliquem rudem: si ante subtilis fuit Sed quando primo veniunt non credunt quod alius sit intellectus nisi secundum corticem literae. Dico quod aliquantulum facit ipsum rudem. Ideo ne ad istam scientiam illatis manibus veniant: melius est antea aliquid audire.' (Petrus de Bellapertica, *Lectura Institutionum* to I. 1.1.1.)

[28] Meijers, *supra* n. 19, pp. 111–12. A similar conclusion was reached by Chevrier, 'Sur l'art de l'argumentation chez quelques Romanistes médiévaux au XIIe et au XIIIe siécle', *Archives de philosophie du droit*, 11 (1966), 115 at 140–5; Feenstra, 'L'Influence de l'enseignement du droit romain à Orléans sur les nations étrangères', *Actes du congrès sur l'ancienne Université d'Orléans (XIIIe–XVIIIe siècles*, (Orléans, 6–7 May 1961) (Orleans, 1962), 45. 52.

[29] P. Stein, *Regulae Iuris: From Juristic Rules to Legal Maxims* (Edinburgh, 1966), 153.

thought ingenious,[30] and of St Catherine of Siena's criticism of those who preach 'more to please men and to delight the ear' than to honour God.[31]

On occasion, Iacobus and Petrus do make use of the new Aristotelian learning. In an environment like Orléans, it is not surprising that they would be interested in it as well as defensive about the value of their own legal training. For example, Iacobus discusses the material, formal, final, and efficient causes of law.[32] Petrus makes use of a 'Parisian' opinion, presumably derived from the *Ethics*, that ethics and law have the same subject, man, and that 'man is part of the state insofar as he makes contracts and commits delicts'.[33] In these instances they may have found some general remark of Aristotle's useful, or, as Richardus suspected, they may have merely wished to display their erudition. They were not applying Aristotle seriously to doctrinal problems. Indeed, when we examine their writings on contract law, we will find hardly an instance in which their insights seem to have been suggested by Aristotle.

Although no systematic attempt to prove the point will be made here, the use of Aristotle by Italian jurists in the early fourteenth century seems to have been equally casual. As has long been recognized, the work of Cinus de Pistoia is much like that of the ultramontanes. A lost commentary of Cinus rediscovered by Domencio Maffei may indicate Cinus was more original than once supposed, but it contains few if any direct citations to Aristotle.[34] One can find applications of Aristotelian concepts such as the four causes or the distinction between substance and accidents in the works of Iacobus Butrigarius, Olradus de Ponte, Raynerius Forlivensis, Jacobus de Belvisio, and, for that matter, Albericus de Rosate.[35] These applications seem to have been occasional and not to have entailed any major recasting of legal doctrine.

In contrast, as we shall see, a quite serious attempt to apply Aristotle to problems of contract law was made by two of the

[30] 'Per apparer ciascun s'ingegna e face | sue invenzioni; e quelle son trascorse | da' predicanti e 'l Vangelio si tace.' (Dante Alighieri, *La divinia commedia*, C. H. Grandgent edn. (Cambridge, Mass., 1972), Paradisio xxix. 94–6.)

[31] 'Le loro predicazioni sono fatte più a piacere degli uomini, e per dilettare le orecchie loro, che ad onor di me [i.e. God].' (N. Tommaseo, *Le lettere di Santa Caterina* (Rome, 1860), p. lxxviii.)

[32] Iacobus de Ravanis, *Super Institutionibus commentaria* under 'Quaeritur primo' before the Proemium, nos. 1, 8.

[33] Petrus de Bellapertica, *Lectura Institutionum*(to rubric no. 23).

[34] D. Maffei, *La 'Lectura super Digesto veteri' di Cino da Pistoia Studio sui Mss Savigny 22 E Urb. Lat. 172'* (Milan, 1963), 34, n. 98.

[35] e.g. Albericus de Rosate, *Commentaria in primam Digesti veteris partem*, Proemium (on the subject of *iustitia civilis* according to Aristotle and on the four causes of *scientia legalis*).

greatest medieval jurists, Cinus's pupil Bartolus de Saxoferrato (d. 1357) and Bartolus's pupil Baldus de Ubaldis (d. 1400). They did not attempt a synthesis of Aristotelian philosophy and Roman law like the late scholastics of the sixteenth century. Their object, like that of their predecessors, was to understand their Roman texts in terms of each other, and their methods remained much the same. Nevertheless, they knew Aristotelian philosophy quite well, and they trusted it. When they looked at problems of Roman contract law, they tended to see Aristotelian answers.

That Baldus did so is not surprising. He regarded moral philosophy as the 'mother' of law.[36] His interest in Aristotelian philosophy is well known.[37] Norbert Horn counted the number of times Baldus cites non-legal authorities directly and found 103 citations to Aristotle, 17 to Cicero, 10 to Boethius, 8 to Thomas Aquinas, 7 to Averroes, 6 to Seneca, 6 to Saint Augustine, 4 to Albertus Magnus, and 2 to Plato.[38] The large proportion of citations to authors squarely in the Aristotelian tradition (Aristotle, Averroes, Albertus Magnus, Thomas Aquinas) is some indication of the importance of this tradition to Baldus. A still better indication is the fact that one can scarcely turn two or three pages of his commentaries without finding some use of the Aristotelian philosophical vocabulary.

Bartolus's interest in Aristotle is more in dispute. His learning extended well outside the field of law. After receiving his doctorate in law at the age of twenty, he spent a number of years reading and studying by himself.[39] His library eventually included thirty-four volumes on theology in addition to thirty on law.[40] He was undoubtedly familiar with the works of Aristotle, whom he described as a paramount authority in philosophy.[41] Nevertheless,

[36] '[philosophia moralis] . . . est legum mater et ianua.' (Baldus de Ubaldis, *Commentaria* to D. 1.1.1.2.) Similarly, 'ius nostrum applicat sibi totam moralem philosophiam.' (Ibid., under rubric to D. 1.1.1, no. 21.)

[37] e.g. Horn, *supra* n. 16, at 124, 134; Ullmann, 'Baldus' Conception of Law', *Law Quarterly Review*, 58 (1942), 386 at 387.

[38] Horn, *supra* n. 16, p. 110.

[39] Bartolus de Saxoferrato to Prima constitutio (Omnem, § Haec autem tria), p. 13, §2, Dig. vet. Pt. 1.

[40] F. C. von Savigny, *Geschichte des Römischen Rechts in Mittelalter*, 2nd edn. (Heidelberg, 1850; repr. Homburg, 1961), vi. 152. Savigny cites Diplovatacius, according to whom Bartolus had a library of 54 books of which 30 were on civil and canon law and 34 were on theology. As Savigny notes, one of these numbers is wrong.

[41] Speaking of various types of authority, Bartolus said: 'Quaedam sunt scripturae, quae procedunt disponendo et determinando, non enunciando, et in his advertendum quid servant studia. Quaedam nota scripturae, tanquam authenticae in studiis reputantur, ut dicta Aristotelis, et Hippocratis et similium, quae tanquam scripturae authenticae in studiis servantur, et istis est standum. . . . Quaedam sunt scripturae quae a studiis non approbantur, nisi probentur per rationem, et istae discuntur

the influence of Aristotle on Bartolus has been doubted since 1913, when C. N. S. Woolf took issue with the earlier conclusions of Luigi Chiapelli.[42] Chiapelli had said that Bartolus 'constantly followed' Aristotle. Woolf doubted that Bartolus was either a profound student of Aristotle or deeply influenced by his political thought. Woolf's evidence, however, was that Bartolus made continual use of Roman law and only occasional use of Aristotle.[43] A more recent and more balanced view is that of Diego Quaglioni, who has shown that his use of Aristotle and Thomas, though occasional, was original, often profound, and the result of a thorough knowledge of their philosophy.[44] As we shall see, so also was the way Bartolus applied Aristotelian and Thomistic ideas to contract law.

THE MEDIEVAL JURISTS AND THE LAW OF CONTRACT

Bartolus and Baldus anticipated the late scholastics by reading Aristotelian ideas into a number of Roman texts. In some instances, however, they or other medieval jurists moved in the direction the late scholastics were to take not because of the influence of Aristotle, but because they considered a particular problem more abstractly than the Romans or raised an issue the Romans had not considered. We will examine some of these instances first, and then turn to interpretations of Roman law that were inspired by Aristotle.

magistrales probationes, non tamen necessariae. . . . Istis quidem non est standum si contrarium videretur, et nisi quatenus necessario concluderent.' (*Commentaria* to D. 12.1.1, nos. 22–3.)

[42] C. N. S. Woolf, *Bartolus of Sassoferrato: His Position in the History of Medieval Political Thought* (Cambridge, 1913), 384–7; Chiapelli, 'Le Idee Politiche del Bartolo', *Archivio giuridico*, 28 (1881), 433 at 433–4. See Horn, *supra* n. 16, pp. 131–2.

[43] For example, as evidence Woolf pointed to a treatise by Bartolus, the *Tractatus de regimine civitatis*. There Bartolus argued that the three forms of legitimate government that Aristotle had described are suited to states of different sizes: democracy to city-states, aristocracy to larger cities and provinces, monarchy to kingdoms and to the Empire. As Woolf correctly observes, 'the authority to which Bartolus primarily turns, here as elsewhere, is not Aristotle, but "leges nostrae", the Roman law'. (Woolf, *supra* n. 42, p. 387.) Nevertheless, the fact that most of the time Bartolus cites Roman texts to deal with Roman legal problems does not make his use of Aristotle shallow or unimportant, as Woolf seems to think. Bartolus organized this treatise around Aristotle's three forms of government, an idea which he applied in a striking and original way.

[44] Quaglioni, '"Regnativa prudentia", Diritto e teologia nel "Tractatus testimoniorum" bartoliano', presented at the conference on 'Théologie et droit dans la science politique de l'Etat moderne', (Theology and Law in the Political Thought of the Modern State), Rome, 12–14 November 1987 (publication forthcoming).

The Role of Consent

A number of medieval jurists concluded that, in principle or by nature, contracts were binding by consent. The distinction between nominate and innominate contracts was merely a matter of Roman or positive law. The late scholastics found this conclusion congenial because, like Thomas, they regarded promises as binding and thought that consent was essential to a promise.[45] Nevertheless, the medieval jurists did not arrive at it by borrowing ideas from Aristotle or Thomas. Nor did they do so, as has sometimes been suggested, by borrowing the teaching of the Canon law that it is sinful to break a promise.[46] They arrived at this conclusion gradually through reflection on their Roman texts. It was not alien to the texts themselves. Indeed, one cannot point to a moment when this opinion represented a genuinely new insight.

Accursius said:

> There are two roots of an effective obligation. One is natural. The natural root arises out of consent which can be given by all men, even slaves. D. 2.14.1.3. . . . Nevertheless this natural root does not have the force to compel performance of the obligation. It does prevent a person who has performed from taking back his performance. D. 46.1.17.2. To this natural root a civil root is sometimes joined which gives efficacy or form or clothing to the natural root so that it can produce an obligation.[47]

In this passage, Accursius pulls together two lines of Roman authority. The first is the text he cites as an example of a natural obligation, D. 2.14.1.3. This is the text already mentioned that says that all contracts require consent, real and formal contracts as well as consensual contracts. The second is the Roman distinction between natural and civil obligations. Natural obligations were created by certain contracts that were not directly enforceable, such as a contract made by a slave or by a father with his son. These contracts nevertheless had certain legal consequences, two of which are mentioned in D. 46.1.17, the last text Accursius cites: a natural

[45] See Ch. 1, pp. 11–12.

[46] e.g., J. Roussier, *Le Fondement de l'obligation contractuelle dans le droit classique de l'église* (Paris, 1933), 20–94, 177–216; A. Solmi, 'Elementi del diritto medioevale italiano', in *Contributi alla storia del diritto comune* (Rome, 1937), 147 at 223; F. Schupfer, *Il diritto delle obbligazioni in Italia nell'età del risorgimento* (Milan, 1920), i. 51. As Astuti has pointed out, however, the differences between the civilians and canonists arose not from a difference in theory or principle but from a difference in the end they had in view. The canonists were concerned not with whether a promise was actionable in civil law, but with whether breaking a promise was sinful. (Astuti, 'I principii fondamentali dei contratti nella storia del diritto italiano', *Annali di storia del diritto*, 1 (1957), 13 at 34–7.)

[47] Accursius, Gloss to I. 3.14 pr. to *necessitate*.

obligation could be the subject of a guarantee, and it could be raised as a defence if a party performed and later sued to recover his performance.[48] In Accursius's view, then, consent to real and formal contracts produces a natural obligation which must then be 'clothed' by the delivery of the object or the formality to produce a civil obligation.

Another Roman text said that 'an obligation is a legal bond which ties us to the necessity of delivering some thing in accordance with the laws of our state'. Accursius thought that the text applied to both natural and civil obligations. Since the civil law did not compel performance of a natural obligation, Accursius concluded that 'whenever a person is said to be bound by a natural obligation, the statement should be understood of the *ius gentium*'.

For the Romans, the *ius gentium* was a law governing matters such as sales that applied to people regardless of their nationality. It was distinguished from the *ius civile*, which governed such matters as marriage and applied only to Romans. In several Roman texts, the distinction is dressed up with some philosophical speculation. The *ius gentium* is the law 'established among all men by natural reason'.[49] The *ius gentium* emerged in response to human necessities; to it pertain such things as war, captivity, and slavery, since by the law of nature all were born free. 'And by the *ius gentium*, nearly all contracts were introduced such as sale and purchase, lease and hire, partnership, loan for consumption and others without number.'[50]

Iacobus de Ravanis and Petrus de Bellapertica took this line of argument farther. According to them, the formal contracts belonged to the *ius civile* because the 'form' or 'substance' of those contracts was the 'intrinsic solemnity' prescribed by the *ius civile*.[51] In contrast, the contracts of the *ius gentium* were 'naturally invented' and gave rise to a 'natural obligation'. The *ius civile* did not 'introduce' or

[48] On the Roman distinction, see Kaser, *supra* n. 3, at i. 480; ii. 245.

[49] The *ius gentium* is 'quod vero naturalis ratio inter omnes homines constituit'. (I. 1.2.1.) The same phrase appears in D. 1.1.9.

[50] The *ius gentium* was established 'usu exigente, et humanis necessitatibus'. (I. 1.2.1.) By the *ius gentium*, . . . bella etenim orta sunt et captivitates secutae et servitutes, quae sunt iuri naturali contrariae. Iure enim naturali ab initio omnes homines liberi nascenbantur.' (Ibid.) 'Ex hoc iure gentium omnes pene contractus introducti sunt, ut emptio et venditio, locatio et conductio, societas, depositum, mutuum, et alii innumerabiles.' (Ibid.)

[51] *Stipulatio* is from the *ius civile* because 'formam recipit de iure civili debet ei attribui'. (Petrus de Bellapertica, *Lectura Institutionum* to I. 1.2.1, no. 25.) '. . . per ius civile additur forma stipulationi ex qua nascit civilis'. (Iacobus de Ravanis, *Super Institutionibus commentaria* to I. 3.14.1, no. 9.) 'Et est solennitas intrinseca, ut substantialia prius tractantur, ut in stipulatione est videre, de cuius substantia est interrogatio praecedens responsio sequens. . . . Item substantia venditionis est res, et pretium'. (Ibid., to I. 3.20.3 [Vulgate 3.21], no. 9.)

'invent' these contracts but merely gave them its 'approbation' by making them actionable.[52] Indeed, underlying even the *stipulatio* was a 'natural obligation' based on consent, although not one the *ius civile* would enforce.[53]

Iacobus concluded that the distinction between nominate and innominate contracts was also created by positive law:

If I agree that you give me ten for my horse there is an action on the agreement. But if I agree that you give me your ass for my horse there is no action on the agreement. If a layman were to ask the reason for the difference it could not be given for it is merely positive law. And if you ask why the law was so established, the reason can be said to be that the contract of sale is more frequent than that of barter. And more efficacy is given to sale than barter.[54]

Bartolus did not reject the view that consent gives rise to a natural obligation by the *ius gentium*. Nevertheless, he tried to find a basis

[52] 'Dico in obligationibus iurisgentium nulla est obligatio nisi naturali inventione cum non necessarium fuit obligationem civilem introducere'. (Petrus de Bellapertica, *Lectura Institutionum* to I. 1.2.1, no. 30.) '. . . non necessarium fuit obligationem civilem introducere [cit. omitted] sed approbatione sic, quia ius civile approbat [cit. omitted] non est tunc reperire in contractibus iuris gentium obligationem civilem sed naturalem'. (Ibid.) 'Nam iure gentium erat quis naturaliter obligatus, tamen contractus, et omnes obligationes fuerunt introducti de iure gentium. . . . sed ius civile dabat istis obligationibus efficaciam agendi. . . . Et istam naturalem . . . posse dici approbationem civilem. . . . obligationes aut legibus sunt inventae aut legibus approbatae.' (Iacobus de Ravanis, *Super Institutionibus commentaria* to I. 3.14.1, no. 3.)

[53] In a *stipulatio*, 'naturalis [obligatio] introducitur propter consensum civilis propter solennitatem'. (Petrus, *Lectura Institutionum* to I. 1.2.1, no. 31; similarly, Iacobus de Ravanis, *Super Institutionibus commentaria* to I. 3.14.1, no. 9.) Azo had felt compelled by his texts to add *emphyteusis*, which resembled a long-term lease, to the contracts that belonged to the *ius civile*. (Azo Portius, *Summa Institutionum* to I. 1.2.1, no. 6.) Accursius had also added *sponsalicia largitas* which was a gift a man gave to his fiancée. (Accursius, Gloss to I. 1.2.1 to *pene*.) Petrus fitted these contracts into his scheme by explaining, rather lamely, that they owed their 'form' to the *ius gentium* but their 'name' to the *ius civile*. (Petrus de Bellapertica, *Lectura Institutionum* to I 1.2.1, nos. 26 and 27.)

[54] Iacobus de Ravanis, *Lectura Super Codice* to C. 4.64.3: 'Si ego conveni quod pro equo meo dares michi x potest agi ex ista conventione. Sed si ego conveni quod pro equo dares michi asinum ex ista conventione agi non potest. Si laicus querat rationem diversitatis reddi non potest nam hoc est mere ius positivum. Et si tu queras quare sic fuit constitutum, potest dici quod illa fuit ratio, quia contractus venditionis frequentior est permutatione. et ideo maior efficacia data est venditioni quam permutationi.' Similar are his remarks to C. 2.3.10. He distinguishes the 'consent' which is a requirement in all contracts from the 'consent' which makes consensual contracts binding by saying that in the latter case consent is 'special'. 'Si tu queras quare est speciale. dico sic placuit legislatori. unde si placeret legislatori quod ex permutatione solo consensu oritur actio: sicut ex venditione. et tamen possible esset. unde ius impositum est. Si velis rationem iure positivi quare est hoc quod ex solo consensu in obligationibus que oriuntur solo consensu oriatur actio: potest esse ratio frequentia istorum contractuum. . . .'

in the *ius gentium* for the distinction between consensual and real contracts. He claimed that the *ius gentium* gave these contracts their 'name'. The 'name' made these contracts actionable, for 'nominate contracts give rise to an action by this alone: that they exist and have a name'.[55] Consensual contracts were binding on consent and real contracts only on delivery of an object, because of a difference in their names. Consensual contracts such as sale took their names from an act a party performs by agreeing: I can sell you my house today by so agreeing even if I do not deliver it to you until next month. Real contracts such as deposit took their names from an act a party performs by delivering: I cannot say I am depositing an object with you unless I am actually depositing it right now.[56]

His pupil Baldus described this distinction in the names of real and consensual contracts without approval or interest.[57] He was content to say, like Iacobus and Petrus, and, indeed, like Accursius, that natural obligations arise by mere consent.[58]

[55] 'Pactum seu conventio nuda . . . est illud quod stat in puris, et nudis finibus conventionis: Illud dicitur vestitum, cui post originem vel in sui origine aliquid superadiicitur. Illud nota quod superadiicitur, dicitur vestamentum.' (Bartolus, *Commentaria* to D. 2.14.7.5, no. 14.) 'Dic ergo quod pactum vestitur quandoque a iure gentium, quandoque; a iure civili. a iure gentium tribus modis: primo vestitur nomine [cit. omitted.] et hoc comprehendit contractus quae celebrantur re, vel consensu. Ideo nota dictitur vestiti, quia iure gentium sibi nomen est additum, Secundum vestimentum est rei interventus, seu implementum iustae causae [cit. omitted]. Tertium vestimentum est cohaerentia contractus.' (Bartolus, *Commentaria* to D. 2.14.7.5, nos. 15–16.) '. . . contractus nominati producunt actionem eo ipso quod sunt, et nomen habent.' (Bartolus, *Commentaria* to D. 2.14.7, no. 2.)

[56] '. . . quidam contractus denominatur ab actu paciscendi, seu conveniendi, quidam denominatur ab actu exequendi. Si loqueris in primis, quando denominatur ab actu paciscendi, statim facto pacto habent nomen, et producunt actionem, exemplum in emptione, venditione, locatione, conductione, societate, mandato, et similibus. Si accipis secundo modo, quando denominatur ab actu, exequendi, non habent nomen, nisi facta executione. exemplum in contractibus, qui re contrahuntur, ut depositum, commodatum, mutuum, qui ab actu exequendi denominantur, ut patet ad sensum. Et ideo si facio pactum de deponendo, commodando, vel mutuando, non est contractus nominatus, nec actionem producit, nisi habeat alia vestimenta.' (Bartolus, *Commentaria* to D. 2.14.7, no. 2.) He goes on to show that *pignus* is derived from a word referring to an act of execution, and that *donatio* belongs with the nominate contracts *re*.

[57] Baldus, *Commentaria* to D. 2.14.7, no. 10.

[58] '. . . naturalis obligatio pendet a facto id est consensu, civilis autem a iuris solennitate'. (Baldus, *Tractatus de pactis*, no. 29.) 'Si agimus tu, et ego nudo pacto de permutando meum librum cum tuo ab initio non nascitur aliqua obligatio civilis, sed naturalis propter consensum, et illi naturali additur civilis, et sic pactum vestitur rei interventu. . .'. (Ibid., no. 30.) Elsewhere he says, 'Vestimentum, ex quo actio oritur, est duplex, scilicet nativum, seu naturale, et hoc modo contractus vestitur re, verbis, et consensu. Istud vestimentum est inseparabile: et est idem, quod propriam essentia contractus, sicut corpus vestiens animam est idem, quod propria substantia hominis. Quoddom vestimentum est dativum, seu accidentale, quod est sub predicamento accidentis. Istud vestimentum pactum non habet ex se, sed accomodatum sibi extrinsecus.' (Commentaria to C. 2.3.10, no. 4.) He did not mean, however, that the

That opinion seems more significant in retrospect than it did at the time. To modern eyes, it seems important practically as a step towards the abolition of the Roman rules, and theoretically as a discovery about the role of consent in contract formation. As Astuti has noted, however, this 'affirmation of principle' of the medieval jurists 'is not linked to any concrete theoretical development in the sense of some extension of the binding force of agreements'.[59] The medieval jurists were not criticizing Roman law. They were simply observing that the rule that one could not enforce a real contract until delivery of an object, or a formal contract until completion of a formality, was a pecularity of Roman law, unlike the requirement that the parties consent, which belonged to the very nature of contracts. As we have seen, one cannot point to a moment when the significance of consent in contract formation was first discovered.

Indeed, the Romans might not have found these ideas particularly novel. The first text Accursius cited said that all contracts require consent. The second, D. 46.1.17.2, implied that when a contract is enforceable a natural and a civil obligation are present together, the natural obligation arising, presumably, from consent. According to another text, 'sale belongs to the *ius gentium* and so is concluded by consent'.[60] The medieval jurists seem to be clearer about the role of consent in contract formation, less because they thought differently from the Romans than because they put all the Roman texts together.

Offer and Acceptance

Another instance in which the medieval jurists moved in the direction later taken by the late scholastics was in raising the question of whether a contract is formed when an offer is revoked before acceptance. This question had not been directly addressed by the Romans. It was of theoretical interest to the late scholastics because they believed, like Thomas, that all promises were binding by the virtue of fidelity. Consequently, it seemed puzzling that an offer might not be binding until acceptance. Again, however, the medieval jurists who raised the problem did not have Aristotle or Thomas in mind.

distinctions among contracts *re*, *verbis*, and *consensu* are 'natural' in the sense that they come from the natural law. He meant that, in the case of these contracts, the 'clothing' that makes them actionable cannot be separated from the contract itself. The 'clothing' of the civil law contract of *stipulatio*, for example, is the formality, which is the very feature that makes the contract a *stipulatio*.

[59] Astuti, *supra* n. 46, p. 30.

[60] 'Est autem emptio iuris gentium: et ideo consensu peragitur: et inter absentes contrahi potest, et per nuntium, et per litteras.' (D. 18.1.1.2.)

The Roman text just mentioned, which said that a sale is concluded by consent because it belongs to the *ius gentium*, went on to say that a sale 'can be contracted by parties not present together either by messenger (*nuntius*) or by letters'.[61] In his gloss to this text, Accursius asked, 'what if before the letters or messenger reach him, the seller revokes?' Following the opinion of Aldericus and earlier Glossators, he decided that a contract entered into would be valid despite the revocation.[62]

To Petrus, Cinus, and Bartolus, the obvious difficulty with this position is that the seller becomes bound to a contract to which he did not consent at the moment it was formed. The issue in Accursius's mind, however, was not whether the seller had consented but the moment at which a communication is effective. That is the issue raised by the texts he cited for and against his position. A partner who renounces the partnership remains liable for all losses, and shares any gains, that are realized before the other partners learn of his renunciation.[63] Since the renunciation of the partnership is not effective instantly, neither, Accursius concluded, is the seller's revocation. He acknowledged, however, that a marriage can be dissolved by a document that never reaches the other spouse;[64] and that a father's revocation of his order to his son to manumit a slave is effective even if the son acts on the order before receiving the revocation.[65]

For Petrus, Cinus, and Bartolus, however, the principle at stake was that 'without the consent of the owner the contract is not valid'.[66] The messenger (*nuntius*) was a 'mere minister', a transmitter of the wishes of another, and if these wishes should change, there was no contract. Petrus, however, followed by Cinus and Bartolus, distinguished the mere messenger from the *procurator*. By appointing a procurator, a person contracts, as Bartolus put it, 'through another as by himself but by the other's act'.[67] He chooses,

[61] See n. 60, *supra*.

[62] 'Item quid si antequam literae vel nuntius ad eum perveniant, venditor renuntiat? quidam dicunt non valere contractum. . . . sed Ald. dicit tenere, quod puto verum. . . .' (Accursius, Gloss to D. 18.1.1.2 to *et per literas*.)

[63] D. 17.2.17.1.

[64] C. 5.17.6.

[65] D. 40.2.4.

[66] 'Et ratio est, quia quando intervenit, ut nuncius non contrahit, sed dominus per eum, et sine consensu domini non valet contractus.' (Cinus, *Commentaria* to C. 4.35.15, no. 4, describing the position taken by him and Petrus.) Similarly, according to Bartolus, 'ubi penitet mandantem, statim deficit eius consensus. Quod ergo postea sequitur, non potest effectum sortiri.' (Bartolus, *Commentaria* to D. 15.4.1.2.) In support, Bartolus cites D. 44.7.2 and D. 2.14.2 for the principle that there must be consent or agreement to form a contract.

[67] Bartolus, *Commentaria* to D. 15.4.1.2. Petrus's opinion is described and adopted by Cinus, *Commentaria* to 4.35.15, no. 4. It is described and rejected by Baldus, *Commentaria* to C. 4.35.15, nos. 28–9.

in effect, to have the procurator's decision count as his own. Therefore, although contracts require consent, the procurator can sell property even if, unknown to him, the owner has written instructing him not to sell.

This distinction between a mere messenger and a procurator was part of a medieval effort to turn the procurator into an agent in the modern sense. The ancient Romans did not recognize the principle that a person could contract, in Bartolus's words, 'through another as by himself'. A person could appoint a procurator to enter into contracts on his behalf, but he could not sue on these contracts unless the procurator assigned him the right to do so. He could be sued by the persons with whom the procurator contracted, but the reason, according to Buckland, was not that the procurator's act counted as his own, but that these people had suffered because he did business through a procurator.[68]

Consequently, Petrus, Cinus, and Bartolus found no direct support for their distinction in the Roman texts. The powers of a mere messenger were analogized to those of a son who frees a slave by his father's authority,[69] a son who accepts an inheritance on his father's instructions,[70] and a wife who contracts in her husband's name.[71] The powers of a procurator were analogized to those of an agent for a municipality, the *tutor* of a minor, and the *curator* of a lunatic.[72] One Roman text said a manumission performed on a father's instructions was invalid if the father had changed his mind;[73] another said that a gift was invalid if the donor died before his messenger had delivered the money to the donee.[74] They were cited to show that the authority of a mere messenger could be revoked before he learns of the revocation. Other texts said that one who revoked another's authority could be sued by him if he had exercised that authority without knowing it had been revoked.[75] They were cited to show that the authority of some persons did not end before

[68] Buckland, McNair, and Lawson, *supra* n. 1, pp. 217–21. See Buckland, *supra* n. 5, pp. 168, 302, 310–11; Kaser, *supra* n. 3, at ii. 99–107.

[69] D. 40.2.4; D. 40.1.22; D. 40.1.16; D. 37.14.13, cited by Cinus, *Commentaria* to C. 4.35.15, no. 4. D. 40.2.4 is also cited by Bartolus, *Commentaria* to D. 15.4.1.2, and in Baldus's account of Petrus's position, *Commentaria* to C. 4.35.15, no. 28.

[70] D. 29.2.25.11, cited by Cinus, *Commentaria* to C. 4.35.15, no. 4.

[71] C. 4.50.6, cited by Cinus, *Commentaria* to C. 4.35.15, no. 4; Bartolus, *Commentaria* to D. 15.4.1.2.

[72] D. 13.5.5.9, cited by Cinus, *Commentaria* to C. 4.35.15, no. 4.

[73] D. 40.2.4, cited by Cinus, *Commentaria* to C. 4.35.15, no. 4; Bartolus, *Commentaria* to D. 15.4.1.2; Baldus describing Petrus's position, *Commentaria* to D. 4.35.15, no. 28.

[74] D. 39.5.2.6, cited by Cinus, *Commentaria* to C. 4.35.15, no. 5.

[75] D. 17.1.15; D. 12.4.5.1, both cited by Bartolus, *Commentaria* to D. 15.4.1.2.

they learned of the revocation. The reason was supposed to be that these persons were procuratores.[76]

Bartolus was not wholly satisfied with this solution because he thought that, in cases 'where no prejudice is caused, a revocation ought to consist in the pure and simple will' to revoke, whether or not authority had been given to a procurator.[77] He pointed to the text on the renunciation of a partnership that Accursius had cited. The renunciation was given legal effect, but in such a way that no other partner could be hurt.[78]

For Baldus, this concern about who might be hurt by the revocation was the key to the entire problem. He returned to what he took to be the solution of Accursius: the revocation was ineffective until the messenger knew about it. 'And if it is said that consent is at an end and therefore the act is invalid, I answer that the act is valid not by reason of consent but by reason of a wrong done, for consent is deemed to endure on account of a wrong.'[79]

Although the medieval jurists did not analyse the problem of offer and acceptance in the same way as the late scholastics, or reach the same conclusions, they raised the problem for the first time. Moreover, later discussions of the problem were to mention the same concerns as the medieval jurists, concerns about the moment a communication was effective, the need for both parties to consent, the nature of agency, and the harm that one party's revocation might cause another. The medieval jurists responded to these

[76] There remained problems. For example, D. 12.1.41 put the case of a man who put a slave in charge of his business out in a province and then died. His will, read in Rome, freed the slave and named him heir to part of the master's estate. Not knowing his master had died, the slave continued to lend the dead man's money and to receive payment of the loans. According to the text, the slave was unable, after his master's death, to alienate money of greater value than his own share in the estate. Nevertheless, debtors who paid the slave not knowing of the master's death were discharged. According to Petrus, the slave was a procurator, but his loans were not valid after the master's death because certain acts, such as transferring property, require the consent of the owner. (Cinus, *Commentaria* to C. 4.35.15, no. 4; Baldus describing Petrus's position, *Commentaria* to C. 4.35.15, no. 28.) Cinus added another epicycle: the debtors are discharged because of a special exception the law creates in their favour. (Cinus, *Commentaria* to C. 4.35.15, no. 4.)

[77] '. . . ubi nullum preiudicium generatur, revocatio debet consistere in pura, et mera voluntate'. (Bartolus, *Commentaria* to D. 15.4.1.2.)

[78] D. 17.2.17.1. Bartolus also thought that the authority to make a gift was revocable without notice, and that this was the true explanation of D. 39.5.2.6, the case in which a gift was revoked by the donor's death before his messenger delivered the money to the donee. He gave a different reason, however: 'quia requiritur interventio personae medie vere, vel ficte prestantis ministerium . . .'. (*Commentaria* to D. 15.4.1.2.)

[79] '. . . et si dicatur, cessat consensus, ergo non valet actus. Respondeo valet actus non tam ratione consensus quam ratione doli: quia ratione doli fingitur consensus durare.' (Baldus, *Commentaria* to C. 4.35.15, no. 29.)

concerns, however, without stating them as principles to be fitted together in a system or elucidated through an abstract discussion.

The Doctrine of Causa

In other instances, the medieval jurists reached much the same conclusions as the late scholastics, and did so because they, too, had read Aristotle. The formulation of the doctrine of *causa* by Bartolus and Baldus is one such instance. According this doctrine, the consent of the parties is binding, in principle, only if it is given for one of two reasons or *causae*: liberality, or the receipt of something in return for what one gives. The doctrine thus went further than the Romans, who had distinguished contracts to make gifts from contracts to exchange, and further than Bartolus's predecessors, who had distinguished contracts made *causa lucrativa* and *causa onerosa*.[80] The late scholastics found the doctrine congenial because they, like Thomas, thought the fundamental distinction among contracts was between acts of liberality and acts of commutative justice.[81] As we shall see, in all likelihood Bartolus and Baldus formulated the doctrine with this distinction in mind. Nevertheless, they were not attempting to explain Roman law systematically by Aristotelian principles. They merely found Aristotle helpful in interpreting their Roman texts.

One key text stated: 'When there is no *causa*, it is accepted that no obligation can be constituted by an agreement; therefore a naked agreement does not give rise to an action although it does give rise to a defence (*exceptio*).'[82] Buckland has called this text 'the famous passage on which the whole theory of *cause* was based'. According to Buckland, although 'it was taken to mean that every contract must have a *cause*, in reality [it] says nothing of the kind'. Clearly, he said, the text is referring to innominate contracts which do not give rise to an action but do create a defence if a party performs and then tries to reclaim his performance.[83] Interestingly enough, Bartolus interpreted the text in the same way as Buckland, as referring to innominate contracts. Thus, rather than inspiring his doctrine of *causa*, the text was an obstacle in Bartolus's way. He wanted to establish that one sort of *causa* was the receipt of a return performance. In discussing sales, he had said that the *causa* of the seller was to obtain the price and that of the buyer was to obtain the

[80] e.g. Petrus de Bellapertica, *Commentaria in Digestum Novum Repetitiones Variae* to D. 44.7.53 [vulgate 44.7.52], D. 44.7.54 [vulgate 44.7.53].

[81] See Ch. 1 above, pp. 12–14.

[82] D. 2.14.7.1.

[83] Buckland, McNair, and Lawson, *supra* n. 1, pp. 229–30.

object sold.[84] Therefore, innominate contracts ought to have a *causa*; for example, in a horse swap each party wants to obtain the horse of the other. Yet here was a text that plainly said they had no *causa*. Bartolus solved the problem in a scholastic fashion by reading a bit more into the text. 'No *causa* means [no *causa*] fulfilled, but the agreement was certainly made for a *causa*.'[85] Thus it was established, less because of the Roman texts than in spite of them, that one sort of *causa* was the receipt of something in return.

The other critical text said that the formal contract *stipulatio* must have a *causa*.[86] The text seems to have meant originally that such a contract would not be enforced unless there was some good reason or *causa* why the promise was made. Bartolus explained that the *causa* of a *stipulatio* might be the receipt of something in return. That alone was not enough, however, since a *stipulatio* was binding even if a promise was gratuitous. In that case, Bartolus explained, the *causa* was 'liberality'. There were then two kinds of *causa*.[87]

This conclusion had not leapt to the minds of the Glossators or the ultramontanes when they read the same texts. Azo, Accursius, and Iacobus describe the *causa* referred to in the text on innominate contracts simply as 'something given or done'.[88] Azo and Accursius describe the *causa* referred to by the text on *stipulatio* as *re* or *spe*, a thing or the hope of a thing.[89] When Iacobus and Petrus discuss that text, they simply note that a *stipulatio* is void if the promisor mistakenly believes there is a *causa* for his promise, but it is valid if he knows there is no *causa* for then he is deemed to be making a gift.[90] They do not arrive at a uniform doctrine of *causa*, let alone one that resembles the Aristotelian distinction between commutative justice and liberality.

Bartolus and Baldus not only did so, but couched their doctrine in a specifically Aristotelian vocabulary. While the Roman texts speak merely of *causa*, which in Latin simply means a reason, Bartolus

[84] Bartolus, *Commentaria* to D. 12.4.16, no. 13, speaks of the price as the *causa finalis* of a sale: 'Sed quare magis rescinditur contractus, quando non adempletur pactum appositum iuxta venditionem, quam si non solvat pretium, non video: imo magis videtur contrarium, quia magis est causa finalis solo pretii, quam pactum appositum iuxta eam.'

[85] Bartolus, *Commentaria* to D. 12.4.7.2: 'nulla subest causa, scilicet impleta, sed conventio bene fuit ob causam'.

[86] D. 12.7.1; see also D. 44.4.2.3.

[87] Bartolus, *Commentaria* to D. 44.4.2.3.

[88] Accursius, Gloss to D. 2.14.7.1 to *causa*: 'Id est, datio vel factum, quod vestiet pactionem.' Iacobus de Ravanis, *Lectura super Codice* to C. 2.3.10: 'pactum nudum est cui causa non subest, id est cui non subest datio vel factio'.

[89] Accursius, Gloss to D. 44.4.2.3 to *idoneam*.

[90] Iacobus de Ravanis, *Lectura super Codice* to C. 2.3.5; Petrus de Bellapertica, *Commentaria in Digestum novum* to D. 44.4.2.

and Baldus speak of the *causa finalis*, or, when they are being very careful, the *causa finalis proxima* of the contracting parties.[91]

They were fully aware of the technical meaning of this term in Aristotelian and Thomistic philosophy. As we have seen, Thomas Aquinas thought that one could define the essence of a human action in terms of its end or *causa finalis*. The end or *causa finalis* of the action itself corresponded to the proximate end or *causa finalis* of the person performing the action.[92] Bartolus and Baldus were quite familiar with the Aristotelian terminology. Bartolus distinguished the 'substantial' and 'accidental' forms of things.[93] He described legal institutions such as contract as a sort of incorporeal thing. He explained that man-made things 'take their substantial form from some aptitude which they have toward a certain end for which they were made by their maker'.[94] To know the end of the maker is to know the end and hence the substantial form or nature of the thing made. Thus, Bartolus moves back and forth between talking about the *causa finalis* of a contract and talking about its substance or nature.[95] Similarly, according to Baldus, 'in a contract

[91] See n. 84 *supra*, and nn. 95, 96, and 104 *infra*.

[92] See Ch. 1, pp. 20–2. Thus, as Thomas said (*Summa theologica* I–II, q. 1, a. 3 *ad ter.*), 'idem actus numero, secundum quod semel egreditur ab agente, non ordinatur nisi ad unum finem proximum, a quo habet speciem: sed potest ordinari ad plures fines remotos, quorum unus est finis alterius. Possibile tamen est quod unus actus secundum speciem naturae, ordinetur ad diversos fines voluntatis: sicut hoc ipsum quod est occidere hominem, quod est idem secundum speciem naturae, potest ordinari sicut in finem ad conservationem iustitiae, et ad satisfaciendum irae.'

[93] 'Nota quod quando forma est perempta, perit res, sed solum cum perit propria forma rei. Quae igitur sit ista propria forma, videamus. Unde sciendum est, quod quaedam est forma substantialis, alia accidentalis. De accidentali non potest intelligi hic, quia licet una res mutet sua accidentia . . . per hoc non desinit esse idem [cit. omitted] et ideo dicimus quod plus et minus non faciunt res differre specie [cit. omitted] [o]pportet ergo, quod hoc intelligatur de propria forma scilicet substantiali. De ista igitur videamus qualiter cognoscatur.' (Bartolus, *Tractatus de alveo*, § Stricta ratione, nos. 1–3.)

[94] '. . . rerum quaedam sunt corporales, quaedam incorporales. Item corporales aliae naturales, aliae artificiales.' (Bartolus, *Tractatus de alveo*, § Stricta ratione, no. 3.) 'Quinto videndum est de rebus artificialibus. Circa quae dico, quod iste assumunt formam substantialem ex quadam aptitudinem, quam habent ad illum finem, ad quem per artificem factae sunt domus: tunc nota dicitur domus, cum habeat debitas partes compositas, ita quod est apta ad habitandum.' (Ibid., no. 19.) 'Sexto videndum est de rebus incorporalibus, ut sunt iura, servitutes, actiones, et obligationes, et similia.' (Ibid., no. 20.) Contracts are another example. (Ibid., nos. 22–3.)

[95] Here is an illustration. 'Sed quare magis rescinditur contractus, quando non adempletur pactum appositum iuxta venditionem, quam si non solvat pretium, non video: imo magis videtur contrarium, quia magis est causa finalis solo pretii, quam pactum appositum iuxta eam. Ideo credo aliter dicendum, quia aut illud pactum appositum iuxta venditionem facit transire in naturam contractus innominati, ut quando vendebam tibi Codicem, ut tu dares mihi decem et Digestum tuum: unde in isto casu magis habet naturam permutationis, quam venditionis: ideo censet contractus innominatus. [cit. omitted] quia tunc potest rescindi contractus, nisi

of sale, the *causa finalis* with respect to the buyer is the object and with respect to the seller is the price';[96] alternatively, he says that 'the essential or substantial' terms 'in a contract of sale are the object and the price'.[97] Indeed, Baldus described the efficient, formal, material, and final causes of a contract, giving examples of each. His example of the final cause is a gift given to accomplish a particular purpose, absent which it would not have been given.[98] He explained the final cause with a series of Aristotelian or Thomistic phrases: 'the final cause is the object of the intellect as an image is the object of vision or a port is the object of navigation, and whatever we do, we do for an end';[99] 'the final cause is the first principle in intention although it is the last in execution';[100] it is 'the cause of the other causes'.[101]

Further evidence that Bartolus and Baldus were trying to remain faithful to the technical meaning of *causa finalis* lies in an instance

servetur pactum. [cit. omitted] Aut non facit transire in naturam contractus innominati, quia minus valet, quod continetur in pacto, quod contineat pretium tunc non rescindit contractus. [cit. omitted] Quandoque est permixtus contractus nominatus cum innominato. Exemplum vendo tibi fundum pro centum hoc pacto, ut des mihi librum. Nam hic primo est contractus nominatus quia vendo, et est mixtus cum contractu innominato: vendo nota ut des. Aliud est exemplum, dono ut aliquid facias, vel ut aliquid des, vel promitto per stipulationem ut aliquid des, vel facias. In his vides permixtum contractum nominatum cum innominato. Et breviter ubicunque contractus nominatus celebratur ob aliquam causam extrinsicam extra substantiam ipsius contractus potest dici permixtus contractus nominatus.' (Bartolus, *Commentaria* to D. 12.4.16, nos. 13–14.)

[96] '. . . in contractu emptionis et venditionis respectu emptoris. causa finalis est res et respectu venditoris est pretium': (Baldus, *Commentaria* to C. 8.40.7 [vulgate 8.41.7], no. 3.)

[97] '. . . quaedam pacta dicuntur essentialia sive substantialia, quia tangunt id, quod habet ipsum actum substantiare, et dare sibi esse, sicut in contractu emptionis et venditionis sunt res et pretium. illa ergo appelantur substantialia, sine quibus contractus esse non potest.' (Baldus, *Commentaria* to D. 2.14.7.7.) Similarly, he speaks of both the final cause and the essence or substance of a contract as the 'root' of the contractual obligation. (Baldus, *Commentaria* to C. 6.44.1, no. 12 ('illa est causa finalis, de cuius radice emanat obligatio'); see n. 135 *infra*.)

[98] 'Debes scire, quod quattuor sunt causae cardinales, ut sic dixerim. Causa efficiens, finalis, formalis et materialis. et ex defectu cuiuslibet istarum causarum, quae sunt radices actuum hominum potest ista condictio oriri. . . . Item pone exemplum in causa finalis ut quando non erat alias daturus. ista dicitur causa finalis.' (Baldus, *Commentaria* to C. 4.6.8, nos. 10–11.)

[99] '. . . causa enim finalis est obiectum intellectus, sicut signum est obiectum visus; et portus est obiectum navigantium, et quicquid agimus, propter finem agimus.' (Baldus, *Commentaria* to C. 6.44.1, no. 17.) He would have been more faithful to Thomas had he borne in mind that 'obiectum intellectus est primum principium in genere causae formalis . . . sed obiectum voluntatis est primum principium in generae causae finalis. . .'. (Thomas Aquinas, *De malo* q. 6, a. 1, in *Opera Omnia*, ed. P. Fiaccadori (Parma, 1852–73), viii. 219 at 310.)

[100] '. . . causa finalis est primum principium intentionis, licet sit ultimum executionis'. (Baldus, *Commentaria* to C. 5.12.6, no. 24.)

[101] See n. 105 *infra*.

in which they corrected the terminology of the Glossators. The Glossators themselves had used the term *causa finalis* in their discussions of the Roman *condictio causa data causa non secuta*. In Roman law, a party used this *condictio* when he had given something to another party in expectation of an event that did not take place. For example, if he had performed his part of an innominate contract expecting the other party to perform in return, he could bring this *condictio* if the other party refused to do so. If he had paid money to his daughter's fiancé in expectation of their marriage, he could bring this *condictio* if the marriage did not occur.[102] The problem for medieval jurists was to distinguish these situations from others in which the *condictio* was not available, for example situations in which a person gave a gift merely hoping that the recipient would use it in a certain way. The Glossators said that the *condictio* could be brought when the expectation of an event was the *causa finalis* of the person who had parted with something, but not when this expectation was the *causa impulsiva* or *causa efficiens*.[103]

As already noted, the Glossators knew of Aristotle's four causes only as trivialized by Boethius. Bartolus and Baldus, however, knew that it was nonsense in Aristotelian philosophical terms to describe the legally insignificant expectations of a donor as a *causa impulsiva* or *efficiens*. *Causa impulsiva* is not an Aristotelian term at all. *Causa efficiens* is not a motive or purpose, nor is it the opposite of *causa finalis*, nor could anything exist without a *causa efficiens* any more than it could exist without a *causa finalis*. Following a hint given by Petrus, Bartolus and Baldus straightened out the Glossators' terminology. A gift, or for that matter a legacy, a contract, or a

[102] See D. 39.5.2.7; D. 12.6.52; D. 35.1.17.3; C. 5.12.25.

[103] Accursius, Gloss to D. 39.5.2.7 to *causa magis*: 'id est modus liberalitatis: et sic fuit impulsiva, non finalis causa'; D. 39.5.3 to *conditio*: 'scilicet finalis. et ita causa fuit finalis'; D. 39.5.3 to *causa*: 'scilicet impulsiva'. Azo, *Summa Codicis* to C. 4.6.7, nos. 3 and 4: 'Inducit autem istam actionem causae defectus . . . hoc ita, si causa fuerit finalis, id est, qua finita vel non completa voluit uterque restitui quod datum est. Secus si fuerit impulsiva causa, id est, in corde tradentis retenta ob quam impellebatur animo suo ad dandum.' Odofredus, *Lectura super Codice* to C. 2.3.1, no. 15: 'Est causa finalis et est causa impulsiva. Causa finalis dicitur ob cuius finem quis dat, alias non daturus: et in ista causa est vera regula, cessante causa etcetera [i.e., cessante causa cessat effectus] [cit. omitted]. Causa impulsiva est ob cuius impulsionem quis dat: sed alias daturus erat. sed citius ob causam dat.' He expressly treats the difference between expressed and unexpressed *causae* as a separate distinction. 'Vel potest dici quod est duplex causa, expressa et tacita.' (Ibid., no. 16.) Meyers is sceptical as to whether this groping resulted in more than the legal conclusion that a cause was final when it had legal effect and impulsive when it did not. (Meyers, 'Les théories médiévales concernant la cause de la stipulation et la cause de la donation', *Tijdschrift voor Rechtsgeschiedenis*, 14 (1936), 365 at 379–8.) Accursius, Gloss to C. 5.12.25 to *mulier*: 'non enim fuit haec conditio sed causa scilicet impulsiva vel efficiens non finalis'.

statute, was ineffective if the purpose that was thwarted was the *causa finalis proxima* of the person making such a disposition; it was effective if the purpose thwarted was a *causa finalis remota*.[104] This formulation was at least a legitimate use of the philosophical vocabulary. As just mentioned, whatever a person's remote ends for performing an action might be, he must have a *causa finalis proxima* or immediate end that corresponds to the end by which the action is defined. Baldus explained that 'the *causa impulsiva* is not properly speaking the cause but some motive' of the act; in contrast, 'Aristotle said that the *causa finalis* is the cause of the other causes. Therefore, when this cause ceases, the effect ceases.'[105]

The fact that Bartolus and Baldus were drawing on the Aristo-

[104] Bartolus, *Commentaria* to D. 35.1.17.2, no. 13: 'ut quando causa non erat obligatoria, tunc non dicitur coherere legato, hoc est nunquam dicitur causa proxima et finalis, quia causa proxima, et finalis est mera liberalitas: legatum non est donatio [cit. omitted] et in donatione causa proxima est liberalitas [cit. omitted] ergo illa inserta, est remota, non coherens legato, et dicitur impulsiva, et illa, si est falsa, non vitiat legatum.' Baldus, *Commentaria* to D. 17.2.61.2, nos. 3 and 4: 'causam remotam non considerari, sed tamen proximam. . . . Ex his apparet quod causa remota aequiparatur causae impulsivae, non causae finali.'

Despite their knowledge of Aristotle, the ultramontanes continued to speak of *causa finalis* and *causa impulsiva*. (Iacobus de Ravanis, *Lectura super Codice* to C. 2.3.1; to C. 4.6.7; Petrus de Bellapertica, *Quaestiones vel distinctiones*, q. 142.) Nevertheless, according to Baldus, Petrus had described the *causa impulsiva* as a 'remote occasion' (*occasionem aliquam remotam*) of an act and therefore not properly a cause (*non proprie . . . de genere causarum*). Baldus, *Commentaria* to C. 1.3.51, no. 10; similarly, Cinus, *In Codicem commentaria* to C.1.3.52, no. 6. Meyers has noted that in this formulation, for the first time, the final cause of an act was said to differ from other motives of the actor only by its proximity to the act itself. (*supra* n. 103, p. 383.) Petrus, moreover, was familiar with the Aristotelian distinction between remote and proximate final causes; indeed, he distinguished the remote and proximate final causes of his law book. Petrus de Bellapertica, *Lectura Institutionum*, to rubric no. 30: 'Est causa finalis. quae est causa finalis, quaedam est propinqua, quaedam remota.')

Bartolus and Baldus continued to speak of the final cause as that absent which the new action would not have been taken, as indeed, by the new view, it was. Bartolus, *Commentaria* to D. 35.1.17.2, no. 13; Baldus, *Commentaria* to C. 4.6.8, no. 10. They stopped equating *causa impulsiva* with efficient cause. As Söllner and Meyers have noted, however, when they speak of efficient cause it is in a completely different sense. (Meyers, *supra* n. 103, p. 388, n. 1; Söllner, 'Die causa im Kondiktionen- und Vertragsrecht des Mittelalters bei den Glossatoren, Kommentoren und Kanonisten', *Zeitschrift der Savigny-Stiftung für Rechtsgeschichte Rom. Abt.* 77 (1960), 182 at 209.) e.g. Baldus to C. 4.6.8 no. 11: 'Pone exemplum in causa efficienti de minore xxv annis ut manumittat servum proprium, hic est defectus istius causae efficientis, id est minoris, qui habet efficere istam manumissionem in servo alieno.' They also stop saying the impulsive cause 'impels' one to act and begin saying this of the final cause; e.g. Bartolus, *Commentaria* to D. 35.17.2, no. 2: 'quod impellimur, ut aliquid disponamus').

[105] '. . . causa impulsiva proprie non est causa, sed est quoddam motivum: sed hic loquitur in causa finali, quod proprie est causa. Imo dicit Aristoteles quod causa finalis est causa aliarum causarum. hac ergo causa cessante cessat effectus . . .'. (Baldus, *Commentaria* to C. 1.3.51 [vulgate 1.6.41], no. 5.)

telian idea of *causa finalis* to formulate their doctrine of *causa* does not, of course, prove that they were also drawing on the Aristotelian distinction between acts of liberality and acts of commutative justice. It would be remarkable, however, if they arrived at their distinction between two types of *causa*, which is so close to the Aristotelian distinction and which had escaped their predecessors, drawing explicitly on what Aristotle said about *causa finalis* in the *Physics* and *Metaphysics*, and with a blind eye to what he had said about contracts in the *Ethics*.

In any event, whatever may be the case as to Bartolus, by the time Baldus had put the doctrine of *causa* in final form, the fit with Aristotelian ideas of liberality and commutative justice had become remarkable indeed. According to Baldus, the rationale of the doctrine was that 'without a *causa* equity will not say that an action arises lest one party use his substance badly and the other be unjustifiably enriched'.[106] Baldus apparently meant that when a party gives out of liberality, he does not use his substance badly and the other party is not enriched unjustifiably; when the parties exchange, neither party is unjustifiably enriched. That statement makes sense, however, only if one thinks of the distinction between the two kinds of *causa* exactly as Aristotle thought of the distinction between liberality and commutative justice. Liberality, for Aristotle, does not simply mean giving wealth away, but giving 'to the right people, the right amounts, and at the right time'. Commutative justice does not simply mean that the parties exchange, but that they exchange so that neither party is enriched at the expense of the other. Baldus's assertion that a contract could lack a *causa* is meaningful only because for him, as for Aristotle, liberality meant more than giving without receiving, and exchange meant more than giving and also receiving. Therefore, the doctrine meant more than the tautology that a party either does or does not get something when he gives.

That Baldus did think of liberality as right management of wealth is confirmed by a statement he makes elsewhere. One contested issue in his day was whether the notarial document—which had come to be accepted as a substitute for *stipulatio*—had to state expressly the *causa* on which the promise was made. Baldus said that it did, for otherwise one should presume the contract was the result of 'foolishness' rather than 'liberality'.[107] To act out of

[106] '. . . non enim debet esse nudum causa quia sine causa aequitas non dictat actionem nasci, ne qui male utatur substantia sua, et alius immerito locupletetur.' (Baldus, *In Decretalium volumen commentaria* to X. 1.4.11, no. 30.)

[107] '. . . sicut ergo nulla inserta causa presumitur stultitia, non liberalitas . . .'. (Baldus, *Commentaria* to C. 4.30.13, no. 14.)

liberality, then, one must give money away sensibly. Otherwise one was simply being foolish.

One can see from other remarks of Baldus that he believed that neither party to an exchange was to be enriched at the other's expense. A famous Roman text gave a remedy to people who sold land at less than half its just price. The Glossators extended the remedy to buyers as well as sellers and to analogous contracts. While the Glossators themselves had not supplied any principled explanation of this doctrine, Baldus did. An unjust price violated 'natural equity'.[108] By equity, Baldus had in mind a principle of equality, since he often used the terms interchangeably, as when he said that 'in contracts, equity or equality must be served. . . '.[109] In this case, he had a particular reason for speaking of 'natural equity' since, according to another famous Roman text, 'By the law of nature it is equitable that no one should be enriched by another's loss or injury.'[110] Elsewhere Baldus said that this principle underlies the Roman remedies for unjust enrichment. Here he implies that it underlies the remedy for an unjust price as well.

For Baldus, then, the *causa* of liberality meant right giving, not merely giving without return; the *causa* of receiving something in return meant receiving something of equivalent value. A contract with neither *causa* was an act of folly. Consequently, the requirement of a *causa* transcended the rules of Roman positive law. It expressed a general truth about when a promise ought to be enforced. Baldus read this truth into the Canon law. Under Canon law, an informal executory agreement was binding in principle and without regard to the Roman rules. That was so, Baldus explained, provided the agreement had a *causa*.[111]

[108] '. . . equitas huius legis extendit se ad contractus stricti iuris, in quibus hincinde par debet nasci obligatio secundum naturalem aequitatem . . .'. (Baldus, *Commentaria* to C. 4.44.2, no. 18.)

[109] '. . . quaero nunquid lex natura habet locum econtra, scilicet decepto emptore ultra dimidiam iusti pretii? Respondeo sic. quia in contractibus est servanda aequitas, vel aequalitas, tam in interpretandis, quam in ipsis iustificandis.' (Baldus, *Commentaria* to C. 4.44.2, no. 48.)

[110] 'Iure naturae aequum est neminem cum alterius detrimento et iniuria fieri locupletiorem.' (D. 50.17.206.)

[111] '. . . iure canonico oritur actio ex nudo pacto, dummodo habeat causam . . .'. (Baldus, *Commentaria* to C. 3.36.15, no. 3.) See Baldus, *In Decretalium volumen commentaria* to X. 1.35.1. As Söllner and Nanz have noted, Baldus was the first to graft the requirement of *causa* onto the Canon law rule that informal agreements are binding. (Söllner, *supra* n. 104, p. 250; K. Nanz, *Die Entstehung des allgemeinen Vertragsbegriff im 16. bis 18. Jahrhundert*, Beiträge zur neueren Privatrechtsgeschichte, 9 (Munich, 1985), 54.) Roussier claimed that Baldus could not have done so. He does not cite earlier Canonists who mention *causa*. He argues that the tradition of Christian morality would never have enforced an 'abstract act' without regard to whether there was a 'duty in conscience' to perform the promise. (Roussier, *supra* n.

It is hard to believe the doctrine would have been formulated in this way and would have taken on this significance had Bartolus and Baldus not been drawing on their knowledge of Aristotle and Thomas.

Mistake

Just as the Romans did not discuss when, in principle, promises or agreements ought to be binding, so they did not discuss what constitutes consent. They recognized mistake, fraud, and duress as defences. In the *Corpus iuris*, however, mistake is discussed in some confused remarks inserted in a title on the law of sales. Fraud is discussed in the context of the *actio de dolo*, and duress in the context of the *actio metus causa*.

The medieval jurists added little to Roman discussions of fraud and duress that the late scholastics were to find helpful. Bartolus and Baldus did, however, give an Aristotelian interpretation to the Roman law of mistake. They concluded that a contract was void for an error in 'substance' by which they meant, as we will see, 'substance' or 'essence' in the Aristotelian sense. Thus their conclusion was like that of Thomas, who, as noted earlier, said that a marriage was void for an error in 'essentials'.[112]

The text from which they extracted this conclusion was D. 18.1.9, which said:

> In contracts of sale there must be consent; the sale is invalid if there is disagreement either as to the fact of sale (*in ipsa emptione*) or the price or any other matter. If therefore I thought I was buying the Cornelian estate and you that you were selling the Sempronian, the sale is void on the ground that we were not at one as to the thing sold (*in corpore*). . . . Then next comes the question whether there is a good sale if there is no mistake as to the identity of the thing (*in corpore*), but there is in regard to its substance (*in substantia*), for example where vinegar is sold for wine, or copper for gold, or lead or something else resembling silver for silver. Marcellus . . . writes that there is a good contract, because there has been agreement as to the specific thing, though mistake as to the material (*in materia*). I take the same view in the wine case, because the *ousia* is pretty much the same, if the wine has just gone sour; but if it is not wine gone sour, but was in origin a specially prepared vinegar, then it appears that one thing has been sold for another. In the remaining cases, however, I hold that whenever there is a mistake as to material, there is no sale.

46, pp. 179–81.) That may be, but it is one thing to refuse to enforce any promise and another to formulate a doctrine of *causa* to explain which promises will not be enforced.

[112] Ch. 1, p. 16.

In this text, practical examples are punctuated by philosophical jargon—words such as *corpus*, *substantia*, *materia*, and *ousia*. All that is clear is that the author could not have been using these terms in an Aristotelian sense. He fails to distinguish clearly between substance (*substantia*) or essence (*ousia*), on the one hand, and matter (*materia*) on the other. For an Aristotelian, the distinction is fundamental. The substantial form or essence makes a thing what it is; the material cause or matter is what a thing is made out of. Moreover, the author claims that, if wine is prepared as wine and turns to vinegar, the *ousia* or essence of the wine and the vinegar is pretty much the same. For an Aristotelian, however vinegar is vinegar if it has the essence or substantial form of vinegar, and it does not matter whether the vinegar was prepared as vinegar or not. And wine and vinegar ought to differ in *ousia*, essence, or substantial form.[113]

The Glossators did not try to find a general principle. They confined themselves to listing the different types of errors that, according to this text and others, would void a sale. According to Azo and Accursius, there were six types of mistake that would have this effect, four of which were taken from the text already quoted. They were: (1) error in 'the fact of sale', (2) error in price, (3) error in *corpore*, (4) error in *materia*, (5) error in *ousia* or *substantia*, and (6) error in sex.[114] Azo and Accursius thus identified error in *ousia* with error in *substantia*: Accursius explained that *ousia* means *substantia*. Error in sex was taken from the strange text of Digest 18.1.11.1, which said that if a person buys a female slave mistakenly thinking her to be a virgin, the sale is valid; but the sale is not valid if he thinks he is buying a male slave, and the slave in question turns out to be a woman.

Azo and Accursius did try to explain why the *ousia* of wine and vinegar is 'pretty much the same'. Their explanation shows how little Aristotelian philosophy they had learned from Boethius. Accursius says, following Azo,

> a substantial quality of the wine and the vinegar is the same with respect to the taste although vinegar is stronger. [The text] says 'much the same' because wine is warm and moist but vinegar is cold and dry. One cannot

[113] According to Aristotle and Thomas, wine loses its form when it becomes vinegar. (Aristotle, *Metaphysics*, VIII. v. 1044^b–1045^a; Thomas Aquinas, *In duodecim libros metaphysicorum Aristotelis expositio*, lib. 8, lec. 4.) That is why, according to Thomas, one could no more celebrate the Eucharist with vinegar than with bread that had become totally corrupted. (*Summa theologica*, iii, q. 74, a. 5, ad 2.)

[114] Accursius, Gloss to D. 18.1.9 to *aliquo alio*.

deny, however, that the individual thing (*corpus*) that both parties perceived was the same.[115]

In Aristotelian terms, the substantial qualities define what a thing is. It does not make sense to say two things have the same substantial quality 'with respect to taste' although one has it more strongly. Moreover, the fact that the individual thing that both parties perceived is one and the same has nothing to do with whether the essence is the same.

Instead of speaking, as Azo and Accursius do, about errors in *corpore*, *materia*, and *substantia*, Petrus simply speaks of an error in *substantia*. He may have had in mind the Aristotelian idea that an individual thing or substance is a composite of its substantial form and its matter. Thus, an error in *corpore*, or *materia*, would also be an error in *substantia*.[116]

Bartolus and Baldus go further. They try to find a sound Aristotelian explanation of the wine that changes to vinegar.

In his *Tractatus de alveo*, Bartolus said that a thing perishes when it loses its 'proper form' or 'substantial form' but not when its 'accidental' form changes.[117] He then applied this Aristotelian distinction to a number of legal problems, one of which was the case of the wine. He said:

> one and the same thing is taken in different ways according to a difference in the way it is considered, as will now be seen. A field may be considered with regard to its matter, which is earth, and then if a river makes a channel through it, it does not cease to be earth, and so the earth remains something of the same kind. It can also be considered as earth suitable for the driving (*agi*) of animals, that is, earth on which animals are led and can labor, and it is from this use that 'field' (*ager*) receives the name which is proper to it. . . . Taken in this way, it loses its proper form [if the river makes channels through it]. . . . It is much the same with the wine. If it is made vinegar, it is still of the same substance insofar as its matter is considered. Properly considered, however, it is not wine but another kind of thing, and it does not come under the name wine.[118]

[115] Accursius, Gloss to D. 18.1.9 to *ousia*: 'id est qualitas substantialis, eadem vini et aceti est quo ad saporem, licet acetum fortius sit, prope autem ideo dicit, quia vinum est calidum et humidum, sed acetum frigidum et siccum, corpus autem idem esse negari non potest, de quo utrunque sentit.'

[116] Petrus de Bellapertica, *Quaestiones vel Distinctiones*, q. 391. Perhaps that is why he also says that an error as to the person one is contracting with prevents a transfer of ownership when it falls on the substance of the person (*circa substantiam persone*). (Ibid.)

[117] See n. 93 *supra*.

[118] 'Sciendum est etiam circa predicta, quod una, et eadem res secundum diversas considerationes diversimode accipitur, ut ecce. In agris potest considerari respectu materiae, quia terra est, et tunc ibi si flumen faciat alveum, non desinit esse terra, et

Thus Bartolus, like Thomas, recognized that the essence of a thing may depend on the point of view from which it is considered. When the field is considered from the standpoint of human needs, it is not simply earth but an object defined by the end it serves, which is the way man-made objects and human actions are defined. But this explanation still does not account for the wine that changes to vinegar. It is hard to see how the vinegar can be 'still of the same substance insofar as its matter is considered' since the 'matter' common to the wine and the vinegar is not, from any point of view, a substance in its own right the way the earth of the field is. Even supposing it were, it is hard to see why the substance of the vinegar is considered according to its matter when the wine accidentally turned sour and not when the wine was deliberately soured to produce vinegar.

Baldus confronted the same problem and came up with an ingenious solution. Admittedly, wine and vinegar do not have the same substance or essence or *ousia*. Nevertheless, Baldus found a reason why, if the wine had soured into vinegar instead of being prepared as vinegar, the buyer could not claim there was an error in substance:

> Note as to a quality that sometimes it is substantial and sometimes it is not said to be substantial; thus, wine is not said to be wine unless it has the substance of wine and the taste of wine; vinegar is always vinegar and is not said to be wine. But if it was wine in the beginning, then remnants of the wine are still left.[119]

And so it turns out, when wine sours to vinegar, that the reason the buyer is not mistaken as to its essence is that the wine has not been completely transformed and remnants of it remain. Baldus presumably thought that no such remnants remain when the wine

sic terra remanet in suo genere. Potest etiam considerari prout est terra apta, ut per eam possit agi, hoc est animalia duci et laborari, a quo ager recipit propriam denominationem, ut dictum est in principio huius libri. Et isto modo perdit propriam formam. Ita loquitur hic textus. non enim ipsam materiam primam debemus inspicere, sed illam qualitatem, a qua denominationem recipit, et sub illa denominatione apud nos sic appellatur. sic simile in vino. si enim fiat acetum adhuc eadem substantia est secundum considerationem materiae, ut ff. de contrahenda emptione 1. in venditione [D. 18.1.9], secundum considerationem propriam non est vinum, sed alia species est, et vini appellatione non continetur.' (Bartolus, *Tractatus de alveo*, § Stricta ratione, nos. 6–7.) The derivation of *ager* (field) from *ago* (drive) is given by Varro, *De lingua latina* (Cambridge, Mass., 1977) v. 34 at 32.

119 'Item nota de qualitate, et quaedam est qualitas substantialis, quaedam non dicitur substantialis: unde non dicitur vinum, nisi habeat qualitatem substantialem vini, et saporem vini. acetum nota quod semper sit acetum, non dicitur vinum: sed si a principio fuit vinum, remanent reliquiae vini.' (Baldus, *Commentaria* to D. 18.1.9, no. 2.)

was deliberately soured to be sold as vinegar. With an excess of ingenuity, then, a Roman text was squared with the Aristotelian understanding of substance.

For Azo and Accursius, error in substance or *ousia* was one of six types of error that would void a contract. Baldus seemed willing to let this type of error assimilate the others. A contract was vitiated, he said, for 'error in identity, substance or object' on the one hand as opposed to an error in 'accidents' on the other.[120] He explained error in the sex of a slave by saying, 'this error is set equal to (*aequiparatur*) an error in kind (*in specie*)'.[121] Although Baldus did not speak of the issue, he would probably have regarded errors in the 'fact of sale' and in the price as affecting the substance or essence of the contract, since he said 'consent . . . must be given equally as to the thing and the price, and these are the essentials of the contract'. In contrast, the 'intrinsic or extrinsic goodness of a thing' was a 'quality as to which the parties to a valid contract might be mistaken.[122]

Thus again, because they had read Aristotle, Bartolus and Baldus anticipated a conclusion of the late scholastics. Again, they did so in the context of particular Roman texts.

The Natural Terms of a Contract

Another such instance was a distinction Baldus drew among three types of terms a contract might have: its 'essential', its 'natural', and its 'accidental' terms. The parties had to agree to the 'essential' terms to form a contract. The 'natural' terms followed from the 'essential' terms, and therefore the parties were bound by them even though they had not agreed on them expressly. The 'accidental' terms did not follow from the 'essential' terms and so were part of the contract only if the parties expressly provided for them. Again, though Baldus claimed to find this distinction in his Roman texts, it is hard to imagine he would have arrived at it but for the influence of Aristotle and Thomas. His distinction was like the one Thomas drew between the 'essentials' of marriage, on which the spouses must

[120] 'Error contrahentis in corpore, in substantia, vel in re, vitiat contractus. secus si erretur in accidentalibus, et inspiciatur persona contrahentis.' (Baldus, *Commentaria* to D. 18.1.9, no. 1.)

[121] '. . . nam aequiparatur error iste [in sexu] errori in specie.' (Baldus, *Commentaria* to D. 18.1.11.)

[122] 'Dictum est supra de precio, et re: nunc dicit de consensu, quia habet cadere pariter super re et precio, et ista sunt essentialia contractus. bonitas, autem intrinseca vel extrinseca rei, dicitur qualitas.' (Baldus, *Commentaria* to D. 18.1.9, no. 1.) 'Nota quod error in corpore, et error in materia, vitiat. sed error in bonitate, vel qualitate, non vitiat.' (Ibid. to D. 18.1.9, no. 2.)

agree, and the obligations that they might not have in mind but which were consequences of their agreement.[123]

The Glossators had distinguished between the 'substantial' and 'accidental' terms of a contract. In this instance, they were indebted to Aristotle. According to one Roman text, since 'the substance of a sale consists in the price', parties who agree to sell and subsequently agree on a different price are not modifying their original contract but are making a new one.[124] The reason, Azo explained, is that a change in price affects the 'substance' of the contract as opposed to its 'accidentals'.[125] Accursius added that the 'substance' of a contract includes those matters 'without which it cannot be'; in a sale, they are the price and the object sold.[126] In order to reach this conclusion, Azo and Accursius needed to know only that, in Aristotelian philosophy, a thing becomes a different thing when it changes its substance but not when it changes its accidents.

According to another Roman text, the parties to a contract that requires good faith should abide by the terms on which they have agreed, but if they have made no express agreement they must fulfil those obligations that 'naturally' belong to their contract.[127] Azo and Accursius explained that the natural terms were not the substantial terms nor merely accidents.[128] They defined the natural terms rather inadequately as those that concerned what was natural

[123] See Ch. 1, p. 16.

[124] 'Pacta conventa, quae postea facta detrahunt aliquid emptioni, contineri contractui videntur, quae vero adiiciunt, credimus non inesse. Quod locum habet in iis, quae adminicula sunt emptionis, veluti ne cautio duplae praestetur, aut ut cum fideiussore cautio duplae praestetur. Sed quo casu agente emptore non valet pactum, idem vires habebit iure exceptionis agent venditore. An idem dici possit, aucto postea, vel deminuto pretio, non immerito quaesitum est, quoniam emptionis substantia consistit ex pretio. Paulus notat, si omnibus integris manentibus de augendo vel de minuendo pretio rursum convenit, recessum a priore contractu, et nova emptio intercessisse videtur.' (D. 18.1.72.)

[125] 'Sciendum est autem quod pactorum quae fiunt inter emptorem et venditorem alia sunt de substantia contractus ut de augendo, vel diminuendo pretio. Quaedam sunt accidentalia. . . .' (Azo, *Summa Codicis* to C. 4.54, no. 1.)

[126] 'Quia sine pretio esse venditio non potest [cit. omitted]. Item si fiat super re vendita augenda vel minuenda [cit. omitted] cum res similiter sit de substantia emptionis, nec sine ea esse possit.' (Accursius, Gloss to D. 18.1.72 to *ex pretio*.)

[127] 'Ex empto actione is, qui emit, utitur. Et in primis sciendum est, in hoc iudicio id demum deduci, quod praestari convenit. Cum nota bonae fidei judicium sit, nihil magis bonae fidei congruit quam id praestari, quod inter contrahentes actum est. Quod si nihil convenit tunc ea praestabuntur, quod naturaliter insunt huius iudicii potestate.' (D. 19.1.11.1.)

[128] Another Roman text said that an action on a sale could not be brought on an agreement entered into after the sale that was outside the nature (*extra naturam*) of the sale. (D. 2.14.7.5.) Accursius and Azo explained that in this text 'nature' referred not to the 'natural terms' of the contract but to its 'substance'. (Azo, *Summa Codicis* to C. 4.54. no. 2; Accursius, Gloss to D. 2.14.7.5 to *extra naturam* ('id est, substantiam'); to D. 18.1.72 to *nova emptio*.)

to a contract even though the contract could exist without them. Their example of such a term was what a modern lawyer would call a warranty of title.[129] Accidental terms are 'extraneous' to the contract. Their examples were an agreement that the seller can reclaim his goods if he returns the price by a certain day, an agreement that the buyer will pay interest on overdue portions of the price, and an agreement that a church will or will not be built on the land acquired.[130] Natural and accidental terms were similar in that attempts to modify them were not attempts to create a new contract.[131]

Petrus de Bellapertica distinguished substantial, natural, and accidental terms in much the same way as Azo and Accursius.[132] So did Bartolus, adding that natural terms are presumed by the law to have been tacitly agreed on by the parties.[133]

Baldus developed a more complete account that was Aristotelian not only in its vocabulary, but in its central ideas. The 'essential' or 'substantial' terms of a contract could not be taken away without a change in the 'essence' of the contract. The substantial or essential terms of a contract of sale, as the Glossators had said, were consent as to the object and the price.[134] While the essential terms are the 'original root' (*radix originalis*) of the contract, to which it is 'principally' ordered, the natural terms are 'an extension of this root to the production of mere qualities', to which the contract is

[129] 'Sed nos dicimus pactum esse de natura quod sit super eo quod est naturalis contractus. ut de evictione praestanda certo modo vel nullo modo.' (Azo, *Summa Codicis* to C. 4.54, no. 2.) 'Sed nos pactum de natura dicimus esse quod sit super id quod est naturale, ut de evictione praestanda.' (Accursius, Gloss to D. 18.1.72 to *nova emptio*.)

[130] 'Quaedam sunt accidentalia sive extranea. ut de dando codice exemplaris loco ut aliquo simili non attingenti venditioni. ut puta si venditor restituat emptori pretium intra certum diem reddatur ei res vel ut emptor praestat venditori usuram pretii tardius soluti vel ut emptor faciat vel ut non faciat monumentum vel ecclesiam in fundo vendito.' (Azo, *Summa Codicis* to C. 4.54, no. 1.)

[131] Azo, *Summa Codicis* to C. 4.54, no. 3; Accursius, Gloss to D. 18.1.72 to *an idem*; to *nova emptio*.

[132] Petrus de Bellapertica, MS. Borghese 277, to l. pacta conventa (D. 18.1.72) fo. 69^{v}, at fo. 70ra–70rb; *Commentaria* to D. 2.14.7.6. Elsewhere, however, he merely contrasts the 'accidentalia contractus' with the 'essentialem naturam contractus': *Quaestiones vel Distinctiones*, q. 66.

[133] 'Pactum super accidentalibus contractibus seu super naturalibus ex intervallo appositum, ad exceptionem tantum prodest: sed si apponatur super substantialibus prodest etiam ad actionem.' (Bartolus, *Commentaria* to D. 18.1.72.) '. . . illud, quod venit ex natura contractus presumitur a iure tacite agi inter partes.' (Ibid. to D. 12.1.3.)

[134] '. . . [substantiala] nec per pactum removeri, salva essentia contractus: sicut in emptione, et venditione est res, et precium, et consensus.' (Baldus, *Commentaria* to D. 18.1.72.1, no. 3.

'consecutively' ordered.[135] While the natural terms are 'according to the nature' of the contract, other terms, the 'accidents', are 'beyond' its nature.[136] They are joined to the contract in 'a special way or by agreement, and this form can be added or subtracted without a substantial change in the subject'.[137] Consequently, while the natural terms 'tacitly' belong to the contract, the accidental terms belong to it only if the parties expressly agree.[138]

For Thomas, the essence of a marriage was defined in terms of its ends. An action was contrary to the nature of marriage if it hindered those ends.[139] Similarly, Baldus concluded that there was a limit to how extensively the parties could modify the natural terms of their contract by express agreement. If the parties added a provision that would remove the 'natural effect' of the type of contract they had entered into, the provision was void since to remove the 'natural effect is to remove the species'.[140] Indeed, 'agreements that cannot attain their due end according to the nature given them are deemed to be imperfect', and cannot be enforced until the imperfection is removed.[141] Thus for Baldus, as for Thomas, the nature of an

[135] The substance of a contract is its 'radix originalis,' and the natural terms are 'extensio illius radicis ex mera qualitate producta'. (Ibid. to C. 4.38.13, no. 6.) The accidental terms are not included *virtute contractus*, because 'nec principaliter, nec consecutive contractus ordinabatur ad hoc.' (Ibid.) Since he has just distinguished essential and natural terms, principal ordering is presumably done by the former and consecutive ordering by the latter.

[136] 'Conclude ergo quod accidentalia sunt praeter naturam: naturalia sunt secundum naturam . . .' (Baldus, *Commentaria* to D. 18.1.72.1, no. 4.)

[137] '. . . aliud vocatur accidens, quod est forma quaedam superaddita supra substantiam, et naturam ex aliquo speciali modo, vel pacto: et quae forma potest adesse et abesse sine substantiali transmutatione subiecti'. (Ibid. to C. 4.38.13, nos. 6 and 7.)

[138] '. . . in contractibus est reperire quaedam accidentalia quae non insunt tacite [cit. omitted] ut pactum de Cundo Romam. quaedam naturalia, quae tacite insunt ut quod debentur evictio et de caveatur . . .'. (Baldus, *Commentaria* to D. 18.1.72. 1, no. 1.)

[139] See Ch. 1, p. 16.

[140] '. . . quaeritur, quid si apponatur pactum, quod removet a contractu naturalem eius effectum . . .? Resp. non tenet venditio, quia a quo removetur naturalis effectus, removetur species. . . .' (Baldus, *Commentaria* to C. 4.38 (rubric), no. 19.)

[141] '. . . unde conventiones, quae non possunt attingere debitum finem secundum naturam eis datam, reputant imperfectae.' (Baldus, *Commentaria* to C. 4.38.13, no. 5.) Imperfect agreements are not valid unless they can be perfected in some way; see ibid., nos. 24 and 25. For example, the contract could not provide that one of the parties would not be liable for future wrongdoing. 'Dolus futurus per pactum remitti non potest.' (Baldus, *Commentaria* to D. 2.14.27.4, no. 1.) '. . . dolus in contractu bonae fidei est contra naturam essentialem.' (Ibid. to D. 4.3.7, no. 9.) Similarly, the parties could not provide for arbitration in such a way that the arbitrator would have to countenance the wrongdoing. 'Sed quaerit Guilielmus utrum per pactum possit remitti reductio ad arbitrium boni viri? et dic, quod non, quia istud pactum tenderet ad delinquendum, et est contra naturam compromissi in bonum virum, quia si assumitur ut bonus vir, est implicare contraria, quod possit inique arbitrari.' (Ibid. to D. 2.14.27.4, no. 3.)

agreement depended on its end, and any provisions the parties made had to be consistent with this end.

The Just Price

Baldus also found an Aristotelian meaning in texts dealing with a one-sided exchange.

As mentioned earlier, one Roman text gave a remedy to a person who sold land at less than half its just price.[142] At a very early date, the Glossators had extended this remedy to sellers as well as buyers and to parties to analogous contracts.[143]

The Glossators identified the just price of goods with their market price. According to one Roman text, 'the prices of things are taken, not from the desire or utility of individuals, but from those of people commonly'.[144] Accursius explained that the just price was not what two or three people would pay for an object but what it could be sold for commonly.[145] Since the just price was the common price, it differed from day to day and region to region. As Accursius noted, 'according to diversity of place, the prices of goods are diversely established'.[146] Similarly, Accursius said, one who sold an object for less than half the amount he paid for it might not be entitled to relief, since 'it could be . . . that when the sale of the object to him occurred, it was worth more than when he now sells'.[147]

The Glossators arrived at these conclusions with no theory in mind as to what a just price might be. They did not need a theory to identify the just price with the price for which goods were commonly traded. That conclusion was suggested by their Roman texts. Moreover, it was just the conclusion that jurists with no theory would reach, since any other conclusion would have invalidated thousands of seemingly innocent market transactions.

The Glossators' closest approach to theory was to relate the remedy for an unjust price to their analysis of fraud. As mentioned earlier, the Glossators distinguished fraud in the *causa*, which led a

142 C. 4.44.2.

143 The *Brachylogus*, written at the beginning of the 12th c., does not speak of land but of objects sold (*Brachylogus* III. xiii. 8). The *Dissensiones dominorum* of the early 13th c. reports a dispute in which all participants take it for granted that the buyer has a remedy. The dispute is over whether he must pay twice or one and a half times the just price before he can seek rescission. The participants are said to be Placentinus and Albericus, who wrote in the 12th c., and Martinus, a student of Irnerius. (Hugolinus de Presbyteris, *Diversitates sive dissensiones dominorum* §253.)

144 'Pretia rerum non ex affectu nec utilitate singulorum sed communiter funguntur.' (D. 35.2.63. Similarly, D. 9.2.23.)

145 Accursius, Gloss to C. 4.44.2 to *autoritate iudicis*; to D. 35.2.63 to *funguntur*; to C. 4.44.6 to *non est*.

146 Accursius, Gloss to D. 13.4.3 [vulgate 13.4.4] to *varia*.

147 Accursius, Gloss to C. 4.44.4 to *autoritate iudicis*.

person to contract who otherwise would not have contracted, from incidental fraud, which led a person to contract on worse terms than he otherwise would have accepted. Incidental fraud was distinguished into fraud *ex proposito* if it was practised intentionally, and fraud *ex re ipsa* if a party paid too much or too little though the other party had done nothing intentionally to defraud him. In the first case, the victim had an action for the difference between the amount he paid and the amount he should have paid, however small that difference might be. In the case of fraud *ex re ipsa*, as the Roman text said, he had an action only if the difference exceeded half the just price. This distinction seems first to have been drawn in a gloss to the *Liber pauperum* of the eleventh-century jurist Vacarius,[148] and it was subsequently picked up by Azo and Accursius.[149]

Whatever its merits, it was not a theory of why relief for an unjust price should be given. The Glossators were not saying, as certain nineteenth-century jurists said, that a price too low or too high was evidence of fraud in any normal sense, and that therefore a remedy should be given. They were simply noting that remedies for intentional incidental fraud and remedies for an unjust price were aimed at the same evil: in both cases, a party had paid too little or too much. The Glossators assumed that a price above or below the normal market price was an evil, but they never explained why.

Later jurists who had read the *Ethics* often gave explanations of the just price that are so sketchy that it is difficult to tell whether they had the Aristotelian theory in mind. For example, Iacobus de Ravanis and Petrus de Bellapertica imply that an unjust price violates 'natural equity'.[150] The expression 'natural equity' seems to be a reference to a Roman text that said 'by the law of nature it is equitable that no one should be enriched by another's loss or injury'.[151] Thus they seem to have believed, as Aristotle and Thomas did, that an unjust price was wrong because it violated a principle of equality.[152]

[148] Vacarius, *Liber pauperum*, iv. 51 to D. 19.2.23.3.

[149] Azo, *Summa Codicis* to C. 2.20, no. 9. See *Summa trecensis*, lib. 4, tit. 41; Rogerius, *Summa Codicis* to C. 4.44; Hostiensis, *Summa aurea*, iii. 17, par. 7. See also G. Fransen, *Le Dol dans la conclusion des actes juridiques* (Gembloux, 1946), 49–55.

[150] See Iacobus de Ravinis, *Super Institutionibus Commentaria* to I. 3.24.1; Petrus de Bellapertica, *Lectura Institutionum* to I. 3.14 pr. [vulgate 3.15 pr.].

[151] See n. 110 *supra*.

[152] They spoke of the opposite of 'natural equity' as 'iniquity', a word traditionally used to describe *dolus ex re ipsa* (e.g. Vacarius, *Liber pauperum*, iv. 51 to D. 19.2.23.3). They said that 'natural equity' is present along with consent in a sale. (Iacobus de Ravinis, *Super Institutionibus commentaria* to I. 3.14.1, no. 5; Petrus de Bellapertica, *Lectura Institutionum* to I. 3.14.1, nos. 13 and 16.)

One can be more confident that Baldus was drawing directly on Aristotelian ideas of equality. Baldus explained that the Roman text just quoted enshrined a principle of 'natural equity' on which remedies for unjust enrichment were based.[153] An unjust price also violates 'natural equity'.[154] Thus, by equity Baldus had in mind a principle of equality. As he said elsewhere, 'in contracts, equity or equality must be served, both in interpretation and in justifying the contract itself'.[155] Moreover, as we have already seen, Baldus seems to have drawn on the Aristotelian distinction between liberality and commutative justice to develop the doctrine that a contract could have two kinds of *causa*, liberality and the receipt of something in return. At one point, Baldus argued that 'without a *causa* equity will not say that an action arises lest one party use his substance badly and the other be unjustifiably enriched'.[156] He meant, presumably, that when each party gives in order to receive something in return, neither is unjustifiably enriched because they trade at a price that preserves equity or equality. It would be odd if a jurist so familiar with Aristotle arrived at this conclusion without having distinctly in mind the Aristotelian principle that acts of commutative justice require equality.

CONCLUSION

As we shall see, the Aristotelian ideas that Baldus, and sometimes Bartolus, read into their Roman texts were later to be central to the late scholastic synthesis. Yet Bartolus and Baldus did not attempt to reorganize Roman law around Aristotelian principles. Their use of Aristotle was limited and, one might almost say, conservative.

The reason was not the principles they espoused, which were like those of the late scholastics, but the project in which they were engaged, which was like that of earlier medieval jurists. They wished to understand every Roman text in terms of every other. Like the Glossators, they presented their conclusions as interpretations of Roman texts, not as consequences of philosophical

[153] e.g. 'praeest aequitas naturalis etiam sine consensu, ut patet in quasi contractibus ut infra de negotio' gest. 1.3, § pupillus, ((D. 3.5.3.4) Baldus, *Commentaria* to D. 2.14.1.) Similarly, he speaks of 'illa aequitas, neminem locupletari cum aliena iactura.' (Baldus, *Commentaria* to I. [illegible].2 pr.) For Baldus's use of the term 'aequitas' in connection with unjust enrichment, see N. Horn, *Aequitas in den Lehren des Baldus* (Cologne, 1968), 114–16.

[154] Baldus, *Commentaria* to C. 4.44.2, no. 18.

[155] Baldus, *Commentaria* to C. 4.44.2, no. 48.

[156] See n. 106 *supra*.

principles.[157] After reading a philosophical principle into a text, they would then cite the text rather than the philosopher as authority for the principle. That is why a rather technical analysis has been necessary to establish the source of their principles. Indeed, the medieval jurists were so much more concerned with texts than with principles that the present chapter is almost misleading. It gives the impression that finding Aristotelian meanings in Roman texts was a major concern to Bartolus and Baldus, when in fact it was a comparatively minor part of their work, significant in retrospect because it anticipated the late scholastics.

Because the medieval jurists were engaged in this project, they analysed legal problems by studying the relations among texts. Their formal education was centred almost entirely around texts. In their books, they explained the law text by text, rather than doctrine by doctrine. For them, to be a doctor of law was to be an expert in Roman texts, not in philosophy or theology. They used Aristotelian principles when they found them helpful to the project in which they were engaged. They could not have reorganized Roman law around these principles, however, without changing their project and with it their legal method, their educational curriculum, their style of legal writing, and their sense of identity as scholars.

[157] Thus, I see a continuing tension between a Roman legal tradition and a Greek philosophical tradition. Harold Berman, in contrast, emphasizes the features that medieval philosophy, theology, and law had in common, features that broke with past traditions (H. J. Berman, *Law and Revolution: The Formation of the Western Legal Tradition* (Cambridge, Mass., 1983), 151–64.)

4
SYNTHESIS

A SYNTHESIS between Roman law and Aristotelian and Thomistic moral philosophy was finally achieved in the sixteenth and early seventeenth centuries. It was part of a larger intellectual movement: the revival of Thomistic philosophy.[1] The movement began in 1503, when a professor at the University of Paris named Pierre Crockaert underwent an intellectual conversion. He rejected the nominalist philosophy of William of Ockham in which he had been educated and turned to that of Thomas Aquinas. He joined the Dominican order to which Thomas himself had belonged. In 1512 he published a commentary on the last part of Thomas's *Summa theologica* with the help of his pupil Francisco de Vitoria. Vitoria returned to his native Spain where, as a professor at the University of Salamanca from 1526 until his death in 1546, he founded the so-called Spanish natural law school. He published nothing himself, and his ideas are known only through the handwritten notes of his lectures that have survived. Nevertheless, he trained scores of highly influential pupils. Among them were the jurist Diego de Covarruvias (1512–77) and the theologian Domingo de Soto (1494–1560), the latter a fellow Dominican who had been his pupil in Paris and became his colleague in Salamanca.

For Vitoria and his school, the philosophy of Thomas was the cure for the chief intellectual, spiritual, and political evils of the age.

[1] For a general description of the movement, see J. A. Fernandez-Santamaria, *The State, War and Peace: Spanish Political Thought in the Renaissance* (Cambridge, 1977); B. Hamilton, *Political Thought in Sixteenth-Century Spain: A Study of the Political Ideas of Vitoria, De Soto, Suarez, and Molina* (Oxford, 1963); Q. Skinner, *The Foundations of Modern Political Thought* (Cambridge, 1978), ii. 135–73. For a description of its influence on law, see *La Seconda scolastica nella formazione del diritto privato moderno* (Florence, 16–19 October 1972), (ed. P. Grossi) (Milan, 1973); M. Diesselhorst, *Die Lehre des Hugo Grotius vom Versprechen*, Forschungen zur neueren Privatrechtsgeschichte, 6 (Cologne, 1959); M. Villey, *La Formation de la pensée juridique moderne*, 4th edn. (Paris, 1975), 343–55.

The significance of the late scholastics for the development of private law has been appreciated only recently; see Ch. 1, pp. 5–6. Coing notes the need for further research: H. Coing, *Europäisches Privatrecht*, i. *Alteres Gemeines Recht (1500 bis 1800)* (Munich, 1985), 191. Although he does not discuss the influence of the late scholastics at length, he does describe the general characteristics of continental law in the early modern period. It will be seen in this chapter that most of the characteristics he describes have late scholastic antecedents. See ibid. 398–422.

Its members disliked nominalism in philosophy, Protestantism in religion, and absolutism in politics. The source of these errors, they thought, was scepticism about the existence of an order in the world that human reason could discover. Because of that scepticism, nominalist philosophers claimed that abstract concepts were creations of the mind rather than discoveries about the world. Lutherans and Calvinists claimed that the Fall had so debased man that he could neither discover nor do what is good. Princes claimed that the law depended on their will alone. The antidote was Thomism with its confidence in natural reason, and particularly Thomistic ideas of natural law.

In some areas, such as their political philosophy, the late scholastics owed a large and unacknowledged debt to the Scotists and nominalists from whom they tried to break free.[2] In their contract doctrine, as we shall see, the debt, if any, was small. They may have found it easier in treating contract to remain faithful to Thomas's method with its combination of teleological and conceptual reasoning. In any case, Thomas had given many more hints than Scotus or Ockham as to how concrete problems of contract law could be analysed. Nearly always, they took these hints as their starting points.

Vitoria's interest in natural law can be seen in his lecture notes. His pupils, Covarruvias and Soto, began to fit Thomistic ideas and Roman rules together. Covarruvias, like the medieval jurists, thought his primary task was to explain the Roman texts. Nevertheless, he explicitly addressed questions about justice raised by Thomistic philosophy. Soto, a philosopher and theologian, tried to apply Thomistic and Aristotelian principles to problems of property, contracts, and torts familiar from Roman law.

The work commenced by these Dominicans or pupils of Dominicans in the early part of the sixteenth century was completed in the later sixteenth and early seventeenth centuries by Jesuits. Francisco Suarez (1548–1617), Luis de Molina (1535–1600), and Leonard Lessius (1554–1623) all belonged to that order. Although Suarez's writings on metaphysics and political and legal philosophy have made him the most famous member of the school, he wrote little about legal doctrine. Molina and Lessius, however, reorganized Roman law in its vast detail and presented it as a commentary on the

[2] On their political theory, see Skinner, *supra* n. 1. Paolo Grossi has claimed that the property law of the late scholastics also shows such a debt. (Grossi, 'La proprietà nel sistema privatistico della seconda scolastica', in *La seconda scholastica*, *supra* n. 1, p. 117.) Be that as it may, I have not found a similar influence on their contract law.

Aristotelian and Thomistic virtue of justice. The traditions of Roman law and Greek philosophy were united more closely than they ever had been before or were to be again.

In the seventeenth century, the doctrines of the late scholastics were taken over intact and popularized by the founder of the northern natural law school, Hugo Grotius (1583–1645). Indeed, the doctrines remained much the same in the work of his successors, Samuel Pufendorf (1632–94) and Jean Barbeyrac (1674–1744), and in that of the French jurists Jean Domat (1625–95) and Robert Pothier (1699–1772), who were to have a great influence both on the drafters of the French Civil Code and on the nineteenth-century common lawyers. While these jurists preserved the late scholastic doctrines, however, they no longer explained them by Aristotelian and Thomistic principles. Nor did they find any new philosophical explanation for them. Consequently the meaning of the doctrines became unclear. The jurists often preserved the Aristotelian terminology in which these doctrines had been formulated, but one cannot be sure what meaning they attached to it. In the work of some eighteenth-century jurists such as Christian Wolff (1679–1754), the late scholastic doctrinal formulations began to disappear. A general reformulation of contract doctrine did not occur, however, until the nineteenth century.

As we shall see, the formulation of these doctrines by the late scholastics and their dissemination by the northern natural law school had few practical consequences. Few of the rules in force changed, and these changes had little economic significance. The great change was in the way contract law was understood.

We will examine that change by seeing how the late scholastics and northern natural lawyers answered three questions: When is a contract binding? When have the parties given their consent? What is the content of a contract?

THE BINDING FORCE OF CONTRACT

The late scholastics analysed the binding force of contracts in terms of the Aristotelian and Thomistic virtues of promise-keeping, commutative justice, and liberality. The Romans had not analysed the problem that way. Indeed, they had scarcely analysed it at all. Gaius had simply observed that different contracts are formed in different ways: by consent, by delivery, by writing, and by words.[3] Nevertheless, the late scholastics read references to promise-keeping, commutative justice, and liberality into particular Roman texts.

[3] See Ch. 3, pp. 31–2.

They read texts that mentioned *pollicitatio* or *pactus* to refer to promise-keeping. As mentioned earlier, by a *pollicitatio*, a person undertook to support public works or to do something for the city in gratitude for an honour he had received.[4] One Roman text observed that a *pollicitatio* was the consent of one party only, as distinguished from a *pactus* or agreement which was the consent of both.[5] Another text said that a *pactus* was the consent of two or more parties to one thing.[6] Lessius and Molina concluded that a promise was a *pollicitatio*, and a promise accepted by the other party was a pact or agreement.[7]

In entering into an agreement, they said, a person performed either an act of commutative justice or an act of liberality.[8] Soto distinguished these acts in a paraphrase of Thomas.[9] Molina raised a doubt as to whether acts of both kinds could be called 'contracts'. To resolve the doubt he cited Roman legal texts, some of which used the work *contractus* to include gifts, but one of which said a contract is a 'mutual obligation' (*ultra citroque obligatio*).[10] In the strict sense, he concluded, contract meant mutual obligation and hence an act of justice, while in a broader and less proper sense it included gifts that were 'an act of liberality of the promisor and not of justice'.[11] Lessius read the same Aristotelian distinction into the Roman texts that Molina had cited.[12] He injected an additional scholastic quibble: why couldn't a gift be an act of the virtue of gratitude rather than an act of liberality? He resolved the doubt scholastically by explaining that the virtue of liberality in a fashion

[4] See Ch. 3, p. 32.

[5] D. 50.12.3.

[6] D. 2.14.1.

[7] L. Lessius, *De iustitia et jure* (Paris, 1628), lib 2, cap. 17, dub. 1; L. Molina, *De iustitia et jure tractatus* (Venice, 1614), disp. 252.

[8] For a valuable and sensitive account of the way in which the late scholastics used Thomistic concepts of promise-keeping, liberality, and commutative justice, see P. Cappellini, *Schemi contrattuali e cultura teologico-giuridica nella seconda scolastica: verso una teoria generale*, thesis, University of Florence, 1978/9, 120–64. His story, however, is one in which Thomistic concepts were 'secularized' to form modern contract law. (Ibid. 138–40, 253, 529–30.) I do not think these concepts needed to be 'secularized'. They came originally from Aristotle, and although Thomas had applied them to problems of moral theology, he resolved moral problems by appeal to natural law. Cappellini is right, for example, that Thomas discussed promises in contexts such as vows and oaths, but Thomas himself thought that promises created a natural obligation which he explained in Aristotelian terms. My view, as will be seen, is that the intellectual problem of the late scholastics was not to turn religious into secular concepts but to turn the general principles of Aristotelian and Thomistic ethics into legal doctrine.

[9] D. Soto, *De iustitia et iure libri decem* (Salamanca, 1553), lib. 3, q. 5, a. 1.

[10] D. 50.16.19.

[11] Molina, *supra* n. 7, disp. 252.

[12] Lessius, *supra* n. 7, lib. 2, cap. 17, dub. 1.

includes that of gratitude.[13] Contracts, in the broad sense, were either acts of commutative justice or acts of liberality.

Through an analysis of these virtues, the late scholastics reached a conclusion that was to outlast the authority of Aristotle: promises are enforceable in principle if they are made for a good *causa* and accepted by the promisee. Any modern civil lawyer would recognize the conclusion. He would be unlikely to know that it emerged from a debate over the meaning of Aristotelian virtues.

The Enforceability of Promises

As we have seen, medieval jurists had concluded that in principle contracts were binding because of the consent of the parties. They had also said that the Roman rules were creations of positive law. The late scholastics, however, had tried to reach this conclusion by arguing from principles drawn from Aristotle and Thomas.

Thomas had said that 'man is obligated to man by any promise, and this is an obligation of natural law'.[14] The late scholastics agreed that it would be wrong to break any promise, whether the act promised was one of commutative justice or of liberality. Thomas did not consider, however, whether it would be not merely wrongful, but unjust, to break a promise to perform an act of liberality. Commutative justice preserves the share of wealth a citizen possesses. The promisee may be disappointed when he does not receive a gift he was promised, but he may be no worse off than if the promise had never been made.

The Dominican theologian Cajetan considered the problem in his commentary on Thomas's *Summa theologica*. He concluded that the promisor was bound only as a matter of truth or faith. The promisee was owed nothing as a matter of justice unless he had suffered damage because the promise was first made and then broken.[15] The French jurist Connanus took the same position. He supported it not only with arguments about the nature of commutative justice, but with questions about the seriousness of those who promise gifts and the prudence of those who believe such promises. He cited the example of Roman law which did not enforce informal promises to make gifts.[16]

This position, in its pure form, was rejected by Soto, Molina, and Lessius, and later by Grotius, Pufendorf, and Barbeyrac. They

[13] Ibid., lib. 2, cap. 18, dub. 2.

[14] *Summa theologica*, II–II, q. 88, a. 3, ad 1.

[15] Cajetan, *Commentaria* (Padua, 1698), to *Summa theologica*, II–II, q. 88, a. 1; q. 113, a. 1. See Cappellini, *supra* n. 8, pp. 326–31.

[16] F. Connanus, *Commentariorum juris civilis libri X* (Naples, 1724), lib. 1, 6, v. 1.

claimed that infidelity was a kind of injustice. Soto quoted a statement by Cicero that good faith is the foundation of justice, and the statement was repeated by the others.[17] None of them explained very clearly how infidelity could be a violation of commutative justice as Aristotle conceived it. According to Lessius, whatever was owed as a matter of fidelity was owed 'imperfectly' but nevertheless owed, so that fidelity was an inadequate or imperfect form of justice (*justitia inadequate concepta*).[18]

Lessius was clear, however, about why he found Cajetan's position unacceptable. The difference between a promise to do something and a mere statement that one would do it was that the promise entailed an obligation that the statement did not. By Cajetan's view, it was hard to see how a promise could entail this obligation. Consequently, it was also hard to see why executory promises to exchange were enforceable. Granted, the obligation of these contracts was the 'more perfect one of equality', but why were they binding in advance of performance if not because of the promises the parties had made? Lessius concluded that all promises were naturally enforceable, although Roman law sometimes required a formality to ensure that a promise was made after deliberation.[19]

Molina opposed Cajetan with a different argument and reached a different conclusion. He noted that in Roman law the actual delivery of a gift made it the property of the donee. If the intention of the donor was clear, there was no reason, in principle, to require actual delivery. A gratuitous promise ought to be sufficient to create a debt enforceable by the promisee. The only question was whether the promisor intended the promise to have that effect. If he did not so intend, Molina concluded, he was obligated merely as a matter of 'honesty'; if he did, he was obligated as a matter of 'justice' and the promise was enforceable. A court would have to determine what the promisor intended by examining the 'circumstances'. If the promisee had completed the formality required by Roman law, however, he would be taken to have obligated himself as a matter of justice.[20]

According to Lessius, Molina failed to recognize that promises obligate simply because they are promises and not because of the precise intention with which they are made.[21] Nevertheless, Grotius

[17] Soto, *supra* n. 9, lib. 8, q. 2, a. 1; Molina, *supra* n. 7, disp. 262; Lessius, *supra* n. 7, lib. 2, cap. 18. dub. 2; H. Grotius, *De iure belli ac pacis libri tres* (Leiden, 1939), II. xi. 1, 5; S. Pufendorf, *De iure naturae et gentium libri octo* (Amsterdam, 1688), III. v. 9.

[18] Lessius, *supra* n. 7, lib. 2, cap. 18, dub. 2.

[19] Ibid.

[20] Molina, *supra* n. 7, disp. 262.

[21] Lessius, *supra* n. 7, lib. 2, cap. 18, dub. 2.

adopted Molina's position. To be enforceable, a promise must be 'perfect'; that is, Grotius explained, the promisor must not merely signify that his 'will [was] determined for the future with a sufficient sign to indicate the necessity of persevering'; he must also add 'a sign of wishing to confer a proper right on another'. He repeated Molina's argument that a delivered gift becomes the property of the donee.[22] Pufendorf and Barbeyrac agreed with Grotius.[23] According to Baberyrac, to say that the promisee had suffered no injustice because he had lost nothing was to assume that the promisee had no right to the gift promised him, which was the very point in dispute.[24]

Although Grotius, Pufendorf, and Barbeyrac continued the late scholastic debate, they made the arguments simpler and also less precise. They did not clearly distinguish Lessius's position and try to answer it. Grotius and Pufendorf adopted Molina's position but gave Lessius's explanation of the Roman formalities rather than Molina's: the formalities are a sign that a promise was deliberately made, not that the promisor meant to confer a right on the promisee.[25]

With Wolff, however, the late scholastic debate finally dropped out of sight. He defined promise by borrowing from Grotius and Pufendorf, and indirectly from Molina: 'one who sufficiently indicates that he wishes to perform or give or do something for another person, and to transfer to that person the right to require that he perform or give or do it, is said to promise that person something'.[26] Nevertheless, he did not discuss whether such a promise was binding as a matter of justice or merely as a matter of fidelity. He proved that the promise was enforceable from the

[22] Grotius, *supra* n. 17, II. xi. 1, 3–4.

[23] Pufendorf, *supra* n. 17, III. v. 5–11. The principal difference is that Pufendorf described imperfect and unenforceable promises as though they were rather exotic fauna. Some jurists, he said, were hard put to find any examples of them. He believed there were instances; for example, a person might ask another to 'take his word' that he would perform so that his performance would appear due to 'the impulse of [his] own virtue'. (Ibid. III. v. 6.) In sharp contrast, Molina had said that promises involving obligations of 'honesty' were 'more frequent among men' than those involving obligations of 'justice'. (Molina, *supra* n. 7, disp. 262.) Nevertheless, Pufendorf claimed that gratuitous promises were to be deemed imperfect if the promisor used words of the future tense: 'I will give' instead of 'I am giving'. (Ibid. III. v. 8.)

[24] Barbeyrac on Pufendorf, n. 10, to III. v. 9; see Barbeyrac on Grotius, n. 2 to II. xi. 1; n. 1 to II. xi. 3.

[25] Grotius, *supra* n. 17, II. xi. 4, 2; Pufendorf, *supra* n. 17, III. v. 11. Barbeyrac seems to have been agnostic about whether *stipulatio* served any useful purpose. (Barbeyrac on Pufendorf, n. 2 to III v. 11; Barbeyrac on Grotius, n. 7 to II. xi. 4.)

[26] 'Qui sufficienter declarat, se aliquid alteri praestare seu dare vel facere velle, ac in ipsum jus transfert a se exigendi, ut praestet, seu det vel faciat, is ei quid promittere dicitur.' (C. Wolff, *Ius naturae methodo scientifica pertractatum* (Frankfurt-on-Main, 1764), iii, §361.)

definition of a promise which gave the promisor the right to enforce it. 'The promisor, indeed, transfers to the promisee the right to require performance of the promise, and consequently the promisee can force him to perform if he does not wish to perform himself.'[27] Wolff, then, no longer explained the binding force of promises in terms of virtue, even in a vaguely Aristotelian sense.[28] Instead, promises were enforceable by definition. In that respect, as we shall see later, he anticipated the nineteenth-century jurists.

These discussions all concerned the theoretical reasons for enforcing promises, not the reform of the Roman rules. Most of the jurists accepted the Roman rules as valid positive law established, no doubt, for sound practical reasons. Eventually, however, the rules were changed throughout continental Europe by statute or judicial decision or by scholars who announced that certain Roman rules had not been received. Contracts of exchange became enforceable without regard to whether they were nominate or innominate. Promises to make gifts remained enforceable only if a formality had been completed.

But for the late scholastic debate, this change would probably not have taken the form it did. It is unlikely that all of continental Europe would have decided to enforce contracts of exchange had not the theorists first concluded that, in principle, they were enforceable as a matter of justice. The Roman refusal to enforce some of them then became an anomaly. Although initially jurists assumed there was some sound pragmatic reason for the refusal, such as preventing litigation, such a reason was hard to find. Bartolus had observed in the fourteenth century that the rule had few practical consequences since innominate contracts were routinely notarized, and Molina repeated his remark.[29] They meant, presumably, that important contracts such as exchanges of land would be notarized anyway, and so the only innominate contracts denied enforcement were occasional horse swaps. At any rate, continental courts, legislators, and scholars eventually decided there was no sufficiently strong reason to deviate from the principle

[27] 'Promissor enim transfert in promissarium jus a se exigendi praestationem promissi [§361], consequenter ipsum cogendi ut praestet, nisi sua sponte praestare velit.' (Ibid. iii, §363.)

[28] Wolff was willing to talk about virtue. He defined virtue as the habit of directing one's actions by the natural law: 'virtus sit habitus actiones suas legi naturali conformiter dirigendi . . .'. (Ibid., 'Prolegomena', §6.) Unlike Aristotle or Thomas, however, he tried to establish what virtue or natural law requires by arguing from a definition, not by an independent argument about the relationship of a virtue or an action to man's ultimate end.

[29] Bartolus de Saxoferrato, *Commentaria* to C. 4.6.2; Molina, *supra* n. 7, disp. 255.

that contracts of exchange should be enforced. To question the deviation, however, they first had to see the principle.

According to the majority of participants in the debate, the Roman rule requiring a formality to make promises of gifts enforceable was also a deviation from principle. The practical consequences of abolishing this rule would have been substantial, however, and continental legal systems were unwilling to tolerate them. Nevertheless, the theoretical debate had an influence. Had the minority position prevailed, it might have seemed anomalous to enforce any gratuitous promises. The rule that such promises could be made enforceable by a formality might eventually have been abolished. Its place might have been taken by the rule Cajetan advocated and which some American jurists such as Melvin Eisenberg now advocate: that gratuitous promises should be enforced only to the extent that the promisee has suffered damages by relying upon them. Instead, Grotius adopted the majority position and later jurists followed Grotius. Reluctance to enforce gratuitous promises was explained as a deviation from principle, and the formality was retained.

Nevertheless, the practical significance of the debate just described was quite small. The debate contributed only indirectly to the reform of the Roman rules concerning the enforceability of innominate contracts, and, as Bartolus and Molina observed, those rules had few practical consequences. The significance of the debate was that, for the first time, the theoretical question of when a contract should be enforced was argued among jurists.

Causa

According to the doctrine of *causa*, every enforceable contract had to be made for one of two *causae* or reasons: 'liberality', or the receipt of a performance in return for one's own. As we have seen, the doctrine was stated this way in the fourteenth century by Bartolus and Baldus. It was stated in much the same way in the seventeenth and eighteenth centuries by Domat and Pothier.[30]

We have seen that Bartolus and Baldus formulated the doctrine with the Aristotelian distinction between liberality and commutative justice in mind. They formulated the doctrine, however, in order to explain their Roman texts. Doubtless, the late scholastics were gratified that the doctrine explained these texts, but, unlike the medieval jurists, their great interest was theory. For them,

[30] J. Domat, *Les Loix civiles* (Paris, 1713), I. i. 1, 5–6; I. i. 5, 13; R. Pothier, *Traité des obligations* (Paris, 1861), §42.

the doctrine expressed the theoretically important idea that, by promising, one could perform acts of commutative justice or acts of liberality. If one promised neither to give 'to the right persons, the right amounts, at the right time' nor to receive an equivalent in return, one was exercising neither virtue. One was lacking in prudence or else dishonest.

Indeed, the late scholastics usually express this idea simply by classifying contracts as either onerous or gratuitous, as made either *causa gratuita* or *causa onerosa*.[31] Grotius, in *De iure belli ac pacis*, classifies all contracts as gratuitous or onerous—in his terminology, as 'beneficial or permutorial'—and mentions *causa* only to say that contracts made for a dishonest *causa* (*causa vitiosa*) are invalid. It is doubtful that Grotius would have seen any difference between speaking this way and saying outright that every valid promise must be made *causa gratuita* or *causa onerosa*.[32]

The doctrine of *causa* has puzzled modern scholars because it seems to be a tautology: the promisor either gets nothing in return for his promise or he gets something. For the late scholastics, the doctrine was not a tautology, because 'liberality' does not mean merely that one gets nothing in return and 'commutative justice' does not mean merely that one gets something. It is true, however, that the doctrine imposed no practical limit on the enforcement of promises. Had the doctrine never been invented, courts still would not have enforced illegal or immoral contracts. Despite the doctrine, courts often enforced foolish gifts. No one expected them to ask whether the promisor had really been giving 'the right amounts to the right people at the right time' as liberality required.

Supposedly, the enforceability of promises was limited by the rule that the *causa* of a promise must be stated in the notarial document which had taken the place of the Roman formalities.[33] Some of the late scholastics said that this rule created a presumption; if the *causa* was not stated, the promisee had the burden of proving that the promise was made out of liberality.[34] Assuming that notaries were reasonably competent in drafting documents, it is unlikely that this rule provided much of a check on folly.

[31] For late scholastic systems of classifying contracts, see pp. 102–5 below.

[32] Grotius, *supra* n. 17, II. xii. 1–7. In his *Introduction to Dutch Law*, he used the word 'cause' to draw what must be the same distinction. He said that, while the Romans sometimes required a *stipulatio*, the 'Germans from of old' have enforced 'all contracts which proceed from any reasonable causes'. A 'reasonable cause' (*redelicke oorzacke*) exists 'whenever the contract or promise takes place by way of gift or is incidental to some other transaction (*handelinge*)'. (H. Grotius, *Inleiding* . . . (Oxford, 1926), III. i. 53.)

[33] D. 44.4.2.2. See Accursius to D. 44.4.2.2 to *sine causa*; Baldus to C. 4.30.13.

[34] e.g. Molina, *supra* n. 7, disp. 257.

To see the doctrine of *causa* as an attempt to limit the enforcement of promises by courts is to miss its real significance. It made the theoretically important claim that there are two good reasons for promises to be made or enforced: the exercise of the virtues of liberality and commutative justice.

Offer and Acceptance

As we have seen, although the Romans dealt with the question only obliquely, the medieval jurists considered whether an offer is not binding until it is accepted by the other party. The late scholastics tried to find an answer that would fit with their theory of contract. The answer was not obvious. If all promises were binding, it was not clear that a promise needed to be accepted. It was not even clear that it needed to be communicated to the promisee.

Thomas had said that a promise must be communicated to be binding. As noted earlier, his reason was that promises established an order of one man to another, just as an oath establishes an order between a man and God. Since God knows our thoughts, words or signs are not necessary to establish such an order with Him, but with men they are necessary.[35]

Soto and Molina seem to have thought that this argument proved only that positive law could not enforce a promise until it had been outwardly expressed. If the promisor really willed to obligate himself, even if he said nothing, then in principle and by natural law he was obligated. The will, after all, was the reason a promise was binding. They pointed out that even by positive law the unexpressed will of a person was sometimes given effect, as for example when he willed to abandon property.[36]

Lessius disagreed. The real force of Thomas's argument, he said, is that words are not merely signs that something has been promised. The words actually effectuate what they signify.[37] He thus anticipated by several centuries Austin's concept of speech-acts.[38] Grotius agreed with Lessius that an outward expression of the promisor's will was required by natural law, and Pufendorf again followed Grotius.[39]

[35] *Summma theologica* II–II, q. 88, a. 1. See Ch. 2, p. 12.

[36] Soto, *supra* n. 9, lib. 8, q. 2, a. 1. Molina, *supra* n. 7, disp. 266. See Cappellini, *supra* n. 8, pp. 500–12.

[37] Lessius, *supra* n. 7, lib. 2, cap. 18, dub. 5 ('Ratio est; quia promissio et donatio sunt signa quaedam practica, efficientia idipsum quod significant'). See Cappellini, *supra* n. 8, pp. 513–19.

[38] J. L. Austin, *How to Do Things with Words* (New York, 1962).

[39] Grotius, *supra* n. 17, II. xi. 11; Pufendorf, *supra* n. 17, III. vi. 16.

Supposing the promise had been communicated, a further question was whether it had to be accepted. Covarruvias,[40] Soto,[41] and Molina said that, since all promises were binding, an acceptance was not necessary in principle. As Molina explained, the promisor is obligated to perform just because he promised, for it is the promise, not the acceptance, that gives rise to that obligation. Admittedly, promises to enter into onerous contracts were not binding until the other party accepted, but that was a rule peculiar to onerous contracts. Since onerous contracts create a mutual obligation, they require mutual assent and hence an accepted promise. In support of his position, Molina pointed to the Roman institution of *pollicitatio*. As mentioned earlier, a *pollicitatio* was a promise made to a city to contribute to public works or to do something in return for an honour conferred on the promisor. According to one Roman text, although a *pactus* or agreement was constituted by the consent of both parties, a *pollicitatio* required the consent of only one.[42] Molina admitted that *pollicitatio* was an institution of Roman positive law. Nevertheless, positive law should not deviate from natural law in a way that caused unnecessary injustice. It would be unjust to require performance of an unaccepted *pollicitatio* if by natural law the promisor was not obligated to perform. Therefore, if one assumed that the Roman rules were just, natural law obligated a promisor to perform an unaccepted promise.[43]

Lessius disagreed. He conceded that, as all promises were binding, it was the promise, not the acceptance, that was the source of the promisor's obligation. An acceptance was necessary, however, because it was the promisor's *sine qua non* condition for being bound to his promise. Only in this way could one explain why one who promised to enter into an onerous contract could revoke his promise before acceptance even though all promises were binding. Moreover, if acceptance was the promisor's *sine qua non* condition for being bound, one could easily explain how Roman positive law, without injustice, could enforce an unacceptable *pollicitatio*. Positive law was not creating an obligation where none existed before. It was simply prohibiting revocation of a promise before the *sine qua non* condition of acceptance had been met.[44]

Lessius then turned to the question of the moment at which an acceptance was effective. Since acceptance was the promisor's *sine*

[40] D. Covarruvias, *Variarum ex iure pontificio, regio et caesareo resolutionum* (Lyons, 1568), p. 2, §2, no. ult., §4, no. 6.

[41] Soto, *supra* n. 9, lib. 3, q. 5, art. 3.

[42] D. 50.12.3.

[43] Molina, *supra* n. 7, disp. 263.

[44] Lessius, *supra* n. 7, lib. 2, cap. 18, dub. 6.

qua non condition, that moment was the one the promisor would have chosen for it to be effective. In onerous contracts, according to Lessius, the promisor would not wish to be bound until after he learned of the acceptance; in gratuitous contracts, he would wish to be bound even before he did so.[45]

Lessius expressed some doubts as to whether a promise was binding before acceptance. Nevertheless, Grotius endorsed Lessius's position without betraying any uncertainty. He used Lessius's argument as to why positive law will sometimes enforce an unaccepted promise. He also drew an analogy to a gratuitous transfer of ownership which is not effective unless the donee accepts what he is given.[46] Pufendorf, Barbeyrac, and Pothier agreed with Grotius,[47] and the doctrine that all promises require an acceptance to be binding became entrenched as a principle of natural law.

Grotius and Pufendorf also adopted Lessius's opinion as to the moment at which an acceptance was effective: as soon as the promisee signified assent in gratuitous contracts; as soon as the promisor learned he had done so in onerous contracts. They said, like Lessius, that these were the times at which the promisor would have wanted to become bound.[48] Since the matter depended on the intention of the promisor, other solutions were possible. Barbeyrac said that an acceptance could be revoked only if the promisee took time to deliberate instead of accepting as soon as he learned of the offer.[49]

With Wolff, however, one senses again that the terms of the late scholastic debate are dropping out of sight. For the late scholastics and the natural lawyers who followed them, promises were binding as a matter of fidelity. A reason consequently had to be found why an unaccepted promise would not be binding. In contrast, as we have seen, Wolff proved that a promise is binding from the definition of a promise.[50] Similarly, he defined the transfer of a right to require the consent of the transferee, and then proved the need for an

[45] Ibid.

[46] Grotius, *supra* n. 17, II. xi. 14.

[47] Pufendorf, *supra* n. 17, III. vi. 15; Barbeyrac on Grotius, n. 1 to II. xi. 15; Pothier, *supra* n. 30, §4. Pufendorf claimed, however, that Grotius's explanation of *pollicitatio* was inconsistent with the text of D. 50.12.3, which described *pollicitatio* as the act of one party only, not as a promise which is irrevocable pending the acceptance of the other party. His own solution was that the state—the other party to a *pollicitatio*—should be deemed to have accepted the promise in advance.

[48] Grotius, *supra* n. 17, II. xi. 15; Pufendorf, *supra* n. 17, III. vi. 15.

[49] Barbeyrac on Grotius, n. 1 to II. xi. 15; Barbeyrac on Pufendorf, n. 10 to III. vi. 15.

[50] See pp. 75–6 above.

acceptance from this definition.[51] Pothier, in like fashion, proved the need for an acceptance from the definition of contract as mutual consent and tried to deduce from the definition the moment at which a contract is binding.[52] As we shall see, in attempting to unpack these conclusions from a definition, they anticipated the jurists of the nineteenth century.

CONTRACTUAL CONSENT

We have just seen that the late scholastics explained the binding force of promises in terms of the Aristotelian virtues of promise-keeping, liberality, and commutative justice. Out of their analysis came a proposition familiar to every modern civil lawyer: that promises are binding in principle if made for a good *causa* and accepted. We will now see that the late scholastics analysed contractual consent by applying Aristotelian and Thomistic ideas about the human intellect and will. Out of that analysis came the proposition, equally familiar today, that duress, mistake, and fraud can invalidate contractual consent. The Romans had known that the parties must consent to form a contract. They gave relief in instances of duress, mistake, and fraud. The late scholastics organized the Roman rules into doctrines and provided them with a theory.

According to Thomas, a person is responsible if his action proceeds from his reason and will. He must have known the essential features of the action and chosen to perform it. Otherwise, he is not acting *qua* human being.[53] Thomas followed Aristotle, who had said that an action is involuntary unless it proceeds from the specifically human principles within a person. An action is not voluntary if a person does not know what he is doing, or if he does know but does not choose because his body is moved by force. An action is voluntary if a person knows what he is doing even if he chooses the action as the lesser of two evils, as when a captain decides to jettison cargo in a storm.[54]

Duress

In analysing duress, the late scholastics had not only these general remarks to build on but Thomas's discussion of the binding force of

[51] Wolff (*supra* n. 26) proves that 'a promise may be revoked before acceptance' (iii, §596) from the proposition that 'a promise is not valid without an acceptance' (iii, §365), which he proves in turn from the proposition that 'ownership or a right of some kind of one's own cannot be transferred except to one who accepts' (iii, §7).

[52] R. Pothier, *Traité du contrat de vente* (Paris, 1861), iii. 1, §32.

[53] *Summa theologica*, I–II, q. 6, aa. 6, 8.

[54] *Nicomachean Ethics*, III. i. 1119^{a}–1110^{b}.

an oath extorted by duress. According to Thomas, one who promises under oath normally incurs two obligations: one to the promisee and the other to God. If the promisee had extorted the promise by duress, then the first of these obligations was removed. '[H]e that used force deserves that the promise to him should not be kept.' The obligation to God was a more difficult matter since one ought to suffer a loss rather than disregard such an obligation. Nevertheless, an oath to God could not obligate a person to do evil. It would be unjust and therefore evil to allow the promisee to inflict a loss on the promisor. Therefore, the promisor could go to court to recover the loss even if he had sworn not to.[55] Thomas made a similar argument in discussing matrimony.[56] Thomas thus remained faithful to the principle he had taken from Aristotle: consent given under duress was nevertheless consent. Coerced oaths and marriages were not binding because of the injustice that had been done.

Soto, for once, could not agree with Thomas and Aristotle. He knew that, by Canon law, if a woman vows to enter a religious order because she is threatened, the vow is not binding. The reason, he said, is that she does not desire what she vows, and therefore the vow is not voluntary. In contrast, the vow would be binding if she took it to obtain divine help in a storm at sea because then she would desire what she was getting. Aristotle said, Soto acknowledged, that consent given under duress is nevertheless consent. But if that were so, a woman who made a vow because of threats would be bound in conscience even though Church courts would not hold her to it. Soto claimed that the reason Canon law does not hold her to it is that the law presumes that she did not consent.[57]

[55] *Summa theologica*, II–II, q. 89, a. 7, ad 3.

[56] Thomas first discussed promises other than those people make when they marry. If made under duress, such promises were not absolutely void, but the promisor could be released from his obligation. The reason was that promises are binding because of the virtue of faith or truth. But a person who promised under duress did not lie. At that moment he genuinely wished the lesser of two evils, which was to give what he had promised. Later, however, he could sue to be released from his promise and to receive back whatever he had given. Suppose, then, he had promised not to sue or to take back what he had given. Thomas answered with the same argument he had made in considering oaths: a promise to condone injustice was a promise to do evil, and such promises could not be binding. (*Summa theologica*, suppl. q. 47, a. 2, ad 4.) According to Canon law, a marriage entered into under duress was absolutely void. The reason, Thomas explained, was that marriage was indissoluble. One could not consent to be married without consenting at the same time to stay married for ever, and not to seek rescission once the unlawful threat had been removed. But, again, a promise not to seek rescission given under duress was not binding because it was a promise to condone the injustice of which one was the victim. Therefore, the coerced consent to marry was void from the beginning. (Ibid., suppl. q. 47, a. 3.)

[57] Soto, *supra* n. 9, lib. 8, q. 2, a. 1.

Molina and Lessius considered the effect of duress on ordinary promises and arrived at a solution that would accommodate the Aristotelian and Thomistic theory of the voluntary. A party who promised under duress really did consent, and therefore his promise was not radically void. Nevertheless, the promise was voidable at his option because, by threatening him, the promisee had done him an 'injury'.[58] Duress, in other words, was a tort or delict to be remedied by allowing the victim to escape from his promise. This position seemed to imply that, if a person promised because of the threats of a third party, and these threats were made without the knowledge of the promisee, the contract would be valid since the promisee had done no injury. The promisor's only remedy would be to sue the third party. Nevertheless, as Lessius acknowledged, such a contract was not binding under Roman law. Although Lessius expressed some doubts, he suggested that the Roman rule was merely one of positive law.[59]

This theory did not easily explain why coerced vows were not binding. In the case of a vow, the promisee was God, and the unlawful threat was necessarily made by a third party. Lessius argued that, although coerced consent was nevertheless consent, a vow had to be taken without coercion to be binding because, in deciding to take a vow, 'man is a law unto himself and arbitrator'.[60] Unfree consent was not the kind of consent that would make a vow binding. Lessius quoted in support of his position a famous Roman text that said 'nothing is more contrary to consent' than duress.[61]

Could one not apply this same argument to contracts in general and conclude that they also require a consent uninfluenced by unlawful pressures? At one point Lessius came very close to saying so: 'one who is compelled by duress is deprived through an injury of his liberty; therefore he must be restored to his original state so that he can freely approve or disapprove the contract'.[62] Coerced consent was still consent. But, Lessius suggests, there are certain relationships in which one cannot be bound by consent that is coerced and therefore unfree.

Grotius, Pufendorf, Barbeyrac, and Pothier—and, this time, even Wolff—preserved the positions taken by the late scholastics. Grotius began his discussion of duress by announcing that the subject had become 'entangled' by distinctions 'between fear impressed justly and unjustly, by the promisee, or by another', and

[58] Molina, *supra* n. 7, disp. 352; Lessius, *supra* n. 7, lib. 2, cap. 17, dub. 6.
[59] Lessius, *supra* n. 7, lib. 2, cap. 17, dub. 6.
[60] Ibid., cap. 40, dub. 3.
[61] D. 50.17.117.
[62] Lessius, *supra* n. 7, lib. 2, cap. 2, dub. 6.

so forth. Having led us to believe he will blaze new trails, he then devotes four sentences to the topic in which he adopts a pure form of the delictual theory of Molina and Lessius. 'He who has promised anything under fear is bound: for here was consent, not conditional, as in the case of erroneous promises, but absolute,' as Aristotle said discussing the person who throws goods overboard to avoid shipwreck. Nevertheless, if the promisee produced the fear unjustly, then the promisor at his option is not bound, 'not because the promise was invalid but on account of the damage wrongfully done'. If the fear was unjustly caused by a third party, the promisor has a right to avoid the contract only as a matter of positive rather than natural law.[63]

Pufendorf adopted the delictual theory with a modification. A person who consented through fear had nevertheless consented. Still, the reason a promisee could not enforce a promise extorted by duress was that he could not acquire a right through his own wrong. One should not talk as though he had acquired a right which he was now compelled to relinquish.[64] Barbeyrac returned to the position of Lessius: 'the consent is not completely free in the way required by promises and agreements, which are voluntary commitments'.[65] The views of Grotius, Pufendorf, and Barbeyrac were discussed at length by Pothier, who was content to say that, even if the promise were binding by natural law, the injustice committed would obligate the perpetrator to release the victim.[66] Wolff said that one could not acquire a right because 'it is not lawful to extort consent by force or duress'.[67]

Mistake and Fraud

Aristotle said that to act voluntarily a person must be aware 'of the particular circumstances of the action'.[68] Thomas explained that an act is involuntary 'when a man is ignorant of some circumstance . . .

[63] Grotius, *supra* n. 17, II. xi. 7.

[64] Pufendorf, *supra* n. 17, III. vi. 12.

[65] Barbeyrac on Pufendorf, n. 5 to III. vi. 10. Domat said an agreement was void (*nulle*) if a party 'did not have the liberty to consent'. Thus, agreements 'in which liberty is injured by some sort of duress are . . . void'. (Domat, *supra* n. 30, I. i, pp. v, 10.) Despite the way he expressed himself (which, as will be seen, may have influenced the way the French Civil Code was drafted), it is hard to believe he meant consent was completely absent. He was a traditionally minded jurist and he does not claim he has any new theory of consent. It is more likely he meant to take the position of Lessius and Barbeyrac.

[66] Pothier, *supra* n. 30, §§22–3.

[67] Wolff, *supra* n. 26, iii, §574, which proved that one could not use force or duress to extort a promise (iii, §575), which proved that one could not acquire a right if one did (iii, §576).

[68] *Nicomachean Ethics*, III, i. 1111[a].

and therefore does what he would not do if he knew . . .'.[69] Ignorance interferes with choice when it is 'the cause of willing what otherwise a man would not will'.[70] This conclusion fitted easily into Aristotle's and Thomas's conception of how choices are made. A human being acts to achieve an end, and wants to achieve this end as a means to further ends which are, at the end of the series, means to his ultimate end. A circumstance of which a person was ignorant at the moment he chose may frustrate the attainment of these more remote ends and so render the action, to that extent, involuntary.

Suppose, however, a murderer were to argue that he never consented to the deed because he was ignorant of one circumstance but for which he would not have killed: the circumstance that he would be caught. Or suppose a spouse were to argue that he never consented to the marriage because at the time he was ignorant of his partner's temper or drinking habits. Thomas's answer was that it is not of the essence of murder that the perpetrator escape or of the essence of marriage that one have a considerate or sober spouse. As long as the felon knew the essentials that made his act a murder, he did choose to murder though he did not choose to be caught. As long as the spouse knew the essentials that made the act marriage, he chose to be married though he did not choose the bad temper or drunkenness of his partner.[71] Thomas presumably thought this analysis applied to other contracts as well, since in discussing consent to marriage he drew an analogy to sale.[72]

Nevertheless, even if one understood the essentials, there were, in Thomas's view, certain circumstances in which an oath, vow, or promise would not be binding. He based this view on Aristotle's concept of equity in the application of laws. As we have seen, for Aristotle and Thomas, the ultimate good for man had the character of an end. One's conclusions about the means necessary to attain that end will be right only in the majority of cases. Consequently, whenever a law is made, particular circumstances can arise under

[69] *Summa theologica*, I–II, q. 6, a. 3.

[70] *Summa theologica*, I–II, q. 6, a. 3.

[71] Thus, according to Thomas, a marriage is void if a party was mistaken as to matters that are 'of the essence of matrimony' (*de essentia matrimonium*). (*Summa theologica* Suppl. q. 51, a. 2.) An example would be a mistake as to the identity of the person one is marrying, since it is of the essence that one be joined to a particular person. Such a mistake destroys consent. In contrast, a mistake as to other matters, such as the spouse's 'nobility' or 'dignity', does not concern the essence of matrimony and therefore the marriage is valid. (Ibid., ad 5.) Thomas draws the analogy to wrongful acts. (Ibid., ad 3.) To be excused, the perpetrator must be ignorant of the attributes of his action that make it wrongful. Otherwise he is still to blame whatever he might not have known.

[72] Ibid. Suppl. q. 51, a. 2, ad 7.

which the law-giver himself never meant the law to be applied. As a matter of 'equity', the law should not be applied under such circumstances.[73] Oaths, vows, and promises, Thomas explained, are a sort of law one prescribes for oneself. They are not binding under circumstances under which the promisor did not intend to be bound.[74] Thomas recognized, of course, that, as in the case of a losing bet or a bad marriage, the promisor might be bound under circumstances so unpleasant that he would not have promised had he known these circumstances would arise. In the case of a bet, and, in Thomas's view, a marriage, there are reasons why, in order to attain his objectives, the promisor must agree to be bound under these circumstances. Other circumstances, however, not only are unpleasant but lie outside his commitment, and then he is not bound. A parent may commit himself to take a child to the zoo rain or shine, even though he will regret his promise if it rains; but the promise is not binding if the child gets sick.

According to Thomas, then, any action is involuntary to the extent that the ultimate purposes of the actor are not achieved. An action is nevertheless involuntary in a much more radical sense if the actor has not understood the essentials of what he is doing. In that event, he has not chosen to perform an action of that kind at all. Moreover, if a promisor understands the essentials of an oath, vow, or promise, he is still bound only under the circumstances that lie within the commitment he intended. The late scholastics drew on all of these views in discussing mistake and fraud.

As mentioned earlier, one Roman text said that a party to a sale did not consent if he made an error in substance.[75] The words 'substance' and 'essence' had similar meanings in Aristotelian philosophy although the author of this text clearly did not have these meanings in mind.[76] Nevertheless, Lessius and Molina cited the text in support of Thomas's conclusion about the effect of a failure to understand the essentials of an act.[77] Lessius explained that, if a party committed an error in the substance of what he contracted for, as for example if he sold a gem as glass, the 'substance of consent is lacking for he did not consent to this thing but another which he believed to underlie its accidents'.[78] As we have seen, Bartolus and Baldus had read the same philosophical conclusion into the text in the fourteenth century.

[73] Ibid. II–II, q. 120, a. 1.
[74] Ibid. II–II, q. 88, a. 10; q. 89, a. 9.
[75] D. 18.1.9. [76] See Ch. 3, pp. 57–8.
[77] Molina, *supra* n. 7, disps. 340, 342.
[78] Lessius, *supra* n. 7, lib. 2, cap. 17, dub. 5.

The late scholastics read Thomas's other views about involuntariness into the Roman texts that dealt with fraud. These texts occasionally referred to the *causa* or reason a person contracted. From the twelfth century, these references had been interpreted to mean that a contract was voidable if the fraud concerned the *causa* of a contract. Fraud in the *causa* was explained as fraud that led a party to contract who otherwise would not have contracted.[79] A traditional example had been selling a person a horse by fraudulently convincing him that his own horse was of no further use.[80] Another traditional example had been buying a copy of the Decretals (part of the Canon law) by telling the seller that it would soon be superseded by a new set of decretals.[81] Fraud in the *causa* was contrasted with 'incidental fraud'. The victim of 'incidental fraud' would have contracted absent fraud but on more favourable terms. He did want a horse but was defrauded as to the qualities of the one he bought. His remedy was not to avoid the contract but to sue for the amount by which the fraud had affected the contract price.

Late scholastics such as Conradus interpreted these traditional rules to mean that fraud in the *causa* destroyed consent. Conradus argued, citing Aristotle's *Ethics*, that, if a party would not have consented but for the fraud, then by natural law there was no consent and no contract.[82] On the surface, this solution was Aristotelian and Thomistic. As we have seen, Thomas had said that an act is involuntary 'when a man is ignorant of some circumstance . . . and therefore does what he would not do if he knew'. If we take fraud in the *causa* to mean fraud in any further purpose or *causa finalis*, however remote, that induces a person to act, the fraud would seem to make the act involuntary.

As just noted, however, Thomas thought that, even if an act was involuntary in the sense that it failed to achieve the actor's ultimate objectives, the actor consented to an act of that type as long as he understood its essentials. Consequently Molina claimed that Conradus was wrong. Only an error in substance or essence destroyed consent; fraud in the *causa* did not. Relief for fraud was given only because of the injury one party had done to the other. Thus, according to Molina, fraud affected a contract in the same way as duress. It constituted a tort or delict or injury.[83] In the case of

[79] Rogerius to C. 4.44. See Vacarius, *Liber pauperum* (London, 1927), IV. 51 to D. 19.2.22.3 to *quaemadmodum*; Distinctiones, Collectio senesis xxviii.

[80] Vacarius, IV. 51 to D. 19.2.22.3 to *quaemadmodum*.

[81] Hostiensis 'de pactis', *Summa aurea* (Venice, 1574), III. 17, par. 7.

[82] Conradus Summenhart, *De contractibus licitis atque illicitis tractatus, compendium* (Venice, 1580), q. 57, p. 22.

[83] Molina, *supra* n. 7, disps. 340, 352.

causal fraud, the injury was repaired by releasing a party from a contract to which he would not otherwise have consented. In the case of incidental fraud, it was repaired by giving damages.

This position, Molina claimed, provided the best account of Roman and Canon law. It explained why Roman law gave no remedy if fraud were committed by a third party without the promisee's knowledge: the promisor had consented and the promisee had not done him an injury. It explained why a marriage was not void even for fraud in the *causa*. (By Canon law, a marriage was not voidable for this reason either, but, Molina argued, that was due to the indissolubility of marriage.) It also explained why onerous contracts were voidable for fraud in the *causa* but were neither void nor voidable for a mistake in the *causa* that was not the result of fraud. In all these respects, Molina said, positive law followed 'the nature of the thing itself'.[84]

Lessius agreed with Molina that despite fraud in the *causa* there is still 'consent in the substance', and therefore the contract is not radically void. In such cases 'there is no error in the substance of the thing but only in the *causa* that inclines or disinclines one to contract'. The parties did agree 'here and now to this thing', and the error 'is not about the substance of the thing but only about what is extrinsic'.[85]

Lessius distinguished error in the substance from error in what is extrinsic in the same way as Thomas. For Thomas, as we have seen, an action was defined by its proximate or immediate end. An error as to this end would therefore be an error in the essence of the action. An error as to the more remote ends to which the immediate end was a means would be an error only in an accident. Lessius, like Thomas, distinguished errors in the 'principal *causa*' or immediate end 'giving the act its species' and errors in the 'accidental conditions and secondary *causae*'. Error in the principal *causa* radically vitiated consent because the party was in error as to 'the substance of the act itself'. Error as to the secondary *causae* did not.[86]

Lessius argued, however, that fraud or error in these secondary *causae* could still have an effect on consent. He adopted Thomas's view that promises are binding only under circumstances in which the promisor intended them to be binding. 'The reason', Lessius said, 'is that a promise only has force because of the will and intention of the promisor . . .; therefore, it cannot bind beyond that intention either as expressed or as prudently interpreted.'[87] Using

[84] Ibid., disp. 352.
[85] Lessius, *supra* n. 7, lib. 2, cap. 17, dub. 5.
[86] Ibid., cap. 18, dub. 17.
[87] Ibid., cap. 18, dub. 10.

Thomas's analogy, he explained that promises are like laws. However absolute their wording, laws 'do not obligate in those cases which the legislator expressly or by interpretation wished to except, and a promise is a sort of particular statute which one freely imposes on oneself'.[88]

Lessius concluded that, unlike contracts made under duress, which could be rescinded 'only by reason of the injury', contracts induced by fraud could be rescinded 'by reason of the injury and by reason of a defect in consent'.[89] Consent was not radically absent, as it would have been had he made an error in the essence of what he was contracting for. Nevertheless, 'no one intends to abide by a contract in such a way that he cannot withdraw even if he only contracted because of a grave error, and therefore full consent is lacking'.[90] Surely, Lessius said, a gratuitous promise ought to be revocable when 'fraud or error in motive gave it its *causa*', because the 'normal and tacit intention of the parties is to be regarded'. Although an onerous contract depends on the consent of two parties rather than one, still the most reasonable conclusion is that it, too, can be revoked as long as the revoking party is not at fault and the positions of the parties have not changed (*res . . . est integra*). If their positions have changed, then the party who did not revoke can sue for compensation for any harm he has suffered.[91]

The late scholastics had tried to synthesize Thomas's ideas with inherited and supposedly Roman rules about mistake and fraud. In the seventeenth century, the positions they had taken were recapitulated by Grotius, Pufendorf, Barbeyrac, Pothier, and Wolff. These authors, however, reproduced the solutions of the late scholastics without reproducing their analysis, and perhaps without understanding the concepts on which it was based.

According to Grotius,

> The discussion of agreements made in error is sufficiently perplexed. For a distinction is commonly made between an error which is in the substance of a thing and one which is not in the substance; as to whether fraud gave the contract its *causa* or not; as to whether the other party to the agreement participated in the fraud or not. . . .
>
> But the way to find the natural truth is opened to us by a principle concerning the force and efficacy of statutes which is universally accepted. If a statute is founded on a presumption as to some fact and the fact is really otherwise, then the statute is not binding for the entire foundation of the statute fails if the truth of the fact fails. When a statute is founded on such, a presumption is to be gathered from its matter, words and circumstances.

[88] Lessius, *supra* n. 7, lib. 2, cap. 17, dub. 10.
[89] Ibid., cap. 17, dub. 5.
[90] Ibid.
[91] Ibid.

Similarly, therefore, we say that if a promise is founded on a presumption as to some fact that is really otherwise by nature the promise has no force because the promisor does not consent except on a certain condition which in reality is not met.[92]

Though he again claimed to be blazing new trails, Grotius merely restated Lessius's position as to error in *causa* while ignoring what he said about error in substance. He made the same argument as Lessius and Thomas about the force of statutes. Like Lessius, moreover, he concluded that 'if the promisor was negligent in inquiring into the matter or in expressing this meaning, and the other party has thereby suffered damage, the promisor will be bound to compensate him. . . .'[93]

One wonders, however, how much of Lessius's position Grotius really preserved. Where Lessius spoke of the *causa* of a promise, Grotius spoke of the 'presumption' on which a promise was 'founded'. He never explained whether 'presumption' carried a different meaning than *causa*. He mentioned fraud in the *causa* along with a number of other late scholastic distinctions, but he observed that they were in 'greater part from Roman rather than natural law', and that 'some of them are not sufficiently true or accurate'.[94]

The meaning of error as to a 'presumption' becomes even harder to understand when one considers Grotius's discussion of changed circumstances. Lessius had explained both error in *causa* and the effect of changed circumstances by the same Thomistic principle: a promise, like a statute, is not binding under circumstances in which it was never meant to apply. According to Grotius, the change of circumstances must concern the 'unique reason' for giving a promise 'of which we have spoken'.[95] He had spoken of this 'unique reason' earlier as 'the unique and efficacious cause which moved the promisor', without which the promise becomes 'unjust and useless'. The words of a promise should be extended beyond their literal significance to include cases within that 'unique reason'.[96] Grotius does not explain how this 'unique reason' or 'unique and efficacious cause' differs from the *causa* of the late scholastics. He does not explain how it differs, if at all, from a presumption on which a promise is founded. One rapidly becomes lost in phrases of uncertain meaning produced *ad hoc* to attack particular problems. It is hard to find an underlying theory of consent that would give these phrases meaning.

[92] Grotius, *supra* n. 17, II. xi. 6.

[93] Ibid. II. xi. 6. 3.

[94] Ibid. II. xi. 6. 1.

[95] Ibid. II. xvi. 25. 2.

[96] Ibid. II. xxi. 20. 2.

One has the same sense reading Pufendorf, Barbeyrac, and Wolff. They say that a promise is not binding when an error concerned 'the presumption of some fact' on which consent was conditioned (Pufendorf),[97] or when the error was the 'unique cause' for consenting (Barbeyrac)[98] or a 'unique reason' absent which a promise would not have been made (Wolff).[99] None of them explains more clearly than Grotius what this error is. Pufendorf and Barbeyrac do not explain how it is related to fraud in the *causa* for which, they say, a contract can be rescinded.[100]

Indeed, it is harder to understand Pufendorf and Barbeyrac than Grotius, since they also thought a contract was void for an error in 'essentials' as distinguished from 'accidentals', an error that Barbeyrac called 'efficacious' as distinguished from 'concomitant'. It is hard to tell how they conceived this kind of error, let alone thought that it was related to an error in a 'presumption' or 'unique cause'. According to Pufendorf, 'the common saying that an agreement is made void by an error in essentials' means that the agreement is void not merely for an error in 'those things that enter into the physical essence of the matter over which the agreement is made', but also for an error in 'those qualities which the maker of the agreement had especially before his eyes'. The reason is that 'it often happens that . . . the quality of a thing is regarded as of the first importance while its physical substance is regarded only as a necessary accessory'.[101] While Pufendorf preserves the formula 'error in essence', he does so without any real commitment to the theory of human choice from which he is borrowing. Error in essence seems to mean only what in some undefined way is important to a party. At the beginning of his work, he gave a vaguely Aristotelian account of how voluntary action presupposes understanding, but one that does not mention essences at all.[102]

Barbeyrac claimed that Pufendorf's discussion was too Aristotelian. His reason shows that Aristotelian philosophy was ceasing to be understood even by educated men such as himself. He said: 'Our author [Pufendorf] with the moralists follows the opinion of the Peripatetics [the Aristotelians] who distinguish the different sorts of error or ignorance by the regret or repentence shown or not shown by the actor after the action. See Aristotle, *Nicomachean Ethics* III ii.'

[97] Pufendorf, *supra* n. 17, III. vi. 6.

[98] Barbeyrac on Pufendorf, n. 3 to III. vi. 6.

[99] Wolff, *supra* n. 26, iii, §504. See ibid. iii, §§569–70. Again following Grotius, Wolff says that, if the mistake was due to the negligence of one party, he must pay whatever damages the other party has suffered. (Ibid. iii, §571.)

[100] Pufendorf, *supra* n. 17, III. vi. 8; Barbeyrac on Pufendorf, n. 2 to III. vi. 8.

[101] Pufendorf, *supra* n. 17, III. vi. 7.

[102] Ibid. I. iii. 10.

That was wrong, Barbeyrac said, since then 'anyone by a simulated repentence could escape responsibility. . . .' After expressing this opinion, which seems quite unrelated to anything in Book III, Chapter ii of the *Ethics*, or for that matter in Pufendorf, Barberyac presents the view of Titius, another jurist, which turns out to be nothing more than Aristotle, watered down and unexplained: ignorance excludes consent when it concerns 'those matters that the nature of the thing necessarily requires'.[103]

Pothier followed Pufendorf. Error excludes consent not only if it falls on the 'thing itself' but also when it concerns 'the quality of the thing that the contracting parties had principally in view and which constitute the substance of the thing'.[104] A contract is not absolutely void for fraud, but relief is given on account of the injustice.[105]

Grotius, Pufendorf, Barbeyrac, Wolff, and Pothier nevertheless preserved, in words if not in spirit, the solutions to the problem of ignorance which the late scholastics had built on Thomas's theory of human choice. They also preserved the theoretical reorganization of Roman law wrought by the late scholastics. Mistake had ceased to be a special topic of the law of sales and fraud a commentary on the *actio de dolo*. The rules of mistake and fraud, like those of duress, had been organized into doctrines which supposedly followed from general principles.

These changes must, again, have had the most minimal significance in practice. Cases of mistake do not arise very often. One wonders, in any case, if many judges would arrive at a different result trying to follow Grotius or Pufendorf instead of Lessius or Molina or the Roman texts. Lessius's and Molina's delictual theory of duress did cast doubt on the Roman rule that a contract could be avoided for duress committed by a third party. Both jurists, however, accepted the rule as valid positive law, and, again, cases calling for its application are rare. This change, like the others we have seen, was in the way contract law was understood.

THE CONTENT OF A CONTRACTUAL OBLIGATION

A modern civil lawyer, though unfamiliar with Aristotelian virtues, would recognize the principle that promises are binding if made for a good *causa* and accepted. Though unfamiliar with Aristotelian theories of human choice, he would be conversant with the doctrines of duress, mistake, and fraud. In contrast, late scholastic ideas about the content of the parties' contractual obligations have left

[103] Barbeyrac on Pufendorf, n. 2 to I. iii. 10; n. 2 to III. vi. 6.

[104] Pothier, *supra* n. 30, §18.

[105] Ibid., §29.

few traces in modern law. Modern lawyers are familiar only with the problems the late scholastics used these ideas to resolve: What terms in a contract are fair? What terms belong to a contract other than those on which the parties expressly agreed?

In explaining these matters, the late scholastics again followed Thomas. Thomas, as we have seen, thought that one could start with the definition of a particular transaction and move to a description of the obligations that this transaction entails. These obligations either were included in the concepts used to formulate the definition or were means to the end in terms of which the transaction has been defined. Thus, after defining commutative justice in terms of equality, and sale as an act of commutative justice, Thomas explained the obligations of seller and buyer as following from the concept of equality. We will examine, first, what the late scholastics said about equality, and then what they said about the obligations entailed by particular contracts.

Equality in Exchange

According to Aristotle and Thomas, acts of commutative justice required equality. The late scholastics found it easy to integrate this requirement with Roman law. As we have seen, the Glossators interpreted Roman law to provide a remedy for a severely unjust price.[106] Baldus had said the remedy was based on 'natural equity'.[107] The late scholastics explained that Roman law gave a remedy because commutative justice required equality. Admittedly, Roman law provided a remedy only for deviations from the just price of more than one-half, but that was because of pragmatic concerns about unsettling commerce or encouraging litigation. Similarly, Thomas had explained that Roman law corrected only large deviations because human law could not command all acts of virtue.[108]

The question that has puzzled modern scholars is what the late scholastics and others in the Aristotelian tradition meant by equality in exchange. Certainly, they did not mean an equality in the personal benefit or advantage the parties gained from the transaction. On the contrary, they maintained that a seller should not charge more than the just price of goods even if the buyer benefited by a much greater amount from having received them.[109] Accordingly, some scholars once thought that they imagined goods to have some mystical intrinsic value. Others have thought that they equated the value of goods with their cost of production. As we shall see, the correct

[106] Ch. 3, p. 65.

[107] Ch. 3, p. 67.

[108] *Summa theologica*, II–II, q. 77, a. 1, ad 1.

[109] e.g. Lessius, *supra* n. 7, lib. 2, cap. 21, dub. 4; Molina, *supra* n. 7, disp. 348.

view is that of more recent scholars: they identified the just price with what we would call the price on a competitive market, a price that varies from day to day and region to region. The question we will have to address is why they thought this fluctuating price preserved equality.

The idea that the scholastics conceived of the just price as a mystical intrinsic value goes back to the writings of Christian Thomasius in the eighteenth century. Those who believe in a just price, he said, regard value as an intrinsic property of things, like colour. The doctrine was founded on sand because value depends 'on the mere judgment of men'.[110] The late scholastics, however, had no such concept of value in mind. They seem to have enjoyed pointing out that the just price of goods did not correspond to their intrinsic worth or usefulness. In a non-economic sense, a man was of more intrinsic worth than an animal and an animal of more worth than a stone; bread which sustains life was intrinsically more useful than luxuries such as diamonds. According to the late scholastics, economic value therefore did not correspond to intrinsic worth or usefulness. Otherwise, a diamond would sell for less than a mouse, which has greater intrinsic worth, or for less than a loaf of bread, which is more useful.[111]

Recognizing that the scholastics had neither a 'subjective' theory in which the value of goods was the benefit conferred on their purchaser, nor an 'objective' theory in which value was an intrinsic property of goods, some scholars claimed that they equated the just price of goods with their cost of production.[112] This interpretation seemed to explain why they believed that exchange at a just price would preserve equality. The seller would recover only his own expenses and labour. Thus the sale would make him neither richer nor poorer. Similarly, the buyer would become neither richer nor poorer since he could always resell the goods for the price he had paid less any amount he had consumed.

[110] C. Thomasius, *De aequitate cerebrina legis II: Cod. de rescind. vendit. et eius usu practico*, cap. II, §14, printed as Dissertatio LXXIII in his *Dissertationum Academicorum varii inprimis iuridici argumenti* (Halle-on-Saale, 1777), III. 43.

[111] Covarruvias, *supra* n. 40, II, iii, no. 4; Molina, *supra* n. 7, disp. 348; Soto, *supra* n. 9, lib. 6, q. 2, a. 3. See Cappellini, *supra* n. 8, p. 184.

[112] e.g. S. Hagenauer, *Das 'justum pretium' bei Thomas von Aquino* (Stuttgart, 1931). Hagenauer was following still earlier scholars who distinguished the 'subjective' factors of need and scarcity from the 'objective' factors of labour and expenses, and believed that Thomas had emphasized the latter: e.g. R. Kaulla, *Die geschichtliche Entwicklung der modernen Werttheorien* (Tubingen, 1906), 53; E. Schreiber, *Die volkswirtschaftlichen Anschauungen der Scholastik seit Thomas von Aquin* (Jena, 1913), 120.

These scholars pointed out that often writers in the Aristotelian tradition seem to say that goods should sell for the amount it costs to produce them. Aristotle said that, in an exchange between a house-builder and a shoemaker, the house must be to the shoes as the builder is to the shoemaker.[113] Thomas and his teacher Albertus Magnus took him to mean that the price of houses must be to the price of shoes as the expenses of producing the one are to the expenses of producing the other. If the price of houses were lower, Albertus said, then houses would not be built.[114] The late scholastics, Grotius and Pufendorf, explained that the cost of production is one factor on which the just price depends.[115]

Nevertheless, none of these writers could have meant that the just price of goods was always equal to the cost of producing them. They all believed that, in the absence of public regulation, the just price was the price for which goods were commonly traded. Albertus said that the just price is the amount goods are worth in the estimation of the market (*fori*) at the time of the sale.[116] Thomas put the case of a merchant who arrives with grain at a famine-stricken city having passed several other grain-bearing ships on the way. For him the question was not whether the famine price of grain was just, but whether the merchant can sell at that price without revealing that the other ships are about to relieve the famine. Thomas answered that as a matter of justice the merchant can remain silent and sell.[117] Soto, Molina, Lessius, Grotius, and Pufendorf explained that, if no price is set by public authority, the just price is the price for which goods are commonly traded as long as there are no monopolies. Therefore the just price varies from day to day and region to region. They said that the just price depends not only on the cost of production, but also on the need for the goods and on their scarcity.[118] As Odd Langholm has noted, the late scholastics were hardly being original, since all three factors had been mentioned over and over in medieval commentaries to

[113] *Nicomachean Ethics*, v. 1133^{a}–1133^{b}.

[114] Thomas Aquinas, *In decem libros ethicorum Aristotelis ad Nicomachum expositio* (Turin, 1934), lib. 5, lec. 9; Albertus Magnus, *Ethica* (Paris, 1890), v. ii, 9–10.

[115] See n. 118, *infra*.

[116] Albertus Magnus, *Commentarii in quattuor libros sententiarum Petri Lombardi* (Paris, 1890), dist. 16, art. 46.

[117] *Summa theologica*, II–II, q. 77, a. 3, ad 4.

[118] Soto, *supra* n. 9, lib. 6, q. 2, a. 3; Molina, *supra* n. 7, disp. 348; Lessius, *supra* n. 7, lib. 2, cap. 21, dub. 4; Grotius, *supra* n. 17, II. xii. 14; Pufendorf, *supra* n. 17, v. i. 6. See Cappellini, *supra* n. 8, pp. 184–96.

Aristotle's *Ethics*.[119] For that matter, all three had been mentioned, albeit cryptically, by Thomas.[120]

More recently, scholars such as Noonan and de Roover have concluded that, absent public regulation, the just price according to these writers was simply the competitive market price.[121] That thesis must be correct given the evidence we have just seen. Nevertheless, it cannot be the whole story. Why, if the just price was the competitive market price, did the late scholastics believe that public authority could set a different price which would then be the just price? How could the late scholastics have expected a fluctuating market price to preserve equality?

We can answer the first of these questions if we examine how the late scholastics thought that markets worked. They believed that in competitive trading prices were set in response to the cost of production, scarcity, and need, much the way modern economists believe that prices are set in response to supply and demand. The difference is that modern economists believe that there is a unique equilibrium price at which supply equals demand and the market clears. The late scholastics did not know of an equilibrium price or a market mechanism that would uniquely determine one proper price. When Covarruvias, Soto, Molina, Lessius, Grotius, and Pufendorf describe how the market price or just price is determined, they say that under given conditions of need, scarcity, and cost there will be a range of prices which are more or less just. The price at which people trade will be set by the *communis aestimatio*, by the judgment of buyers and sellers as to the price that best reflects need, scarcity and cost.[122] To have conceived of a unique equilibrium price, the late scholastics would have had to imagine separate schedules of supply and demand. This they failed to do. While they knew which factors led prices to rise and fall, they did not study each

[119] O. Langholm, *Price and Value in the Aristotelian Tradition* (Bergen, 1979), 61–143.

[120] Aquinas, *supra* n. 114, lib. 5. lec. 9 (mentioning labour and expenses and *indigentia* or need). The role of scarcity is recognized implicitly in his case of the grain merchant.

[121] J. Noonan, *The Scholastic Analysis of Usury* (Cambridge, Mass., 1957), 82–8; de Roover, 'The Concept of the Just Price Theory and Economic Policy', *Journal of Economic History*, 18 (1958), 418. Similarly, Ambrosetti, 'Diritto privato ed economia nella seconda scolastica', in *La seconda scolastica nella formazione del diritto privato moderno*, *supra* n. 1, 23 at 28.

[122] Covarruvias, *supra* n. 40, II. iii, no. 4; Soto, *supra* n. 9, lib. 6, q. 2, a. 3; Molina, *supra* n. 7, disp. 348; Lessius, *supra* n. 7, lib. 2, cap. 21, dub. 2; Pufendorf, *supra* n. 17, v. i. 8. Grotius apparently held a similar view since he says the price is determined by 'taking account' of these various factors, and he uses the phrase *communis aestimatio* to describe how a risk is priced in an insurance contract. (Grotius, *supra* n. 17, II. xii. 14, 23.)

factor separately as an independent variable. As Langholm has noted, this 'basic failure to separate demand and supply as separate arguments in the value formula' was 'a defect in the Aristotelian market model that was never quite straightened out in the scholastic tradition'.[123] Not knowing of a unique equilibrium price, then, they thought that need, scarcity, and cost were more or less adequately reflected at a range of possible prices. Not knowing of an inexorable but invisible mechanism by which supply and demand reach equilibrium, they ascribed to human judgment the role of taking proper account of need, scarcity, and cost.

We can understand, then, why the late scholastics, Grotius and Pufendorf, were critical of monopolies but open to price regulation by public authority. Monopolies were bad because the market price was supposed to reflect need, scarcity, and cost rather than the desire of a few people to enrich themselves.[124] Regulated prices were legitimate because in establishing them public authority was merely substituting its own judgment about the price that best reflected need, scarcity, and cost for the *communis aestimatio* of buyers and sellers.[125] Since the late scholastics believed that need, scarcity, and cost were reflected more or less adequately at a range of prices, they did not have a modern economist's fear of upsetting a unique equilibrium and thereby causing scarcities or queues of buyers.

The remaining question is why they thought a fluctuating market price, however it was determined, would preserve equality. The problem is that, as recent scholars have pointed out, these writers believed that the just price depended on need and scarcity as well as on the cost of production. Nevertheless, as an older generation of scholars pointed out, only if the just price equalled the cost of production could equality be preserved. Only then would seller and buyer become neither richer nor poorer, since the seller would receive exactly the amount of his expenses and labour and the buyer could always resell for his cost of acquiring the goods. Thus Langholm has noted that what these writers said about equality and cost would converge with what they said about need and scarcity 'only if the just price idea had expressed exactly what we now call long-run

[123] Langholm, *supra* n. 119, p. 116.

[124] e.g. Soto, *supra* n. 9, lib. 6, q. 2, a. 3; Lessius, *supra* n. 7, lib. 2, cap. 21, dub. 21; Grotius, *supra* n. 17, II. xii. 16.

[125] Molina, *supra* n. 7, disp. 347; Lessius, *supra* n. 7, lib. 2, cap. 21, dubs. 2 & 4. Similarly, Grotius and Pufendorf describe the regulated price as one that will accord with the range of just prices the market sets. (Grotius, *supra* n. 17, II. xii. 14; Pufendorf, *supra* n. 17, V. i. 8.)

equilibrium price'.[126] In a long-run equilibrium, a market price set in response to scarcity and need would exactly cover the cost of production. But, he observes, that cannot be what the earlier writers meant since their just price was a fluctuating market price. Moreover, as we have seen, they did not know of an equilibrium price, let alone a long-run equilibrium.

To solve the problem, let us again consider the passage in Aristotle about the house-builder and the shoemaker. Albertus and Thomas interpreted it to mean that the price of houses must be to the price of shoes as the labour and expenses of producing the one are to the labour and expenses of producing the other. Albertus says that if the price of houses were lower the builder would cease to build. We know that Albertus and Thomas thought of the just price as a fluctuating market price. Therefore we have to read their comments on this passage to mean that the builder and shoemaker should recover their cost of production (although they will not do so in every transaction), and that if they do not do so (normally or eventually) they will cease to produce. Normally or eventually, then, the seller should recover his costs, but it does not seem to have troubled Thomas or Albertus that he would not do so in every transaction.

One reason it may not have troubled them that the seller would sometimes recover more or less than his costs may be that they knew prices must fluctuate to take account of need and scarcity. If these fluctuations were necessary lest worse evils ensue, then the inequalities they produced in individual transactions had to be tolerated. If they were not necessary, then, as the late scholastics said, public authority could intervene and establish a regulated price. Thus, absent a regulated price, the competitive market price was just in the sense that it preserved equality to the extent possible if need and scarcity were to be taken into account. In contrast, there was no justification for tolerating the further inequalities that arose when, as Lessius put it, one party took advantage of another's 'ignorance' or 'necessity' to sell to him for more than the market price or to buy from him for less.[127] Similarly, there was no justification for allowing a monopoly to raise prices for its own profit.

There may have been another reason why writers in the Aristotelian tradition were not disturbed that market prices often failed to equal costs of production. They may have thought that, as long as the

[126] Langholm, *supra* n. 119, p. 34.

[127] Lessius, *supra* n. 7, lib. 2, cap. 21, dub. 4. Similarly, Soto, *supra* n. 9, lib. 6, q. 3, a. 1.

seller recovered these costs eventually or normally, it did not matter that he recovered more or less in any particular transaction. Over enough contracts, the end result will be equal. Moreover, in any particular transaction, the seller who received less than his costs of production could just as easily have received more. Thus, that transaction would be equal in the sense that a bet is fair when each party has an equal risk of gain and loss.

Soto makes such an argument to explain why market prices are fair:

> It is a most fallacious rule that one should always sell for the amount for which he buys plus the amount of labor and risk he incurs plus his profit. Rather, if a merchant lacking in skill and ignorant of business buys for more than is just, or if bad fortune buffets him, for example, because an unexpected abundance of goods mounts up, he cannot justly exact the expenses that he incurred. And conversely, if someone is more diligent or more fortunate because he happens to buy for less or because fortune smiles on him and later there is an unexpected scarcity of goods, surely he may justly sell for more, and, indeed, he may do so on the same day and in the same place even though the merchandise has not been improved in any way. For as the business of buying and selling is subject to fortuitous events of many kinds, merchants ought to bear risks at their own expense, and on the other hand, they may wait for good fortune.[128]

Other late scholastic writers were less explicit about the risk of price fluctuations. Nevertheless, they understood that a contract could be fair because it gave a party the chance to gain as well as to lose. Molina defended the rule that the risk of physical destruction fell on the buyer even before delivery by observing that, as he could lose if the goods perished, so he could gain if their condition improved.[129] He also noted that the sellers's costs included 'risk', such as the risk of destruction before sale, as well as 'labour' and 'expenses'.[130] A price that compensated him for the risk he had borne was not unfair even when the risk had failed to materialize. Similarly, Lessius observed that 'this is the condition of merchants, that as they may gain if they receive goods at small expense, so they may lose if the expense was disproportionate or extraordinary'.[131] Molina and Lessius thus recognized that a contract could be equal because a party had a chance to gain as well as to lose, even though

[128] Soto, *supra* n. 9, lib. 6, q. 2, a. 3.
[129] Molina, *supra* n. 7, disp. 366.
[130] Ibid., disp. 348. Similarly Pufendorf, *supra* n. 17, v. i. 10.
[131] Lessius, *supra* n. 7, lib. 2, cap. 21, dub. 4.

they did not apply this analysis as clearly as Soto to the risk of market price fluctuations.[132]

There are two reasons, then, why writers in the Aristotelian tradition may not have been troubled by the fact that market prices fluctuate and do not always equal the costs of production. They may have thought that the inequalities caused by price fluctuations had to be tolerated because prices must adjust to need and scarcity. They may have thought that price fluctuations did not destroy equality because the party who failed to recoup his costs might as easily have made a gain. These writers were often not explicit, but then they saw no need to be. No one had yet accused them of defending a mystical and paradoxical notion of value.

When Thomasius made this accusation in the eighteenth century, the earlier conception of equality in exchange was ceasing to be understood. Otherwise Thomasius would not have insisted that his opponents were conceiving of value as an intrinsic property of a thing like its colour. Barbeyrac sympathized with Thomasius.[133] Pothier and Wolff reaffirmed the need for equality in exchange, but they may not have had the earlier conception in mind. Pothier said a remedy must be given for *lésion* because 'equity must reign in conventions', and 'equity, in acts of commerce, consists in equality'. He added, however, that there is an 'imperfection in the consent of the injured party', since he only contracted because he thought he was receiving something worth what he gave.[134] The reference to an imperfection in consent may not represent a change in underlying theory, since, as will be seen later on, the late scholastics and natural lawyers also thought the parties would normally want to contract at a just price.[135] Still, Pothier apparently felt the doctrine needed an additional justification which earlier writers had not supplied.[136] Wolff tried to prove that one must sell at a just price from the propositions that no one is obliged to give gratis when he can get something in return, and that a price is a judgment as to what should be given in return.[137] The earlier ideas of commutative justice and equality in exchange have been blurred beyond recognition.

[132] Similarly, Ambrosetti concluded that the just price was fair, for the late scholastics, because losses were the result of either misfortune or incompetence. (Ambrosetti, *supra* n. 121, pp. 31–2.)

[133] Barbeyrac on Pufendorf, nn. 1 and 2 to v. iii. 9.

[134] Pothier, *supra* n. 30, §33.

[135] See pp. 109–11 below.

[136] Domat did not give this explanation either. He simply said that relief should be given for *lésion*. (Domat *supra* n. 30, I. i, vi. 9.)

[137] Wolff, *supra* n. 26, iv, §§268, 271, 273, 322.

In any event, the late scholastics had given the requirement of a just price a general theoretical justification, and the attempt to provide one for it survived even in the work of Pothier and Wolff. Once again, the change was one in theory with few practical consequences. As we have seen, the Glossators had no theory of why a price was just. Nevertheless, they conceived of the just price in much the same way as the late scholastics. It was the price for which goods were traded at a given place and time. The Glossators had allowed a party to renounce the remedy in his contract. Bartolus and Baldus allowed him to do so in principle although they found ways to invalidate some renunciations. The late scholastics' position as to the validity of these renunciations was too ambiguous to have worked any decisive change in positive law. Some argued that the same ignorance or necessity that led a party to contract at an unjust price might also lead him to waive the remedy.[138] Some argued that renunciations were written into contracts more because they appeared in notaries' form books than because of the consent of the parties. They claimed that such renunciations should either be invalid or be upheld only if the parties had requested such a clause or if it had been read to them or put in their own handwriting.[139] More typically, however, the late scholastics either ignored the problem or compromised as Bartolus and Baldus had done. A renunciation would be upheld, but it had to be specific and could not be made by persons of less than normal sophistication, such as 'women, children, and rustics'.[140] Moreover, a party could not renounce the remedy if the deviation went well beyond half the just price, if it was not only *enormis* but *enormissima*.[141] While there may have been a continuing pressure, then, to limit the circumstances under which renunciations would be upheld, any change in the law in force was probably minor.

Types of Contracts and Natural Terms

For the late scholastics, as for Thomas, once one had defined a transaction one could move from the definition to a description of the obligations that the transaction entails. One defined a transaction by identifying its end and placing it in some larger type or category of actions to which it belongs. Thus, as we have seen, Thomas

[138] See P. Parisius, *Consilia* (Venice, 1543), cons. xii, no. 88. The argument is discussed by Covarruvias, *supra* n. 40, II. iv, no. 3; Molina, *supra* n. 7, disp. 349.

[139] These arguments are discussed by Covarruvias, *supra* n. 40, II. iii, no. 4. He was critical of them.

[140] See Covarruvias, *supra* n. 40, II. iv, no. 3; Parisius, *supra* n. 138, cons. xii, no. 5; P. Decius, *Consilia* (Venice, 1570), cons. clxxx, no. 4.

[141] Covarruvias, *supra* n. 40, II. iv, no. 5; Molina, *supra* n. 7, disp. 349; Parisius, *supra* n. 138, cons. xii, nos. 80–1; J. Rubeus, *Consilia* (Lyons, 1540), cons. ci, no. 2.

classified the contracts familiar from Roman law by identifying them as acts of liberality or commutative justice and by identifying the end that each serves. Some contracts transfer ownership of a thing, as in a sale, some the use of a thing, as in a lease, and some transfer the thing for safe keeping, as in a deposit, or to secure an obligation, as in pledge and suretyship.[142]

The late scholastics, for the most part, took over Thomas's scheme for classifying contracts with only minor changes. Molina and Lessius tinkered with it to find a place for the feudal fief and a somewhat analogous Roman institution called *emphyteusis*; in both cases, they explained, neither ownership nor merely use was transferred but something in between, which, following others, they called *dominium utile*.[143] Lessius reclassified deposit by saying it was a kind of lease, a lease of one's services in taking care of the thing deposited.[144] Soto subclassified contracts in which a party transferred the use of a thing for recompense: such a contract was a lease if the thing could be used without consuming it, and the illegal contract of usury if it could not.[145] Otherwise, these jurists preserved Thomas's system virtually intact.

Thomas's classification nevertheless suggested the possibility of a grander enterprise going beyond what Thomas himself had attempted: to devise a system of classification that would encompass all possible contracts and reduce them to a set number of natural types. It was not clear on Thomistic principles that such a system was theoretically possible. Cajetan claimed that the only natural division of human agreements was into acts of liberality and acts of commutative justice. Thomas's subclassifications were merely instances in which an 'equivalent' is given 'in such and such matter (*materia*)'. 'The species of commutative justice are not multiplied' by such classifications.[146]

Nevertheless, some late scholastics were not dismayed by the theoretical difficulties. Conradus, who in another age might have made a brilliant botanist, claimed that there were thirty natural types of contracts.[147] Soto, who had preserved Thomas's system almost intact in one part of his work, claimed in another part to have reduced all possible voluntary commutations to seven types which could in turn be reduced to five. In barter (*cambium*) one thing is

142 *Summa theologica*, II–II, q. 61, a. 3. See Ch. 2, pp. 14–15.
143 Molina, *supra* n. 7, disp. 259; Lessius, *supra* n. 7, lib. 2, cap. 17, dub. 3.
144 Ibid., lib. 2, cap. 17, dub. 3.
145 Soto, *supra* n. 9, lib. 3, q. 5, a. 3.
146 Cajetan, *supra* n. 15, to *Summa theologica*, II–II, q. 61, a. 3.
147 Summenhart, *supra* n. 82, q. 18, p. 51.

given for another; in sale (*emptio*) a thing is given for a price; in loan for consumption (*mutuatio*, apparently meaning something more than the Roman *mutuum*) a thing is given to receive the same thing or the same amount in return; in *emphyteusis* (meaning more, again, than the Roman *emphyteusis*) the use of a thing and its fruits (*ususfructus*) is given for a price; in loan for consumption (*commodatio*) the mere use of a thing is given gratis; in loan–barter (*permutata accommodatio*) use of one thing is given for use of another; and in lease (*locatio*) the use is given for a price. Soto then tried to reduce barter to sale and loan–barter to lease.

Soto's system thus rested on the idea that there are two natural ways to distinguish contracts. The first is according to whether something is given gratuitously or for recompense. The second is according to whether it is the ownership of a thing that is given, which Soto describes as 'power over its substance', or the use of a thing and its fruits, which Soto describes as 'power over its qualities and accidents', or merely the use of a thing.[148] One wonders, of course, why the transferable interests in a thing have to be divided up in exactly that way, and why Soto does not consider other logically possible transfers of these interests, such as the use and fruits of one thing given for those of another.

Perhaps the most beautiful all-encompassing system was built by Grotius, who stayed closer than Soto to the contracts familiar from Roman law. According to Grotius, sometimes a benefit is conferred 'beneficially' (i.e. gratuitously) and sometimes 'permutatorially' (i.e. for a benefit received in return). A benefit conferred beneficially is transferred sometimes immediately and sometimes in the future, as in a promise to make a gift. Sometimes its transfer creates an obligation on the part of the recipient. In the latter case, the contract is a loan for use (*commodatio*) if the recipient is given the use of goods, or a gratuitous agency (*mandatum*) if the recipient is given services. Grotius then divides 'permutatorial' contracts into those that produce a community of interest, such as partnership (*societas*), and those that separate the parties. The latter are then further distinguished according to what is given in exchange. In barter, a thing is exchanged for a thing; in sale, a thing for money; in currency exchange, money for money; in lease, the use of a thing (including a service) for money, unless the service is a guarantee against risk, in which case the contract is insurance.[149]

In this scheme, Grotius has presented a virtual periodic table of

[148] Soto, *supra* n. 9, lib. 4, q. 1, a. 1; lib. 6, q. 2, a. 1.
[149] Grotius, *supra* n. 17, II. xii. 1–7.

types of contracts which he describes as 'natural' and 'simple'.[150] His definitions are based on distinctions that seem so basic they would appear in any developed society. In this sense, at least, they are 'natural' types. By combining the elements of these 'simple' contracts, Grotius explains, one can make others which are 'mixed', such as the feudal fief which combines elements of a gratuitous contract with elements of a lease. Thus the simple contracts are the building blocks from which the others were made, and by understanding the simple ones one can understand the rest. Still other systems of classification were proposed by Pufendorf and Pothier.[151]

Not all the late scholastics tried to classify contracts exhaustively into a number of simple and natural types. Nevertheless, they all tried to define each type of contract properly. For them, as for Thomas and Grotius, definition was the first step towards understanding. Starting from the definition, they believed they could identify the obligations to which a party to that type of contract should normally be bound.

These obligations were, as the medieval jurist Baldus had said, 'natural' to that type of contract. Baldus, it will be remembered, developed a threefold distinction among contractual terms that was to be repeated until the time of Pothier.[152] The 'essential' terms were necessary for a contract of a given type to exist and were the 'original root' from which the 'natural' terms arose. The 'natural' terms were read into a contract when the parties had made no other express provision. The 'accidental ' terms were binding only if the parties mentioned them expressly. In developing these distinctions, as we have seen, Baldus himself had been influenced by Aristotelian philosophy. For the most part, the late scholastics, like Baldus, assumed that the terms 'natural' to a given type of contract were those that Roman law read into such a contract absent express provision by the parties. The late scholastics tried to find Aristotelian and Thomistic explanations of why they were 'natural'.

An example is the late scholastic analysis of the duty of a seller to disclose defects in his goods. Roman law, as interpreted by medieval jurists, gave the buyer two remedies if the seller had failed to disclose a defect: he could rescind the contract, or he could demand

[150] He contrasts the 'natural' types of contracts, which exist by natural law, with the distinctions among nominate and innominate contracts established by positive law. 'At ius naturae ignorat haec discrimina: neque vero qui innominati ab illis dicuntur contractus, aut minus sunt naturales, aut minus antiqui. . . .' (Grotius, *supra* n. 17, II. xii. 3. 3.) He distinguishes the 'simple' types of contracts from the 'mixed' contracts which are created by combining them. (Ibid. II. xii. 7; II. xii. 5.)

[151] Pufendorf, *supra* n. 17, v. ii. 8–10; Pothier, *supra* n. 30, §§9–15.

[152] See Ch. 3, pp. 63–5. The distinction appears in Pothier, *supra* n. 30, §§6–8.

the difference between the value of the defective goods and the price he had paid on the assumption that they were sound. The late scholastics explained this rule as an application of Thomas's principle that a seller must disclose defects in order to avoid loss to the buyer and hence injustice and inequality in the contract. Molina and Lessius said that the seller is obligated to disclose 'by his office' (*ex officio*) since, as Molina explained, he has more knowledge of his goods and he offers them 'in order to receive a just price'.[153]

Lessius and others found an explanation for why there should be two Roman remedies, rescission or recovery of the difference in price. The first was appropriate when, had he known of the defect, the buyer would not have contracted, and thus the seller's non-disclosure amounted to fraud in the *causa*. The second remedy was appropriate when non-disclosure merely affected the price the buyer paid.[154] The Roman remedies were thus explained by the same principles by which Lessius and others had explained involuntariness.

Neither the Romans nor their medieval interpreters had been particularly clear about what constituted a defect. They may have simply regarded goods as defective when they were damaged or broken. The late scholastics enlarged the concept of a defect by drawing directly on Thomas's account of what a defect was. In discussing metaphysics, Aristotle had said that things can change in four respects: in substance, in quantity, in quality, and in location.[155] Thomas explained that a seller must answer if his goods were defective in their substance, as when his wine was watered; in their quantity, as when he used false weights; or in a quality, as when he sold a sick horse as sound.[156] Generally, the late scholastics gave the same explanation.[157]

On other questions the implications of Thomas's principles were less clear and the late scholastics were divided. For example, suppose that a seller who had failed to disclose defects nevertheless sold his goods at a price that would be just for goods with these defects. Cajetan and Soto argued that the buyer had no remedy since, having received the goods at a just price, he had suffered no injury.[158] Molina claimed that the buyer could seek rescission if the defect made the goods 'notably' unfit for the purpose for which they

153 Lessius, *supra* n. 7, lib. 2, cap. 21, dub. 11; Molina, *supra* n. 7, disp. 353.

154 Lessius, *supra* n. 7, lib. 2, cap. 21, dub. 11.

155 *Physics*, III. 200^b–201^a.

156 *Summa theologica*, II–II, q. 77, a. 2.

157 e.g. Soto, *supra* n. 9, lib. 6, q. 3, a. 2; lib. 2, cap. 21, dub. 11 (mentioning quality and quantity but not substance).

158 Cajetan, *supra* n. 15, to *Summa theologica*, II–II, q. 77, a. 3; Soto, *supra* n. 9, lib. 6, q. 3, art. 2.

were sold; otherwise, the buyer had no remedy since he had not been injured.[159] Lessius seems to have confined Molina's solution to cases in which the seller had been asked about the goods by the buyer and had failed to tell the truth. A buyer who does not ask 'trusts his own judgment' and has no remedy as long as he receives the goods at a just price. Lessius noted that this solution seemed to clash with a Roman text that said 'the seller should disclose all hidden defects to the buyer',[160] and otherwise the buyer had a right of rescission. He answered that the text either described positive law or assumed that the buyer had asked about the goods.[161] Thus, in different ways, the late scholastics accommodated their theories of the voluntary, their theories of commutative justice, their sense of the practical, and their Roman texts.

Neither Grotius nor Pufendorf made much change in late scholastic doctrine. Grotius again neglected much of its detail while preserving the principle. 'In contracts, nature requires equality', and this requirement extends to 'preceding acts' so that 'he who makes a contract about any thing ought to make known the defects of the thing so far as he knows them, which is not only the usual rule of civil law but also agreeable to the nature of the act'. In words that recall what Molina and Lessius had said about the 'office' of the seller, Grotius explained that the seller has a duty to disclose because, in a contract that is made for the 'common utility', there is a 'connection' or 'union' between the parties that is 'closer' than in other relationships.[162] In speaking of this 'closer connection' Grotius seems to have meant merely that the relationship of parties to an onerous contract is one that requires equality and hence disclosure. Pufendorf, in rejecting his explanation, took him to mean either that the 'bond of humanity' is 'more tightly drawn' in such a contract, or that the parties have assumed duties 'over and above those required by the nature of a contract'. Nevertheless, Pufendorf explained the rule in the same way as his predecessors: the seller must disclose defects, because otherwise the parties cannot set a just price that will preserve equality.[163]

In considering undisclosed defects, the problem for the late scholastics was to work out the details of a solution Thomas had given to the very problem they were addressing. Fortunately for them, this solution seemed to fit neatly into the Roman law of sale.

[159] Molina, *supra* n. 7, disp. 353. [160] D. 19.1.14.
[161] Lessius, *supra* n. 7, lib. 2, cap. 21, dub. 11.
[162] Grotius, *supra* n. 17, II. xii. 9. 1.
[163] Pufendorf, *supra* n. 17, v. iii. 1–3. Since Barbeyrac was sceptical about the doctrine of a just price, he was sceptical about this reason as well. (Barbeyrac on Pufendorf, n. 3 to v. iii. 2.)

Most of the time, however, the implications of their Aristotelian and Thomistic principles were unclear. Roman law, however, contained a vast number of specific solutions to the problems they were attempting to solve. The late scholastics typically accepted the Roman solution as a rule of natural law and then devised an explanation for it. Perhaps inevitably, these explanations were only partially successful. The late scholastics usually did account for the rule in a manner consistent with their larger principles, but they failed to show that the rule is the only one consistent with those principles.

For example, Thomas never dealt with the problem of when the risk of physical destruction of goods passes to the buyer. According to Roman law, even though the risk of destruction normally rests on the owner, and even though the buyer does not become owner until the goods are delivered, nevertheless the risk falls on the buyer before delivery as long as the seller had used care to preserve the goods.[164] The late scholastics and the northern natural lawyers accepted the Roman rule and then invented explanations for it.

According to Molina, while the seller owned the goods before delivery, he owed them to the buyer and could pay this debt by delivering the goods in whatever shape they happened to be. That result was fair because, as the buyer can profit if the goods improve, so he must suffer if they are destroyed.[165] According to Lessius, by natural law the buyer owned the goods as soon as the contract was made. Positive law could modify natural law, and the Romans had done so in this instance by providing that the seller owned the goods until delivery. The Romans had not modified one consequence of the natural law rule, however: that the risk of loss immediately passed to the buyer. That is where the risk should be since the parties to a sale intend the buyer to lose or gain from future changes in the condition of the goods.[166] According to Grotius, while 'ownership may be transferred at the moment of contracting without delivery', and this is 'most simple', nevertheless, the 'rule that the thing is necessarily forthwith at the risk of the buyer' is a 'fiction' of civil law. There was no reason why the parties could not pass ownership at some other point in time.[167] According to Pufendorf, the risk of loss ought to remain on the seller before delivery as long

[164] W. W. Buckland, *A Manual of Roman Private Law* (Cambridge, 1953), 282; M. Kaser, *Das Römische Privatrecht*, 2nd edn. (Munich, 1971), i. 552.

[165] Molina, *supra* n. 7, disp. 366.

[166] Lessius, *supra* n. 7, lib. 2, cap. 21, dub. 12; lib. 2, cap. 3, dub. 3.

[167] Grotius, *supra* n. 17, II. xii. 15. 1. This point was hardly an innovation. Molina and Lessius had observed that the parties could expressly contract that the risk of loss would pass to the buyer at any point in time. (Molina, *supra* n. 7, disp. 366; Lessius, *supra* n. 7, lib. 2, cap. 21, dub. 12.)

as the reason the goods were not delivered immediately is that the seller needed time to make delivery; it should be on the buyer if delivery was delayed to accommodate him.[168] We have, then, a series of solutions, each one plausible, and yet none of them the same. It proved difficult to reach a consensus when there were no Thomistic or Aristotelian principles that clearly addressed these problems.

However imperfect the synthesis achieved, the late scholastics provided the Roman law of particular contracts with a theory. The Romans said much about the rules of particular contracts but little about the general principles of contract law. The late scholastics and natural lawyers tried to bridge the gap between general principles and particular contracts with their systems of classification and their doctrine of natural terms. Alan Watson has observed, speaking of Grotius's scheme of classification, that it was a most un-Roman way to speak about the Roman contracts.[169]

The theory they built had an interesting property which modern theories of contract do not. Modern theories tend to set in opposition, on the one hand, the will of the parties, and on the other any attempt by a court or legislature to judge the fairness of the contract. For the late scholastics and the natural lawyers, there was no such radical opposition.

To hold the parties to the terms natural to the type of contract they entered into was to effectuate their will. In Thomistic terms, the essence of each type was defined by the end it served, and the terms were means to that end. As Domat explained, contracts are formed by mutual consent. But different parties had different needs, and corresponding to each was a different type of contract:

> Agreements are engagements formed by the mutual consent of two or more persons who themselves make a law between themselves to do that which they promise each other. The use of agreements is a natural consequence of the order of civil society and the bonds that God forms between men. For He has made necessary for all their needs the reciprocal use of their industry and their work and various commerce in things, and it is principally by agreements that these needs are met. Thus, for the use of industry and

[168] Pufendorf, *supra* n. 17, v. v. 3. According to Barbeyrac, if the goods were not present when the sale was concluded, the parties should be presumed to want the risk to be borne by the seller, since a buyer would not normally be willing to take the chance of any accident that might occur. (Barbeyrac on Pufendorf, n. 8 to v. v. 3.) According to Domat, the moment the parties agree is the moment when the thing pertains to the buyer rather than the seller, and hence the moment when the risk passes. (Domat, *supra* n. 30, I. ii. vii. 1, 2.) But the risk remains with the seller if he delays delivery. (Ibid. I. ii. vii. 3.)

[169] A. Watson, *The Making of the Civil Law* (Cambridge, Mass., 1981), 94–6.

work, men associate and hire and act in various ways for each other. Thus, for the use of things, when they need to acquire or alienate them, they enter into commerce through sales and barter, and when they only need to have them for a time, they rent or borrow them. And so, according to other and different needs, there are different types of agreements.[170]

Once one enters in an agreement of a given type, Domat said, one is bound 'not only by what is expressed, but also to everything that is required by the nature of the agreement, and to all the consequences that equity, statute and usage give to the obligation one has undertaken'.[171] Nevertheless, the parties could vary the terms of their contract according to differences in their needs:

> [S]ince voluntary engagements among individuals must be proportional to the different needs that make the use of them necessary, all persons capable of such engagements are free to bind themselves by all kinds of agreements, as seems good to them, and to diversify them according to the differences in affairs of all kinds, and according to the infinite diversity of the combinations which are joined in these affairs and the circumstances.[172]

While the terms natural to a contract corresponded to the will of the parties, these terms were also fair. In a contract of exchange, these terms maintained equality in the value of what was given and received. To Thomas, the late scholastics, Grotius, or Domat, the requirement of equality was not something imposed on the parties against their will. The parties to an exchange could only have intended that the contract preserve equality. If either party had wished to enrich the other party at his own expense, he would have wished to make a gift, not an exchange. As Grotius said, 'Nor is it enough for anyone to say that what the other party has promised more than equality is to be regarded as a gift. For such is not the intention of the contracting parties, and is not to be presumed so, except it appear.'[173] For Grotius then, as for the late scholastics, to require equality in an onerous contract in which neither party wished to make a gift was to honour and not to thwart the intention of the contracting parties.

The parties could set aside the terms natural to their contract by an express provision in the contract. The natural terms are means to

[170] Domat, *supra* n. 30, *livre preliminaire*, introduction.

[171] Ibid. I. i. iii. I.

[172] Ibid., 'Traité des loix', vi. 9. Provided, he adds, that the contract is not illicit and contrary to the order of society. (Ibid. vi. 10.) Similarly, in *Les Loix civiles*, I. i. 4. I: 'As agreements are *arbitraires* and diversify themselves according to needs, one can, in all kinds of agreements, contracts and accords (*traitez*), add all kinds of agreements, conditions, restrictions, reservations, *quittances generales*, and other provisions, provided that there is nothing contrary to law and good morals.'

[173] Grotius, *supra* n. 17, II. xii. 11. I.

the end of their contract and, as Thomas said, under particular circumstances the means most appropriate to an end will vary. Nevertheless, they could not do so in a way opposed to the nature of the contract itself. Thus, as Molina and Domat explained, the parties could agree that the seller would not be liable for undisclosed defects. They could do so, however, only if the seller reduced the price so as to preserve equality.[174] Molina and Domat did not think they were disregarding the intentions of the parties. They were honouring the intention that any parties to an exchange must have. A person who did not intend to make a gift could not simultaneously will to enrich the other party at his own expense.

This way of analysing the content of a contractual obligation has become strange to us. It has become strange because the Aristotelian metaphysics of essences on which it was based fell from favour at the very time the northern natural law school was disseminating the doctrines of the late scholastics.

[174] Domat, *supra* n. 30, I. iv. 2. Molina added that this equality could be preserved only if the seller did not know of a specific undisclosed defect when he disclaimed liability (Molina, *supra* n. 7, disp. 353).

5
DISCONTINUITY IN THE NATURAL LAW TRADITION

AS WE have seen, the contract law of the late scholastics depended on a series of Aristotelian ideas. The binding force of contract, and consequently the requirements for contract formation, were explained by Aristotelian virtues of promise-keeping, liberality, and justice. Contractual consent was explained by an Aristotelian theory of choice in which, in order to act *qua* human being, one had to understand the essence of one's action. The consequences of a contract were thought to follow from its essence, either because they were included in its definition or because they were means to the end in terms of which the contract was defined.

In the seventeenth century, the entire edifice was threatened by philosophers such as Descartes, Hobbes, and Locke. They attacked the most fundamental principles of Aristotelian metaphysics, for example the idea that an object has a substantial form and a final cause or end. They themselves were aware that, if those metaphysical principles were false, so also was Aristotle's account of morality, choice, and knowledge. There could be no virtues in the sense of acquired faculties by which one moved towards one's end. There could be no essences in the sense of concepts through which one grasped the substantial form of a thing or an action. Choice could not depend on knowing the essence of one's action. Knowledge could not be acquired by capturing an essence in a definition and then drawing out its consequences.

It would seem that, if the philosophical attack on Aristotle succeeded, the legal doctrines of the late scholastics would have to be rebuilt on new foundations. Paradoxically, the attack on Aristotle did succeed in the eyes of most educated people, and yet, as we have seen, for a long time contract doctrine remained much the same. When Grotius wrote, Aristotelian philosophy dominated the universities of the Protestant north as well as the Catholic south. In the mid-seventeenth century, Hobbes complained that 'the Philosophy-schooles, through all the Universities of Christendome' followed Aristotle.[1] When the century ended, Aristotle was losing his hold over curricula. Educated people were coming to agree with Dryden:

> Longer tyranny ne'er swayed
> Than that wherein our ancestors betrayed
> Their freeborn reason to the Stagyrite
> And made his torch their universal light.

Nevertheless, jurists such as Pufendorf and Barbeyrac, who agreed with Dryden, preserved the doctrines of the late scholastics, and, indeed, disseminated them ever more widely at the very time the authority of Aristotle was crumbling. Aristotelian concepts and principles began to blur and, in the writings of Wolff, to drop out. Yet there is far more continuity than one would expect. To understand the paradox, we must first examine the philosophical challenge to Aristotle.

THE CHALLENGE OF THE NEW PHILOSOPHERS

One reason the seventeenth- and eighteenth-century philosophers distrusted Aristotle's metaphysics was that they were impressed by the physical discoveries of Galileo and, later, of Newton. The reason these discoveries aroused distrust was not merely that they revealed phenomena of which Aristotle had been ignorant, such as the position of the sun in the heavens; people already thought Aristotle had been ignorant of many important things, for example the fitness of non-Greek peoples for constitutional government and the redemption of the world by Christ. Nor did the distrust arise simply because these discoveries were made by a method that stressed experimental observation and mathematics. It took people a long time to see the difference between this method and one that stresses definition. The fundamental problem was that the new science described the motions of objects without regard to their substantial form or end. It described them by mathematical rules to which, for no discernible reason, the motions conformed. It seemed as though objects did not have substantial forms or ends.

Though impressed by these discoveries, the new philosophers put their critique of Aristotle on a different basis. They returned to an epistemological problem that had been noted, but not pushed to its logical conclusions, by the medieval nominalists. In Aristotelian philosophy, substances exist, such as men and pear trees, and yet we know of their existence by perceiving their accidents, such as their

[1] T. Hobbes, *Leviathan* (Cambridge, 1935), I. i at 2.

colour and shape. On the basis of what we perceive, we form a concept in our mind, the essence, which corresponds to the substantial form of the man or the pear tree. As the medieval nominalists pointed out, however, one cannot logically demonstrate that the substance exists from the fact that the accidents are perceived.[2] Descartes made the same point by asking how he could prove to himself that the objects around him really existed. He might be dreaming or the victim of illusions created by an evil demon.[3]

Descartes tried to demonstrate the existence of the outside world by proving first his own existence, and then that of God. God, he argued, would not permit the outside world to be a mere illusion.[4] According to this solution, however, one could prove nothing about the outside world on the basis of one's perceptions alone. Indeed, it was not clear how one's perceptions were related to the outside world. Descartes seemed to be asking God to guarantee the truth of assertions about the outside world that went beyond any evidence one had to support them.

Philosophers such as Hobbes and Locke concluded that one ought not make assertions about the outside world that went beyond one's experience. This experience, Locke explained, could be the kind we associate with the presence of external objects: we see colours and shapes, we feel heat or cold, and so forth. Alternatively, it could be the experience of what is going on inside us, of 'operations of the mind', such as thinking, reasoning, feeling satisfied, or feeling uneasy. To be meaningful, the words we used should refer to an experience or a combination of experiences.[5]

Therefore, according to Hobbes and Locke, the fundamental terms of Aristotelian metaphysics such as substantial form, nature, essence, and final cause or end were meaningless, or, as Locke put it, not 'significant'. To speak of the 'substantial form' or 'end' of a man or a pear tree was to describe neither its colour nor its shape, nor any experience or combination of experiences one could have of it. Such terms described neither one's experience nor anything one could infer from one's experience.[6] Locke regarded the use of such terms as a great source of philosophical error. The prime offenders,

[2] e.g. William of Ockham, *Scriptum in librum primum sententiarum ordinatio*, lib. I, prologus, q. I, in *Opera theologica* (St Bonaventure, NY, 1970), i. 38–9.

[3] R. Descartes, *Méditations* méd. I, in *Oeuvres* (Paris, 1967), ii. 404–13.

[4] Ibid., méd. 6, in *Oeuvres*, ii. 480–505.

[5] J. Locke, *Essay on Human Understanding*, II. i. 2, in *The Works of John Locke* (London, 1823), i. 82–3. See T. Hobbes, *Leviathan* (Cambridge, 1935), I. i at I; I. iv at 18–20.

[6] Locke, *supra* n. 5, II. xiii. 19, in *Works*, i. 166–7; II. xxiii. 1–2, in *Works*, ii. 1–5.

'the great mint-masters of this kind of terms', were the disciples of Aristotle, the 'Schoolmen and Metaphysicians'.[7]

Human thought would therefore have to be explained without using the concept of essence, and morality without using the concept of the end of man. According to Hobbes and Locke, human thought proceeds not by abstracting the essence of an object, but by grouping experiences together.[8] Locke called the experiences themselves 'simple ideas'.[9] We combine them to make 'complex ideas'.[10] Sometimes we combine them because we observe that a number of simple ideas 'go constantly together'.[11] For example, having observed certain colours, lines, and shapes together, we combine them to make the complex idea we call 'pear tree'. Sometimes we combine simple ideas 'very arbitrarily, . . . without patterns, or reference to any real existence'.[12] Mathematicians do so when they make complex ideas such as 'triangle' by combining simple ideas such as straight, side, figure, and three. Since we make these complex ideas ourselves, their meaning is exactly fixed by the way we have defined them.[13] Therefore, our knowledge of them is 'infallibly certain'.[14]

Similarly, a new basis would have to be found for moral philosophy. One could no longer speak of activities that contribute to the end of man or the virtues that make such activities possible. According to Locke, 'the philosophers of old did in vain inquire whether the *summum bonum* consisted in riches, or bodily delights, or virtue or contemplation; and they might have as reasonably disputed, whether the best relish were to be found in apples, plums or nuts'.[15] One could only say that a person felt certain experiences to be agreeable and others disagreeable. Hobbes spokes of these feelings as 'appetite' and 'aversion', which he described physically as 'small beginnings of Motion, within the body of Man', towards or away from something.[16] Locke spoke of the pursuit of pleasure and the avoidance of pain, pleasure meaning whatever one found agreeable and pain whatever one found disagreeable. He redefined good, happiness, and obligation in terms of the pursuit of pleasure. 'What has an aptness to produce pleasure in us is that we call good, and what is

[7] Ibid. III. x. 2, in *Works*, ii. 269. Similarly, see Hobbes, *supra* n. 5, I. i at 2; I. iv at 19–20.

[8] Ibid. I. i at 1; I. iv at 18–20; I. v at 21–2.

[9] Locke, *supra* n. 5, II ii. 1, in *Works*, i. 99–100.

[10] Ibid. xii. 1, in *Works*, i. 153–4

[11] Ibid. xxiii. 1, in *Works*, ii, 1.

[12] Ibid. III. v. 3, in *Works*, ii. 196.

[13] Ibid. ii. 15–16, in *Works*, iii. 297–9.

[14] Ibid. IV. iv. 5, in *Works*, ii. 386.

[15] Ibid. II. xxi. 55, in *Works*, i. 273.

[16] Hobbes, *supra* n. 5, I. vi at 28–9.

apt to produce pain in us we call evil'.[17] For one person, study might be good, for another hawking, for another 'luxury and debauchery'.[18] 'Happiness' is 'utmost pleasure'.[19] We have a 'duty' and 'obligation' to pursue it.[20]

If that were so, it might seem one could have no 'obligation' except to pursue pleasure and avoid pain in any way one could. To avoid this conclusion, Hobbes and Locke turned to the idea of contract. Contract seemed to transmute self-interest into a limitation on the pursuit of self-interest. Each party to a contract gives up something in order to obtain an advantage for himself. Hobbes and Locke explained society as a contract in which each person limits the ways he pursues pleasure and avoids pain in order to benefit from the limitations assumed by others.[21]

Contract, then, was supposed to explain how there could be obligations in a world in which the critical terms of Aristotelian philosophy were not 'significant'. For this explanation to work, however, contract itself would have had to be explained by principles entirely different than those of the late scholastics. For the late scholastics, contract law, like other branches of law, presupposed Aristotelian concepts such as virtue and essence that Hobbes and Locke were trying to do without. Contracts were binding because of a virtue of fidelity. Each type of contract had an essence a person must understand in order to consent. Certain terms followed from the essence of a contract, so that a person would be bound by these terms even if he had not considered them.

It was not clear how contract law could be explained without these concepts. For Hobbes and Locke, there were no virtues in the Aristotelian sense. Indeed, there was no ultimate standard of conduct beyond the conflicting interests of the parties. Yet, supposedly, people were obligated by a contract even when they could get away with violating it. There were no essences. Yet, supposedly, complex phenomena such as government could be understood through a simple formula, the social contract, from which a variety of consequences followed.

The explanation of Hobbes and Locke seems to have been that one could formulate definitions even in a world without essences, and from these definitions one could extract all the consequences necessary to their theory. People were bound by a contract, according

[17] Locke, *supra* n. 5, II. xxi. 42, in *Works*, i. 263. Similarly, see Hobbes, *supra* n. 5, I. vi at 30.

[18] Locke, *supra* n. 5, II. xxi. 54, in *Works*, i. 273.

[19] Ibid. 42, in *Works*, i. 262.

[20] Ibid. 52, in *Works*, i. 271.

[21] J. Locke, *Two Treatises of Government*, II. viii. 95, in *The Works of John Locke* (London, 1823), v. 394; Hobbes, *supra* n. 5, II. xvii at 119.

to Hobbes and Locke, because a contract by definition was binding. As Hobbes said, a 'mutuall transferring of Right, is that which men call CONTRACT'.[22] As Locke said, in his *Second Treatise of Government*,

> Every man, by consenting with others to make one body politic under one government, puts himself under an obligation to every one of that society, to submit to the determination of the majority and to be concluded by it; or else this original compact, whereby he with others incorporate into one society, would signifie nothing, and be no compact, if he be left free, and under no other ties, than he was before in the state of nature.[23]

The obligations of those who entered into the social contract were supposed to follow from its definition by deductive logic. Hobbes claimed to have proven that the people had a duty to obey a sovereign in almost everything.[24] In his *Second Treàtise of Government*, Locke claimed to have shown that the people had a duty to obey the majority; that the majority had a right to delegate power to 'oligarchs' or to a 'monarch'; that the government must rule 'by promulgated standing laws' enforced by 'authorized known judges'; that the government could not 'destroy, enslave or designedly impoverish the subjects' or 'take from any man any part of his Property without his own consent' except by proportional taxation.[25]

Argument from a definition, however, was no longer possible in the same way as in the world of Thomas. In that world, the essence of a moral action had been defined by an end that was itself a means to man's ultimate end. For that reason, one could move from the definition to a large number of consequences. Now, definitions would have to be formulated and consequences extracted in some other way.

Locke tried to explain how one could formulate definitions in his *Essay on Human Understanding*. Definitions were 'complex ideas' which were made by combining simple ideas. The simple ideas were combined either because they were observed to 'go constantly together', or 'very arbitrarily, . . . without patterns, or reference to any real existence'. Definitions of moral ideas such as 'government' and 'contract' were not made in the first way. One did not define government to entail a social contract, because one frequently observed that people subject to governments had made social contracts. One did not define contract to entail an obligation

[22] Ibid. I. xiv at 89.

[23] Locke, *supra* n. 21, II. viii. 97, in *Works*, v. 395.

[24] Hobbes, *supra* n. 5, II. xviii at 120–8.

[25] Locke, *supra* n. 21, II. viii. 97, in *Works*, v.395; II. ix. 132, in *Works*, v. 415; II. xi. 136, in *Works*, v. 419; II. xi. 135, in *Works*, v. 418; II. xi. 138, in *Works*, v. 421.

because one frequently observed that the persons who made contracts also happened to be bound by obligations. Therefore, definitions of moral ideas were made by combining simple ideas arbitrarily. If that were so, however, it would seem that the conclusions drawn from these definitions must be equally arbitrary. As Locke himself asked, if 'moral knowledge be placed in the contemplation of our own moral ideas' and these 'be of our own making', will there not be 'a confusion of virtues and vices, if everyone may make what ideas of them he pleases'?[26]

One answer Locke gave is that the definer is arbitrary only in choosing a name for a given combination of simple ideas. There would be

> no confusion or disorder in the things themselves, nor the reasonings about them; no more than [in mathematics] there would be a disturbance in the demonstration, or a change in the properties of figures, and their relations one to another, if a man should make a triangle with four corners, or a trapezium with four right angles: that is, in plain English, change the names of the figures, and call that by one name, which mathematicians call ordinarily by another. For, let a man make to himself the idea of a figure with three angles, whereof one is a right one, and call it, if he please, equilaterum or trapezium or anything else; the properties of, and demonstrations about that idea will be the same as if he called it a rectangular triangle.[27]

The philosopher David Hume recognized that this answer was not satisfactory. He therefore denied the very possibility of grounding moral obligations on reason. Locke's answer presupposed that simple ideas were related in some way that did not depend on the arbitrary choice of the definer. Mathematical demonstrations were possible because the definer could not 'make to himself' the idea of a plane figure with any number of right angles. Indeed, if definitions were entirely a matter of arbitrary choice, demonstrations would tell us nothing except which arbitrary choices the definer had made. For example, Locke's demonstrations would be impossible if one could define government either to require or not to require a social contract; if one could define contract either to be binding or not to be binding; if one could define the social contract either to require or not to require obedience to the majority, and so forth.

According to Hume, the 'simple ideas' composing a definition could be related in precisely four ways, none of which had anything to do with law or morals. They might be related by resemblance (like similar shapes or similar emotions); in quantity (like lines of

[26] Locke, *supra* n. 5, IV. iv. 9, in *Works*, ii. 388.
[27] Ibid.

different length); in the degree to which they possess a common quality (like shades of a colour); or by contrariety, that is, one might necessarily exclude the other. In those four cases, although the ideas are given by experience, one can speak of a relationship among them that must hold whenever they are experienced: for example that one shade of colour is redder than another, or that the hypotenuse of a right triangle is longer than its side. Moral reasoning was not demonstrative because it was not concerned with any of these four relationships:

If you assert, that virtue and vice consist in relations susceptible of certainty and demonstration, you must confine yourself to those *four* relations, which alone admit of that degree of evidence; and in that case you will run into absurdities, from which you will never be able to extricate yourself.[28]

Perhaps glimpsing these difficulties, Locke had given another answer as well:

complex ideas . . . depend on the mind and are made by it with great liberty, yet they are not made at random, and jumbled together without any reason at all. Though these complex ideas be not always copied from nature, yet they are always suited to the end for which abstract ideas are made.[29]

To whose 'end', however, are some definitions more suited than others? One could no longer speak of an ultimate end of man but only of the different and conflicting ends of individuals. Moreover, in Locke's world, unlike that of Aristotle or Thomas Aquinas, definitions are made not by an act of abstraction, but by grouping simple ideas together. If the simple ideas really have no relationship to each other before the definer groups them together, it is hard to see how one such arbitrary combination could be of more use than another.

Hume was willing to face the intellectual consequences. He concluded that morality could not rest on reason. 'Reason is the discovery of truth or falsehood.' Truth or falsehood depended either on 'real relations of ideas' of the four kinds just mentioned or on 'real existence and matter of fact', that is, on the relations among simple ideas that had actually been experienced. Therefore, statements about morality were statements about feelings for which no reasons could be given.[30] 'So that when you pronounce any action or character to be vicious, you mean nothing, but that from the

[28] D. Hume, *A Treatise of Human Nature* (London, 1886), bk. 3, pt. 1, sect. 1 at ii. 240.

[29] Locke, *supra* n. 5, III. v. 7, in *Works*, ii. 199.

[30] Hume, *supra* n. 28, bk. 3, pt. 1, sect. 1, at ii. 236.

constitution of your nature you have a feeling or sentiment of blame from the contemplation of it.'[31]

Hume tried to free his own discussion of contract law of a virtue of fidelity however disguised. There is no reason why a contract should be binding. The problem is to explain why people feel bound anyway. The feeling cannot be instinctive since ideas such as contract are 'infinitely complicated', and 'to define them exactly, a hundred volumes of laws, and a thousand volumes of commentators, have not been found sufficient'.[32] Therefore, this feeling must have first developed in societies so small that contracts would be kept out of self-interest alone, since, if a person violated his contract, others would immediately lose their motive for co-operating with him. When society became larger, people were already accustomed to seeing contracts kept, and so they felt displeasure at seeing them violated even when they were not the ones to suffer.[33] As Charles Fried noted, Hume's explanation gives a person no reason whatever to abide by a contract, and indeed, by showing him there is no such reason, can encourage him to break it.[34]

Nor did Hume believe that the rules contained in the 'hundred volumes of laws, and . . . thousand volumes of commentators' could be extracted from a definition of the 'infinitely complicated' idea of contract. Sometimes, one could arrive at these rules by considering the 'public interest', which Hume conceived as an aggregate of the interests of individuals. Often, one could not. Then the rules must be made arbitrarily or on the basis of psychological associations, 'fancy', and 'imagination'. 'The slightest analogies are laid hold of, in order to prevent that indifference and ambiguity, which would be the source of perpetual dissension. . . . Many of the reasonings of lawyers are of this analogical nature, and depend upon very slight connexions of the imagination.'[35] According to Hume, 'there are, no doubt, motives of public interest for most of the rules, which determine property; but still I suspect, that these rules are principally

[31] Hume, *supra* n. 28, bk. 1, pt. 1, sect. 1, at ii. 245.

[32] D. Hume, *An Enquiry Concerning the Principles of Morals*, sect. 3, pt. 2, in *Essays* (London, 1882), ii. 195.

[33] Hume, *supra* n. 28, bk. 3, pt. 2, sect. 2, at ii. 262–4, 270–2; bk. 3, pt. 2, sect. 4, at ii. 283–4; bk. 3, pt. 2, sect. 5, at ii. 284–93.

[34] C. Fried, *Contract as Promise: A Theory of Contractual Obligation* (Cambridge, Mass., 1981), 15.

[35] Hume, *supra* n. 32, sect. 3, pt. 2, in *Essays*, ii. 189–90. Thus, 'many of the reasonings of lawyers' are 'dependent on a kind of capricious analogy'. (Ibid., sect. 4, in *Essays*, ii. 201.) Hume noted the similarity between the reasoning of lawyers and that of the scholastics. The 'casuistical subtleties' of 'Jesuits' with their 'habit of scholastic refinement' and of 'metaphysical schoolm[e]n' 'may not be greater than the subtitles of lawyers, hinted at above'; but 'the former are *pernicious*, and the latter *innocent* and even *necessary*'. (Ibid., sect. 3, pt. 2, note, in *Essays*, ii. 193, n. 1.)

fix'd by the imagination, or the more frivolous properties of our thought and conception'.[36] Presumably, he held the same view of the rules of contract law.

Hobbes and Locke had claimed that by abandoning Aristotelian metaphysics and ethics one could have a new moral philosophy in which, Locke said, 'from self-evident propositions, by necessary consequences, as incontestable as those in mathematics, the measures of right and wrong might be made out'.[37] Hume exploded these claims. Reason could not measure right and wrong, moral science was impossible, and legal reasoning, even about positive law, was mostly arbitrary.

THE RESPONSE OF THE JURISTS

These philosophical developments seemed to cry out for a response by the jurists. Grotius wrote before they had taken place—indeed, just as Descartes launched the attack on Aristotle. One would have expected Pufendorf and Barbeyrac, however, either to defend Aristotle or to reject his principles and reformulate their contract doctrine along the lines suggested by Hobbes and Locke, or to succumb to scepticism as Hume was to do. Instead, Pufendorf and Barbeyrac preserved the doctrines of the late scholastics while rejecting Aristotle. They rejected Aristotle without genuinely embracing the philosophy of Hobbes or Locke or even coming to terms with the problems these philosophers were raising. Thus, although they claimed that their legal doctrines rested on higher philosophical principles, these doctrines lost their original moorings in Aristotelian philosophy without finding a new philosophical anchorage. Legal doctrine and moral philosophy began to drift apart.

Historians, however, have usually taken a quite different view of the work of Grotius, Pufendorf, and Barbeyrac. They have seen them as participants in the revolt of the philosophers. It is true that Grotius broke with the scholastic tradition of legal writing. Pufendorf and Barbeyrac imitated Grotius and saw, in the break he made with the past, the creation of a new legal science. It is misleading, however, to identify their rejection of the scholastic tradition with the new philosophers' rejection of scholastic and

[36] Hume, *supra* n. 28. bk. 3, pt. 2, sect. 3 n., at ii. 275, n. 1. 'I shall continue to explain these causes,' Hume said, 'leaving it to the reader's choice, whether he will prefer those deriv'd from publick utility, or those deriv'd from the imagination.' (Ibid.)

[37] Locke, *supra* n. 5, IV. iii. 18, in *Works*, ii. 368–9.

Aristotelian philosophy. The jurists were engaged in a different kind of revolt that had little relation to that of the philosophers.

Grotius was at home in an Aristotelian world and disinclined to question its assumptions. As scholars such as Chroust, Thieme, Feenstra, Wieacker, and Wolf have pointed out, the idea that Grotius rebelled against the scholastic philosophical tradition is a myth.[38] Historians have perpetuated this myth by characterizing his opinions in a way that makes them sound modern, or at least non-medieval, non-scholastic, or non-Aristotelian. Almost invariably, however, the opinions in question might have been held by a late scholastic or any other writer in the Aristotelian tradition.

For example, Grotius said that, because God created man with a rational and social nature, man was subject to a natural law, the first principles of which he could comprehend by an act of abstraction like that of a mathematician who abstracts figures from physical bodies. Since the natural law followed from man's nature, once God created that nature, He could no more abrogate that law than He could ordain that two times two is unequal to four. Indeed, although atheism is 'utmost wickedness', there would be natural law even if there were no God.

All of these statements, including the hypothetical one about the non-existence of God, were made by medieval authors, indeed, by authors in the Thomistic and Aristotelian tradition.[39] Yet they have been used as evidence, and usually as the only evidence, that Grotius broke with that tradition. Because Grotius believed in principles of natural law grounded in human nature and valid if there were no God, he has been called a 'stoic'.[40] For the same reason, and because he did not explain these principles in the course

[38] Chroust, 'Hugo Grotius and the Scholastic Natural Law Tradition', *The New Scholasticism*, 17 (1943), 101; Thieme, 'Qu'est ce-que nous, les juristes, devons à la seconde scolastique espagnole?' in *La seconda scolastica nella formazione del diritto privato moderno* (Florence, 16–19 October 1972), ed. P. Grossi (Milan, 1973), 9–10; Feenstra, 'L'influence de la pensée juridique de Grotius', *XVIIe Siècle*, 35 (1983), 487 at 493; K. Wieacker, *Privatrechtsgeschichte der Neuzeit under besonderer Berücksichtigung der deutschen Entwicklung*, 2nd edn. (Göttingen, 1967), 270, 291, 299; Wieacker, '*Contractus* und *Obligatio* im Naturrecht zwischen Spätscholastik und Aufklärung', in *La seconda scolastica*, *supra* n. 38, 223–5, 238; E. Wolf, *Grosse Rechtsdenker der deutschen Geistesgeschichte*, 3rd edn. (Tubingen, 1951), 256–60.

[39] On the hypothetical statement see Chroust, *supra* n. 38, pp. 114–16; M. Villey, *La Formation de la pensée juridique moderne*, 4th edn. (Paris, 1975), 346–7, 611–13.

[40] M. Diesselhorst, *Die Lehre des Hugo Grotius vom Versprechen*, Forschungen zur neueren Privatrechtsgeschichte, 6 (Cologne, 1959), 40; Villey, *supra* n. 39, pp. 613–16; E. Cassirer, *The Myth of the State* (New Haven, Conn., 1946), 172. Wieacker notes that, while Stoicism may have influenced Grotius, his work is 'essentially bound to the classical tradition of Aristotelian and Thomistic thought'. (Wieacker, '*Contractus*', *supra* n. 38, p. 224.)

of a treatise on moral theology, he is said to have developed a secular, non-theological theory.[41] Because he said jurists abstract in a way similar to mathematicians and denied that God could will either violations of natural law or mathematical contradictions, he has been called a 'rationalist'.[42] He has been compared to Hobbes and even Galileo because, like them, he wished to base his system on nature.[43]

Similarly, the fact that Grotius was not a Catholic (did not believe in an 'independent ecclesiastical authority') has been cited as evidence that, unlike the scholastics, he regarded reason as 'a function of the individual mind'.[44] His comparatively minor disagreements with Aristotle have been characterized as 'an open attack on the basis of Aristotelian ethics'.[45] He has been called an 'individualist' because

[41] A. P. d'Entrèves, *Natural Law: An Introduction to Legal Philosophy*, 2nd edn. (London, 1970), 54–5; C. J. Friedrich, *Inevitable Peace* (Cambridge, Mass., 1948), 120–1; R. Tuck, *Natural Rights Theories: Their Origin and Development* (Cambridge, 1979), 76; Nutkiewicz, 'Samuel Pufendorf: Obligation as the Basis of the State', *Journal of the History of Philosophy*, 21 (1983), 15 at 18; Hofmann, 'Hugo Grotius', in *Staatsdenker im 17. und 18. Jahrhundert*, ed. M. Stolleis (Frankfurt-on-Main, 1977), 51 at 74; F. Todescan, *Le radici teologiche del giusnaturalismo laico*, i. *Il problem della secolarizzazione nel pensiero giuridico di Ugo Grozio* (Milan, 1983), 96–7, 100, 106. It is, of course, important that Grotius wrote a book about law that was not also about moral theology, and one can call that development, in Wieacker's words, the emergence of 'an independent legal theory from general moral doctrine'. (Wieacker, 'Contractus', *supra* n. 38, p. 237.) The view that Grotius secularized legal theory, however, has been criticized by Wieacker himself (*Privatrechtsgeschichte*, *supra* n. 38, pp. 266, 270–1, 301) as well as by Villey (*supra* n. 39, pp. 611–13), Feenstra ('La Pensée juridique de Grotius', *supra* n. 38, p. 493), and G. Ambrosetti (*Diritto naturale cristiano Lineamenti storici* (Rome, 1964), 152.)

[42] d'Entrèves, *supra* n. 41, pp. 55–6. See Todescan, *supra* n. 41, p. 101. Similar ideas seem to underlie Krause's claim that Grotius thought an entire system of law could be grounded on reason, whereas the late scholastics believed natural law was an invisible 'Rahmenrecht' that 'only made its appearance when positive law contradicted it'. (O. W. Krause, *Naturrechtler des sechzehnten Jahrhunderts: Ihre Bedeutung für die Entwicklung eines natürlichen Privatrechts* (Frankfurt-on-Main, 1982), 147. As Wieacker has pointed out, however, Grotius was not a rationalist. He reached conclusions not by deduction from axioms but by citation of theological and humanistic authorities. (Wieacker, *Privatrechtsgeschichte*, *supra* n. 38, p. 270.) His appeal to self-evident principles was characteristic of pre-Cartesian thinkers in the Platonic and Thomistic traditions. (Ibid., 270, 291.)

[43] Cassirer, *supra* n. 40, p. 165.

[44] Friedrich, *supra* n. 41, p. 117.

[45] According to Tuck (*supra* n. 41, p. 74), 'Grotius made the non-Aristotelian character of his theory of justice clear in a more technical way in his discussion of the meaning of *ius* in Book I.' Tuck quotes *De iure belli ac pacis*, I. i. 4–8, in which Grotius identifies a 'perfect right' or 'faculty' with Aristotle's commutative justice, and an 'imperfect right' or 'aptitude' with Aristotle's distributive justice. Grotius's point is that persons who are entitled to something as a matter of commutative justice must be given that to which they have a right. In contrast, persons who are entitled to be considered for an office, or something else they are to receive as a matter of distributive justice, merely have a right to fair consideration. Grotius also says Aristotle was wrong to define distributive justice as justice that follows a geometrical proportion since the same proportion is followed in the law of partnership. Tuck then

of theories of government he shared with the late scholastics,[46] or on the basis of no evidence at all except a supposed 'shifting of accent on these commonplaces of natural law theory'.[47] He has been called a 'voluntarist' or 'consensualist' on account of beliefs he shared with the late scholastics about natural law, the binding force of promises, and the effect of error on consent.[48]

says: 'Grotius' open attack on the basis of Aristotelian Ethics immediately aroused his Protestant contemporaries.' It is hard to see in this passage an 'open attack' on Aristotle. To prove that it antagonized Protestant Aristotelians, Tuck quotes a criticism of Grotius by Johannes Feldman. The criticism, however, was not that Grotius attacked Aristotle but that he imitated 'the ineptitudes of the scholastics' and ignored the 'Civilians'. (Ibid. 75.)

According to Augé, one can see the individualism of Grotius in his reference to man's desire for society (*appetitus societatis*), 'an idea that is Ciceronian rather than Aristotelian'. (Augé, 'Le Contrat et l'évolution du consensualisme chez Grotius', *Archives de philosophie du droit*, 13 (1968), 99 at 111.) As Grotius himself said, this idea was familiar to the Stoics. Nevertheless, it is hard to see why Grotius's use of that idea is supposed to be a sign of 'individualism'. However, as Chroust observed, it is also hard to see any break with the Aristotelian tradition. (See Chroust, *supra* n. 38, at 131–2.) Grotius used the idea to argue that man, by nature, aims not merely at his own advantage, but desires 'life in a community' and 'not any life, but one that is peaceful and organized to suit the measure of his intelligence, with persons of his own kind'. ('Prolegomena' §6.) He could have made the same point by quoting Aristotle's view that 'man is a political animal'.

[46] For example, Augé asks: 'l'idée même d'une analyse contractualiste de l Etat n'est-elle pas un critère de individualisme?' (Augé, *supra* n. 45, p. 111.) Historians of political thought, however, have traced this idea back through Grotius to the late scholastics and thence to the conciliarists of the 15th c. (See Q. Skinner, *The Foundations of Modern Political Thought* (Cambridge, 1978), ii. 135–73; Salmon, 'An Alternative Theory of Popular Resistance: Buchanan, Rossaeus, and Locke', in J. H. M. Salmon, *Renaissance and Revolt: Essays in the Intellectual and Social History of Early Modern France* (Cambridge, 1987), 136 at 136–8.) According to Salmon, since the time of the Council of Constance, 'the theorists of resistance held that political authority was created by the consent of the entire community and that, if it were exercised in a way contrary to the welfare of the community, it could be withdrawn'. 'The mainstream of resistance theory', however, 'considered the community as a self-sufficing Aristotelian entity, and lacked the individualist premises to speculate about a state of nature and a social contract prior to the contract of government.' The break with the past was made not by Grotius, but by Locke. Although Grotius 'commented upon' these ideas, 'little or nothing along the highroad from Constance to 1688 . . . suggested the sudden emergence of Locke's individualistic presuppositions'. (Ibid. 136–7.)

[47] d'Entrèves, *supra* n. 41, p. 58.

[48] Diesselhorst, *supra* n. 40, pp. 34–5, 40, 50–1, 97–9; Augé, *supra* n. 45, pp. 100–1, 104, 111–12; M. Lipp, *Die Bedeutung des Naturrechts für die Ausbildung der Allgemeinen Lehren des deutschen Privatrechts* (Berlin, 1980), 133–41. Diesselhorst (pp. 50–1), Lipp (pp. 140–1), and Augé (p. 104) point to Grotius's observation that a perfect promise is binding because the promisor alienates either a thing or a portion of his liberty. (H. Grotius, *De iure belli ac pacum libri tres* (Leiden, 1939), II. xi. 4; H. Grotius, *Inleiding* . . . (Oxford, 1926), II. i. 1. But one has to read a lot into that statement before it becomes more 'voluntarist' or 'consensualist' than those of Molina and Lessius, who said that the promisor transfers a right to the promisee to require performance. Moreover, Molina drew a similar analogy between a promise and a conveyance of property. (L. Molina, *De iustitia et iure tractatus* (Venice, 1614),

The fact that Grotius's works have been mined so carefully for modern views with so little result is excellent evidence that he did not hold such views.

In contrast, Pufendorf and Barbeyrac borrowed ideas freely from the new philosophers. Pufendorf was sympathetic to Descartes, and, indeed, was the pupil of a Cartesian. Barbeyrac admired Locke. They both asserted their independence of Aristotle and their dislike of scholasticism. Nevertheless, the revolt against Aristotle had a different significance to them than it did to philosophers such as Descartes, Hobbes, and Locke. These philosophers disagreed with Aristotle over the most basic principles of metaphysics and ethics. Pufendorf and Barbeyrac did not present their differences with Aristotle and the scholastics as a disagreement over philosophical principles.

Their attack on Aristotle sounded more like Dryden. The problem is not so much that Aristotle was wrong but that for centuries people thought he was invariably right. Thus, Pufendorf mocked those who regarded Aristotelian philosophy as a summit beyond which the mind could not go.[49] Nevertheless, he cited Aristotle frequently and quite often with approval. Similarly, Barbeyrac's primary concern was to show that Aristotle too could make mistakes, and, indeed, had made many. He had been overly influenced by the Greek forms of government, he had treated some matters too lightly or too obscurely, had not had ideas 'bien nettes' about human equality, and, indeed, had 'expressed himself in a manner that allows one to think that some men are natural slaves'. Moreover, in permitting abortion, 'this great natural genius, this philosopher for whom so many have such a great veneration, grossly ignored and trampled under foot without scruple one of the most evident principles of natural law'.[50] Unlike contemporary philosophers, however, Barbeyrac's point was that Aristotle had often been wrong, not that his fundamental principles were wrong.

disp. 262; L. Lessius, *De iustitia et iure, ceterisque virtutibus cardinalis libri quatuor* (Paris, 1628), lib. 1, cap. 18, dub. 8. See Wieacker, *supra* n. 38, pp. 228–30.) Augé (p. 112) claims that Grotius's 'new dichotomy of promise and contract' indicates 'a more and more pronounced repudiation of the Roman rules'. Feenstra seems to agree. (Feenstra, *supra* n. 38, pp. 496–7.) As we have seen, however, Grotius's distinction between promise and contract is like that of the late scholastics between promising and the acts of liberality and commutative justice one can perform by promising. He explains the binding force of promises and the types of contracts and their obligations in much the same way as the late scholastics. And, like the late scholastics, he regarded the Roman rules as matters of Roman positive law rather than natural law.

[49] S. Pufendorf, *De iure naturae et gentium libri octo* (Amsterdam, 1688), I. ii. I.

[50] Barbeyrac on Pufendorf, 'Préface du traducteur', §24, p. lxxxviii.

Similarly, though Pufendorf and Barbeyrac detested the scholastics, they did not quarrel with them over philosophical principles. Pufendorf described them as self-interested, misguided ecclesiastics.[51] He would not cite them. Barbeyrac criticized their 'barbarous language and ridiculous subtleties'.[52] He said that Aristotelian philosophy had engendered the 'barbarity' of scholasticism, a 'patchwork', a 'confused collection without any rule or fixed principles' that had 'spread itself all over Europe'.[53] The main criticism, then, was not that the scholastics had the wrong principles. Nor could it have been that they had the wrong legal doctrines, since, as we have seen, those of Pufendorf and Barbeyrac were the same, although expressed in a language which, while possibly less barbarous, was certainly less precise.[54]

Moreover, Pufendorf and Barbeyrac were never genuinely committed to any definite set of modern philosophical principles. Pufendorf made several great philosophical departures from the Aristotelian tradition, but in each instance with enough qualifications to bring him almost back to the point from which he had departed. Like the new philosophers, Pufendorf separated the physical and moral world in a way alien to the Aristotelian tradition. He distinguished 'physical entities' from 'moral entities'. The latter exist by the 'imposition' of human or divine will.[55] Thus, moral obligation exists only through the will of a superior, a position

[51] Pufendorf, *supra* n. 49, I. iii. 4; I. iii. 5.

[52] Barbeyrac on Pufendorf, 'Préface du traducteur', §30, p. cvi.

[53] Ibid., §28, p. civ.

[54] Nevertheless, according to Nanz, Pufendorf's new philosophical principles led him to 'some of the most important elements of the modern concept of contract'. Among them are: (1) that the parties stand in a relationship of equality to each other; (2) that each party enjoys 'freedom of contract', both as to whether to enter into a contract and as to the contractual terms ('Abschluß- und Inhaltsfreiheit'); (3) that a contractual relationship is created by consent; and (4) that the parties are bound by 'the natural law command of fidelity' ('Vertragstreue'). (K. Nanz, *Die Entstehung des allgemeinen Vertragsbegriff im 16. bis 18. Jahrhundert*, Beiträge zur neueren Privatrechtsgeschichte, 9 (Munich, 1985), 151–2. As we have seen, however, for Pufendorf, as for Grotius and the late scholastics, contracts were formed by consent, were binding on account of fidelity, and required equality in their terms. Consequently, it is hard to see (1) that Pufendorf's philosophical observations about equality produced any change in contract doctrine, if, indeed, they were an innovation in philosophy: (2) that the 'Abschluß- und Inhaltsfreiheit' of his parties was any more extensive; or (3) and (4) that the consent of these parties was any more necessary or was necessary on any different principle. Again, Nanz sees an anticipation of the 19th c. in Pufendorf's conclusion that a contract arose from 'two independent consents'. Yet a similar conclusion had been drawn by many of the late scholastics.

[55] Pufendorf, *supra* n. 49, I. i. 1–4. See L. Krieger, *The Politics of Discretion: Pufendorf and the Acceptance of Natural Law* (Chicago, 1965), 57–8, 74; H. Welzel, *Die Naturrechtslehre Samuel Pufendorfs Ein Beitrag zur Ideengeschichte des 17. und 18. Jahrhunderts* (Berlin, 1958), 19–30; Wolf, *supra* n. 38, pp. 338–40.

which, Pufendorf admitted, approached that of Hobbes.[56] Nevertheless, Pufendorf explained, having created man with a certain nature, God imposes those obligations appropriate to that nature.[57] Similarly, to impose an obligation, a human authority requires not mere force, but just reasons, reasons that again depend on man's nature.[58] In the end, Pufendorf's moral law depends on a concept of human nature that bridges the moral and the physical world.

Similarly, Pufendorf gave an account of how 'sociability' develops out of more primitive human inclinations that owed a debt to Hobbes and, indeed, anticipated Hume.[59] Pufendorf's early men, however, unlike those of Hobbes and Hume, have an inclination to observe a natural law that is proportioned to their nature and conducive to their own good.[60] Instead of explaining moral law by human inclination, Pufendorf, in the end, explained human inclination by moral law.

Again, like Hobbes, Pufendorf claimed that moral reasoning must proceed by demonstrations from first principles like those of mathematics.[61] Indeed, despite the opinions of Aristotle and Grotius, he said that the moral conclusions thus derived are unchangeable rather than subject to correction in the light of new circumstances.[62] Consequently, Wieacker concluded that Pufendorf's innovation was his use of such a method. Indeed, Wieacker divided the natural law school into an early phase to which Grotius belonged and a second phase founded by Pufendorf which he calls 'systematic' or 'mathematical'.[63]

[56] Pufendorf, *supra*, n. 49, I. iv, 1; I. iv. 5.

[57] Ibid. II. iii. 5. Thus, Barbeyrac explains that Pufendorf's term 'institution' will be misunderstood if we fail to recognize that, according to Pufendorf, 'there are two kinds of institution, one purely arbitrary, and the other founded on the thing itself and a necessary consequence of what one has already freely decided'. Thus, God was free to create or not to create 'man, that is, a rational and sociable animal', but having done so He 'could only impose on him the obligations that are necessarily appropriate to the constitution of such a creature'. (Barbeyrac on Pufendorf, n. 4 to I. i. 4.)

[58] Pufendorf, *supra* n. 49, I. vi. 9; I. vi. 18. See Krieger, *supra* n. 55, pp. 85–6.

[59] Pufendorf, *supra* n. 49, II. iii. 14–15. See Welzel, *supra* n. 55, pp. 41–50; Wolf, *supra* n. 38, pp. 345–6.

[60] Pufendorf, *supra* n. 49, II. iii. 16.

[61] Ibid. I. ii. 2. Indeed, he gives moral science a rationalist programme. The proper programme of metaphysics is to 'place accurately in classes all the beginnings of which one can form an idea, and then to develop, by sound general definitions, the nature and constitution of each kind of being that belongs to these classes'. He wishes to follow a similar programme in describing 'moral entities'. (Ibid. I. i. 1.)

[62] Ibid. I. ii. 1.

[63] Wieacker, *Privatrechtsgeschichte*, *supra* n. 38, pp. 270–1, 301, 307–8. Similarly, Denzer has said that Pufendorf's goal was a closed system based on reason. (Denzer, 'Samuel Pufendorfs Naturrecht im Wissenschaftssystem seiner Zeit', in *Samuel von Pufendorf 1632–1982*, Ein rättshistoriskt symposium i Lund, 15–16 January 1982 (Lund, 1986), 17 at 19.

There is no reason, however, to take Pufendorf's statements about method any more seriously than his other borrowings from the new philosophers. He wrote a book in his youth on *Elements of Universal Jurisprudence* in which he really did try to present the natural law in a series of axioms and quasi-mathematical proofs. Nevertheless, in his main work, *De iure naturae et gentium*, he imitated the method of Grotius. He quoted classical poets, Roman law, scripture, and ancient and modern philosophers. He did not distinguish sharply between axioms and propositions that are proved from axioms. He did not dress up his arguments to make them look like mathematical proofs. Indeed, had Pufendorf not announced that he was producing a complete system of moral law based on strict deductions from principles, no one would have suspected him of attempting an innovation in method. His announcement is one more instance in which he made a bold claim inspired by contemporary philosophers and then ignored its implications.

While Pufendorf borrowed from the new philosophers, then, he defaulted on every intellectual debt he incurred. His biographer, Leonard Krieger, put the matter in a more kindly spirit:

> Pufendorf possessed, as a secondary thinker, a great comparative advantage over his mentors. He was an occasional philosopher—that is, he worked up philosophical analyses only on those occasions in which his more mundane concerns required footing—and the scope of the analysis was defined by the occasion which it served. His occasional philosophy sufficed to keep the intellectual faith of his age continuously relevant, albeit at the cost of its logical integration. What had been a rigorous system became with him a plastic set of assumptions, which were thereby rendered separable and susceptible to autonomous development subject to the more flexible limits of psychological rather than logical coherence.[64]

Similarly, although Barbeyrac believed that a great break had been made with the past, he did not think of it primarily as the rejection of an old philosophy in favour of a new one. He thought that Grotius first 'broke the ice' and raised the science of morality from the dead.[65] He praised Grotius, however, not for the discovery of new principles, but for his 'extraordinary *netteté d'esprit*, exquisite discernment, profound thought, universal erudition, prodigious reading, . . . and a sincere love of the truth'.[66] He credited Grotius with having grasped 'the true fundamental principle of the natural law'. Nevertheless, Barbeyrac did not identify this principle, and it

[64] Krieger, *supra* n. 55, p. 50.
[65] Barbeyrac on Pufendorf, 'Préface du traducteur', §28, p. civ; §29, p. civ.
[66] Ibid., §29, p. civ.

is doubtful that he had any definite discovery in mind.[67] He praised Pufendorf, who more fully 'disengaged himself from the prejudices of the School [the scholastics]'[68] and 'established and developed the fundamental maxims of natural law distinctly'.[69] Again, however, Barbeyrac did not seem to have in mind particular philosophical discoveries. When he explained why Pufendorf's work was superior to that of Grotius, he mentioned not Pufendorf's principles, but his more popular style, the 'order and disposition' of his work, and the fact that it was a 'complete system'.[70] Indeed, Barbeyrac praised Pufendorf for having 'followed the spirit and method of Grotius'.[71] When he mentioned the debt Pufendorf owed to 'the new philosophy' (that of Descartes), he spoke not of Cartesian principles, but of how this study enabled Pufendorf 'to perfect his natural talents and to render him capable of so great a work'.[72] Barbeyrac himself was attracted to Locke, but he did not think Locke's discoveries required that law be rebuilt on new foundations. If he had, he would not have devoted himself to writing translations and commentaries on Grotius and Pufendorf.

There is no doubt that Pufendorf and Barbeyrac believed they were engaged in an intellectual revolt begun by Grotius against the scholastic tradition. Oddly enough, however, it seems to have been a revolt without principle. Pufendorf and Barbeyrac were not committed to any new philosophical principles. Grotius had not broken with those of Aristotle and the scholastics.

Such a revolt is not the contradiction in terms it might appear. We have already seen examples of intellectual continuity despite a change in philosophical principle, and of great change despite continuity in principle. What matters is not only the principles but the project or task to which the principles are applied. Post-Glossators such as Bartolus and Baldus believed in Aristotelian principles unknown to the Glossators, yet little change took place. The project remained the same: to fix the meaning of each Roman legal text in the light of all the others. The late scholastics believed in the same Aristotelian principles as Bartolus and Baldus. Nevertheless, their project was different. They wished to synthesize Aristotle and Thomas with Roman law. The result was a massive intellectual change.

Grotius, Pufendorf, and Barbeyrac broke with the past by engaging in a different project from that of the late scholastics. That is why

[67] Ibid., §31, p. cx. In any case, Barbeyrac notes that Grotius made little use of this principle. He merely mentioned it in the introduction to his book. (Ibid.)

[68] Ibid., §31, pp. cx–xci.

[69] Ibid., p. cxi.

[70] Ibid., p. cx.

[71] Ibid., §30, p. cvii.

[72] Ibid., p. cvii.

they broke with the scholastics without joining the revolt of the new philosophers. Their project was to bring legal science within the domain of *belles-lettres*. Law and moral philosophy were to be the affair not of technically trained specialists, but of liberally educated, intelligent men. By making moral knowledge more accessible, they expected to raise the moral level of human conduct.

This project demanded a change in the way law books were written. Indeed, the most obvious break these jurists made with the scholastics was in their methods of presentation. Grotius invented a style of legal writing which could reach the non-specialist. Unlike the scholastics, he did not try to present every argument for or against a conclusion or to trace each concept and doctrine back to its ultimate philosophical foundation. His book was elegant and simple. It was ornamented with quotations from classical literature attractive to the educated readers of his day. It avoided technicalities. It was written so that gentlemen with no formal philosophical or legal training could understand it. This style was imitated by Pufendorf, Barbeyrac, Domat, and Pothier, and it eventually inspired the simple and elegant texts of the French Civil Code.

The jurists did not think they were engaged in a merely literary endeavour. They thought that to express the truth elegantly and simply was almost the same as to discover it. Like the scholastics themselves, they believed that true moral philosophy consisted of simple principles and clear demonstrations. They meant, however, that the meaning of principles and the force of demonstrations had to be easy to grasp, whereas the scholastics had sought simplicity and clarity in technical terminology and complicated arguments, in what Barbeyrac called 'barbarous language and ridiculous subtleties'. Thus, it was not hypocritical of these jurists to denounce the scholastics and then present scholastic conclusions as their own discoveries. They were the first to express these conclusions in a manner that was easy to grasp. Indeed, because Pufendorf and Barbeyrac identified readily intelligible arguments with clear and valid arguments, they sincerely believed that Pufendorf had, in Barbeyrac's words, 'established and developed distinctly the fundamental maxims of the natural law, and deduced from them, by a fairly exact chain of consequences, the principal duties of man and of the citizen'.[73]

By expressing moral truth simply, they hoped they would enable this truth to influence human conduct. As Grotius explained in the introduction to his book, everywhere people were disregarding the

[73] Barbeyrac on Pufendorf, 'Préface du traducteur', §31, p. cxi.

most elementary principles of justice, most of all when they went to war. The scholar's contribution to ending injustice, limited as it might be, was to place before mankind a law founded on nature and reason.

According to Pufendorf, the people's knowledge of the natural law depended on the scholar. While 'the natural law is known to all men who have the use of reason', only some were 'capable of methodically demonstrating its maxims'. Nevertheless,

> the more mediocre spirits can at least comprehend these demonstrations when they are proposed to them, and recognize the truth of them clearly by comparing them to their natural condition. Even the vulgar, who are acquainted with the law of nature from popular sources and general custom, could be sufficiently assured of its truth by the authority of their superiors . . ., by the impossibility of finding any apparent reason that can destroy or shake their certainty, and by the manifest utility which one sees in them all the time.[74]

Barbeyrac praised Pufendorf for contributing to this diffusion of knowledge. Although Grotius wrote with 'purity and exactness', with 'marvellous elegance and facility', he was 'too concise'. 'He assumes matters that demand rather great study so his work is for few beyond the savants, in contrast to that of Pufendorf which is within the reach of all.'[75] Barbeyrac intended to make the law of nature more accessible still. He intended his translation of Pufendorf for 'young men who are aiming at political and ecclesiastical careers'. These men often have 'no inkling of the most general principles of a science so universally necessary', as well as a knowledge of Latin too poor to attempt Pufendorf in the original. Barbeyrac also wished to reach, if not the 'peasant' or the 'day labourer', at least moderately educated 'common people or people without letters', for among them 'there reigns such a great ignorance' of these same principles. They would find the book comprehensible and free from 'the subtleties of the bar'.[76]

The sense of mission is also reflected in the people the new moral scientists regarded as their enemies. Rarely do they treat anyone as an enemy, even Aristotle, simply because he reached a sound moral conclusion from the wrong principles or by an invalid argument. Enemies are those who interfere with the moral education of mankind. The scholastics did so by making moral truth obscure and inaccessible. The still greater enemy, however, is the moral sceptic, the person who, as Barbeyrac describes him, doubts for the sake of

[74] Pufendorf, *supra* n. 29, II. iii. 13.
[75] Barbeyrac on Pufendorf, 'Préface du traducteur', §31, p. cx.
[76] Ibid., §32, pp. cxii–cxiii.

doubting and so calls all moral truth into question.[77] Grotius attacked him in an imaginary debate with the ancient sceptic Carneades,[78] Pufendorf in a series of skirmishes with Hobbes.

In one sense, this project succeeded. Knowledge of legal principles came to be recognized as indispensable to a liberal education. Law books and legal ideas were disseminated among multitudes of non-lawyers. Lawyers who were not philosophers were encouraged to think in terms of general legal principles rather than technical professional solutions.[79]

A special case of this dissemination of natural law doctrine will be considered in the next chapter. Anglo-American lawyers, after neglecting theory and system for centuries, began to incorporate this doctrine into the common law, drawing on the works of Grotius, Pufendorf, Barbeyrac, Domat, and Pothier. While the Anglo-Americans might have sought after more general legal principles anyway, the natural lawyers encouraged them by placing such principles within easy reach.

Offsetting the gain in accessibility, however, was a loss in philosophical depth and in rigour of argument. As we have seen, the truly fundamental philosophical problems of the age were sidestepped. Concepts and principles were stated in elegant language, but so imprecisely that often one cannot be sure of their meaning. The links between philosophical principles and the legal doctrines supposedly founded on them were left obscure.

This lack of rigour camouflaged the difficulties of preserving late scholastic legal doctrines while repudiating the Aristotelian principles on which they had been founded. Pufendorf and Barbeyrac could speak about the virtue of fidelity or about the essence, substance, or nature of a contract without considering closely what these terms could mean in the non-Aristotelian world they thought they were inhabiting.

Wolff broke with the tradition Grotius had founded. It seemed to have led to unsound principles obscurely linked to still more obscure doctrines. He tried to found a moral science in which, as Hobbes and Locke desired, doctrines could be strictly deduced from first principles by arguments as rigorous as those of mathematics. He

77 Barbeyrac on Pufendorf, 'Préface du traducteur', §3, p. xiv.

78 H. Grotius, *De iure belli ac pacis*, *supra* n. 48, 'Prolegomena'.

79 On the popularity of Grotius's *De iure belli ac pacis*, see Feenstra, *supra* n. 38, pp. 493–4. On the dissemination of the works of Pufendorf and Barbeyrac, see S. Othmer, *Berlin und die Verbreitung des Naturrechts in Europa Kultur- und sozialgeschichtliche Studien zu Jean Barbeyracs Pufendorf-Übersetzungen und eine Analyse seiner Leserschaft* (Berlin, 1970); Luig, 'Zur Verbreitung des Naturrechts in Europa', *Tijdschrift voor Rechtsgeschiedenis*, 40 (1972), 539.

wrote like a mathematician in a series of numbered propositions and deductive arguments. The first principles, however, were not those of Hobbes and Locke. They were a rationalist version of Aristotle. The law of nature is 'to be demonstrated from the essence and nature of man himself'.[80] 'Virtue' is the 'habit of directing one's actions in conformity with the law of nature'.[81] One must follow the law of nature to reach 'happiness', the 'summum bonum', and 'perfection'.[82]

Yet paradoxically, as we have seen, in the writings of Wolff, late scholastic doctrines, preserved by Pufendorf and Barbeyrac, start to disappear. Indeed, as we shall see, some of his conclusions anticipate those of the nineteenth-century jurists. The reason, I believe, is that, as has often been pointed out, Wolff really did not understand the Aristotelian tradition he was attempting to modernize and revive. Consequently, he did not understand the Aristotelian doctrinal formulations that Pufendorf and Barbeyrac had preserved. Unlike them, he aimed at a rigorous system in which all doctrines were precise. Consequently, he eliminated the doctrines he did not understand. As we will see, the nineteenth-century jurists were to proceed in the same way, reformulating the doctrines of Grotius, Pufendorf, Barbeyrac, Domat, and Pothier, by eliminating Aristotelian formulations that no longer seemed meaningful. It is not surprising, then, that some of their reformulated doctrines resemble those of Wolff.

The difference is that Wolff thought that the marriage of moral philosophy and legal doctrine that had existed since the time of the late scholastics could be preserved. Jurists such as Pufendorf and Barbeyrac had allowed philosophical principle and legal doctrine to drift apart. The solution was to be a rigorous deduction of legal conclusions from a modernized version of Aristotelian principles. The difficulties are clearer in retrospect than they were at the time. After the Aristotelian tradition had been in disfavour for a century, merely understanding it required an historical effort that Wolff was not equipped to make. To defend it against the attack of the new philosophers was a task of which few, if any, were capable, and Wolff certainly was not. Indeed, by the end of the century it was clear that his doctrinal conclusions were only flimsily tied to the philosophical principles from which they were supposed to be derived.

In the nineteenth century, the marriage of philosophy and legal doctrine that Wolff had tried to preserve ended in divorce.

[80] C. Wolff, *Ius naturae modo scientifica pertractum* (Frankfurt-on-Main, 1764), 'Prolegomena', §2.

[81] Ibid., §6.

[82] Ibid., §§7–8.

6
THE ANGLO-AMERICAN RECEPTION

As one nineteenth-century common lawyer observed, at the time of Blackstone 'the science of law in all that relates to contracts was left almost without cultivation'.[1] The first treatise on contract law was published by Powell in 1790. Before that time, as Simpson has noted, there was scarcely any common law literature on contracts beyond a few pages in Blackstone and the reports of decided cases.[2] The law of contract did not have a theory or a systematic doctrinal structure. It was organized not by definitions, doctrines, and principles, but in the common law courts by writs such as covenant and assumpsit, and in the courts of equity by a series of vaguely conceived grounds for relief.

Beginning with Powell, the treatise writers gave the law of contract a systematic doctrinal structure it had previously lacked. They did so, as we will see in this chapter, by borrowing doctrines from natural lawyers such as Grotius and Pufendorf and from jurists influenced by them such as the French jurists Domat and Pothier. The doctrines they borrowed were then borrowed in turn by common law judges. We will be concerned with the work of the judges only to the extent necessary to show its dependence on that of the treatise writers.

The treatise writers were thus borrowing doctrines which the natural lawyers themselves had taken from the late scholastics who had founded them on the philosophy of Aristotle and Thomas Aquinas. This philosophy was almost unintelligible to nineteenth-century jurists. Consequently, the treatise writers often borrowed superficially, repeating the phrases of the natural lawyers with little understanding of their original meaning. They often borrowed selectively, neglecting doctrines that seemed alien and repugnant.

As time went on, the common lawyers looked for substitutes for the phrases they borrowed but did not understand. They also bent

[1] Carey, 'A Course of Lectures on the Law of Contract: Lecture I', *The Law Times*, 4 (1845), 463 at 463.

[2] Simpson, 'Innovation in Nineteenth Century Contract Law', *Law Quarterly Review*, 91 (1975), 247 at 250–1.

and stretched the doctrines they had borrowed to make them do the work of those they had not. Their continental contemporaries were engaged in a similar effort to reshape doctrines inherited from the natural lawyers to make them acceptable in the nineteenth century. In the next chapter we will examine these efforts. First, however, we must see what the common lawyers borrowed.

THE BINDING FORCE OF CONTRACT

The Enforceability of Promises

The natural lawyers had said that contracts are entered into by the agreement of the parties. The nineteenth-century common law treatise writers defined contract in terms of agreement or assent. Comyn did so in 1809, followed by Newland in 1821, Chitty in 1826 (who added that an agreement is the mutual assent of the parties), Kent in 1827, Dodd in 1836, William Story in 1844 (who spoke of contract as an 'engagement'), Carey in 1845, Parsons in 1860, and Leake in 1867.[3]

As will be seen in the next chapter, these definitions were both a borrowing from and a break with the natural law tradition. The common lawyers borrowed the idea that contracts are made by consent. They did not borrow the ideas that consent was binding because of a virtue of promise-keeping, or that by giving consent the parties exercised virtues of liberality or commutative justice.

The point that concerns us now is that for the common lawyers it was an innovation not only to define contract in terms of agreement, but to define contract at all. The extent of the innovation is shown by the authority they cite. The authors just mentioned cite Comyns's *Digest* or Plowden or Blackstone. Comyns's *Digest* contains a brief entry under the word 'agreement' which says that an agreement is a mutual assent or *aggregatio mentium*, citing Plowden.[4] Plowden reports the case of *Reniger* v. *Fogossa* decided by the Exchequer in

[3] S. Comyn, *Contracts and Agreements Not Under Seal* (Flatbush, 1809), i.*2 [NB: an asterisk before the page number in a citation means that the pagination is that of an original edition, which has been preserved in the edition cited]; J. Newland, *A Treatise on Contracts* (Philadelphia, 1821), 1; J. Chitty, *A Practical Treatise on the Law of Contracts* (1826), 3; J. Kent, *Commentaries on American Law* (Boston, 1884), ii.*450; Dodd, 'On the Construction of Contracts–Assent–Construction', *The Legal Observer*, 12 (1836), 249 at 249; W. W. Story, *A Treatise on the Law of Contracts* (Boston, 1851), 1; Carey, *supra* n. 1, p. 464; T. Parsons, *The Law of Contracts* (Boston, 1860), i.*6; S. Leake, *Elements of the Law of Contracts* (London, 1867), 7–8.

[4] J. Comyns, *A Digest of the Laws of England*, 4th edn. (London, 1800), i. 400.

the reign of Edward VI.[5] A merchant's cargo had been seized for non-payment of a customs duty despite an arrangement with a customs official to have the cargo weighed before the duty would be paid. The merchant invoked a statute which said that an 'agreement' with a customs official would be a defence to non-payment of the duty. The lawyer for the Crown argued that the merchant had no agreement because he had nothing legally enforceable. The merchant's lawyer responded that an agreement was an '*aggregatio mentium*', a meeting of the minds. One could scarcely imagine more wretched authority for the proposition that a contract at common law is a mutual agreement.[6]

The remaining authority was Blackstone. In the few pages he wrote on contract in the later eighteenth century, he embarked on the task the common lawyers of the nineteenth and early twentieth centuries were to complete: to bring system and doctrinal coherence to the law of contract. To do so, he drew continually on the works of natural and civil lawyers. He defined contract as 'an agreement upon sufficient consideration to do or not to do a particular thing'.[7] There was nothing novel about his definition of contract in terms of agreement save that he claimed to be writing about English law rather than natural law. Since, as we shall see, his discussion of consideration owed a great and obvious debt to the natural lawyers, it is reasonable to suppose that his definition of contract did as well.

Had the nineteenth-century treatise writers or Blackstone hunted a bit further, they could have found occasional remarks by English judges explaining contract as mutual assent. The remarks are occasional, however, and one would have to hunt for them. Blackstone and the nineteenth-century treatise writers defined contract in terms of agreement or mutual assent not because common law judges had done so, but because, in their belief, that was how contract ought to be defined. They were familiar with the writings of the seventeenth- and eighteenth-century natural lawyers who had discussed the need for agreement or assent. Rather than striking out in some completely new direction, they simply applied these discussions to what they called the common law of contract. Indeed, the moment they did so they began to create a common law of contract out of a common law of assumpsit, covenant, and so forth.

[5] *The Commentaries or Reports of Edmund Plowden*, Eng. trans. (Dublin, 1792), i. 1–17.

[6] Carey himself realized that Plowden had little value as an authority: Carey, *supra* n. 1, p. 463.

[7] W. Blackstone, *Commentaries on the Laws of England* (London, 1766), ii. 442.

Causa *and Consideration*

Before the nineteenth century, common law judges had developed a rule that an action of assumpsit would not lie unless there was 'consideration' for a promise. The judges had no clear idea of what consideration meant, and the lack of one had not overly concerned them. The nineteenth-century treatise writers, in contrast, wanted an explanation. The natural lawyers, as we have seen, thought there was a fundamental distinction between promises to give and promises to exchange. According to the doctrine of *causa*, these were the two types of promises that ought to be binding. Borrowing selectively, the common lawyers claimed that their doctrine meant that only the latter type of promise was enforceable.

Actually, the doctrines of consideration and *causa* had little to do with each other. There is a famous and inconclusive debate as to whether the common law judges who originally developed the doctrine of consideration did so under the influence of the doctrine of *causa*. However that may have been, the consideration of the common law judges soon ceased to resemble the *causa* of Bartolus and Baldus, the late scholastics and the natural lawyers. Contracts entered into out of liberality had a *causa*, but, according to the common law judges, liberality did not constitute consideration. Promises to exchange did have a consideration, but the common law judges did not equate consideration with the *causa* of an onerous contract. They found consideration in many transactions that a late scholastic, a natural lawyer, or a person of ordinary common sense would regard as gratuitous. As we shall see, promises to give money to a prospective son-in-law were found to have consideration, as were a variety of gratuitous loans and bailments.

Indeed, it is almost misleading to compare the two doctrines since they were forged for very different purposes. We saw earlier that the doctrine of *causa* was of theoretical rather than practical significance. Inspired by Aristotle's distinction between liberality and commutative justice, the formulators of the doctrine had identified two sensible reasons a person might have for promising: liberality, and the receipt of something in return. The doctrine had little effect on the promises the law actually did enforce. The doctrine of consideration grew up in just the opposite way. The common law judges were not theorizing about why people make promises. They were not particularly concerned about producing a coherent definition of consideration. Their task was the practical one of limiting the promises that could be enforced in assumpsit. They worked pragmatically, striving to find consideration present in cases that seemed particularly deserving of a remedy. Often they succeeded in finding consideration by drawing some tendentious analogy to a contract of exchange, a type of contract that they did seem to regard as the paradigm case in which consideration was present.[8] It does not follow, however, that consideration meant exchange or bargain. Consideration meant that relief would be given in certain cases marked out by precedent such as breach of promises to exchange, and that in dubious cases relief would be limited by the ability and willingness of judges to draw far-fetched analogies to those. Consideration was a technique for limiting the action of assumpsit rather than a concept one can define.

Nevertheless, beginning with Blackstone, common lawyers who wished to find a theory or at least a coherent definition of consideration persistently equated consideration with *causa*. The difficulties of doing so are particularly obvious in Blackstone's discussion. He began by defining consideration much as *causa* had been defined: it is the 'reason one contracts'. Although this phrase suggests that consideration meant *causa* in general rather than merely the *causa* of an exchange, he immediately added that consideration is 'something mutual, reciprocal—something given in exchange'. The rule that consideration is required, he said, was taken from the civil law rule that no action lies on a naked pact. He illustrated the rule with pieces of civilian learning; for example, consideration is present where *do ut des*, *facio ut des*, and so forth. He thus seems to have been equating consideration with the *causa* of an exchange without bothering to explain why liberality is not also a 'reason one contracts'. He then bobbed and weaved to explain why English courts find consideration in contracts that do not look like exchanges. When consideration is 'blood and natural affection', the 'satisfaction' the promisor receives is somehow an equivalent. When money is promised to a prospective son-in-law, the marriage of a daughter is somehow an equivalent. Bonds and notes are evidence of consideration, but Blackstone never explained how that can be.[9]

Despite these difficulties, the early nineteenth-century treatise writers, sometimes quoting Blackstone and sometimes quoting civilian authority directly, continued to identify consideration with *causa*. Kent said:

> A contract without a consideration is a *nudum pactum*, and not binding in law, though it may be in point of conscience; and this maxim of the common

[8] e.g. *Sturlyn* v. *Albany*, Cro. Eliz. 67, 78 Eng. Rep. 327 (QB 1587).

[9] Blackstone, *supra* n. 7, ii. 444–6.

law was taken from the civil law, in which the doctrine of consideration is treated with an air of scholastic subtlety.[10]

Similarly, Powell, Taylor, William Story, Comyn, Parsons, and Smith equated consideration with the civil law doctrine, Comyn explaining that consideration was the 'motive' for contracting, Parsons and Smith insisting that civilian 'cause' and common law consideration meant something narrower than mere motive.[11] As Simpson has observed, the early nineteenth-century treatise writers seemed to regard consideration as a local version of the doctrine of *causa*.[12] Nevertheless, like Blackstone, they seem to have had in mind only the *causa* of an onerous contract since they all explained that purely gratuitous promises will not be enforced.

Offer and Acceptance

As the first common law treatises were published, the first glimmerings of a doctrine of offer and acceptance appeared in the decided cases. In 1789, in *Payne* v. *Cave*, it was held that a bidder at an auction could withdraw his bid before the hammer fell because 'every bidding is nothing more than an offer on one side, which is not binding on either side till it is assented to'.[13] In 1790, in *Cooke* v. *Oxley*, it was held that an offeror who sold the goods to a third party before the offeree accepted was not bound because until acceptance there was no contract.[14] In 1818, in *Adams* v. *Lindsell*, it was held that an offeror who sold the goods to a third party after the offeree mailed his acceptance but before the offeror received it was liable to the offeree. The acceptance completed the contract at the time it was mailed.[15]

Although the rule that offers are not binding until acceptance was new to the common law, it had long been a commonplace among the natural lawyers. Had the common law judges not been familiar with the rule from that source, it is hard to believe they would suddenly have started to invoke it. In *Payne* v. *Cave* the court explained the rule with a civil law expression that the natural lawyers had employed: before acceptance there is a *locus poenitentiae*.[16] Nevertheless, the

[10] J. Kent, *supra* n. 3, ii. 630.

[11] J. Powell, *Essay upon the Law of Contracts* (London, 1790), i. 331; W. Taylor, *The Laws of England and Scotland Relating to Contracts* (London, 1849), 16; Story, *supra* n. 3, 431, at 431, n. 1; Comyn, *supra* n. 3, i. 8; Parsons, *supra* n. 3, i.*355; J. Smith, *The Law of Contracts* (Philadelphia, 1847), 88, n. *a*.

[12] Simpson, *supra* n. 2, at 262.

[13] *Payne* v. *Cave*, 3 Term R. 148, 100 Eng. Rep. 502 (1789).

[14] *Cooke* v. *Oxley*, 3 Term. R. 653, 100 Eng. Rep. 785 (1790).

[15] *Adams* v. *Lindsell*, 1 Barn. & Ald. 681, 106 Eng. Rep. 250 (1818).

[16] 3 Term. R. at 149, 100 Eng. Rep. at 503.

judges seem to have borrowed no more than the bare rule that offers are not binding before acceptance. The result in *Cooke* v. *Oxley*, which later courts overruled, seems to have been their own idea of how that rule should be applied. Similarly, the reasoning employed in *Adams* v. *Lindsell* displays a confusion not found among the natural lawyers. The court argued that, if a contract is not formed until the offeror knows of the offeree's acceptance, then it would not be formed until the offeree knows the offeror has received his acceptance, and if this were true no contract could ever be formed by correspondence since the offeror should then have to know that the offeree knows that the offeror has received the acceptance and so forth, *ad infinitum*.[17] This reasoning confuses the question of when an acceptance is effective with the question of whether a contract can be formed without both parties knowing that they are bound.

When the doctrine of offer and acceptance was still in this embryonic stage, the common law treatise writers erected it into a fundamental principle of contract law. Every contract required an offer and acceptance, according to Kent, Dodd, Carey, William Story, Parsons, Metcalf, Leake, Hammon, and Anson.[18] It is hard to believe they would have reached this conclusion so readily had it not been endorsed by the natural lawyers.

CONTRACTUAL CONSENT

Before the nineteenth century, English courts had given relief for fraud, duress, and mistake. They had done so without concerning themselves with the theoretical problems of what constitutes consent.

They decided cases involving duress and fraud without saying much more than that fraud and duress are bad. Some of the nineteenth-century treatise writers had little more to say.[19] Chitty simply explained that 'the law will not sanction dishonest views and practices. . . '.[20] Joseph Story quoted Cicero to the effect that

[17] 1 Barn. & Ald. at 683, 106 Eng. Rep. at 251.

[18] Kent, *supra* n. 10, ii.*477; Dodd, *supra* n. 3, pp. 249–50; Carey, *supra* n. 1, p. 505; W. W. Story, *supra* n. 3, 370; Parsons, *supra* n. 3, i.*399; T. Metcalf, *Principles of the Law of Contracts* (New York, 1878), 14; S. Leake, *Elements of the Law of Contracts* (London, 1867), 12; Hammon, *General Principles of the Law of Contract* (St Paul, 1912), 38; W. Anson, *Principles of the English Law of Contract* (London, 1898), 13.

[19] e.g., anon., 'On the Law of Fraud in Contracts', *Journal of Jurisprudence and Scottish Law Magazine*, 1 (1857), 488, 513; 2 (1858), 7, 55.

[20] Chitty, *supra* n. 3, 222.

'[f]raud is even more odious than force'.[21] Similarly, William Story simply observed that fraud violates 'the spirit of the law'.

This vague moralizing gradually gave way to a concern about how duress and fraud affected consent. According to some English and American jurists, they vitiated consent.[22] Others argued that relief was given not because consent was lacking, but because an injustice had been committed.[23] We will examine these arguments in the next chapter along with similar ones put forward at the same time by continental jurists. Here we need only note that the theoretical problem of how fraud and duress affect consent was familiar to the natural lawyers but new to the common law. Again, it is unlikely the common lawyers, left to themselves, would suddenly have become interested in the problem.

The development of the doctrine of mistake, however, more dramatically illustrates this new concern with the nature of consent. In the eighteenth and early nineteenth centuries, the common law courts and courts of equity gave relief while avoiding almost entirely the question of the effect of mistake on consent.

Courts of equity in the eighteenth and early nineteenth centuries could reform a written document if it did not conform to the intentions of the contracting parties. If one party was mistaken about what he was to receive under the contract, the courts could deny specific performance or grant specific performance only on condition that the other party paid him some compensation. The courts were far from clear, however, about why in principle relief ought to be given. In some cases, particularly in the earlier eighteenth century, they simply announced that they can give relief for mistake.[24] In other cases they gave brief and cryptic explanations. Typically, however, these explanations were appeals to a vague common-sense notion of fairness.

In *Howland* v. *Norris* in 1784, Chancellor Thurlow spoke of the 'justice' of discharging from a contract a party who 'fairly and conscientiously' relied on a mistaken notion of what he was

[21] J. Story, *Commentaries on Equity Jurisprudence* (Boston, 1918), i. 261–2. Although in the next sentence Story quoted Pothier's definition of fraud, he apparently had no use for Pothier's discussion of the effect of fraud on consent.

[22] e.g. Carey, *supra* n. 1, p. 505; Dodd, 'Contracts Vitiated for Fraud', *The Legal Observer*, 11 (1836), 505 at 505; Hammon, *supra* n. 18, 142, 188; Anson, *supra* n. 18, 156, 203, 218.

[23] e.g. E. Batten, *Specific Performance of Contract* (London, 1849), 27; Leake, *supra* n. 18, 182; F. Pollock, *Principles of Contract* (London, 1885), 390.

[24] e.g. *Martin* v. *Savage*, Barn, Ch. 189, 27 Eng. Rep. 608 (1740); *Henkle* v. *Royal Exchange Assurance Co.*, 1 Ves. Sen. 317, 27 Eng. Rep. 1055 (1749); *Baker* v. *Paine*, 1 Ves. Sen. 456, 27 Eng. Rep. 1140 (1750).

contracting for.[25] In *Calverley* v. *Williams* in 1790, where a seller had mistakenly included an extra seven acres in his advertisement of sale, Thurlow explained that 'neither party may be damaged'. '[I]t is impossible to say one shall be forced to give that price for part only, which he intended to give for whole, or that the other shall be obliged to sell the whole, for what he intended to be the price of part only.'[26] In *Marquis Townshend* v. *Stangroom* in 1801, Chancellor Eldon quoted a remark of Lord Hardwicke's with favour: 'in a moral point of view there is very little difference between calling for the execution of an agreement obtained by fraud, which creates a surprise upon the other party, and desiring the execution of an agreement, which can be demonstrated to have been obtained by surprise'.[27] In *Halsey* v. *Grant* in 1806, Chancellor Erskine spoke generally about the 'healing power of equity' to do 'substantial justice' by 'preserving the substantial part of the contract but not forcing upon the party something different'.[28] These remarks suggest a variety of concerns: the innocent reliance of the mistaken party, the damage a party will suffer if he gives more or receives less than he intended, the immorality of holding the mistaken party to the contract, the healing power of equity. They do not suggest a theoretical interest in the effect of mistake on consent.

When the effect of mistake on consent was mentioned, it was described obscurely and overlaid by other concerns. In 1813, in *Clowes* v. *Higginson*, the Vice-Chancellor found it interesting that the Master of the Rolls, who had heard another action between the same parties, 'seems to think that the Consequence of such a Mistake would be that in Reality there was no Agreement between them . . .'. Here the principle that the Master of the Rolls thought applicable seems to be something like the natural law principle that mistake vitiates consent. In the same sentence, however, the Vice-Chancellor attributed to him the further opinion that 'Contract so founded in Mistake, cannot consistently with Justice be executed: as the Effect would be, that one must pay £2,000 more, or the other receive £2,000 less than he intended.'[29] Elsewhere, the Vice-Chancellor said that mistake may make it 'unconscientious' for a party to insist upon specific performance and 'unjust' for a court to

[25] *Howland* v. *Norris*, 1 Cox 59, 61, 29 Eng. Rep. 1062, 1063 (1784). The Lord Chancellor doubted, however, that English law was as liberal in this respect as he would wish.

[26] *Calverley* v. *Williams*, 1 Ves. Jun. 210, 211, 30 Eng. Rep. 306 (1790).

[27] *Marquis Townshend* v. *Stangroom*, 6 Ves. Jun. 328, 337, 31 Eng. Rep. 1076, 1079 (1801).

[28] *Halsey* v. *Grant*, 13 Ves. Jun. 73, 77–8, 33 Eng. Rep 222, 223 (1806).

[29] *Clowes* v. *Higginson*, 1 Ves. & B. 524, 530, 35 Eng. Rep. 204, 206 (1813).

grant it, 'and therefore not conformable to the Principles on which a Court of Equity exercises this Jurisdiction'.[30] Concern about whether there was consent was never clearly distinguished from a vague concern about fairness.

Since the English chancellors were attempting to do justice in particular cases, not to analyse abstract principles, their lack of clarity is not surprising. Moreover, they were not dealing with cases in which the principle that mistake vitiates consent would have been particularly helpful. They were not dealing with textbook problems of gold sold as copper or wine as vinegar, but with more complicated contracts in which people were more likely to make mistakes. Typically, the parties to a land transaction had failed to describe accurately in a written document the patchwork quilt of rights to be conveyed. The document had erroneously omitted or included a parcel in a larger estate[31] or an outbuilding[32] or liability for tithes[33] or for rents[34] or rights to tithes[35] or to timber[36] or to pasturage.[37] All the remarks just quoted were made in cases of this sort. It is not surprising that attention focused on the unfairness of making a party give more or receive less than he had bargained for. It would not have been very useful to consider at just what point the less or more becomes so substantial that a party did not consent to the contract at all.

The courts of equity never translated their concerns about fairness into a thoroughly satisfactory rule as to when relief should be given. In the leading eighteenth-century case of *Howland* v. *Norris*, Lord Chancellor Thurlow said that the rule he personally favoured was to deny specific performance when the party's mistake made a 'material difference'.[38] Nevertheless, he granted specific performance in the case before him despite a mistake as to whether land was tithe-free and whether it included an unlimited right of common rather than pasturage for sheep only. The reason, he said, was precedent. The remedy had once been denied when the 'whole object' of the buyer had been to obtain a wharf he mistakenly believed to be on the property.[39] With blind unconcern about consistency, the Lord Chancellor then added that he would still deny specific performance

[30] 1 Ves. & B. at 527, 35 Eng. Rep. at 205.
[31] *Marquis Townshend* v. *Stangroom*, 6 Ves. Jun. 328, 31 Eng. Rep. 1076 (1801).
[32] *Stapylton* v. *Scott*, 13 Ves. 425, 33 Eng. Rep. 353 (1807).
[33] *Howland* v. *Norris*, 1 Cox 59, 29 Eng. Rep. 1062 (1784).
[34] *Halsey* v. *Grant*, 13 Ves. Jun. 73, 33 Eng. Rep. 222 (1806).
[35] *Drewe* v. *Hanson*, 6 Ves. Jun. 675, 31 Eng. Rep. 1253 (1802).
[36] *Clowes* v. *Higginson*, 1 Ves. & B. 524, 35 Eng. Rep. 204 (1813).
[37] *Howland* v. *Norris*, 1 Cox 59, 29 Eng. Rep. 1062 (1784).
[38] *Howland* v. *Norris*, 1 Cox 59, 61, 29 Eng. Rep. 1062, 1063 (1784).
[39] 1 Cox at 61, 29 Eng. Rep. at 1063.

if a party had purchased 'purely for the sake of this particular wanting'.[40] Two early nineteenth-century cases explicitly repudiated the case of the wharf and opted for less rigid formulations of the rule. In *Stapylton* v. *Scott*, the court said it would deny specific performance if the respondent could establish that the presence of a certain outbuilding on the property had been a 'strong inducement' to the purchase.[41] In *Halsey* v. *Grant*, although the court granted specific performance despite a mistake as to certain fixed charges to which land was subject, it said it would deny the remedy if the property had been 'substantially different' than the buyer thought.[42] For present purposes, the important point is that these formulas—'material difference', 'whole object', 'particular wanting', 'strong inducement', 'substantially different'—were not answers to the question of when mistake destroys consent. They were attempts to find a short formula that would reflect a range of non-theoretical, unsystematized, and often inarticulate concerns about the fair thing to do.

In the common law courts, as Simpson has noted, very little was said about the effect of mistake on consent until the nineteenth century.[43] In one early nineteenth-century case, *Thornton* v. *Kempster* in 1814, the court endorsed the principle that, when 'the parties had never agreed that the one should buy and the other accept the same thing . . . there was no agreement subsisting between them'.[44] If the court had in mind some larger ideas about how mistake affects consent, its opinion contains no trace of them. Moreover, *Thornton* was just the sort of case in which the court could make such a remark without being drawn into the difficult theoretical problem of what it means to agree on the same thing. In *Thornton*, a broker had handed the seller and buyer documents which described the goods differently: as 'Petersburgh clean hemp' in the one and as 'Riga Rhine hemp' in the other. It was quite easy to say that the parties had never reached agreement.

In some subsequent cases, the question of whether the parties had agreed to the same thing would, a theoretician might think, have been presented rather clearly. Yet the common law judges consistently avoided that question. For example, in 1815, in *Cox* v. *Prentice*,[45] the buyer had purchased a bar of silver under a mistake as to how many ounces of silver it contained. The court treated the

[40] 1 Cox at 61, 29 Eng. Rep. at 1063.
[41] *Stapylton* v. *Scott*, 13 Ves. 425, 426, 33 Eng. Rep. 353, 354 (1807).
[42] *Halsey* v. *Grant*, 13 Ves. Jun. 73, 76, 33 Eng. Rep. 222, 223 (1806).
[43] Simpson, *supra* n. 2, pp. 265–9.
[44] *Thornton* v. *Kempster*, 5 Taut. 786, 788, 128 Eng. Rep. 901, 902 (1814).
[45] *Cox* v. *Prentice*, 3 M. & S. 344, 16 Rev. Rep. 288 (1815).

problem as one of implied warranty without getting to the question of what sort of mistakes vitiate consent. In 1835, in *Dobell* v. *Hutchinson*,[46] the buyer purchased land described in a bill of particulars as containing a yard which it in fact did not contain. The court voided the contract because the yard was 'an essential part of the premises' but had little more to say on why a contract should be void for such a mistake. In 1846, in *Smith* v. *Jeffryes*,[47] the seller had agreed to sell 'ware potatoes' and the buyer later claimed he had intended to buy a particular kind of ware potatoes, 'Regent's wares', whereas the seller had insisted he take 'Kidney wares'. The court denied relief because, it said, the description 'ware potatoes' in the contract unambiguously referred to any kind of ware potatoes, and therefore, under the parol evidence rule, testimony as to the buyer's understanding was inadmissible. In 1858, in *Scott* v. *Littledale*,[48] the seller sold one hundred chests of Conguo tea, the cargo of the ship *Star of the East*, having shown by mistake a sample of a quite different tea to the buyer. The seller, on discovering his mistake, refused to deliver. Without considering the principle that the parties must agree to the same thing, the court denied relief. The court's argument was that even a court of equity would not void such a contract but would merely require the buyer to compensate the seller for the difference in quality.

These cases have been described here because, unlike the typical cases in equity, and unlike many others that could have been described, they seem to cry out for some statement, even a vague one, as to the effect of mistake on consent. Yet the courts did not resolve them by exploring the principle espoused in *Thornton* that the parties to a contract must agree on the same thing.

In 1864 the famous case of *Raffles* v. *Wichelhaus*[49] was decided, which common law treatise writers were to cite ever after for the principle that mistake destroys consent. The contract was for the sale of one hundred and twenty-five bales of Surat cotton to arrive 'ex *Peerless*' from Bombay. There were two ships *Peerless* sailing from Bombay, and the seller had one in mind, the buyer the other. The court held there was no valid contract. The opinion was *per curiam* and gave no reasons. Pollock indicated in his remarks to counsel that he thought the case was like one in which one party intended to sell goods in a particular warehouse and the other party intended to buy goods of the same description in another, or one

[46] *Dobell* v. *Hutchinson*, 3 Ad. & El. 355, 11 Eng. Rep. 448 (1935).
[47] *Smith* v. *Jeffryes*, 15 Mee. & W. 561, 71 Rev. Rep. 761 (1846).
[48] *Scott* v. *Littledale*, 8 Eliz. & Bl. 815, 120 Eng. Rep. 304 (1858).
[49] *Raffles* v. *Wichelhaus*, 2 H. & C. 906, 159 Eng. Rep. 375 (1864).

party wished to sell wine coming from one estate in France or Spain and the other wished to buy wine coming from a different estate of the same name. Counsel at one point remarked that without a *consensus ad idem* there could not be a binding contract, but he explored the implications of that remark no further than the *Thornton* court did. *Raffles* v. *Wichelhaus* was a different case from *Thornton*, since here the parties' minds supposedly had not met, whereas in *Thornton* their very documents disagreed. This was the point that irritated plaintiff's counsel, who argued that '[i]ntention is of no avail, unless stated at the time of the contract'.

Thus, even in 1864, counsel could still argue that an unstated intention is of no avail, and courts could still reply with cryptic utterances. In contrast, by that date a series of common law treatise writers had explained the effect of mistake on consent in the very words of the natural lawyers. According to Powell, Kent, Joseph Story, William Story, and Fry, to void a contract a mistake must be in 'essence' or 'substance'.[50] They all cited civilian authority. Sometimes they explained the doctrine with other Aristotelian terms that the natural lawyers had preserved. Powell said that a mistake as to whether an estate is tithe-free should not void a contract, because 'whether it be so or no is an accident and has nothing to do with the essence of the contract'.[51] According to Joseph Story, a mistake voided a contract when it was 'an efficient cause of its concoction'.[52] According to Fry, the mistake had to be one in 'substance' as opposed to 'quality or accident'.[53] Once again, the nineteenth-century treatise writers organized the common law of contract by borrowing from the natural lawyers.

THE CONTENT OF A CONTRACT

Almost as significant as the instances in which the common lawyers borrowed from the natural lawyers are those in which they did not do so. They did not borrow the doctrine that contracts of exchange require equality. They did not borrow the doctrine that contracts could be classified into natural types, each with a set of natural obligations to which a party to that type of contract was bound. In the nineteenth century, these doctrines appeared too strange and

[50] Powell, *supra* n. 11, i. 147–8, 151; Kent, *supra* n. 10, ii.*477 (adding that this is 'a clear principle of universal jurisprudence'); J. Story, *supra* n. 21, i. 213–14; W. W. Story, *supra* n. 3, 419, 424–6; E. Fry, *Specific Performance of Contracts* (London, 1892), 371.

[51] Powell, *supra* n. 11, i. 148.

[52] J. Story, *supra* n. 21, i. 213.

[53] Fry, *supra* n. 50, 371.

wrongheaded to be worth appropriating. Nevertheless, the refusal to borrow them did not leave the common law where it had been in the eighteenth century. Unlike the eighteenth-century courts, the nineteenth-century treatise writers were seeking system and theory. By refusing to borrow these doctrines, they committed themselves to building a coherent theory without the use of them.

Equality in Exchange

The nineteenth-century treatise writers discussed equality in exchange in the context of two inherited rules. One was the rule that a common law court could not examine the adequacy of consideration. As we shall see in the next chapter, they interpreted this rule to mean that there was no requirement of equality in exchange. Such a requirement, they said, would be paternalistic. Moreover, to speak of equality in exchange involved swampy and mystical notions of economic value. The other rule was that a court of equity would give relief from an unconscionable bargain. As we shall see, according to the treatise writers, this rule did not require equality in exchange. Relief was given not because a bargain was unequal, but because the harshness of its terms was evidence of fraud.

The treatise writers explained the law as they did because Aristotelian ideas about equality were out of favour. Had these ideas still been in vogue, the treatise writers could as easily have proceeded in the opposite way. They might have discovered the principle of equality in the rule allowing relief for unconscionable bargains and explained away the rule that common law courts would not examine the adequacy of consideration. Actually, either of these ways of proceeding would have been an innovation. The common law courts had not rejected the principle of equality, and the courts of equity had not endorsed it.

As Simpson has pointed out,[54] the judges who fashioned the rule against examining the adequacy of consideration were not confronting the problem of what to do about hard bargains. They were deciding what promises to enforce. Some limit had to be imposed on the enforcement of promises through an action in assumpsit, and the English courts had imposed one by requiring that a promise have consideration. In a two-party exchange, that requirement was rather straightforward. The consideration for a promise was found in what the promisor was to receive in return. Had these been the only promises common law judges wished to enforce, the rules about consideration might have developed quite differently. Instead,

[54] Simpson, *supra* n. 2, pp. 445–9.

they chose to enforce some promises involving three parties or detrimental reliance as well as certain gratuitous arrangements such as gifts to prospective sons-in-law and gratuitous loans and bailments.[55] Although the judges often found consideration in these cases by drawing far-fetched analogies to contracts of exchange, the consideration was not a recompense in any ordinary sense of the word. In these cases, to demand that consideration be adequate would have defeated the very purpose the judges were trying to achieve, which was to enforce promises in which the consideration was not a recompense. Thus it came to be said, in the famous words of *Sturlyn* v. *Albany*,[56] that 'when a thing is done, be it never so small, this is a sufficient consideration to ground an action'. In *Sturlyn*, plaintiff had leased to a third party who granted his estate to the defendant. The plaintiff demanded rent from the defendant, who promised to pay if the plaintiff would show him a deed proving the rent was due. The showing of the deed was said to be consideration. As Simpson points out, the case has nothing to do with the enforcement of hard bargains.[57] Admittedly, the enforcement of hard bargains was the occasional consequence of the rule against examining the adequacy of consideration. Nevertheless, the judges who developed the rule were not confronting the problem of equality in exchange.

Moreover, in granting relief from unconscionable bargains, the courts of equity were not espousing the principle of equality in exchange. The principle was surely known to them from the works of the natural lawyers, yet it does not seem to have influenced either the rule they developed or the way they explained it. Before 1750, nearly all the cases in which courts of equity found a contract to be unconscionable concerned either necessitous heirs who sold their inheritance at a low price or the repercussions of the South Sea Bubble.[58] The fact that courts would help necessitous heirs does not

[55] Simpson, *supra* n. 2, pp. 416–52.

[56] *Sturlyn* v. *Albany*, Cro. Eliz. 67, 78 Eng. Rep. 327 (QB 1587).

[57] Simpson, *supra* n. 2, p. 447.

[58] See Simpson, 'The Horwitz Thesis and the History of Contracts', *University of Chicago Law Review*, 46 (1979), 533 at 562–6. A few cases involved neither necessitous heirs nor the South Sea Bubble. Even in these cases, however, the courts did not endorse a principle of equality in exchange. *Osmond* v. *Fitzroy & Duke of Cleveland*, 3 P. Wms. 129, 24 Eng. Rep. 997 (1731), did not involve an exchange, let alone an unequal one. The court set aside, for breach of trust, a bond for £1,000 obtained by a servant from a 27-year-old lord whom the servant cared for as a child. In *Willis* v. *Jernegan*, 2 Atk. 251, 26 Eng. Rep. 555 (1741), the plaintiff bought lottery tickets from the defendant, it having been agreed that the plaintiff could keep all the profits from reselling them. The court denied relief, commenting that, if it were 'a very hard and unconscionable bargain, if a person will enter into it with his eyes open, equity will not believe him upon this footing only, unless he can shew fraud . . .'. (2 Atk. at 251, 26 Eng. Rep. at 555.) The exchange, however, had not

indicate, of course, that they subscribed to some general principle that exchange must be equal. The courts may merely have been concerned about the squandering of family estates.[59] Moreover, the relief given in the South Sea Bubble cases was actually inconsistent with what natural lawyers such as Grotius had said about equality. For Grotius, as for the late scholastics, the just price in the absence of state regulation was the market price. In the South Sea Bubble cases the value of landed estates had been pushed up by the rise in the price of South Sea Company stock. Those who bought land at this high price were sometimes given relief not because they had paid more than the market price, but because the price of land was due to a 'delusion'.[60]

Moreover, it is almost impossible to find even a reference to the principle of equality in exchange as such in the arguments of counsel or the opinions of the court in the cases decided from the time the doctrine of unconscionability originated through the end of the eighteenth century. There is a great deal of talk about whether a bargain is 'unreasonable',[61] 'unjust',[62] 'unequitable and

been shown to be unequal. According to the reporter, 'plaintiff might have sold them to very great advantage but, by . . . insisting on an exorbitant premium, he was a considerable loser'. (2 Atk. at 251, 26 Eng. Rep. at 255.) According to the Lord Chancellor, the plaintiff made the bargain with an 'easy stomach, and a quick digestion'. (2 Atk. at 252, 26 Eng. Rep. at 555.) In *How* v. *Waldon & Edwards*, 2 Ves. Sen. 516, 28 Eng. Rep. 330 (1754), a sailor had sold in advance and for a small sum the right to the prize money to which he was entitled. The Master of the Rolls granted relief, commenting that, 'though the inadequateness of the value will not of itself be sufficient to set aside the contract, yet it is a very material ingredient . . .'. (2 Ves. Sen. at 518, 28 Eng. Rep. at 331.) Again, however, one cannot know how the court would actually have dealt with an unequal bargain entered into without fraud. In *How*, the risk of obtaining the money had been 'greatly misrepresented' to him, a circumstance that, according to the court, constituted 'gross fraud'.

[59] Indeed, the courts mention these considerations. In *Johnson, Ex'r of Hill* v. *Nott*, 1 Vern. 271, 272, 23 Eng. Rep. 464, 465 (1684), the court observed that the 'practice of purchasing from heirs was grown too common'. In *Twistleton* v. *Griffith*, 1 P. Wms. 310, 311, 24 Eng. Rep. 403, 404 (1716), the court spoke of the destruction of heirs through such contracts and of the desirability of curbing their extravagance and forcing them to approach their fathers for money. Similarly, considerations were mentioned in *Earl of Chesterfield* v. *Jannsen*, 2 Ves. Sen. 125, 144–5, 28 Eng. Rep. 82, 93–4 (1750–1).

[60] e.g. *Kien* v. *Stukeley*, 1 Bro. 191, 192, 11 Eng. Rep. 506, 507 (HL 1722), where the defendant argued that 'stocks, lands as well as every thing else, were, raised to an extravagant price' owing to 'the general delusion which all men lay under'. *Savile* v. *Savile*, 1 P. Wms. 745, 746–7, 24 Eng. Rep. 596 (1721), where the court spoke of 'under what a general delusion the nation was at the time when this contract was made . . . when there was thought to be more money in the nation than there really was which induced people to put imaginary values on estates'.

[61] *Earl of Arglasse* v. *Muschamp*, 1 Vern. 237, 238–9; 23 Eng. Rep. 438, 439 (1684); *Earl of Chesterfield* v. *Jannsen*, 2 Ves. Sen. 125, 130, 28 Eng. Rep. 82, 85 (1750–1) (argument for plaintiff).

[62] *Earl of Chesterfield* v. *Jannsen*, 2 Ves. Sen. 125, 130, 28 Eng. Rep. 82, 85 (1750–1) (argument for plaintiff).

unconscientious',[63] 'hard and unequal',[64] or entered into for 'inadequate' or 'grossly inadequate' consideration[65] or through 'imposition'.[66] One is hard put, however, to find a reference to commutative justice, or even a simple statement that exchange in principle requires equality. A few cases briefly mention the civil law rule that relief is available when the contract price deviates by one-half from the just price. Nearly always, however, the civil law rule is contrasted with English law and the principle that exchange requires equality is not mentioned.[67] For example, in the elaborately argued *Chesterfield* case, civil law rules protecting heirs were mentioned many times. The one reference to the civil law remedy for an unjust price was a deprecatory remark by the lawyer arguing that the contract should be upheld. The idea that exchange requires equality was not mentioned in pages and pages of argument.[68]

If the seventeenth- and eighteenth-century courts of equity did not endorse the principle of equality in exchange, neither did they reject it. Sometimes, rather like the nineteenth-century jurists, they spoke of the harsh terms of the bargain as grounding a presumption of fraud.[69] But, as just noted, they also spoke of whether the terms

[63] *Chesterfield* v. *Jannsen*, 2 Ves. Sen. 125, 155, 28 Eng. Rep. 82, 100 (1750–1).

[64] *Kien* v. *Stukeley*, 1 Bro. 191, 192, 1 Eng. Rep. 506, 507 (HL 1722) (argument for defendant).

[65] *Gwynne* v. *Heaton*, 1 Bro. C.C. 1, 6, 28 Eng. Rep. 949, 951 (1778).

[66] *Earl of Chesterfield* v. *Jannsen*, Ves. Sen. 125, 145, 152, 156, 28 Eng. Rep. 82, 94, 98, 100 (1750–1); *Nichols* v. *Gould*, 2 Ves. Sen. 422, 423, 28 Eng. Rep. 270, 270 (1752).

[67] e.g. *Nott* v. *Hill*, 2 Chan. Cas. 120, 121, 22 Eng. Rep. 875, 876 (1682); *How* v. *Weldon & Edwards*, 2 Ves. Sen. 516, 518, 28 Eng. Rep. 330, 331 (1754). In *Gwynne* v. *Heaton*, 1 Bro, C.C. 1, 9, 28 Eng. Rep. 949, 953 (1778), there are references to what the 'excellent writer' Domat said about the contracts of minors and 'the vices of covenants'. What he said about equality in exchange is not so much as paraphrased.

[68] *Earl of Chesterfield* v. *Jannsen*, 2 Ves. Sen. 125, 134, 28 Eng. Rep. 82, 87 (1750–1).

[69] For example, in *Earl of Chesterfield* v. *Jannsen*, 2 Ves. Sen. 125, 155–6, 28 Eng. Rep. 82, 100 (1750–1), Chancellor Hardwicke said that fraud may be 'apparent from the intrinsic nature and subject of the bargain itself; such as no man in his senses and not under delusion would make on the one hand, and as no honest and fair man would accept on the other; which are inequitable and unconscientious bargains . . .'. In addittion, fraud could be 'presumed from the circumstances and condition of the parties contracting . . .'. Hardwicke says little about how apparent fraud differs from presumed fraud except that in the latter case one party has taken 'surreptitious advantage of the weakness or necessity of another; which knowingly to do is equally against the conscience . . .'. Neither does Hardwicke explain whether the harshness of the terms is merely evidence of fraud or actually constitutes fraud. In any event, judicial explanations of the remedy were not consistent. In the same case, Burnett said that a court would give relief not only 'on presuming a man would not enter into [the contract] but by imposition', but also when the court concluded that 'necessity alone could induce to make that bargain'. (2 Ves. Sen. at 145, 28 Eng. Rep. at 94.) Strange claimed that 'want of fraud or imposition' did not preclude relief. (2 Ves. Sen. at 149, 28 Eng. Rep. at 96.)

were 'unreasonable', 'unjust', 'unequitable', 'unconscientious', and 'unequal'. Sometimes, counsel or the court claimed that inequality of itself would not warrant relief. Indeed, the Lord Keeper who decided the Batty case in 1682 made a statement that a natural lawyer would have found appalling: 'One that is necessitous must sell cheaper than those who are not.'[70] Usually in such cases, however, counsel or the court proceeded to argue that the contract was not very unfair after all.[71] In denying that mere inequality did not warrant relief, they had been making one more argument. Unlike the nineteenth-century jurists, they were not mounting a theoretical challenge to the principle of equality. Thus, the nineteenth-century jurists, as Simpson observes, provided the giving of relief in equity with a new rationale. A disparity in price came to be considered as 'evidence of fraud, not as an independent substantive ground, and not as constituting hardship'.[72]

It is important to realize that these changes, like so many others we have considered, affected the way that rules were explained, not the way in which they were applied. According to the treatise writers, the reason the common law courts did not examine the adequacy of consideration was that it would be improper to review the fairness of an exchange. Yet even after their explanation became widely accepted, the rule was rarely invoked to uphold an unfair exchange. The rule was applied in Massachusetts, to uphold an agreement not to run a competing stagecoach line in return for one dollar,[73] and in Minnesota, to uphold the agreement of a corporate treasurer to pay the face value of a bond which she later

[70] *Batty* v. *Lloyd*, 1 Vern. 141, 142, 23 Eng. Rep. 374, 374 (1682).

[71] *Batty* v. *Lloyd*, 1 Vern. 141, 142, 23 Eng. Rep. 374, 374 (1682); *Willis* v. *Jernegan*, 2 Atk. 251, 252, 26 Eng. Rep. 555, 555 (1741); *Kien* v. *Stukeley*, 1 Bro. 191, 192, 1 Eng. Rep. 506, 507 (HL 1722) (argument of counsel); *Earl of Chesterfield* v. *Jannsen*, 2 Ves. Sen. 125, 131–2, 28 Eng. Rep. 82, 85–6 (1750–1) (argument of counsel). In *Earl of Ardglasse* v. *Muschamp*, 1 Vern. 237, 240, 23 Eng. Rep. 438, 440 (1684), the Lord Keeper said that the court could neither set aside the bargain nor presume fraud from an inequality in the bargain. He nevertheless gave relief.

If statements such as these had accurately reflected English law, relief would almost never have been given. These statements also contradicted those of other judges. One can find such contradictions not only between judicial opinions but within them. In *Gwynne* v. *Heaton*, 1 Bro. C.C. 1, 5, 28 Eng. Rep. 949, 951 (1778), Lord Chancelor Thurlow stated that 'an inadequate consideration is not *alone* sufficient to vitiate the contract'. He immediately added that where property 'is sold for a sum grossly inadequate the court has never suffered it to stand'. He then said that a contract could be set aside when an inequality was 'so strong, gross and manifest' as to call forth an 'exclamation' from a 'man of common sense'. (1 Bro. C.C. at 9, 28 Eng. Rep. at 953.)

[72] Simpson, *supra* n. 58, p. 569.

[73] *Pierce* v. *Fuller*, 8 Mass. 223 (1811). However, the party benefiting from the agreement claimed there were other considerations, including his purchase of the competing line.

alleged was worth far less.[74] Nevertheless, in the vast bulk of cases in which the rule has been invoked, the problem involved was quite different.

In some cases in which the rule was applied, the contract price had been set through a procedure designed to prevent questions of unfairness from arising.[75] Some cases involved aleatory contracts in which the consideration does not seem inadequate when one takes into account the risk involved.[76] In others, one of the parties received a *de facto* benefit although the rights he purchased were legally invalid.[77] Many more cases did not involve a two-sided exchange. Some involved gifts, as when a dying man gave a promissory note for a huge sum to those who cared for him in his illness,[78] or a philanthropist promised money to a college that would name a

[74] *Minneapolis Land Co.* v. *McMillan*, 79 Minn. 287, 82 NW 591 (1900).

[75] For cases in which specific performance was granted when the contract was made at an execution sale or at a price fixed by arbitrators, see nn. 105–6 *infra*. One early case often cited for the proposition that the law will not examine the adequacy on consideration involved a procedure of another kind; the defendant denied owing plaintiff $100 but promised to pay the money anyway if the plaintiff would swear that the money was due. The plaintiff's oath was held to be consideration for the $100. *Brooks* v. *Ball*, 18 Johns. 337 (NY 1920).

[76] *Cates* v. *Bales*, 78 Ind. 285 (1881) (contract to buy into an insurance scheme which seems to have had the properties of a chain letter); *Embola* v. *Tuppella*, 127 Wash. 285, 220 P. 789 (1923) (miner borrowed $50 from a friend to go to Alaska to try to recover property worth $500,000, which had been sold by his guardian while the miner was committed as insane; he was to pay his friend $10,000 if he succeeded). Similar are contracts to discontinue suit when there is doubt about the outcome, e.g. *Flannigan* v. *Kilome*, 58 NH 443 (1878); contracts to purchase a quitclaim deed from a party who has no interest in the land when there was doubt about his interest at the time of the purchase, e.g. *Mullen* v. *Hawkins*, 141 Ind. 363, 40 NE 797 (1895); and contracts to protect a party against possible claims even when no claims are forthcoming, e.g. *Hubbard* v. *Coolidge*, 42 Mass. (1 Met.) 84 (1840). Also similar are sales of patents when the sale was made to settle or avoid litigation, e.g. *Hall Mfg. Co.* v. *American Ry. Supply Co.*, 48 Mich. 331 (1882), or when the patented invention later proves to be useless, e.g. *Hardesty* v. *Smith*, 3 Ind. 39 (1851); *Howe* v. *Richards*, 102 Mass. 64 (1869); *Nash* v. *Lull*, 102 Mass. 60 (1869).

[77] e.g. *Bartlett* v. *Holbrook*, 67 Mass. (1 Gray) 114 (1854) (invalid patent nevertheless created *de facto* monopoly); *Marston* v. *Swett*, 66 NY 206 (1976) (same). A case that also turned on the actual effect of a legally invalid transfer of rights—although one that may have reached the wrong result—is *Sanborn* v. *French*, 22 NH 246 (1850). There the court upheld a contract in which a married woman was given a $50 note to convey a life estate to a third party. The court noted that, even if the conveyance were invalid, it would give colour of title to the third party and cloud the woman's own title.

[78] e.g. *Clark's Appeal*, 57 Conn. 565, 19 A. 332 (1889); *Worth* v. *Case*, 42 NY 362 (1870). Similarly, in *Earl* v. *Peck*, 64 NY 596 (1876), the court upheld a note for $10,000 given by a dying man to his housekeeper as a gift and as remuneration for past services. Similarly, courts have enforced contracts in which one family member promised to leave a large amount of property to another who promised to care for him until his death; e.g. *Peter* v. *Griffin*, 184 Iowa 1061, 169 NW 441 (1918); *Thompson* v. *Ramack*, 174 Iowa 155, 156 NW 310 (1916); *Brackenbury* v. *Hodgkin*,

fund after her.[79] Others involved reliance, as when one person guaranteed another's credit.[80] Some involved three-party situations in which the consideration was not inadequate given the role of the third party.[81] As far as one can tell from reported American cases of the nineteenth and early twentieth centuries, the enforcement of

116 Me. 399, 102 A. 106 (1917). In some cases not only did the promisor intend a gift, but the promisee relied, or the consideration may not have been inadequate given the risk that the promisor would live a long time.

[79] e.g. *Allegheny College* v. *National Chautauqua County Bank*, 246 NY 369, 159 NE 173 (1927). Similarly, promises that were intended primarily as gifts have been enforced when the consideration amounted to a pledge to name a child after the promisor, e.g. *Wolford* v. *Powers*, 85 Ind. 294 (1882); *Gardner* v. *Denison*, 217 Mass. 492, 105 NE 359 (1914).

[80] In some of these cases, one party pledged to hold the other harmless if the second party did a certain act, e.g. *Lawrence* v. *McClamont*, 43 US (2 How.) 425 (1844) (mother's promise to guarantee her son's debts if money advanced to him); *Train* v. *Gold*, 22 Mass. (5 Pick.) 380 (1827) (promise by creditor's attorney to indemnify sheriff against claims brought against him for levying execution). In other cases, the contract would not have appeared one-sided to the promisee who relied because the promisor was acting in part out of generosity, or because the contract involved a risk, or because any disparity in the values exchanged was not striking. In *Ga Nun* v. *Palmer*, 216 NY 603, 111 NE 223 (1916), a 70-year-old woman, alone and unmarried, promised $70 per month and $20,000 after her death to the plaintiff if she would come and live with her as a companion. Plaintiff did so, giving up her business as a dressmaker. Cardozo held that the contract was enforceable, giving as one of his reasons that the law will not examine the adequacy of consideration. (Ibid. at 609, 111 NE at 225.)

[81] When three parties are involved, A, B, and C, a court cannot judge whether a contract between two of them is one-sided simply by looking at the value of what each received from the other. It may be that A had previously entered into a fair contract with B, and B with C, and that C then made a seemingly one-sided contract with A, but one that is not unfair since it excuses A from paying B and B from paying C on the earlier contracts. An early example may be *Sturlyn* v. *Albany*, 1 Cro. Eliz. 67, 78 Eng. Rep. 327 (QB 1587), described in the text. In that case, the landowner was merely trying to recover from the person occupying his land the rent due from the owner's immediate tenant. A more modern example is *Manson & MacPhee* v. *Flanagan*, 233 Mass. 150, 123 NE 614 (1919), where a subcontractor who had not been paid for his materials and labour by his general contractor obtained a promise of payment from the homeowner in return for his own forbearance to file a lien. Although the subcontractor would have had the right to file a lien only for the value of his labour, which was a small part of the value of labour and materials for which the owner had agreed to pay, the court enforced the contract, noting that 'mere inadequacy of the consideration' does not invalidate a contract. (233 Mass. at 153, 123 NE at 614.)

Another possibility is that C has promised A a performance to which C is already bound by a previous contract with B. A may be receiving something for little or nothing, but at any rate B is losing nothing. For example, in *Perkins* v. *Clay*, 54 NH 518 (1874), a butcher had sold his business, promising not to compete with the buyer, and later made the same promise to a second party who was purchasing the business from the first buyer. The court found some consideration for the second promise and enforced it, noting that the adequacy of consideration is irrelevant.

A third possibility is that C has promised A that if A will deal with B, C will answer if B fails to perform. This is a special case of the promise to another to hold him harmless if he takes a certain action, a case discussed in n. 80 *supra*. To enforce the unfair bargains has never been more than an occasional consequence of the rule.

Similarly, the practice of the courts of equity did not change even though the courts now said that the disparity in price was relevant only as evidence of fraud. Indeed, had they acted in accordance with this new rationale, they would have stopped giving relief almost entirely. When a fraud is committed there will often be such a disparity, but it will rarely be the only evidence or the best evidence. The victim of fraud in any normal sense will usually know what the other party did to defraud him. A court concerned only about fraud would hear his testimony and that of the other party and then use the disparity in price as evidence of whom to believe. In some cases such a dispute actually occurred, for example over whether a sheriff's sale was collusive.[82] Nevertheless, most often when courts gave relief in the nineteenth and early twentieth centuries, there had been no charge of fraud in the ordinary sense. No one claimed that a fact had been concealed or misrepresented.

In many cases, as one might expect, there was not merely a disproportionate price but some definite reason why the disadvantaged party had difficulty protecting himself. He was drunk,[83] feeble-minded,[84] or a drug addict,[85] or he had contracted with a friend on whose judgment he relied.[86] In other cases there was evidence of some kind of disability, but one that people normally manage to surmount. He was 21 and buying land,[87] or 70 and selling

promise is not to enrich A at C's expense, but to reimburse A for a loss that C has caused him.

A fourth and more troubling possibility is that C has promised to reimburse A for a loss A suffers on his contract with B, but neither A's contract with B nor his loss was caused by C's promise. Normally the doctrine of consideration would prevent C's promise from being enforced. But sometimes courts have found some consideration for the promise and enforced it. Whether or not they should do so, they are at any rate not enforcing a contract that gives one party a windfall and the other a corresponding loss, as they would if they enforced a two-party exchange without regard to the adequacy of consideration. See e.g. *Haigh* v. *Brooks*, 10 Adol. & El. 309, 113 Eng. Rep. 119 (QB 1839); *Hind* v. *Holdshop*, 2 Watts 104 (Pa. 1833). A more typical case is a promise to pay the debts of a relative who has died insolvent. Some courts will enforce such promises, saying that the cancellation of even a worthless note is consideration, e.g. *Judy* v. *Louderman*, 48 Ohio St. 562, 29 NE 181 (1891). Other courts will not enforce them, e.g. *Newman & Snell's State Bank* v. *Hunter*, 243 Mich. 331, 220 NW 665 (1928).

[82] e.g. *Byers* v. *Surget*, 60 US (19 How.) 303 (1856) (collusion suspected in sheriff's sale); *Clement* v. *Reid*, 9 Miss. (9 S. & M.) 535 (1848) (same).

[83] e.g. *Babcock* v. *Eagle*, 58 Mont. 597, 194 P. 137 (1920).

[84] e.g. *Brook* v. *Berry*, 2 Gill 83 (Md. 1844).

[85] *Leathers* v. *Deloach*, 140 Tenn. 259, 204 SW 633 (1918) (morphine addict).

[86] e.g. *Hall* v. *Perkins*, 3 Wend. 626 (NY 1829).

[87] e.g. *Gasque* v. *Small*, 21 SC Eq. (2 Strobb. Eq.) 72 (1847) (purchase by 21-year-old).

a patent;[88] he had been drinking but it is not clear how much.[89] In still other cases, the disadvantaged party seems to have been under no disability except for his failure to know the market price. Relief was given to a physician who had agreed to exchange property worth $11,800 for property worth $15,000 but subject to a $15,000 mortgage that he agreed to pay.[90] Relief was given when a trustee sold land for one-tenth its value,[91] when the owner of a fruit farm parted with it for property worth little more than a mortgage which he also assumed,[92] and when the owner of a four-family block of flats exchanged it for a vacant lot in which he would have an equity worth half the equity he had given up.[93] In 1914, a telephone company was relieved of a contract it had made with a railroad to install telephones in its depot and provide free telephone service forever, the only consideration given by the railroad being its permission to install.[94]

It is hard to tell how consistently the courts of equity were giving such relief. It is striking, in any event, that in the great bulk of the cases in which relief was denied the contract was not simply an unfair exchange. In some cases the contract was not purely an exchange. The party seemingly disadvantaged had intended to benefit the other because of friendship of family ties or gratitude.[95] In other cases the exchange had not been proven unfair. The court found that the consideration was adequate[96] or noted that evidence

[88] e.g. *Gillette* v. *Metzgar Register Co.*, 243 Mich. 48, 219 NW 644 (1928).

[89] e.g. *Rupniewski* v. *Miazga*, 299 Pa. 190, 149 A. 193 (1930).

[90] *State Security & Realty Co.* v. *Shaffer*, 176 Mich. 639, 142 NW 1058 (1913).

[91] *Wright* v. *Wilson*, 10 Tenn. (2 Yerg.) 294 (1829).

[92] *Koch.* v. *Streuter*, 232 Ill. 594, 83 NE 1072 (1908).

[93] *Linsell* v. *Halicki*, 240 Mich. 483, 215 NW 315 (1927).

[94] *Great N. Ry. Co.* v. *Sheyenne Tel. Co.*, 27 ND 246, 145 NW 1062 (1914).

[95] e.g. *Eyre* v. *Potter*, 56 US (15 How.) 42, 60 (1853) (widow conveyed property inherited from her late husband to his children out of 'motives of affection'); *Engle* v. *Engle*, 209 Mich. 275, 176 NW 547 (1920) (admittedly unequal division of property among heirs); *White* v. *Thompson*, 21 NC (1 Dev. & Bat. Eq.) 493, 494 (1837) (father sold land to son out of 'natural love and affection'); *Knobb* v. *Lindsay*, 5 Ohio 468 (1832) (prisoner conveyed land to a friend who had paid his bail); *Fripp* v. *Fripp*, 14 SC Eq. (Rice Eq.) 84, 107 (1839) (man assigned his share of his brother's estate to his sister-in-law as a 'kind and liberal action'); *Sarter* v. *Gordon*, 11 SC Eq. (2 Hill Eq.) 121, 139 (1835) (slaves previously purchased from the buyer's father at a low price were resold to the buyer at a low price; the seller was supposedly acting out of 'humanity'). However, if a contract looks too much like a gift, a court may apply the rule that promises of gifts cannot be specifically enforced, e.g. *Frank* v. *Gaylord*, 119 NJ Eq. 427, 182 A. 614 (1936).

[96] e.g. *Scott* v. *Hobirck*, 188 Iowa 155, 174 NW 1 (1919). In other cases, the court conceded there might be some disporportion, but said it was not very great, e.g. *Hamilton* v. *Hamilton*, 162 Ind. 430, 70 NE 535 (1904); *Herdeman* v. *Berge*, 18 Tenn. (10 Yerg.) 202 (1836); *Simpson* v. *Green*, 231 SW 375 (Com. App. Tex. 1921). In still other cases, the court observed that there was no proof that the consideration was

of value was conflicting.[97] In other cases contract may not have been unfair because it involved a risk such as uncertainty about title,[98] the length of a person's life,[99] the size of mineral deposits,[100] or the value that land would have in the future.[101] In other cases the party seemingly disadvantaged had been seeking some benefit in addition to the price he paid: for example, he sold land to a railroad so that the value of his remaining land would rise.[102] In still other cases the court was not in a position to determine the value of the things exchanged. For example, when two railroad companies agreed that each could build tracks over the other's right of way, and one later

inadequate, e.g. *Hendler Creamery Corp.* v. *Lillich*, 152 Md. 190, 136 A. 631 (1927); *McManus* v. *Boston*, 171 Mass. 152, 50 NE 607 (1818).

[97] e.g. *Nickerson* v. *Bridges*, 216 Mass. 416, 103 NE 939 (1914); *Seymour* v. *Delancy*, 3 Cowers 445 (NY 1824).

[98] e.g. *Sutherland* v. *Sutherland*, 187 Kan. 599, 358 P.2d 776 (1961); *Osgood* v. *Franklin*, 2 Johns. Ch. 1 (NY Ch. 1816).

[99] An example is a contract in which an old person promises a large sum in return for care for life, e.g. *Green* v. *Thompson*, 37 NC (2 Ired. Eq.) 365 (1842). This case involved two other considerations as well: (1) care was to be provided by a relative, and so the payment may have been intended in part as a gift; (2) it was hard to judge the burdens that the agreement imposed on the person rendering care and thus hard to tell if the contract was one-sided. The court remarked that, in view of the personality and drinking habits of the man to be cared for, the service may have been cheap at the price. (37 NC at 369.)

[100] e.g. *Heyward* v. *Bradley*, 179 F. 325 (4th Cir. 1910) (owner agreed to sell phosphate deposits for $20,000 if buyer elected to purchase after making tests; specific performance granted despite the discovery of deposits worth $70,000, since the buyer paid $2,500 for tests which would have been a 'total loss' if paying quantities of ore had not been found).

[101] See *Chicago Title & Trust Co.* v. *Illinois Merchants' Trust Co.*, 329 Ill. 334, 160 NE 597 (1928). Nevertheless, courts have occasionally handled contracts involving a risk in various ways, some of them strange. Sometimes they have simply neglected to take account of the risk and denied specific performance because the end result was one-sided, e.g. *Marks* v. *Gates*, 154 F. 481 (9th Cir. 1907) (a prospector and a backer entered into a grubstake contract, the prospector to receive $1,000 and the cancellation of an $11,225 debt, the backer to receive a one-fifth interest in any property the prospector might acquire in Alaska; specific performance was denied when the prospector acquired property worth $750,000). Sometimes a court has gone to the opposite extreme of refusing to examine whether the consideration was inadequate once it has observed that the contract did involve a risk, e.g. *Marsh* v. *Lott*, 8 Cal. App. 384, 97 P. 163 (2d Dist. 1908) (three-month option to buy land for $100,000 given for 25¢); *Chicago Title & Trust Co.* v. *Illinois Merchants' Trust Co.*, 329 Ill. 334, 160 NE 597 (1928) (no investigation of terms of option); see *Adams* v. *Peabody Coal Co.*, 230 Ill. 469, 82 NE 645 (1907) (option for $1, but the court enforced it without noting that options involved a risk). Sometimes courts have tried to assess the actuarial fairness of the terms, but have gravely overestimated their own abilities; see e.g. *Weeks* v. *Pratt*, 43 F. 2d 53 (4th Cir. 1930), where the court refused to enforce a sale for $100,000 of a formula that would make automobile fuel out of water, observing that the formula must be far more valuable than that. Sibley J, concurring in the result but not on this point, noted that the discovery was of 'undemonstrated value'. (43 F. 2d at 57.)

[102] *Western R.R.* v. *Babcock*, 47 Mass. (6 Met.) 346 (1843).

challenged the fairness of the exchange, the court noted that, 'when the contract, as in this case, furnishes no standard or measure for estimating the relative advantages, it would be extremely hazardous for the court to attempt a solution'.[103] There are also cases in which the court denied relief, and, while the contract may have been unfair, no evidence of a disparity in price appears in the court's opinion.[104] Finally, there are cases in which the price, whether unfair or not, had been set by following some procedure that was supposed to produce fair terms. For example, the property was purchased at a sheriff's sale,[105] or the price was set by arbitrators selected by the parties.[106] Thus, the court had good reason for not allowing the procedure to be called into question.

Certainly, courts of equity were not granting or denying relief according to the likelihood that fraud had actually been committed. They may have occasionally upheld a harsh bargain. On the whole, however, it is hard to believe that they were more inclined to uphold harsh bargains than eighteenth-century courts. For that matter, it is hard to believe that they would have behaved much differently if they had been taking their law from Lessius or Grotius rather than from the nineteenth-century treatise writers.

Admittedly, the relief that courts of equity most often gave was not rescission or reformation but a denial of specific performance. In theory, the advantaged party could still sue on his contract in a court of common law and recover damages. It is doubtful, however, that he succeeded in doing so very often. His damage claim would have required a jury trial, and juries may not have been eager to award damages on such a contract. Moreover, after the merger of law and equity courts, he would usually have to have sought specific performance and damages in one unified proceeding. The very evidence he presented to show that his contract was not unconscionable would usually show that his damages were small. In any event, one scholar has found only two reported cases in which a

[103] *South & N. Ala. R. Co.* v. *Highland Ave. & B.R. Co.*, 98 Ala. 400, 405, 13 So. 682, 684 (1893).

[104] e.g. *Ullsperger* v. *Meyer*, 217 Ill. 262, 75 NE 482 (1905). The court said that inadequacy of consideration, without more, will not defeat specific performance. (217 Ill. at 267, 75 NE at 484.) What a court says it will do, however, and what it actually will do when confronted with convincing evidence of a one-sided contract, are two different things.

[105] e.g. *Erwin* v. *Parham*, 53 US (12 How.) 196 (1851); *Delafield* v. *Anderson*, 8 Miss. (7 S. & M.) 630 (1846). Sometimes, however, purchasers at a sheriff's sale have been denied specific performance when the disproportion was particularly great or where there was suspicion of fraud, e.g. *Modisett* v. *Johnson*, 2 Blackf. 431 (Ind. 1831) (alternative holding).

[106] e.g. *Viele* v. *Troy & B.R.R.*, 21 Barb. 381 (NY 1855).

party who failed to obtain specific performance still managed to obtain damages.[107] That result should not surprise us. If plaintiffs had been flocking into the common law courts with such claims, one would expect to hear something about it in the appellate opinions. Yet, as we have already seen, very few of the cases in which the appellate courts said they could not examine the adequacy of consideration actually involved an exchange in which the consideration was inadequate. The nineteenth-century treatise writers failed to borrow the doctrine of equality in exchange, and yet the greatest change that took place was in theory.

The Terms of Exchange

Unlike the natural lawyers, nineteenth-century treatise writers did not discuss the reasons there were different types of contracts, each with different terms. The treatises written in the earlier part of the century often solemnly define contract in terms of mutual assent and then leap without explanation into the welter of rules applicable to various types of contracts. The question why the parties are bound to these rules to which they never expressly consented is hardly considered.[108] Towards the end of the century, particularly in the works of Langdell and Holmes in the United States and Anson and Pollock in England, the discussion of the particular rules of various types of contracts all but disappears. These authors describe general contract law without trying to relate it to the law of sales, the law of leases, and so forth.

The nineteenth-century jurists did write chapters on how contracts should be interpreted. Typically, however, these chapters do not deal with the problem of why parties to a sale are bound by the law of sales. They are filled with maxims of interpretation: the contract should be construed according to its spirit and not its letter; ambiguous words should be construed against the party who drafted the contract; and so forth.[109] Grotius himself had written such a chapter.[110] Grotius, however, had dealt with the problem of the rules applicable to particular types of contracts not in his chapter on

[107] Newman, 'The Renaissance of Good Faith in Contracting in American Law', *Cornell Law Review*, 54 (1969), 553 at 559.

[108] e.g. W. Story, *supra* n. 3, Parsons, *supra* n. 3, Comyn, *supra* n. 3, Kent, *supra* n. 3, Taylor, *supra* n. 11, Chitty, *supra* n. 3.

[109] e.g. Kent, *supra* n. 3, ii. *552–7; W. Story, *supra* n. 3, pt. 1, ch. 20; Comyn, *supra* n. 3, ii, pt. 4, ch. 1; Parsons, *supra* n. 3 ii, pt. 2, ch. 1; J. Bishop, *Commentaries on the Law of Contracts* (Chicago, 1907), ch. 14; Hammon, *supra* n. 18, ch. 9; Metcalf, *supra* n. 18, ch. 5; Anson, *supra* n. 18, pt. 4, ch. 2.

[110] H. Grotius, *De iure belli ac pacis libri tres* (Leiden, 1939), II. xvi.

interpretation, but in his chapter 'On Contracts', which began by assigning to each type its proper definition.

As the century wore on, the general law of contract bore steadily less relation to the rules governing particular contracts. Observing this development, and working only from American and English sources, Grant Gilmore concluded that no one had arrived at the notion of a general law of contract before the late nineteenth century.[111] In fact, the common lawyers had borrowed their general law of contract from the natural lawyers but failed to borrow the doctrines concerned with particular contracts.

Again, their failure to do so mattered mostly in theory. The rules that nineteenth-century courts applied to particular contracts such as sale and lease were sometimes inherited from the eighteenth century and sometimes forged for the first time. It is possible, of course, that the common lawyers would have arrived at different rules had they been guided by the theories of the natural lawyers. Nevertheless, as we have seen, theory had relatively little impact even on the rules the late scholastics applied to particular contracts. Most of these rules were less the consequences of theory than inheritances from Roman law for which the late scholastics had found theoretical explanations.

The one rule for which the late scholastics had a clear theoretical explanation, although it was also taken from Roman law, was that the seller warrants his goods against defects. In contrast, the common law was uncertain until the late eighteenth century when the courts adopted the rule of *caveat emptor*.[112] Nevertheless, the difference between the results the common law courts were reaching and those the natural lawyers would have approved may not have been very great. According to Lawrence Friedman, 'although common-law courts refused to *imply* warranties, they showed a marked tendency to read *express* warranties into a seller's words, at the slightest provocation. Often, these "express" warranties were much the same as those which the namby-pamby civil law "implied".'[113] Indeed, Kim Scheppele has shown, in a study of nineteenth-century New York cases, that the rule of *caveat emptor* was usually applied to cases in which merchants act as mere conduits between the supplier and the consumer, often dealing in

[111] G. Gilmore, *The Death of Contract* (Columbus, Ohio, 1974), 6; G. Gilmore, *The Ages of American Law* (New Haven, Conn., 1977), 45.

[112] The rule of *caveat emptor* was adopted by Lord Mansfield in *Stuart* v. *Wilkins*, 1 Dougl. 18, 99 Eng. Rep. 15 (1778). In a later opinion, Grose asserted that before *Stuart*, a seller had been liable for defects in his goods: *Parkinson* v. *Lee*, 2 East. 314, 102 Eng. Rep. 389 (1802). There is no way to know if he was right.

[113] L. Friedman, *A History of American Law*, 2nd edn. (New York, 1985), 265.

goods they cannot inspect, of whose desirable properties they are ignorant, and of whose defects they can have no more knowledge than the consumer himself. The courts rarely applied the rule in contracts between the supplier of goods himself and the consumer, as in sales of local horses or foodstuffs. The rule itself began to break down in the late nineteenth century when a greater proportion of the litigated cases concerned contracts made by manufacturers.[114] A natural lawyer might have disagreed with *caveat emptor* in principle but found the results in New York quite tolerable.

[114] K. Scheppele, *Legal Secrets: Equality and Efficiency in the Common Law* (Chicago, 1988), 269–98.

7
THE NINETEENTH-CENTURY REFORMULATION

WHEN the authority of Aristotle collapsed in the seventeenth and eighteenth centuries, the law of contract lost its philosophical foundations. Nevertheless, as we have seen, for a long time doctrine changed very little. Systematic and general reformulation did not come until the nineteenth century, when the Aristotelian origins of contract doctrine were long forgotten and Aristotelian philosophy itself was barely intelligible.

Nineteenth-century jurists no longer claimed that their conclusions followed from larger philosophical principles. They said they were merely describing the law in force in their own countries. In England and the United States they claimed to be interpreting the decisions of judges; in France, the French Civil Code; in Germany, the Roman texts of the *Corpus iuris* which were not replaced by the German Civil Code until 1900. Nevertheless, Anglo-American, French, and German jurists arrived at similar doctrinal conclusions by a similar route. They purged the doctrines of the natural lawyers of Aristotelian concepts and principles that seemed wrong or unintelligible to them. They bent and stretched the ideas they retained to make them do the work of those they had abandoned. Then, as authority for their conclusions, they cited a case, the French Civil Code, or a Roman text.

One of the key concepts they retained was that of the will of the contracting parties. This concept figured so prominently in their work that they are commonly said to have developed 'will theories' of contract. Their innovation was not simply to use the concept of will, but to use it almost exclusively. The late scholastics had discussed not only the will, but the virtues of promise-keeping, liberality, and commutative justice, the final cause and essence of a contract, natural terms, and equality in exchange. The natural lawyers still used these concepts, though often with little knowledge of their original Aristotelian meaning. The nineteenth-century jurists rejected them. They were left with few concepts other than the will of the parties.

Jurists today often speak of the age of the will theories as the last time contract law was coherent. Now, as Grant Gilmore said, describing *The Death of Contract*, 'the systems have come unstuck'.[1] Actually, the will theories were never very coherent, and that is why they came unstuck. Almost every important doctrine raised problems the will theorists tried in vain to resolve. As we will see, these problems arose at just the points where the concept of will had been stretched to make it do the work of some earlier concept that had been abandoned. The will theorists had failed to make their theory work without these earlier concepts.

THE BINDING FORCE OF PROMISES

The Enforceability of Promises

The late scholastics recognized that contracts are formed by the will of the parties. By expressing their will, however, the parties exercised the Aristotelian virtues of promise-keeping, liberality, or commutative justice. The late scholastics analysed the binding force of contract in terms of these virtues, and the natural lawyers preserved much of their analysis. The nineteenth-century jurists eliminated the concept of virtue from their discussions and were left with the concept of the will alone.

Like Wolff, they defined contract or promise in terms of consent, agreement, or expression of will. As we have already seen, English and American jurists defined contract in terms of the agreement or assent of the parties. French jurists typically explained that the wills of two or more parties formed an agreement (*convention*), and that an agreement to create an obligation was a contract.[2] German jurists such as Savigny, Puchta, and Windscheid developed a more technical and precise formulation. In enforcing contracts or testaments, and in similar situations, the law produced a certain result because that result had been willed. The will had to be declared outwardly since, as Savigny said, willing is an 'invisible event'.[3] In German terminology, a person's declaration of his will was a

[1] G. Gilmore, *The Death of Contract* (Columbus, Ohio, 1974), 102.

[2] e.g. M. Duranton, *Cours de droit français* (Paris, 1834–7), x, §§51–2; A. M. Demante and E. Colmet de Santerre, *Cours analytique de Code Civil* (Paris, 1883), v, §§2, p. 2 *bis*, 3; C. Demolombe, *Cours de Code Napoléon* (Paris, 1854–82), xxiv, §12; F. Laurent, *Principes de droit civil français* (Paris, 1869–78), xv, §§424–7; M. L. Larombière, *Theorie et pratique des obligations* (Paris, 1857), i, §41.

[3] F. C. von Savigny, *System des heutigen Römischen Rechts* (Berlin, 1840–8), iii, §134, p. 258.

Willenserklärung. His act in declaring his will so that a legal result would follow was a 'juristic act' or *Rechtsgeschäft*. Juristic acts such as testaments required the declaration of will of one party only. Contracts, in contrast, required the declaration of will of two or more parties.[4]

The nineteenth-century jurists, Anglo-American, French, or German, did not explain why contracts were binding or enforceable. They simply defined binding and enforceable contracts in terms of will or consent. They did not give a reason why the will of the parties ought to be respected. As Ranouil observes of the French will theorists, the binding force of contract was taken for granted rather then demonstrated.[5] She quotes Gounot's description of their view: 'The contract is obligatory simply because it is the contract.'[6]

The most famous critics of the will theorists later attacked them, not simply for emphasizing the will, but for refusing to explain why the will of the parties should be binding. In Germany, Ihering denounced them for ignoring the purposes for which the parties enter into contracts or the law enforces them.[7] Duguit, citing Ihering, made the same arguments in France.[8] In the United States, Roscoe Pound attacked 'mechanical jurisprudence, a condition of juristic thought and judicial action in which deductions from conceptions are developed logically at the expense of practical results . . .'.[9] He was criticizing those who defined contract in terms of the consent of the parties and then, without giving any other reason, insisted that anything to which the parties consented should be enforced.

To have a theory of why the law enforces contracts is more difficult than Ihering, Duguit, and Pound seem to have realized. The theory of the late scholastics relied on the philosophy of Aristotle and Thomas Aquinas, which provided an ultimate standard beyond the immediate and conflicting wills of the contracting parties. Hobbes and Locke had tried to do without this ultimate standard, only to run into the objections raised by Hume.

[4] See ibid., §104, pp. 5–7; G. F. Puchta, *Pandekten* (Leipzig, 1844), §§49, 54; B. Windscheid, *Lehrbuch des Pandektenrechts* (Frankfurt-on-Main, 1891), i, §69.

[5] V. Ranouil, *L'Autonomie de la volonté: naissance et évolution d'un concept* (Paris, 1980), 71–2.

[6] E. Gounot, *Le Principe de l'autonomie de la volonté en droit privé: contribution a l'étude critique de l'individualisme juridique* (thesis, Paris, 1912), 129; quoted by Ranouil, *supra* n. 5, p. 72, n. 31.

[7] R. Ihering, *Zweck im Recht* 3rd edn. (Leipzig, 1898).

[8] L. Duguit, *Les Transformations générales du Droit privé depuis le Code Napoléon*, 2nd edn. (Paris, 1920), 72–3, 97–8.

[9] Pound, 'Liberty of Contract', *Yale Law Journal*, 18 (1908–9), 454 at 457.

The nineteenth-century jurists wished to avoid these philosophical problems.

Nevertheless, by trying to do so, they set themselves an impossible task, as their critics recognized. They had to explain rules that were in force in order to serve human purposes by a definition that abstracted from those purposes. It was like trying to explain a machine without regard to its function. The rules of contract law they were trying to explain did not treat all expressions of the will of the parties the same way. The will theorists could not have explained the differences in treatment without speaking, not merely of the will of the parties, but of the reasons the will should be respected.

Consideration and Causa

For the late scholastics, as we have seen, the parties could promise either an act of liberality or an act of commutative justice. The doctrine of *causa* identified liberality and commutative justice as the two legitimate purposes or good reasons for the parties to contract. For the nineteenth-century jurists, the doctrine of *causa*, and, indeed, the distinction between liberality and exchange, were problematic. These jurists no longer discussed virtues and supposedly were interested only in what the parties willed, not in whether the purposes they sought to achieve were good.

The French jurists nevertheless discussed *cause* (the French word for *causa*). The French Civil Code required a contract to have a *cause*.[10] Here, as elsewhere, the Code had preserved the doctrines of the natural lawyers, which was not surprising since the drafters had taken nearly all the provisions of contracts almost verbatim from the works of Domat and Pothier.

French jurists used traditional formulas to state the doctrine. In gratuitous contracts, the *cause* of an obligation was to perform an act of liberality or render a service.[11] In an onerous contract it was the advantage each party intended to obtain;[12] the *cause* of each party's obligation was the obligation of the other party.[13] Nevertheless, these formulas now had to be explained without referring to the virtues of liberality and commutative justice. For nineteenth-century jurists, liberality no longer meant a virtue of right giving, and exchange no longer meant an act of commutative justice that required equality. Consequently, the doctrine of *cause* began to

[10] According to Article 1131, 'An obligation without a *cause* or on a false *cause* or on an unlawful *cause* can have no effect.' See also Article 1108, trans. in n. 14 below.

[11] C. Aubry and C. Rau, *Cours de droit civil français* (Paris, 1869–71), iv, §345; Demolombe, *supra* n. 2, xxiv, §352; Larombière, *supra* n. 2, i. 272.

[12] Aubry and Rau, *supra* n. 2, iv, §345.

[13] Demolombe, *supra* n. 2, xxiv, §346; Larombière, *supra* n. 2, i. 272.

seem pointless. It seemed to mean merely that a party must have some motive for contracting, and the motive must be either to get something or not to get something.

French jurists were aware of the difficulty. They frequently observed that it was difficult to imagine a contract without a *cause*.[14] Despite their efforts, it remained difficult. Aubry and Rau said the *cause* had to be a 'legally sufficient motive'.[15] As Laurent observed, however, that explanation was not helpful unless one could explain what constituted a legally sufficient motive.[16] Toullier said that a contract without a *cause* must have been one entered into by mistake.[17] If that were so, however, it seemed pointless to have a doctrine of *cause* in addition to a doctrine of mistake. In any case, article 1131 of the French Civil Code said that 'an obligation without a *cause*' was invalid as well as one with 'a false *cause*'. Demolombe suggested that a contract lacked a *cause* if it concerned a non-existent object, for example if the parties sold a harvest that was never produced.[18] Similarly, Larombière suggested that a purchase of one's own property would be a contract without a *cause*. In the end, however, he conceded that such an example was really only another instance of mistake.[19] No one could find a convincing reason for there to be a doctrine of *cause*.

The French also ran into trouble distinguishing between gratuitous contracts and contracts of exchange. They wished to do so not only because these transactions were supposed to have different *causes*, but because they were governed by different rules. In particular, unexecuted promises of a gift of property were not binding unless notarized.

The late scholastics had distinguished gratuitous and onerous contracts with the aid of two concepts the nineteenth-century jurists

[14] C. B. M. Toullier, *Le Droit civil français* (Paris, 1869–78), vi, §166; Demante and Colmet de Santerre, *supra* n. 2, v, §47; Aubry and Rau, *supra* n. 11, iv, §345 n. 7; Demolombe, *supra* n. 2, xxiv, §357. Laurent had a more elaborate argument. According to Article 1108 of the French Civil Code, 'Four conditions are essential for the validity of an agreement: the consent of the party who obligates himself; his capacity to contract; a definite object that forms the matter of the engagement; a lawful *cause* of the obligation.' Since the *cause* of an onerous contract was the obligation of the other party, Laurent argued, there was no difference between saying the contract must have a *cause* and saying it must have a 'definite object'. Thus, the requirement of a *cause* was superfluous. (Laurent, *supra* n. 2, xvi, §§110–11.) In a gratuitous contract, the *cause* was the will to confer a benefit, which meant merely the will to give, and so there was no difference between saying the contract had a *cause* and saying the donor consented. Again, the requirement of a *cause* was superfluous. (Laurent, *supra* n. 2, xvi, §111.)

[15] Aubry and Rau, *supra* n. 11, iv, §345.

[16] Laurent, *supra* n. 2, xvi, §109.

[17] Toullier, *supra* n. 14, vi, §168.

[18] Demolombe, *supra* n. 2, xxiv, §357.

[19] Larombière, *supra* n. 2, i. 273–5.

had abandoned: final cause and equality in exchange. The concept of final cause allowed them to define these transactions in terms of a single purpose or end: in a gratuitous transaction, to perform an act of liberality; in an exchange, to receive an equivalent for what one gave. The concept of equality in exchange allowed them to distinguish the effects of these transactions on the wealth of the parties: in a gift, one party enriched the other; in an exchange, neither party was enriched.

The final cause was the end that defined a type of transaction. In this sense, it was 'the end' of the transaction, even though under the particular circumstances that end might not be accomplished. The parties must have entered into the transaction with that end in view; otherwise, they would have entered into a different type of transaction. In this sense, the final cause was 'the end' of the contracting parties even though they had other ends as well, and these other ends varied from one party to the next.

With the concept of final cause all but forgotten,[20] French jurists found it hard to explain how a transaction could be defined by an end that, under some circumstances, might never be attained. Larombière said that a gratuitous contract must be defined according to 'its nature and conditions *intimes*, independently of extrinsic circumstances that can alter its efficacy and destroy the advantages' it is intended to confer. It remains a gratuitous contract even if it results in no profit for the alleged beneficiary. It does not cease to be an onerous contract even if it procures one party an advantage at the

[20] Demolombe, borrowing a phrase from the past, said that the *cause* was 'in a word, the final cause (*cause finale*) of the obligation itself'. (Demolombe, *supra* n. 2, xxiv, §345.) Demolombe devoted no more than a word to the subject, and it is doubtful that he had the original meaning of the phrase in mind. As Laurent objected, for him 'to say that the *cause* is the final cause is almost to say the *cause* is the *cause*'. (Laurent, *supra* n. 2, xvi, §107.)

A return to the Aristotelian concept of final cause was actually attempted in an article by Labord, 'Applications de la théorie de la cause aux matières du droit et principalement aux obligations', *Revue générale du droit, de la législation et de la jurisprudence en France et a l'étranger*, 5 (1881), 344, 397, 548. He explained that the efficient cause brings a thing into being, and in the case of a voluntary act the efficient cause was the will. Human beings act, however, because of a final cause, 'which is revealed by the very nature of the act, which does not change whatever the circumstances are of time or place in which the act is performed, whatever the person is who performs it', and which is the 'immediate and apparent end' of the act (p. 348). The other motives that inspire the act 'accidentally' are occasional causes (pp. 348–9). As Labord acknowledged, he was not simply applying a 'legal theory'. 'The theory of cause', he said, 'is the greatest that the mind can conceive.' 'It pertains to the domain of philosophy where it explains the origin of things and beings and the different motives of human actions' (p. 348). There was little discussion of Labord's solution among the jurists. It was hardly a feasible project to revive Aristotle's theory of the four causes in a law review article. In any event, the jurists had little desire to enter the 'domain of philosophy'.

expense of the other. Larombière concluded that 'the description of an act is therefore independent of extrinsic events'.[21] He did not explain how that could be except for his mysterious reference to 'nature and conditions *intimes*'.

Other French jurists observed that the *cause* of a given type of transaction must be the same for every party even though different individuals enter into such a transaction with different motives. As Aubry and Rau observed, the buyer of a horse might plan to give the animal to a third party. Nevertheless, the transaction is onerous, and its *cause* is acquiring the horse, not making a gift.[22] As Demolombe said, motives could vary from one individual to the next, but the *cause* of identical types of contracts must be the same no matter who entered into them.[23]

No one, however, found a good way to distinguish the *cause* from the contracting party's other ends or motives. Demolombe, following Toullier and Demante, said the *cause* was a 'determining' rather than 'impulsive' motive.[24] As Laurent pointed out, they left the meaning of 'determining' and 'impulsive' completely obscure.[25] Demante, Demolombe, and Aubry and Rau drew an almost unintelligible distinction: *cause* was the reason or motive for which the party obligated himself, as distinguished from the reasons or motives for which he contracted.[26] Everyone agreed, as Larombière said, that the *cause* was 'something other than a mere motive',[27] but no one including Larombière could explain the difference.

Laurent concluded that *cause* could not be a motive precisely because motives vary from one person to the next while the *cause* had to be the same for a given type of transaction.[28] But then, it seemed, one could not define the difference between gift and exchange in terms of the motive or intention of the contracting parties.

Another concept the nineteenth-century jurists had abandoned was that of equality in the value of the performances exchanged. As we shall see, they thought this concept involved a paternalistic attitude towards the parties and mystical notions of value. Yet the lack of this concept was also a difficulty for French jurists who wished to explain the difference between gift and exchange. If a

[21] Larombière, *supra* n. 2, i. 27.

[22] Aubry and Rau, *supra* n. 11, iv, §345, n. 2.

[23] Demolombe, *supra* n. 2, xxiv, §355.

[24] Toullier, *supra* n. 14, vi, §168; Demante and Colmet de Santerre, *supra* n. 2, v, §46 (by Demante); Demolombe, *supra* n. 2, xxiv, §§345, 354–5.

[25] Laurent, *supra* n. 2, xvi, §107.

[26] Demante and Colmet de Santerre, *supra* n. 2, v, §46 (by Demante); Aubry and Rau, *supra* n. 11, iv, §345, n. 2; Demolombe, *supra* n. 2, xxiv, §355.

[27] Larombière, *supra* n. 2, i. 281–2.

[28] Laurent, *supra* n. 2, xvi, §109.

kindly uncle sells his nephew an expensive car for a small price, the transaction does not seem to be purely a gift or purely an exchange. Yet it is difficult to explain why without speaking of an inequality in the value of the performances. Indeed, Larombière found it necessary to do so. He said that such a transaction is neither gift nor exchange but 'mixed' because the values exchanged are intended to be disparate.[29] He did not explain why he felt entitled to use the concept of equality of exchange in this context and to ignore it in every other.

The German jurists were struggling with a similar problem. They, too, had a rule that unexecuted promises to make gifts of property were not binding unless notarized. For most of the century, they defined a gift as a transfer of property intended by the transferor to enrich the recipient, most of them adding that the recipient must be enriched with his own consent and at the transferor's expense.[30]

The late scholastics had also defined gift in terms of an intention to enrich. They meant, however, that the donor must intend to benefit the donee. Not conceiving of a gift as an act of liberality, the German jurists meant that the donor, for whatever motive, must wish the donee to be richer. Dernburg explained that the 'distant motive' of the donor did not matter. The donor could give out of concern for the donee's well-being. But he could also give to show off or to obtain someone's affection or the protection of a powerful person.[31] A late scholastic would have described all of these cases as instances of liberality, provided the donor intended to confer a benefit on another. To the late scholastic, the gift made to show off would be an act of liberality performed for a bad remote end, as in Thomas's example of almsgiving out of vainglory.[32] The other gifts would be acts of liberality that are also acts of the Aristotelian virtue of friendship (*amicitia*)—in the case of the gift to obtain protection, an act of the special type of friendship Thomas and Aristotle called *amicitia utilis*, friendship based on exchange of favours.[33] In contrast, Dernburg and other German jurists were trying to separate the donor's intention that the donee should have the property from any reason why the donor would wish him to have it.

As some German jurists noted, the ultimate consequence of this way of defining a gift was that one could not speak of the enrichment of the donee as a state of affairs that the donor necessarily desired to

[29] Larombière, *supra* n. 2, i. 26–7.

[30] A. Brinz and P. Lotmar, *Lehrbuch der Pandekten* (Erlangen, 1892), iv, §560; F. von Keller, *Pandekten* (Leipzig, 1861), §63; H. Dernburg, *Pandekten* (Berlin, 1894), ii, §161; Puchta, *supra* n. 4, §68; Windscheid, *supra* n. 4, ii, §365.

[31] Dernburg, *supra* n. 30, ii, §161.

[32] Ch. 2 above, p. 21.

[33] *Nicomachean Ethics*, VIII. iii. 1156ᵃ.

bring about. Although Brinz and Vangerow spoke of an 'intention to enrich', they warned that the concept was entirely 'negative': it meant the absence of an intention to settle a debt or create an obligation.[34] Lenel, after pointing out how varied the motives of the donor might be, argued that one should not define gift in terms of an intention to enrich or any other purpose of the donor. The only distinguishing feature of a gift was negative: 'the purpose must not be directed toward securing a recompense (*Entgelt*)'.[35]

In 1887, two years before Lenel made this suggestion, the First Drafting Commission completed its draft of the German Civil Code. Following the view then held by the jurists, the drafters defined gift in terms of an intention to enrich.[36] The Second Drafting Commission was appointed in 1890 and completed its draft in 1895. Following Lenel,[37] drafters defined gift negatively, by the absence of recompense. Lenel, however, had said that the donor must not have the purpose of securing a recompense. The drafters provided: 'A disposition by which one person enriches another out of his property is a gift if both parties are agreed that the disposition is to occur without recompense (*unentgeltlich erfolgt*).'[38]

The drafters did not explain why they changed Lenel's formula. They may well have noticed that the law of gift was in danger of colliding with the law of unjust enrichment.[39] The aim of the law of unjust enrichment was to prevent transfers of wealth that took place for no good reason. As the law was normally stated, a gift was a good reason; the mere absence of a purpose to seek recompense for the transfer was not. The drafters solved that problem by speaking

[34] Brinz and Lotmar, *supra* n. 30, iv, §560; K. von Vangerow, *Leitfaden für Pandekten-Vorlesungen* (Marburg, 1847), i, §121.

[35] Lenel, 'Die Lehre von der Voraussetzung', *Archiv für die zivilistische Praxis*, 74 (1889), 213 at 232.

[36] Entwurf, §437. The drafters explained that they were following the 'herrschenden Ansicht'. (*Motive zu dem Entwurfe eines Bürgerliches Gesetzbuches für das Deutsche Reich* (Berlin and Leipzig, 1888), ii. 286.)

[37] J. Dawson, *Gifts and Promises* (New Haven, Conn., 1980), 137–9.

[38] Bürgerlichesgesetzbuch, art. 516, par. 1.

[39] Dawson notes that, since no reasons were given for the change, we have to guess why it occurred. (Dawson, *supra* n. 37, p. 139.) His guess, however, is different than mine. He thought the drafters were acting on 'their conviction that gifts, like other contracts, were the product of mutual assent. From this premise it seemed to follow that the agreement of both parties was needed to establish an attribute that had suddenly been made essential: they must have *agreed* to exclude any recompense for the gain to be conferred' (p. 139). I agree that the drafters thought that gifts, like other contracts, required mutual assent, and hence an acceptance by the donee. Nevertheless, they did not simply say the donee must accept the gift; they said that both parties must agree on the absence of recompense. When the First Drafting Commission merely wished to say the donee must accept, it said 'and the other [party] accepts it as a gift'. (Entwurf §437, *Motive*, *supra* n. 36, ii. 286.) It is hard to believe that is all the Second Drafting Commission meant.

not of the absence of such a purpose, but of an agreement by the parties that there would be no recompense. The solution, however, was makeshift. Those who give and receive gifts understand that there will be no recompense, but they hardly ever agree that there will not be. Yet the drafters saw no alternative.

Once again, it had proven difficult to define gift without the older Aristotelian concepts. In the Aristotelian tradition, when jurists said that the final cause of a gift was liberality, they identified both an intention the donor must have and a good purpose he was trying to achieve. To the German jurists, it seemed that donors might have any number of purposes in view, good or otherwise. They tried to define gift without regard to the purposes the donor was pursuing. At some point a conflict with the law of unjust enrichment was inevitable, since it requires that there be a good purpose.

As in France, moreover, it also proved difficult to do without the concept of equality in exchange when discussing mixed transactions in which the parties intended one performance to be worth more than the other. Keller, Vangerow, and the Austrian jurist Unger found it necessary to speak of the 'true worth' of an object. According to them, if the value of one party's performance is above or below the 'true worth' of that of the other party, the transaction is a gift if the party who loses intends to enrich the party who gains.[40] Yet as we shall see, 'true worth' was a concept the jurists found repugnant in other contexts.

In France and Germany, then, the nineteenth-century jurists were unable to explain as basic a distinction as that between gift and exchange. This major failure in theory, however, had little effect upon practice. The chief practical consequence of calling a transaction a gift was that the promisor was not bound before he performed unless his promise was notarized. The courts did not need a theory to apply this rule in ordinary cases. When they deviated from the results common sense would dictate, it was usually to enforce unnotarized promises of gifts to charities and other worthy causes. In such cases, they defied theory and also twisted the rules they were supposed to be applying. The French courts found flimsy excuses for enforcing such contracts. For example, they would call a gift an exchange because the donor had received some intangible benefit.[41]

[40] Keller, *supra* n. 30, §63; Vangerow, *supra* n. 34, §121; J. Unger, *System des osterreichischen allgemeinen Privatrechts* (Leipzig, 1892), ii, §95. Similarly, the First Drafting Commission said that as a matter of common sense such transactions are gifts; see *Motive*, *supra* n. 36 ii.287.

[41] e.g. Decision of 5 Feb. 1923, cass., ch. civ., D. 1923. I.20; Decision of 15 March 1900, trib. civ., Langres, D. 1900.II.422; Decision of 19 July 1894, cass. ch. civ., D. 1895.I.125. See Dawson, *supra* n. 37, pp. 84–96.

By a forced interpretation of the Code, German courts decided that a transfer of property to a charity was not a gift since the charity was a conduit to the ultimate beneficiary.[42] The theorists had purged the law of the concept of virtue, but the courts bent rules to enforce contracts made with virtuous intentions.

The most remarkable response to the problem of distinguishing gift from exchange came from the Anglo-American jurists. They were preoccupied with the meaning of 'consideration'. As described earlier, they had inherited a rule that an action of assumpsit would lie only on a promise that had consideration. The meaning of this requirement was quite unclear. Nevertheless, the early nineteenth-century treatise writers identified consideration with the *causa* of an onerous contract. They were borrowing extensively from continental sources, and *causa* was the only concept they found in these sources that approximated the doctrine they were trying to explain.

For a long time, the common lawyers explained consideration with a formula borrowed from the natural lawyers. Consideration was 'the motive' or 'the reason' for contracting. The difficulties in saying so without using the Aristotelian notion of final cause were not yet apparent. Sometimes they even spoke of consideration as an equivalent in value. Langdell claimed

> that the law has never in theory abandoned the principle that a consideration must be commensurate with the obligation which is given in exchange for it; that, though the smallest consideration would in most cases support the largest promise, this is only because the law shuts its eyes to the inequality between them; and hence any inequality to which the law cannot shut its eyes is fatal to the validity of the promise.[43]

He also spoke of consideration as the sole motive for promising:

> As every consideration is in theory equal to the promise in value, so it is in theory the promisor's sole inducement to make the promise. As the law cannot see any inequality in value between the consideration and the promise, so it cannot see any motive for the promise except the consideration.[44]

These traditional formulas did not seem to work in cases described earlier in which courts had found consideration for a contract even though there was no exchange in any ordinary sense. Langdell explained these cases by having the law close its eyes an improbable amount of the time. A peppercorn would be consideration for a

[42] e.g. Decision of 7 May 1909, Reichsgericht, 7th Civil Senate, 71 Entscheidungen des Reichsgerichts in Zivilsachen 140.

[43] C. C. Langdell, *Summary of the Law of Contracts* (Boston, 1880), 70–1.

[44] Ibid. 78–9.

house. A dollar would not be consideration for a larger sum of money, he explained, because in that case the law could shut it eyes no longer.[45]

Langdell did not explain what he meant by sole motive or equality in the values exchanged. A new theory of consideration was built by Oliver Wendell Holmes and Sir Frederick Pollock, to whom these notions did not make sense. Holmes pointed out that a party does not have *a* reason or motive to contract, but a variety of reasons. 'A man may promise to paint a picture for five hundred dollars, while his chief motive may be a desire for fame.'[46] Pollock introduced his own discussion of consideration by quoting Thomas Hobbes: '[T]he value of all things contracted for, is measured by the appetite of the contractors, and therefore the just value, is that which they be contented to give.'[47]

Holmes and Pollock never doubted that, as Langdell and the earlier treatise writers had said, consideration meant the presence of a bargain or exchange. They tried to explain bargain without depending on such concepts as sole motive or equality in exchange. According to Pollock, whatever 'a man chooses to bargain for must be conclusively taken to be of some value to him'.[48] That was so even if the man himself had received nothing, consideration having moved to a third party. The rule that a court will not 'enter into an inquiry as to the adequacy of consideration' is reached 'by a deduction' from this principle.[49] Therefore, to say that the promisor entered into a bargain simply means that he was induced to give his promise by some change in the position of the promisee. Pollock argued:

> Consideration means not so much that one party is profited as that the other abandons some legal right in the present, or limits his legal freedom of action in the future, as an inducement for the promise of the first. It does not matter whether the party accepting the consideration has any apparent benefit thereby or not. . . .[50]

Using only the notions of detriment and inducement, and without introducing any theoretical requirements of 'equal value' and 'sole motive', Pollock reached essentially the same results as Langdell.

[45] Similar to Langdell's views were those of Edward Q. Keasbey, 'The Origin and Nature of Consideration in the Law of Contract', *New Jersey Law Journal*, 5 (1883), 1, 296, 324. Citing Langdell with favour (p. 325), he said that consideration 'must be some thing which the law may regard as an equivalent' (pp. 300, 325, 328, 330).

[46] O. W. Holmes, *The Common Law* (Boston, 1881), 293.

[47] F. Pollock, *Principles of Contract* (London, 1885), 172. The quotation is from T. Hobbes, *Leviathan*, I. xv. 102.

[48] Pollock, *supra* n. 47 (10th edn. 1936), 172.

[49] Ibid.

[50] Ibid. 164.

Nominal consideration will support a promise because 'the promisor has got all that he bargained for'.[51] Past consideration and performance or promise of performance of a pre-existing duty are not consideration because they are not a legal detriment for which the promisor could have bargained. Pollock expressly dismissed the questions whether equivalent values are exchanged and whether the promisor's sole motive was to obtain the consideration as devoid of legal significance.[52]

Although Pollock worked out this theory in successive editions of his treatise, the core idea was present in the first edition: 'the leading and characteristic point of the modern learning of Consideration [is] that when a thing is done at a man's request the law does not ask whether it is for his apparent benefit, but takes it as against him to be of the value he has himself chosen to put upon it.'[53] Pollock sent a copy of this edition to Oliver Wendell Holmes,[54] and he was greatly impressed. 'I am just now writing that part of my course which deals with contracts,' he wrote to Pollock, 'and am struck anew with the value of your book. I referred to your account of Consideration in one of my articles as the best which I had seen.'[55] In his book *The Common Law*, Holmes espoused much the same theory. Any act or forbearance which the promisee has a legal right to perform or not as he pleases constitutes a detriment, and will constitute consideration if, in addition, the detriment is incurred as an inducement to the making of the promise and the promise is given as an inducement to the incurring of the detriment.[56]

This formulation of the doctrine of consideration became classic, less because it resolved the theoretical problem of distinguishing gift from exchange than because nobody could think of a better alternative. Indeed, problems with the formulation were seen almost immediately. Ames pointed out that, if the value of the performance the promisor bargains for does not matter, it is hard to see why consideration must be a 'fresh' detriment rather than performance of a pre-existing duty.[57] Indeed, Ames argued, all mutual promises ought to be consideration for each other. It should not matter whether the promise could create a new legal obligation or, for that matter, any legal obligation at all. If one party is induced to

[51] Ibid. 175. [52] Ibid. 165, 172.

[53] Pollock, *supra* n. 47 (1st edn. 1876), 150–1.

[54] Letter from Pollock to Holmes, 16 Dec. 1875, in *Holmes–Pollock Letters*, 2nd edn., ed. M. Howe (Cambridge, Mass., 1961), i. 276.

[55] Letter from Holmes to Pollock, 17 June 1880, in ibid. i. 14, 15.

[56] Holmes, *supra* n. 46, pp. 293–4.

[57] Ames, 'Two Theories of Consideration', *Harvard Law Review*, 12 (1899), 515 at 515–17; 13 (1899), 29 at 37–42.

make his own promise by the other party's very act of making his, that act is itself one that the first party desires.[58]

Pollock replied that the promisee was not seeking to obtain 'the utterance of words of promise',[59] but rather 'the assurance of the performance to which the promisor obligates himself'.[60] But this answer was clearly inadequate. Ames's objection to it—as well as Williston's—was that it was circular. The only reason the promisee obtained an 'assurance' of performance was because the promise was legally binding on the promisor; the only reason it was legally binding was because the contract was supported by consideration; and the reason it was supported by consideration was that both sides had given and obtained this 'assurance'.[61] Pollock and Holmes virtually conceded the circularity. They both agreed, as Holmes said, that 'it is a case of jumping in—call one binding and both are. It is more convenient to say both bind than that neither does, therefore *voilà vous êtes* . . .'.[62]

This concession seemed to Ames, to Williston, and later to Corbin to cast grave doubt on the whole theory. It is hard to see the point of a theory of consideration that cannot account for the enforcement of mutual promises. The theory is supposedly based on the principle that bargains should be enforced. Yet, in terms of the theory, an exchange of promises is a bargain only because it is arbitrarily said to be.

Ames's theory, however, was equally hard to accept, or at least it was for most people. If Ames were right, promises to accept gifts would be consideration for promises to give them, and even illusory promises would support a contract.[63] Indeed, if all mutual promises are to be termed 'bargains', the point of enforcing bargains is far from clear, and denying enforcement to promises that are not bargains is almost inexplicable.

Williston suggested:

> [N]o briefer definition of sufficient consideration . . . can be given than this: Mutual promises each of which assures some act or forebearance that will be, or apparently may be, detrimental to the promisor or beneficial to the promisee, and neither of which is rendered void by any rule of law other

[58] Ames, 'Two Theories of Consideration', *Harvard Law Review*, 13 (1899), 29 and 29.

[59] Pollock, *supra* n. 47 (10th edn. 1936), 179

[60] Ibid. 180.

[61] Ames, *supra* n. 57, 13 (1899), 29 at 31; Williston, 'Successive Promises of the Same Performance', *Harvard Law Review*, 8 (1894), 27 at 35.

[62] Letter from Holmes to Pollock, 18 Dec. 1910, in *Holmes–Pollock Letters*, *supra* n. 54, i. 172; Pollock, *supra* n. 47 (19th edn. 1936), 179.

[63] See Williston, 'Consideration in Bilateral Contracts', *Harvard Law Review*, 27 (1914), 503 at 516–18.

than that relating to consideration, are sufficient consideration for each other.[64]

The approach taken here, as Williston notes, is 'to revise slightly the test of consideration in a bilateral contract, seeking the detriment necessary to support a counter-promise, in the thing promised, and not in the promise itself'.[65] In a 'unilateral' contract no revision was necessary, and the detriment could still be found in the thing actually done or given.

Williston's solution was an attempt to define consideration in a manner free from paradox. It did not resolve or even address the theoretical problems that had emerged from the Pollock–Ames debate. Without the concept of equality or some other way of taking economic value into account, there seemed to be no reason for insisting that a detriment be 'fresh'. Without the concept of final cause or sole motive or some other way of distinguishing among the promisor's motives, there seemed to be no way of saying that 'the inducement' was the thing promised rather than the legal obligation created by the promise or the 'utterance of the words of promise', since the promisor desired all of these.

In short, it became extremely difficult to explain the difference between gift and exchange when the only concepts one had to work with were the promisor's will or motives on the one hand and the promisee's ability to do something the promisor wanted on the other.

Offer and Acceptance

The nineteenth-century jurists agreed that an offer had to be accepted to be binding. This conclusion had been reached by some of the late scholastics and most of the natural lawyers. For them, however, this conclusion was far from obvious. Since all promises were binding as a matter of fidelity, Covarruvias, Soto, and Molina had denied that an acceptance was necessary. Lessius had argued it was the promisor's *sine qua non* condition to be bound.

In contrast, like Wolff, the nineteenth-century jurists extracted their conclusions from the definition of contract. The common lawyers defined contract as mutual assent, the French as a concord of wills, the Germans as a two-sided juristic act (*Rechtsgeschäft*) formed by the declarations of will (*Willenserklärungen*) of both parties. Therefore, they concluded, an unaccepted offer is not a contract and is not binding. In England and the United States this argument was made by Kent, Dodd, Carey, William Story, Parsons,

[64] Ibid. 527–8. [65] Williston, *supra* n. 61, p. 35.

Metcalf, Leake, Hammon, and Anson.[66] In France it was made by Aubry and Rau, Demolombe, Larombière, and Laurent.[67] In Germany it was made by Brinz, Puchta, and Windscheid.[68]

Thus, the nineteenth-century jurists defined an acceptance to be necessary without discussion of any purpose that such a requirement would serve. For Thomas and the late scholastics, since the essence of a human action had to be defined in terms of its end, reasoning from a definition and reasoning in terms of purpose went together. As we have seen, however, the nineteenth-century jurists had formulated their definitions of contract without regard to why a contract should be binding. Once they had done so, it was difficult for them to take purposes into account. Consequently it was hard for them to explain why contract should be defined to require an acceptance.

Sir Frederick Pollock was one of the few to point out that contract did not have to be defined in that way. The law could make a promise binding without mutual assent. Indeed, at common law, 'promises' made by deed were irrevocable without any need for an acceptance.[69] Pollock concluded there were 'difficulties . . . in making proposal and acceptance parts of the general conception of contract'.[70] He did not explain why an acceptance was necessary, however. He merely observed that 'in practice' proposal and acceptance 'are the normal and most important elements' of a contract.[71] Like the other jurists, Pollock lacked a starting-point from which to discuss when promises should be binding. The virtue of fidelity had once provided such a starting-point. The nineteenth-century jurists had not found an alternative. It was difficult for them to avoid presenting their conclusions in the form of definitions. Indeed, at one point Pollock fell into the tautology he had just

[66] J. Kent, *Commentaries on American Law* (Boston, 1884), ii.*477; Dodd, 'On the Construction of Contracts–Assent–Construction', *The Legal Observer*, 12 (1836), 249 at 249–50; Carey, 'A Course of Lectures on the Law of Contract: Lecture I', *The Law Times*, 4 (1845), 463 at 505; W. W. Story, *The Law of Contracts Not Under Seal* (Boston, 1851), 370; Parsons, *The Law of Contracts* (Boston, 1860), i.*399; T. Metcalf, *Principles of the Law of Contracts* (New York, 1878), 14; S. Leake, *Elements of the Law of Contracts* (London, 1867), 12; L. Hammon, *General Principles of the Law of Contract* (St Paul, 1912), 38; W. Anson, *Principles of the English Law of Contract* (London, 1989), 13.

[67] Aubry and Rau, *supra* n. 11, iv. §343; Demolombe, *supra* n. 2, xxiv, §45; Larombière, *supra* n. 2, i. 6–7; Laurent, *supra* n. 2, xv, §§468–9.

[68] Brinz and Lotmar, *supra* n. 30, iv, §571; Puchta, *supra* n. 4, §250; Windscheid, *supra* n. 4, ii, §§304–5. Dernburg was one of the few who gave a reason why an offer should have to be accepted. He said that an obligation could not arise against a party's will; therefore the offeree must eventually assent. To explain why he had to assent right away, Dernburg said that it was not desirable for a half-completed legal relationship to persist for a long time. (Dernburg, *supra* n. 30, ii, §12.)

[69] Pollock, *supra* n. 47, 6–7.

[70] Ibid. 9.

[71] Ibid.

criticized: 'before acceptance there is no agreement, and therefore the proposer cannot be bound to do anything.'[72]

The nineteenth-century jurists then considered the moment in time at which a contract became binding. Lessius, Grotius, and Pufendorf had analysed this problem by asking at what moment the offeror would have wished to be bound. The method of the nineteenth-century jurists again committed them to analysing the problem without regard to the purposes of the offeror or anyone else. They again tried to extract a conclusion from their definition of contract. A contract was formed, they argued, as soon as the requirements of the definition were satisfied, that is as soon as there was mutual assent, a concord of wills, or two *Willenserklärungen*. They then discussed whether this moment occurred when the will was expressed or when the expression of will was communicated to the other party or at some other point in time.

As a result, the nineteenth-century jurists found themselves in a dilemma. They wanted their conclusions to follow logically from the definition of contract. On the other hand, since this method did not take account of the purposes of the parties, it could easily produce conclusions that thwarted these purposes. Langdell claimed not to care. He thought an acceptance was effective when communicated even though 'it has been claimed that the purposes of substantial justice, and the interests of contracting parties as understood by themselves, will be best served' if acceptances were effective on dispatch. 'The true answer to this argument', he said, 'is, that it is irrelevant . . .'.[73] Having said so, however, he tried to show that the interests of the parties would be served by the rule he advocated. Few jurists genuinely wished to ignore these interests. Yet their method required them to seem to do so. Consequently, they found themselves playing a strange game. They arrived at conclusions with the parties' needs in mind, and then tried to show that these conclusions could be derived from a definition of contract that disregarded those needs.

Various conclusions could be said with some plausibility to follow from the definition of contract. The trouble was that all of them seemed to frustrate the offeree's need to know whether or not a contract had been formed. According to the French jurists Duranton, Aubry and Rau, and Demolombe,[74] and the German jurists Puchta

[72] Ibid. 23. At another point he said, inconsistently, that nothing but the requirement of consideration prevents an offer from being irrevocable when the promisor has promised not to revoke it (p. 24).

[73] Langdell, *supra* n. 33, pp. 15, 20–1.

[74] Duranton, *supra* n. 2, xvi, §45; Aubry and Rau, *supra* n. 11, iv, §343; Demolombe, *supra* n. 2, xv, §§73–5.

and Windscheid,[75] a declaration of will was effective when the will was declared whether or not the other party had yet learned of the declaration of will. The offeree's acceptance was thus effective at the moment the offeree declared his will. But then, so it seemed, the offeror's revocation of his offer would be effective as soon as he declared his will to revoke. Consequently, the offeree could not be certain that a contract had been formed when he accepted, since it was always possible that the offeror had already revoked, for example in a letter that had not yet reached the offeree. Puchta acknowledged this consequence;[76] Aubry and Rau, Demolombe, and Windscheid tried to find a reason the offeror could not revoke with impunity.

This view had another consequence that jurists at the time found bizarre. The offeree who had mailed his acceptance could not change his mind and revoke it before it came to the attention of the offeror. Aubry and Rau tried to avoid this result by saying that an acceptance was effective only if the offeree lost power over his acceptance, as for example when he used the mails.[77] Windscheid said that the offeree could withdraw his acceptance before the declaration had reached the offeror. The reason was that, until the offeror received it, the declaration still belonged to the offeree. It might seem odd, Windscheid acknowledged, that the offeror was bound as soon as the offeree declared his will to accept but the offeree was not bound until the offeror received his acceptance. But, he argued, nothing in the definition of a two-sided juristic act (*Rechtsgeschäft*) prevents one party from being bound to a contract when the other is not.[78]

Other jurists, such as Langdell in the United States,[79] Larombière, Laurent, and Troplong in France,[80] and Brinz and Vangerow in Germany,[81] said that a declaration of will was not effective until the party to whom it was addressed had actual knowledge of it. They argued that communication or consensus requires not merely that the parties will the same thing, but that they manifest their will to each other. By this view, revocations of offers were not effective until the offeree knew of them. But, it seemed, the offeree could not be sure he had a contract at the moment he dispatched his acceptance,

[75] Puchta, *supra* n. 4, §251; Windscheid, *supra* n. 4, 442 ii, §306.

[76] Puchta, *supra* n. 4, §251.

[77] Aubry and Rau, *supra* n. 11, iv, §343.

[78] Windscheid, *supra* n. 4, ii. §306.

[79] Langdell, *supra* n. 33, pp. 15, 20–1.

[80] Larombière, *supra* n. 2, i. 15–16, 18–19; Laurent, *supra* n. 2, xv, §479; R. Troplong, *De la vente* (Paris, 1837), 36–8.

[81] Brinz and Lotmar, *supra* n. 30, iv, §572; Vangerow, *supra* n. 34, iii, §603.

since it would not be effective until it came to the attention of the offeror.

In England and the United States, theoretical discussion was inhibited by the fact that the courts had arrived at a solution that protected the offeree but was hard to justify theoretically: offers and revocations of offers were effective on receipt but acceptances were effective on dispatch. Thus, the offeree who had not received a revocation knew when he mailed his acceptance that he had a contract. Acceptance had been held to be effective when mailed in *Adams* v. *Lindsell*[82] in 1818, before much theoretical discussion had taken place. Thereafter, the treatise writers usually remarked that, however the matter ought to have been settled, the law was clear.

In France and Germany, increasingly elaborate theories were developed in hopes of arriving at results that both protected the offeree and seemed to follow from the definition of a contract. One solution limited the power of the offeror to revoke his offer. According to the German jurist Vangerow[83] and the French jurists Aubry and Rau, Laurent, and Demolombe,[84] an offer was irrevocable if the offeror promised not to revoke it. The difficulty with this solution was that the promise was itself an unaccepted offer, and so no contract had yet been formed.[85] Vangerow and Demolombe answered that, since this offer was entirely in the offeree's interest, the offeree was deemed to accept it as soon as he had knowledge of it.[86] Demolombe and the German jurist Regelsberger went one step further. An offer should be irrevocable even if the offeror did not expressly promise to keep it open since a promise to do so was implied in the offer. Again, this implied promise was itself an offer that the offeree was deemed to accept as soon as he learned of it.[87] Regelsberger acknowledged that he espoused this position in order to protect the offeree. Indeed, it is hard to believe that without this objective in view he or Demolombe would have developed this contrived account in which an implied offer meets with a tacit acceptance.

Yet another approach was to claim that offers were revocable but that the offeror who revoked had to pay any damages the offeree had suffered (the 'negative Interesse' or, as common lawyers now say, the 'reliance interest'). It was not very clear why the offeror

[82] *Adams* v. *Lindsell*, 1 Barn. & Ald. 681, 106 Eng. Rep. 250 (1818).

[83] Vangerow, *supra* n. 34, iii, §603.

[84] Aubry and Rau, *supra* n. 11, iv, §343; Laurent, *supra* n 2, xv,§476; Demolombe, *supra* n. 2, xxiv, §§59, 65.

[85] Larombière, *supra* n. 2, i. 12.

[86] Vangerow, *supra* n. 34, iii, §603; Demolombe, *supra* n. 2, xxiv, §§59, 65.

[87] Ibid. xv, §66; F. Regelsberger, *Die Vorverhandlungen* (Weimar, 1868), §13.

should have to pay. In France, Aubry and Rau and Troplong gave no reason at all.[88] Demolombe and Larombière said the offeree was entitled to damages under section 1382 of the Civil Code.[89] As Laurent pointed out, however, under that section, a person was liable if he was at fault for causing another harm. If the offer was not binding, it was hard to see how the offeror could be at fault for revoking it.[90] In Germany, Ihering said the reason was *culpa in contrahendo*, 'fault in contracting', but, as he acknowledged, he was not using the word 'fault' in its ordinary sense.[91] Windscheid and Vangerow said the offeror was liable for a violation of trust (*Vertrauen*) or good faith (*bona fides*).[92] They did not explain why it was a violation of trust or good faith to revoke an offer that was not legally binding.

In Germany, the debate ended when the Civil Code provided that offers were irrevocable unless the offeror expressly reserved the right to revoke.[93] Like Regelsberger, the drafters spoke of an implied promise to keep the offer open. Nevertheless, like Regelsberger, they acknowledged that they were trying to protect the offeree, 'who must be able to count on a contract arising when he on his side makes a timely acceptance of the offer'.[94] It is extraordinary that, throughout this debate, theory was a hurdle that had to be leapt in order to provide the protection of the offeree that everyone desired. Apparently, Langdell had been right. Theory took no account of 'substantial justice and the interests of the contracting parties', at least not until it was manipulated to make it do so.

CONTRACTUAL CONSENT

The nineteenth-century jurists retained the concept of will. They had to apply that concept, however, without using others that they had not retained. The late scholastics had said, following Thomas, that to act voluntarily a person must understand the essence of his action. If he does, the action is voluntary even if he chooses the lesser of two evils, as when a captain decides to jettison cargo in a

[88] Aubry and Rau, *supra* n. 11, iv, §343; Troplong, *supra* n. 80, i. 38.

[89] Demolombe, *supra* n. 2, xxiv, §71; Larombière, *supra* n. 2, i. 22–3.

[90] Laurent, *supra* n. 2, xv, §481.

[91] Ihering, 'Culpa in contrahendo oder Schadenersatz bei nichtigen oder nicht zur Perfection gelangten Verträgen', *Ihering's Jahrbücher für die Dogmatik des heutigen römischen und deutschen Privatrechts*, 4 (1861), 1 at 92–106.

[92] Windscheid, *supra* n. 4, ii, §307; Vangerow, *supra* n. 34, iii, §603. In early editions of his treatise, Windscheid argued that the offeror was liable because of a 'tacit guarantee' that he would not revoke. Windscheid finally acknowledged that the liability does not arise from the will of the offeror but is imposed by the law.

[93] Bürgerlichesgesetzbuch, art. 145.

[94] *Motive*, *supra* n. 36, i. 165–6.

storm. The nineteenth-century jurists had to speak about will without using the theory of choice on which the late scholastics were drawing.

They all broke with earlier doctrine, but in different ways. Most French jurists said that fraud, duress, and mistake do not destroy consent but simply render it impure. Most German jurists took a diametrically opposed position: mistake, fraud, and duress, in and of themselves, had no effect upon consent. Relief was given on other grounds. English and American jurists held a variety of opinions, some resembling those of the French or the Germans, and some quite distinctive. Surprisingly enough, there was little difference of opinion about the cases in which relief should be given. The problem was how these cases should be explained.

Duress and Fraud

Unlike the earlier jurists and also unlike the Germans, the French claimed that duress and fraud rendered consent impure. According to Colmet de Santerre, Demolombe, and Laurent, that was the meaning of the Code. It said: 'There is no valid consent if the consent was only given because of error or was extorted by duress or induced by fraud.'[95] According to the Code, in all these cases the contract was not simply void: an action had to be brought to avoid or rescind it.[96]

It is most unlikely that the drafters had any such idea in mind. They themselves claimed to have taken their provisions on mistake, fraud, and duress from earlier jurists such as Pothier and Barbeyrac.[97] According to Pothier and Barbeyrac, the victim of fraud or duress did consent. Relief was given because of the injustice done him, or, in the case of duress, Barbeyrac said, because contractual consent is not binding unless given freely.[98] In all probability, the reason the drafters mentioned fraud and duress together with mistake in one article was that these causes for invalidating a promise were mentioned together in a Roman text in the *Institutes*.[99] Demante, in

[95] Code civil art. 1109.

[96] Code civil art. 1117.

[97] Bigot-Préamenu, Présentation au Corps législatif, in P. Fenet, *Recueil complet des travaux préparatoires du Code civil* (Paris, 1827), xiii. 215, 223.

[98] The drafters are stating Barbeyrac's view when they speak of 'liberty' and hence freedom from duress as necessary for consent to be validly given. (Bigot-Préamenu, Présentation au Corps législatif, ibid. xiii. 223; Mouricault, Discours prononcé devant le Corps législatif, ibid. xiii. 413, 416–17.) Thus these statements are not, as I once thought, evidence that the drafters were 'perhaps anticipating the new approach' of the 19th-c. French jurists. (A. T. von Mehren and J. Gordley, *The Civil Law System*, 2nd edn. (Boston, 1977), 859.)

[99] 'Verbi gratia si metu coactus aut dolo inductus aut errore laspsus stipulanti Titio promisisti, quod non debueras promittere, palam est iure civile te obligatum esse et

his earlier commentary, assumed that the drafters held the same views as Pothier.[100]

The later commentators who espoused the new view gave little justification beyond insisting that this view was enshrined in the Code. Colmet de Santerre accused Demante of substituting his own 'theories' for the expressed will of the legislator.[101] Demolombe said that, while Pothier might be correct 'philosophically', his views were not recognized by the Code.[102] Demolombe noted elsewhere that an opinion could be 'philosophically' sound and still be 'juridically' false, in which event, he implies, the best course of action is to ignore it.[103]

The reason the French jurists did not present a theoretical justification for their conclusions is that they did not have a theory of human choice. As far as one can tell, they had in mind only the naïve idea that to interfere with a person's choice is to hinder his consent. Since fraud and duress, as well as mistake, lead a person to do what he would otherwise not want to do, they were also supposed to vitiate consent. Thus, Aubry and Rau merely stated that fear has a direct and determining influence that can overcome the freedom of the will.[104] Demolombe described the influence of fear in the same way, and added that fraud affects consent because it is mixed with error.[105] Laurent claimed that any 'vice of consent', be it mistake, fraud, or duress, makes the contract voidable when a party otherwise would not have contracted.[106] Similarly, Larombière wrote as though anything regrettable that influences a person's choice hinders his consent. Consent, he said, must be 'enlightened': one must know 'concerning what and why one is contracting'. It must be 'free': as an 'essential act of our will', consent 'presupposes a fullness of liberty in us and a faculty of choice incompatible with the force which annihiliates both'. It must be 'spontaneous': consent must be given by 'a will that is entirely itself' rather than an 'intelligence . . . deceived by perfidious machinations'.[107]

actio, qua intenditur dare te oportere, efficax est: sed iniquum est te condemnari ideoque datur tibi exceptio metus causa aut doli mali aut in factum composita ad impugnandam actionem.' (I. 4.13.1.)

[100] Demante and Colmet de Santerre, *supra* n. 2, v, §§16 (error), 20 (duress), 26 (fraud) (written by Demante).

[101] Ibid. v, §27 *bis* III (written by Colmet de Santerre).

[102] Demolombe, *supra* n. 2, xxiv, §164.

[103] Ibid. i, §181.

[104] Aubry and Rau, *supra* n 11, iv, §343 *bis*.

[105] Demolombe, *supra* n. 2, xxiv, §151 (duress); §184 (fraud).

[106] Laurent, *supra* n. 2, xv, §487.

[107] Larombière, *supra* n. 2, i. 41–2.

Some English and American jurists held a similar view.[108] Dodd thought that fraud, like duress, 'nullifies' the 'assent' of a party.[109] Carey thought that duress destroys 'the free exercise of the understanding and the will'.[110] Hammon said that fraud and duress affect 'the reality of consent'.[111] Anson said that fraud and duress affect 'the reality of consent', although he managed to discuss both doctrines without otherwise mentioning the consent of the parties.[112] The authors seem to have had in mind the same idea as the French: pressures that influence consent interfere with consent. This idea is sufficiently simple that they may have arrived at it without reading the French jurists.

The objections to this view were also fairly obvious. They had been raised since the time of the late scholastics. As the German jurist Savigny pointed out, relief for fraud or duress is given only when the perpetrator acted wrongfully; therefore, the reason for giving relief cannot be their effect on the will. '[I]f freedom were excluded by fear, then it would be entirely irrelevant whether this fear originated simply in the thoughts of the person who is afraid or whether it originated in threats made by another person.'[113] In cases of duress and fraud, the law gives a remedy not because consent is lacking, but because 'a like immorality appears in the actions of another person'.[114]

A similar objection was raised by some Anglo-American jurists. According to Batten, relief was given for duress not merely because of a 'want of will' but because a court of equity would deem it a fraud to take advantage of another's circumstances.[115] Another author noted that, if relief for duress is to 'depend on an esoteric investigation of the will of the contracting parties', there will be 'no safety', since 'in ninety-nine cases out of a hundred the parties are not free agents'. It is wrong to think that 'where pressure meets weakness there is not freedom', for the pressure of circumstances 'is the very motive without which there would be no contract'.[116] Similarly,

[108] I once thought William Story held this view. He said consent 'must be freely and voluntarily given', and duress takes away 'free agency'. (W. W. Story, *supra* n. 66, p. 398.) Most likely, however, he was paraphrasing Barbeyrac.

[109] Dodd, 'Contracts Vitiated for Fraud', *The Legal Observer*, 11 (1836), 505 at 505. The same opinion was expressed in an anonymous article, 'Void and Voidable Contracts', *The Law Times*, 45 (1868), 369 at 370.

[110] Carey, *supra* n. 66, p. 505.

[111] Hammon, *supra* n. 66, pp. 142, 188.

[112] Anson, *supra* n. 66, pp. 156, 203, 218.

[113] Savigny, *supra* n. 3, iii, §114, p. 108.

[114] Ibid. iii, §115, p. 115.

[115] E. Batten, *Specific Performance of Contracts* (London, 1849), 27.

[116] Anon., 'The Doctrine of Free Agency in Contract', *Law Journal*, 22 (1887), 123 at 123.

Leake observed that, although the victim of fraud is mistaken, that mistake 'alone would not vitiate [a party's] dealings with others. . .'. Relief is given because fraud 'precludes the party so occasioning the mistake from holding the other bound . . .'.[117]

The objection is so straightforward and obvious that, again, except in the special case of Sir Frederick Pollock, there is no reason to suppose that the common lawyers borrowed it from the Germans. Pollock also denied that 'consent determined by . . . fraud or duress is no consent'. If that were so, all such contracts would be radically void *ab initio*, and there would be no reason to enquire whether the party who had induced a mistake or applied pressure had acted wrongfully. There is no doubt that Pollock was familiar with Savigny's formulations of these arguments since he cites Savigny.[118]

It is astonishing how little the leading French jurists had to say about this obvious problem. They do not confront it directly. Demolombe and Colmet de Santerre explain that contracts to pay for rescue in a storm or for rescue from brigands are not invalid for duress. They then grope for some other reason why these contracts might be invalid: perhaps for 'temporary dementia', or the disappearance of the party's will through fear. They struggle with the awkward consequence that if the contract is invalid the rescuer apparently cannot recover recompense for his services.[119] Presumably, however, they would not invalidate a contract as readily when fear is not wrongfully induced as when it is. They would not invalidate a contract for a medical operation that will save a person's life. They never explain why they would not if, in all cases, relief is given because of the effects of fear on the consent of the party.[120]

[117] S. Leake, *supra* n. 66, p. 182.

[118] F. Pollock, *Principles of Contract* (London, 1885), 390.

[119] Demante and Colmet de Santerre, *supra* n. 2, v, §20 *bis* (by Colmet de Santerre); Demolombe, *supra* n. 2, xxiv, §150.

[120] One has the same sense reading the later and supposedly more iconoclastic French writer Demogue. 'It little matters that, among exterior circumstances, some have an unjust character . . . provided that they act in a gradual fashion, allowing the spirit to reflect, to be master of itself.' (Demogue, 'De la violence comme vice du consentement', *Revue trimestrielle de droit civil*, 13 (1914), 435 at 437.) Duress is a 'brutal pressure' (p.438). Demogue tries to build a theory in which relief for duress and *force majeure* depend on the principle that decisions made under such pressure are avoidable. He never confronts the difficulty that the 'unjust character' of a threat does matter. As Demogue notes, a party who demands an excessive price for a rescue at sea will be compelled to relinquish part of his gain. (p. 441). But he will not be treated in the same way as a pirate who demands a price for not sinking the ship.

Mistake and Changed Circumstances

Following Thomas, late scholastics such as Lessius said that a promise was radically void if the promisor was mistaken as to the essentials of what he was doing. If he did understand the essentials, he was still not bound if circumstances arose under which he never intended to be committed. For the most part, the natural lawyers also regarded mistake and changed circumstances as distinct grounds for relief although they did not draw the distinction in the same way as Thomas and Lessius.

In the nineteenth century the doctrine of changed circumstances went into eclipse, and little will be said about it here. In contrast, enormous effort was spent trying to clarify the doctrine of mistake.

Changed circumstances In the nineteenth century, the doctrine of changed circumstances had few defenders. They explained relief by saying that the existence of certain circumstances was a tacit or implied condition of the contract. According to the French jurist Larombière, an 'error in motive' affected the validity of a contract only if the parties so wished, but a judge would determine whether they so wished by examining 'according to the circumstances, if the fact alleged as a motive was taken to be the determining reason (*raison déterminante*) and if the consent depended on its reality'.[121] The German jurist Windscheid said that the continuation of certain circumstances could be an 'undeveloped condition' of the contract, 'undeveloped' in the sense that it was not expressly willed by the parties. The doctrine forced itself on the attention of Anglo-American jurists when the Coronation cases were decided in the early twentieth century. Rooms had been rented along the route of the coronation procession of Edward VII for a single day and at a suitably enhanced price. When Edward became ill, the procession was postponed. In *Taylor* v. *Caldwell*, Blackburn granted relief on the grounds, again, that an implied condition of the contract had not been fulfilled. Anglo-American jurists repeated his explanation.

For most nineteenth-century jurists, the obvious objection to the doctrine was that a tacit or undeveloped condition was one that the parties never consciously willed. They had never thought about the change in circumstances, let alone agreed on what should happen if the change occurred. The judge said that the contract was subject to such a condition because he thought that was a sensible and fair result. As Williston said, 'any qualification of the promise

[121] Larombière, *supra* n. 2, i. 282–3.

is based on the unfairness or unreasonableness of giving it the absolute force which its words clearly state'.[122]

Thomas or Lessius would not have thought there was a conflict between interpreting the will of the promisor and asking what was fair and reasonable. They had founded the doctrine on Aristotle's theory of equity. Promises, like laws, prescribed a means to an end, and circumstances could necessarily arise in which the means would no longer be reasonable or fair. The promisor had never agreed to be bound under such circumstances.

Without rejecting this idea outright, most of the nineteenth-century jurists distrusted it. For them, the task of contract law was the enforcement of the will of the parties, by which they meant the enforcement of decisions the parties had consciously made. Whether these decisions were sensible in the light of different circumstances was a matter the parties should have considered. Thus, the doctrine of changed circumstances slumbered during the nineteenth century.

It continues to do so in France, although the administrative courts have developed a version of it called *imprévision*. The drafters of the German Civil Code ignored the doctrine, but the courts brought it back under the pressure of the First World War and the drastic inflation of the 1920s. They held that relief for *Wegfall der Geschäftsgrundlage*, destruction of the basis of the contract, could be given under the most general article of the Code, article 242, which requires that a contract be performed in good faith. The doctrine has been extended in a variety of ways by Anglo-American courts since the Coronation cases. Although today most jurists approve of the doctrine, they regard it as sorely in need of an explanation. Despite all the changes that have occurred since the nineteenth century, the feeling remains that to say what is fair or reasonable is not to interpret the will of the parties but to express a purely subjective opinion.

Mistake The nineteenth-century jurists neglected the doctrine of changed circumstances because they thought the real task of contract law was to enforce the will of the parties. For that same reason, however, they gave considerable attention to the doctrine

[122] S. Williston, *The Law of Contracts* (New York, 1920), §1937. Instead of speaking of implied conditions, Williston said that relief was given because of a 'presumed assumption by the parties of some vital supposed fact'. He acknowledged that '[t]he only evidence, however, of such mutual assumption is, generally, that the court thinks a reasonable person, that is, the court itself, would not have contemplated taking the risk of the existence of the fact in question.' (Ibid.) Thus although Williston did not talk about 'implied conditions', he asked the same question about what it was sensible for the parties to have done.

of mistake. No other legal doctrine raised so squarely the question of whether the parties had consented.

For the late scholastics, a party did not consent if he was mistaken as to the substance or essence of what he was contracting for. In the Aristotelian and Thomistic tradition in which they were writing, the essence of his contract was defined by its end. This end gave the contract, and the object contracted for, their identity. It defined the kind of contract, and the kind of object, for which the parties had contracted.

Nineteenth-century jurists approached the problem of mistake without the concept of essence. When they discussed the kind of mistake that called for relief, they identified it as a mistake in the identity of an object, in the species of an object, or in a characteristic of the object that was important to the parties. However, identity, species, and the ends of the parties were now different ideas, no longer united by the concept of essence. When they thought about the matter, the nineteenth-century jurists usually conceived of the identity of the object apart from any properties at all. A party was getting what he contracted for when he received the particular thing he had in mind: 'this object here'. They conceived of the species of an object as the set of properties which conventional usage regarded as making the object one of a certain kind. They regarded the ends of the parties as any important ends the parties had in mind, not as the proximate final cause for which they contracted. They argued about whether relief should be given for an error in identity or an error in species or an error in characteristics important to the parties. Taken by itself, however, none of these alternatives seemed to work.

French, German, and Anglo-American jurists faced the problem of mistake in different contexts. In France, leading jurists such as Colmet de Santerre, Demolombe, and Laurent distinguished mistakes in the identity of an object, which destroy consent, from mistakes in its 'substance', which merely render consent impure. In the former case, a contract was simply void; in the latter, as in the case of duress and fraud, an action had to be brought to avoid or rescind it.[123]

These French jurists claimed to be following the Code. The Code, however, merely said that an error invalidated consent if it concerned the 'substance' of the performance contracted for.[124] It neither said that such an error affects the purity of consent, nor

[123] e.g. Demante and Colmet de Santerre, *supra* n. 2, v, §§14 *bis*, 16 *bis* I, 26 *bis*, 27 *bis* I–III (written by Colmet de Santerre); Demolombe, *supra* n. 2, xxiv, §§88, 124–7, 164, 171, 181–4; Laurent, *supra* n. 2, xv, §§450–3, 458, 484.

[124] Code civil art. 1110.

distinguished it from an error that destroys consent entirely. Indeed, the drafters of the Code claimed to be following Pothier and Barbeyrac, who, like the late scholastics, said that consent was destroyed by an error in 'substance' or in 'essentials'. The drafters did provide that, as in the case of fraud and duress, an action had to be brought to avoid the contract. They may have done so because they were following a Roman text which said that, in a *stipulatio*, a promise induced by mistake, fraud, or duress is not simply void but gives rise to an exception.[125] Or they may have done so because the requirement made procedural sense, or because they were working in haste, or because they wanted to keep matters simple. It is extremely unlikely that they did so because they held a new view of consent which they never so much as mentioned.

The French jurists' view seems to have been that a party made a mistake in identity when the mistake concerned not the properties of an object, but which individual object he was to receive. He wanted 'this horse here' and contracted for 'that horse there'. Mistakes in 'substance' or 'substantial properties' were not mistakes in identity, but distorted a party's decision to contract. Although he did consent, as in the case of fraud and duress, his consent was impure.

Laurent explained the effect of mistake in just this way. Other commentators seem to have had the same idea in mind except that, as Laurent pointed out, they were inconsistent. If an 'error in substance' was a mistake not in identity, but in a property of importance to a party, then, Laurent noted, any mistake of sufficient importance to a party must be an 'error in substance'. Laurent said that relief should be given whenever a party would not have contracted had he known the truth.[126] Other French commentators, inconsistently, defined an 'error in substance' as one that concerned the nature or species of an object. Colmet de Santerre said the error must concern a quality absent which its 'nature' would be different.[127] Demolombe said the error must concern the 'principal' or 'characteristic' quality of a thing that individualizes it, makes it

[125] See n. 99 above. As mentioned earlier, the drafters also followed this text in writing Article 1109.

[126] Laurent, *supra* n. 2, xv, §487.

[127] Demante and Colmet de Santerre, v §16 *bis* II (written by Colmet de Santerre). According to Colmet de Santerre, a mistake as to whether a horse is lame, a watch is accurate, or a book is well written is not an 'error in substance'; a mistake as to whether goods are silver, candlesticks are modern in style, or a Raphael is a copy is such an error. The characteristic is an 'essential part' of the object and its absence alters its 'nature'. (Ibid.)

proper to a given use, or gives it its name.[128] Aubry and Rau said that a contract was voidable if a party was in error as to 'the properties which, taken together, determine [a thing's] specific nature and distinguish it according to common notions from things of every other species'.[129] As Laurent pointed out, even though these jurists thought an 'error in substance' did not destroy consent, they were defining such an error as though it did concern the identity of an object.[130]

These jurists were not merely being inconsistent. Once Aristotelian metaphysics had been abandoned, it was hard to see how certain properties could determine the nature or species of an object. Aubry and Rau seemed to sense the difficulty since they spoke of the properties that distinguish an object 'according to common notions from things of every other species'. But if things really do not have distinct essences or natures, it is hard to see why 'common notions' would draw such a distinction. One would expect common notions to denote mere family resemblances among things or to classify things in as many different ways as the thing has properties of interest to different groups of classifiers. According to the jurist Fubini, the problem with the 'objective' solution that Aubry and Rau had proposed was that 'species' has no precise meaning. Also, Fubini observed, the parties may have attached importance to characteristics that do not determine the 'species' of an object.[131]

Laurent's alternative was to ask about the importance of a property to the parties. Fubini called this solution 'subjective'. The trouble was, he observed, 'if a contracting party could always have the contract avoided by claiming that he decided to contract because of a quality which had importance for him alone, agreements will be subject to grave uncertainty'.[132] Indeed, whatever Laurent might say, neither he nor anyone else would really have granted relief simply because such a party would not have contracted had he

[128] Demolombe, *supra* n. 2, xxiv, §89. His examples of errors in substance are mistakes as to whether a candlestick is silver, a horse is Arabian, or a painting is by Rubens. In contrast, the absence of 'accidents' does not change one thing into another. Examples of accidents are the purity of a silver candlestick, the agility of an Arab horse, and the excellence of a Rubens painting. (Ibid.)

[129] Aubry and Rau, *supra* n. 11, iv, §343 *bis*. In contrast, an 'error in the origin, the antiquity, or some other more or less important quality of the thing . . . does not make the contract void unless it becomes a condition of the contract, because the parties negotiated with it in view, indicating or specifying it'. (Ibid.)

[130] Laurent, *supra* n. 2, xv, §489.

[131] Fubini, 'Contribution à l'étude de la théorie de l'erreur sur la substance et sur les qualitiés substantielles', *Revue trimestrielle de droit civil*, 1 (1902), 301 at 309–11.

[132] Ibid. 321.

known the truth. Little would have been left of the binding force of contract.

There seemed to be no solution to the problem. One might, Fubini noted, grant relief only if the mistake were made by both parties. But it was hard to justify this limitation by any basic principle of contract law. Moreover, this solution seemed to confuse mistake with the failure of a condition.[133] Fubini offered a solution of his own that, unfortunately, seemed to create several of the difficulties he had mentioned at once.[134]

Savigny led German jurists in the exact opposite direction. The French said that mistake, fraud, and duress rendered consent impure. Savigny said that, in principle, mistake, fraud, and duress did not affect consent. Nevertheless, the same difficulties emerged.

According to Savigny, although mistake, like duress, affected the choice a person made, nevertheless, the person did choose, and that was all that mattered. A party under duress chose one alternative among others open to him. Therefore, he had 'freedom to choose'; 'the freedom of his will must be actually present'.[135] Similarly, if a party was mistaken, '[t]he will can repudiate whatever advantages these possibilities seem to offer because of the error; accordingly, the existence of a free declaration of will is not excluded in any way . . .'.[136]

This solution presupposed that one could clearly distinguish what a person chose from his reasons for choosing it. As Savigny said, a 'sharp distinction' must be drawn 'between the will itself and that which precedes it in the soul of the person who wills'. Once that distinction was drawn, it seemed to follow that a party did will the alternative he selected whatever mistakes might have led him to will that alternative.[137] 'The will itself is an independent event,' Savigny argued, 'and it alone is important for the formation of legal relations.' One cannot 'link this event' with the preceding process as though the process were part of its 'essence'.[138] As Puchta recapitulated the argument,

> An action presupposes the direction of the will to its object. The existence of the will juridically is, as a rule, only what comes to light through the act.

[133] Fubini, *supra* n. 131, 301 at 322.

[134] According to Fubini, the best solution is to combine the objective and subjective theories. A quality is substantial if the nature of the thing agreed upon assigns it this chararcter (i.e. if the thing belongs to a determinate natural genus), or if the quality is one which, according to custom, the parties envisage in this way, or if the quality should be deemed to have been envisaged this way because of the circumstances of the particular case. (Ibid. 323.)

[135] Savigny, *supra* n. 3, iii, §114, p. 102.

[136] Ibid. 113. [137] Ibid. [138] Ibid.

The process of its establishment and hence its motives are irrelevant from a legal standpoint.[139]

Savigny then confronted the question of why the law sometimes gives relief when a party is mistaken. He answered that in these cases the reason for giving relief is not the mistake itself, but rather the failure of the will of the party to correspond to the party's outward declaration of his will. As mentioned earlier, the German jurists typically defined contract as a type of *Rechtsgeschäft*, or 'juristic act'. A party entered into a *Rechtsgeschäft* by making a *Willenserklärung*, or declaration of his will that a certain legal result follow. A valid *Rechtsgeschäft* thus required both that the party will a certain legal result and that he declare his will for it. If a party willed one result and declared his will for another, his *Rechtsgeschäft* was invalid. Such a party will have made a mistake in declaring his will, but the reason for giving him relief is not the mistake itself but the failure of his will to correspond to his declaration.[140] A contract was a *Rechtsgeschäft* that was made by the declaration of will of two or more parties. Consequently, a contract was void if the will of any party did not match that party's declaration, or if the will and declaration of one party did not match those of another.[141]

Savigny's solution, as elaborated by leading jurists such as Puchta and Windscheid, became widely accepted.[142] A version of it eventually passed into article 118 of the German Civil Code, which provides that a *Rechtsgeschäft* is void when a party is in error as to the content of his declaration of will.

Several German jurists put forward rival solutions. Some of them allowed relief to turn on the importance of a mistake to a party. According to Regelsberger, for example, a contract was void if the parties failed to agree on an 'essential point'. A point was 'essential' if it was so 'tightly bound' to the 'interest' of a party that, but for the mistake, the party would not have contracted.[143] He did not explain any better than Laurent why contracts are often binding even then.[144]

[139] Puchta, *supra* n. 4, p. 77.
[140] Savigny, *supra* n. 3, iii, §135, pp. 263–4.
[141] Ibid. 265.
[142] Puchta, *supra* n. 4, p. 77; Windscheid, *supra* n. 4, i, §76.
[143] F. Regelsberger, *Pandekten* (Leipzig, 1893), i, §142.
[144] In discussing error in characteristics, he says that whether the error concerns a party's motive (*Beweggrund*) or his will (*Wollen*) cannot be decisive. (Ibid. i, §142.) He immediately qualifies that remark by saying that the 'subjective conception' of the party is not what matters. (Ibid.) He later says that an error in motive does not usually void a contract. The reason is not sought in 'inner grounds' (i.e. in principle) but in the need for the security of commerce. (Ibid. §143.)

Typically, however, even the German jurists who disagreed with Savigny maintained that mistake did not warrant relief simply because it had led a party to contract.[145] Relief for mistake had to be explained in some other way. Hölder, for example, wanted to ask whether the will of one contracting party corresponded to the will of another. If one party said 'I will buy' when he meant 'I will sell', the contract was void because the parties' wills failed to match, not because of the mistake, and not, as Savigny thought, because one party's will failed to match his own declaration. Words, Hölder argued, are mere signs of thoughts, and it is the thoughts that matter.[146]

Zitelmann's solution was to ask whether a party willed the very legal result which it was now proposed the law should bring about. If he intended some other result, his *Rechtsgeschäft* was void since, by the definition of *Rechtsgeschäft*, the law produces a certain legal result because the party intended it should be produced.[147]

Brinz made the rather bizarre claim that a party who indicated one specific thing when he wanted another was simply unaware of what he was doing. His contract was void because he lacked the will to act, and not, as Savigny thought, because his will did not match his declaration. While a contract was always void for unawareness, Brinz claimed that in principle it was not void for mistake, since to will something in error was to will it nevertheless.[148] Brinz's critics

[145] An exception was Ryck, whose solution resembled that of the late scholastics but was largely ignored. Citing Aristotle three times, Ryck proposed to start from the proposition that man had a distinctive potential to think and to will, and so, unlike other animals, he had a 'thinking will'. When a party contracted, his will was to achieve as an end and through the transaction some principal result (*bezwecken rechtgeschäftlichen Erfolg* or *bezweckten Haupterfolg*). Certain features of the transaction, taken together and as a unity, enabled this result to be achieved. Absent these features, the 'character' of the result achieved was altered so that the result was no longer the same as the one the party willed. Such features were 'essential' (*Essentialen*), and error as to them would void a contract. (Ryck, 'Der Irrthum bei Rechtgeschäften', in *Festgabe für George Beseler* (Berlin, 1885), 117 at 131–42.)

[146] Hölder, 'Die Lehre vom error', *Kritische Vierteljahresschrift für Gesetzgebung und Rechtswissenschäft*, 14 (1872), 561 at 568, 574, 580. Hölder used the term *dissens* to describe the case in which the contract is void because the wills of parties are not in accord. He recognized another case as well in which a contract must be void: that in which one cannot even say there was an act (*Handlung*) because the parties 'willing' (*Wollen*) did not correspond to his 'action' (*Thun*) (p. 580). In such a case, the question is not 'what I wanted to say' but 'whether I wanted to say what I said wholly apart from the meaning to be attached to what I said' (p. 564). In these two cases a contract must be void, and the reason, properly speaking, is not the error itself but the fact that a party did not will what is necessary for a contract or for an action (p. 574). To be distinguished is the case of an *error in substantia* which need not void a contract but sometimes does (pp. 578, 581).

[147] E. Zitelmann, *Irrtum und Rechtgeschaft* (Leipzig, 1879), 341–2.

[148] Brinz and Lotmar, *supra* n. 30, iv, §525. Brinz claimed that the Latin word *error* was more general than the German word *Irrthum*. *Irrthum* meant the falsehood

said that they found this distinction between unawareness and mistake to be baffling. A party who incorrectly designated what he wanted seemed to be no less mistaken than a person acting under any other false impression.[149]

Savigny's solution seemed superior to most German jurists because it appeared to give a unified view of a problem of which the others considered only particular aspects. His requirement that the will correspond to the declaration embraced both Zitelmann's concern that a party have actually willed a legal result and Brinz's insistence that a party have willed the declaration he actually made. The additional requirement that in contracts the will and declaration of each party must match that of the other embraced Hölder's requirement that the wills of the parties correspond. Savigny thus seemed to cover more ground with a few very simple concepts.

In any event, Savigny's solution and those of Hölder, Zitelmann, and Brinz seemed to avoid the difficulties in which the French were finding themselves. Relief was explained without speaking mystically about characteristics that determined the species of an object and without asking about the importance of a mistake to a party.

Nevertheless, these solutions did not avoid the question of what constitutes the identity of the object for which a party contracts. By Savigny's solution, one had to ask whether the object the party willed to have was the same as the object he declared his will to have. Indeed, all these solutions raised the question of what made an object the very object the party willed.

The German jurists answered that the party willed a concrete individual thing. According to Windscheid, a person represented this thing in his own mind, either through an image derived from sense perception or through characteristics that set that object apart from all others. When the person's declaration of will indicated the very object that was thus mentally represented, the juristic act was

of a mental representation (*Vorstellung*), whereas *error* also meant a 'momentary unawareness' (*momentare Besinnungs- oder Bewusstlosigkeit*) of what one was doing. *Error* that is not *Irrthum* excludes the will to act. *Irrthum* does not because what is mistakenly willed is nevertheless willed. (Ibid.)

[149] Zitelmann pointed out that a person has a mental representation (*Vorstellung*) of some sort even in a case of unawareness (*Bewusstlosigkeit*). 'One cannot see why the falsity or absence of a mental representation of the content of a person's own concurrent action should be less an error (*Irrthum*)' than the falsity or absence of other mental representations. (Zitelmann, *supra* n. 147, p. 369.) Similarly, Mandry argued that there cannot be an act without a will of some sort even in a state of unawareness. (Mandry, review of A. Brinz, *Lehrbuch der Pandekten* (Erlangen, 1871), in *Kritische Vierteljahresschrift für Gesetzgebung und Rechtwissenschaft*, 14 (1872), 374 at 380.)

valid. That was so whatever false beliefs a person has about the object's attributes.[150]

Similarly, according to Zitelmann, a person who intends a result must intend a result that is 'concrete' and 'individualized'. To be concrete and individual, however, a result must be perceptible by the senses at a distinct place and time.[151] Consequently, if a party perceives an object physically before him and wills to have it, he gets what he intended as long as he gets the object he perceived.[152] If the object is not before him, he must make an 'act of individualizing choice' by singling it out according to its characteristics. He then gets what he intended as long as he gets the object singled out by those characteristics.[153] In either case, it does not matter what other qualities he believed the object to have.

Similarly, Bechmann distinguished *Identitätsmerkmale*, which single an object out, and *Beschaffenheitsmerkmale*, which denote its qualities.[154] Hesse distinguished the 'definite thing or kind of thing' a party willed from its 'characteristics'.[155] Assolter claimed

150 Windscheid, *supra* n. 4, i, §76a.

151 Zitelmann, *supra* n. 147, pp. 436–42. 'Space and time are the principles of individuation in the world of the concrete. Therefore it is through the perception of an object by the senses at a given place and given time that the concrete object is individually marked out (*bestimmt*)' (p. 439).

152 Ibid. 444–5.

153 Ibid. 447–9. Zitelmann handled the case of a generic sale by saying that there the intention of a party is not fully determined (*bestimmt*). The mental representation (*Vorstellung*) of the party 'includes only the characteristics of a genus' (p. 510). It is normally left to someone else to provide concreteness by choosing any object with these characteristics, just as, if the contract left him free to choose between alternate performances, he would make it concrete by choosing one of them (pp. 510–11). Zitelmann recognized that in a generic sale a party may have in mind not a specific set of characteristics, but the name of a genus. In that event, the party's intention 'embraces all objects that normally in life are taken to belong together to the genus' (p. 511). On the difficulties of determining what does and does not belong to a genus by such an appeal to common usage, see p. 197 below. It is striking that, after writing so much about the ancient metaphysical problem of identity, Zitelmann denied he was doing metaphysics at all. He said that Ulpian, by using the word *ousia* in his classic Roman text on mistake, had wandered off on to 'the dubious path of metaphysics'. Ulpian had confused the 'abstract essence of a thing' with its 'identity' (p. 569). Apparently, the dubious path is trodden by those who speak of essences but not by those who speak of identity.

154 A. Bechmann, *Der Kauf nach gemeinem Recht* (Erlangen, 1884), ii, §241. He admits that, since the same characteristic of a thing can be used as an *Identitätsmerkmal* or a *Beschaffenheitsmerkmal*, it is hard to tell in practice which is which. (Ibid., citing Zitelmann with approval, p. 447, n. 2.) In any event, a contract is void only if an object lacks the *Identitätsmerkmal* that a party used to designate the object he wanted. Bechmann describes that case as *error in corpore*. Nevertheless, relief can be given for an error in a *Beschaffenheitsmerkmal* if the characteristic was decisive for the decision to contract and so gave rise to a warranty or a condition. (Ibid. §242.)

155 Hesse, 'Ein Revision der Lehre von Irrthum', *Ihering's Jahrbücher für die Dogmatik des heutigen römischen und deutschen Privatrechts*, 15 (1877), 62 at 101.

that a party's image (*Bild*) of what he wills is that of an 'individual determinate thing or kind of thing'. A thing's 'characteristics' were not part of that image.[156] Bruns distinguished the 'identity' of a thing from its 'characteristics'.[157] Similar distinctions were drawn implicitly by Brinz[158] and Hölder.[159] Thus the Germans, like the French, found themselves distinguishing the identity of an object from the properties that make it an object of a certain kind or an object that a contracting party desires.

In so doing, they assumed that one can divide the party's many thoughts about an object into two classes: those that establish its identity by setting it apart from all other objects, and those that make it an object of a certain kind or an object he wishes to buy. They also assumed that only the first of these classes is relevant to whether the party is getting the object that he willed. The jurist Ryck pointed out that it was odd to think the human mind worked that way, or that a party's only legally relevant intention was to receive an object so identified.[160] Indeed, the jurists seem to have found these assumptions plausible primarily because they permitted

According to Hesse, 'as a rule, one wants not characteristics (*Eigenschaften*) but a specific thing or a genus to which one ascribes characteristics and, perhaps, because one ascribes to it these characteristics. The essence of a thing is determined not by characteristics but by *Merkmale*' (i.e. by those features used to designate a specific thing or genus) (p. 101). Hesse concluded that a contract was void when the will indicated one specific thing or genus and the expression of will another (pp. 101–3). He termed the first of these cases *error in corpore* (pp. 101–2). The contract was not void for an error in characteristics (*Eigenschaften*) (p. 103).

[156] Assolter, 'Der Irrthum beim Kauf', *Archiv für Bürgerliches Recht*, 6 (1892), 280 at 291–2, 298–9. An error in characteristics (*Eigenschaften*) does not void a contract (pp. 298–9).

[157] Bruns, 'Pandekten-Fragmente: Bestandtheile der Rechtsgeschäft', in C. Bruns, *Kleinere Schriften (Weimar*, 1882), ii. 452 at 481, 484. According to Bruns, that which a party willed must be 'really the same' as that which he declared himself to will. If it is not, the contract is void for an error in 'identity' (pp. 477, 481). A contract is not void in principle for an error in characteristics (*Eigenschaften*) because such an error does not affect 'the existence of the will' (p. 484). *Error in substantia* is an exception to that general rule (p. 485).

[158] Brinz claimed that, in the case of an *error in corpore*, a party was simply unaware of what he was doing. Such a mistake voids the contract because it excludes the will to act. Brinz and Lotmar, *supra* n. 30, iv, §525. In principle, a contract is not void for an *error in substantia* since the party wills to have the thing despite the error in his mental representation of it. Nevertheless, Roman law sometimes gave relief. (Ibid., §§525, 527.)

[159] Hölder thought that the Roman *error in substantia* involved not a lack of accord between the wills of the contracting parties, but a failure of the mental representation of a party to accord with reality (*Wirklichkeit*). Although Roman law sometimes gave relief, such an error would not in principle void a contract. (Hölder, *supra* n. 146, pp. 575, 578, 581.)

[160] Ryck, *supra* n. 145, p. 121. Ryck was speaking of Zitelmann, but his observation applies to the other jurists as well.

one to ignore the properties of an object that determine its species or its desirability to a contracting party.

In fact, however, the German jurists paid attention to such properties despite their assumptions. Had they failed to do so, their solution would have seemed artificial and at odds with the Roman texts which they were supposedly trying to explain. According to the texts, a party received relief when copper was sold for gold but not when a mistake merely concerned names and labels.

Some jurists, such as Hesse, Assolter, and Renaud, did so without admitting it. They simply devised examples in which the characteristic by which a party identified the object he wanted was also a characteristic that made the object particularly valuable to him.[161]

Other jurists confronted the problem head-on. Savigny tried to do so while maintaining the principle that the importance of a characteristic to a party was irrelevant. According to Savigny, the reason relief was given when copper was sold for gold was that some properties of an object were bound up with its identity. These were properties by which a thing was classified as a thing of a certain type 'according to the concepts dominant in actual commerce'.[162] If a party declared his will to contract for an object that he mistakenly believed to have such a property, the contract was void because his will did not correspond to his declaration.[163]

This solution was adopted by Puchta[164] and, with reservations, by

[161] Hesse said that, if a party bought a table mistakenly believing it to be silver, he should obtain relief if he wanted a mere mass of silver but not if wanted a table to which he ascribed the 'characteristic' silver. (Hesse, *supra* n. 155, p. 102.) (The case is drawn from D. 18.1.41.1, a text that upholds a contract despite an error in whether a table is silver.) Assolter said that the buyer of a barrel he mistakenly believed to contain wine should obtain relief if he wanted wine but not if he wanted a particular barrel. (Assolter, *supra* n. 156, pp. 293–4.) Renaud said that, if a party bought a ring mistakenly believing it to be gold, he should obtain relief if he wanted 'a golden something' rather than a 'particular something'. If a Cellini collector bought a Cellini statue falsely believing it to be gold, the contract stands because it can be presumed that he wanted a work of Cellini. But a contract is void if a gilded object believed to be gold is purchased by a goldsmith who works only in gold. (Renaud, 'Zur Lehre von Einflusse des Irrthums in der Sache auf die Gültigkeit der Kaufverträge mit Rücksicht auf v. Savigny: Der *error in substantia*', *Archiv für die Civilistische Praxis*, 28 (1846), 247 at 259, 261.) Without saying so, these authors are allowing relief to turn on whether the party was mistaken about a characteristic that was particularly important to him.

[162] To void a contract, a characteristic 'nach den im wirklichen Verkehr herrschenden Begriffen, die Sache zu einer anderen Art von Sachen gerechnet werden müsste . . .'. (Savigny, *supra* n. 113, iii, §137, p. 283.)

[163] Ibid. iii, §137, p. 283. See P. Haupt, *Die Entwicklung der Lehre vom Irrtum beim Rechtsgeschäft seit der Rezeption* (Weimar, 1941), 44–6.

[164] Puchta, *supra* n. 4, §65. An error in a characteristic of an object was an error in 'identity', or *error in corpore*, when in commercial usage (*Verkehr*) the meaning of the characteristic was equivalent to that of the individual object. (Ibid.)

Windscheid.[165] It became mainstream opinion, or, as the Germans put it, *herrschende Lehre*. A version of it was eventually incorporated in the German Civil Code. After providing that a declaration of will could be invalidated if a party was mistaken as to its 'content', the Code added that a mistake concerning characteristics 'regarded in ordinary dealings as essential' would be 'deemed' to be a mistake in content.[166]

To some German jurists, however, this solution seemed to contradict Savigny's own principles.[167] If the significance of a characteristic to a party did not matter, its significance according to 'commercially dominant concepts' should not matter either. According to Windscheid, Savigny's solution did not work in theory. He accepted it, *faute de mieux*, as an explanation of the Roman texts.[168] Indeed, as Fubini noted, Savigny's solution was much like that of the French jurists Aubry and Rau, who had asked whether a property constituted a difference in 'species' according to 'common notions'.[169] It was open to the same objections. In a world without essences, it was hard to see why common notions or commercial dealings should classify things into species rather than merely reflect various resemblances among them. Moreover, it was hard to see the relevance of such classifications. They would be based on characteristics of an object of importance to people in general. But according to Savigny, the fact that a characteristic was important to the parties themselves was not supposed to matter.

While one can speak of a French approach and a German approach to the problem of mistake, there were almost as many Anglo-American approaches as jurists. Ultimately, however, the English and Americans found themselves confronting the same problems, and with as little success.

Some of them supported the solution that Fubini had said was difficult to justify in theory. They said that to warrant relief a mistake must be mutual: that is, both parties must be mistaken.

[165] Windscheid, *supra* n. 4, i, §76a.

[166] *Bürgerlichesgesetzbuch*, §119.

[167] Bekker, 'Zur Lehre von den Willenserklärung: Einfluss von Zwang und Irrthum', book review of A. Schliemann, *Die Lehre vom Zwange* (Rostock, 1861), in *Kritische Vierteljahresschrift für Gesetzgebung und Rechtwissenchaft*, 3 (1861), 180 at 188–9; Renaud, *supra* n. 161, pp. 247–54; Hesse, *supra* n. 155, p. 101. Mandry raises the problem but is uncertain how to resolve it. (Mandry, *supra* n. 149, pp. 381–2.)

[168] Roman law, Windscheid said, regarded certain 'attributes' as 'so close to defining the essence of a thing' that their presence or absence 'makes the thing a different thing'. Just which attributes did so was not at all clear from the Roman texts. The opinion dominant among German jurists was that 'concepts and views must be involved that are decisive for commercial usage'. (Windscheid, *supra* n. 4, i, §76a.)

[169] Fubini, *supra* n. 131, pp 309–10.

Some Anglo-American courts had adopted this rule in a pragmatic attempt to limit relief, and it was repeated by a number of common law writers such as Joseph Story,[170] Leake,[171] and Leonard.[172] It seemed, however, flatly to contradict the principle on which everyone agreed: that both parties must consent to the same thing to form a contract. Leonard admitted the difficulty and justified the rule by saying that, while there was no contract in principle, nevertheless, 'the rights of one must yield to the rights of many, the individual is subordinated to the state'.[173]

Those who wanted a solution founded on principle looked in the same directions as their continental brethren. They talked about the identity of an object, about the properties that constituted a difference in species, or about properties important to the parties.

Metcalf[174] and Leonard[175] said that a contract was void for a mistake in 'identity'. Similarly, Parsons said that it was void if the parties did not agree 'to the same thing in the same sense'.[176] They did not explain what they meant by 'identity' or 'sameness', and it is unlikely that they could have done so.

Pollock, following Savigny, allowed relief to be given for a mistake about an 'attribute' of an object that constituted a 'difference in kind' according to the 'ordinary course of dealing'.[177] Like Savigny, he claimed that in such a case the party's expression of his will differed from his true will, and therefore no contract was formed.[178] He did not respond to any of the criticisms that had been voiced in the half-century since Savigny wrote.

Many more Anglo-American jurists allowed relief to depend on the importance of a mistake to a party. After saying that a contract is void for a mistake in 'essence' or 'substance', Joseph and William Story revealed how little they understood the original sense of those terms by claiming that the mistake must be 'material'.[179] Later authors such as Bishop[180] and Ashley[181] did not mention 'essence' or 'substance' but stated that a 'material' mistake will void a contract. What Ashley meant by 'material' is far from clear, since his examples

[170] J. Story, *Equity Jurisprudence as Administered in England and America* (Boston, 1918), 152.

[171] Leake, *supra* n. 66, pp. 168–70.

[172] Leonard, 'An Analysis of the Law of Mistake of Fact as Applied in the Avoidance of Contracts', *Albany Law Journal*, 64 (1902), 148 at 152.

[173] Ibid. 152.

[174] Metcalf, *supra* n. 66, p. 30.

[175] Leonard, *supra* n. 172, p. 150.

[176] Parsons, *supra* n. 66, i, *399.

[177] Pollock, *supra* n. 47, p. 436.

[178] Ibid. 392–4.

[179] J. Story, *supra* n. 170, i. 152, 212–13; W. W. Story, *supra* n. 66, pp. 405, 419.

[180] J. Bishop, *Commentaries on the Law of Contracts* (Chicago, 1907), 297–8.

[181] C. Ashley, *The Law of Contracts* (Boston, 1911), 131, 136; Ashley, 'Mutual Assent in Contract', *Columbia Law Review*, 3 (1903), 71 at 72.

are mistakes in the identity of a concrete individual thing.[182] William Story[183] and Bishop[184] explained, however, that a mistake is 'material' if but for the mistake the parties would not have contracted. Surely, however, they would not have been willing to give relief for every such mistake, and they do not explain how relief should be limited.

In the twentieth century, more sophisticated ways were found to describe the significance that a mistake must have to a party to warrant relief. Despite his professed belief in an objective theory of contracts, Williston developed such a solution, one that was eventually incorporated in the First and Second Restatements of Contracts. A party would be given relief when he mistakenly 'assumed the existence of a fact . . . as a basis on which [he] bargained'.[185] Corbin popularized another solution that was also incorporated in the Second Restatement: a party cannot obtain relief when he assumed the risk that the facts are not as he hoped. According to Corbin, a risk is assumed when 'the occurrence of an event is consciously considered in agreeing upon terms', when 'there is an awareness of uncertainty, a conscious ignorance of the future'.[186] The two solutions are like opposite sides of a coin. The first asks what a party assumed to be true, the second what he doubted. Presumably, however, neither Williston nor Corbin nor the drafters of the Restatements really meant that the validity of a contract should turn on what a particular party treated as certain or uncertain. If that were so, the validity of a contract would turn on whether the party was the brash type who always assumes his horse will win, or the nervous or imaginative type who consciously considers every possible catastrophe. Consequently it is not clear what these solutions mean. They seem to mean merely that relief will be given for certain mistakes of significance to a party, but one cannot say which ones.

If the French, German, and Anglo-American jurists failed to find a coherent solution, it was not for want of trying. They faced a new and intractable problem. The concept of essence had enabled earlier jurists to talk about a single set of properties that determined the identity of an object, its species, and the end it served. Various

[182] Ashley, *Law of Contracts*, *supra* n. 181, pp. 136–8; Ashley, 'Mutual Assent in Contract', *supra* n. 131, p. 76.

[183] W. W. Story, *supra* n. 66, p. 419.

[184] Bishop, *supra* n. 180, pp. 297–8.

[185] As the Second Restatement puts it, to invalidate a contract a mistake must concern 'a basic assumption on which the contract was made'. (Restatement (Second) of Contracts, §152(1) (1981).)

[186] A. Corbin, *Contracts* (St. Paul, Minn., 1963) iii, §598. According to the Second Restatement, a party bears a risk when 'he is aware . . . that he has only limited knowledge . . . but treats his limited knowledge as sufficient'. (Restatement (Second) of Contracts, §152 (1981).)

nineteenth-century jurists recognized that mistakes in the identity of an object, its species, and its usefulness did matter. Without the concept of essence, however, they had to discuss each one of these three without regard to the others, and that did not work.

A will theory that cannot explain when a party willed to contract is in serious trouble. In the late nineteenth century, proponents of an 'objective theory' of contract such as Oliver Wendell Holmes in the United States and Siegmund Schlossmann in Germany claimed that the concept of will was not useful. Contract was a series of consequences that law attached to what the parties said and did, whatever their will might be.

To explain relief for mistake, Holmes looked to what the parties said and did, Schlossmann to the consequences the law might wish to impose. According to Holmes, a mistake would prevent formation of a contract only if, because of the mistake, the parties contradicted themselves outwardly. For example, if a party agreed to buy 'these barrels of mackerel', and the barrels contained salt, the language was contradictory and the contract void because no object is both 'these barrels' and 'of mackerel'. The difficulties of ignoring what the parties might want and allowing everything to turn on what they happened to say were obvious even to Holmes. A taciturn party who merely said he wanted 'these barrels' would be bound. A loquacious party who described the goods he wanted in detail would be released if there were the most insignificant discrepancy between the goods and his description. Holmes answered, in a famous phrase he used more than once, 'The distinctions of the law are founded on experience, not on logic.' In other words, Holmes's distinctions were not founded on logic. As we have seen, Williston looked elsewhere for a solution, despite his allegiance to an objective theory and his admiration for Holmes.

Schlossmann thought relief should depend on whether it is 'fair and equitable to grant protection against the legal consequences of his transaction to the person who is in error as to the characteristics of an object'.[187] The reason for giving relief at all is simply 'that the person in error is human, and that it is therefore equitable' to help him 'insofar as it can be done without serious damage to more or equally important interests of another party—in a contract, in particular, those of the other contracting party'.[188] The trouble is that in contract law the question of whether the other party's interests are important usually turns on whether the first party has committed himself and, if so, to what. That is the very question

[187] S. Schlossmann, *Irrtum* (Jena, 1903), 46.
[188] Ibid. 47.

raised in a case of mistake. Schlossmann did not explain how to answer it, and his failure indicates a basic problem with 'objective theories'. It is not helpful to say that contract is a series of consequences the law attaches to the parties' conduct if one cannot explain why the law does so. Very often, the law does so only because the parties did consent.

THE CONTENT OF A CONTRACT

For the late scholastics and the natural lawyers, contracts were entered into by the will of the parties. The parties' obligations, however, depended on the type of transaction they chose to enter into. Each type could be defined by identifying an end the transaction served and a larger type to which it belonged: it is an act of commutative justice or an act of liberality. The obligations of the parties followed from the definition. For example, acts of commutative justice required equality in the value of the performances exchanged.

Again, the nineteenth-century jurists dispensed with the concepts of virtue, commutative justice, essence, and end. This time when they did so almost nothing remained of earlier doctrine. It was no longer possible to speak of equality in exchange or the natural terms of a contract. The nineteenth-century jurists spoke of will instead. The obligations of the parties were whatever the parties willed them to be.

Equality in Exchange

As we have seen, in the late eighteenth century the doctrine of equality in exchange was attacked by Christian Thomasius. He claimed that those who believed in equality in exchange conceived of value as an intrinsic property of things. In fact, value depends on 'the mere judgment of men', and the judgment that mattered was that of the contracting parties themselves, not that of other people.[189] Thomasius thus made two arguments that were repeated thereafter: that value is relative, and that to insist on exchange at a just price is to interfere with the judgment of the contracting parties.

These arguments were made in the late eighteenth and nineteenth centuries when attempts were made to abolish the doctrine in Germany and France. When Prussian law was codified by the

[189] C. Thomasius, 'De aequitate cerebrina legis II: Cod. de rescind. vendit. et eius usu practico cap. II §14, 15, 19, 25', printed as Dissertatio LXXIII, in C. Thomasius, *Dissertationum Academicorum varii inprimis iuridici argumenti* (Halle-on-Saale, 1777), iii. 43. See Ch. 4 above, p. 95.

Allgemeines Landrecht of 1794, Suarez explained for the drafting committee that Thomasius had refuted 'the whole theory' on which relief for an unjust price had rested.[190] The new Code provided that disparity in price would not invalidate a contract 'in and of itself',[191] although error would be 'presumed' when a buyer paid twice the normal price.[192] Relief for an unjust price was abolished in Bavaria in 1861,[193] in Saxony in 1863,[194] and in commercial matters by the Allgemeines Handelsgesetzbuch of 1861.[195] Defending the latter measure in his commentary on commercial law, Endemann argued in much the same way as Thomasius. Value was relative. 'It is wholly unclear what a value corresponding [to the goods] should be taken to mean: the value of goods is one amount here and another there, one amount for the seller and another for the buyer . . .'.[196] Moreover, 'the determination of the price' should 'be left to the free agreement of the parties'.[197]

In France, these same two arguments were made by Berlier to explain why he and the other drafters of the Civil Code proposed to abolish relief for an unjust price. On the one hand, '[t]hings do not in general have a true price; a just price; they are worth less to one person, more to another . . . but the price is known only from the agreement itself.'[198] On the other hand, to give relief would be to interfere with the decision of the parties. 'An adult's duty is to contract with prudence', and therefore '[t]he law owes him no protection against his own acts.'[199] This proposal to abolish relief succeeded only in part. Article 1118 of the Civil Code provided that *lésion* or disparity in value would not invalidate a contract as a general rule.[200] Bonaparte, however, insisted on an exception in the

[190] *Allgemeines Landrecht für die Preussischen Staaten*, 7th edn., ed. C. Koch (Berlin, 1978), i, §58 n. 8.

[191] *Allgemeines Landrecht für die Preussischen Staaten von 1794*, ed. H. Hattenhauer (Frankfurt-on-Main, 1970), i. 77, §58.

[192] Ibid., *supra* n. 191, i. 77, §59.

[193] Landtagsabschiedes of 10 Nov. 1861, §282.4 [1861–2] Gesetzblatt; quoted in M. Danzer, *Das Bayerische Landrecht (Codex Maximilianeus Bavaricus Civilis) vom Jahre 1756 in seiner heutigen Geltung* (Munich, 1894), 229–30. Until then, the remedy of *laesio enormis* had been preserved in the Codex Maximilianeus Bavaricus Civilis, IV. iii, §§19–22 (enacted in 1756).

[194] Bürgerliches Gesetzbuch für des Königreich Sachsen, §864.

[195] Allgemeines deutsches Handelsgesetzbuch, §286.

[196] W. Endemann, *Handbuch* (Leipzig, 1882), ii, §261. III, pp. 555–6.

[197] Ibid. 555.

[198] J. Locré, *La Legislation civile, commerciale et criminelle de la France* (Paris, 1826–31) xii. 65.

[199] Ibid. xii. 188.

[200] Article 1118 provided that *lésion* 'vitiates certain but not all contracts and these only with respect to certain persons, as is explained in the appropriate section'. In addition to the exception, Article 1674 provided for sellers of land, Article 1304

case of sales of land, and article 1674 duly provided for relief when land was sold for less than five-twelfths of its value.

It is worth noting that the reasons Bonaparte advanced had no relation at all to the earlier theory of equality in exchange. He observed that the way a person disposes of land is 'not without importance to society', and that a person should not be allowed to sacrifice 'in a moment of folly the inheritance of his fathers and the patrimony of his children to the violence of his passions'.[201] Bonaparte does not seem to have been concerned about equality as such but about the squandering of family estates.

In France, then, a remedy remained for sale of land at an unjust price. In Germany, the old Roman remedy for *laesio enormis* or gross disparity in price remained except in those areas in which it had been abolished by statute. Whether such a remedy was abolished or retained, however, the older principle of equality in exchange dropped out of treatises on contract law.

In France, some jurists questioned whether relief for *lésion* should be given at all. Like Berlier, Demolombe argued that value was 'subjective', 'variable and relative'.[202] Similarly, Laurent observed that the value of things was not 'absolute': things worth one amount 'from a commercial point of view' might be worth quite a different amount to the parties because of their 'needs, tastes and passions'.[203] Jurists who were more sympathetic to the remedy defended it without invoking a principle of equality in exchange. Thus Duranton, Colmet de Santerre, and Marcadé explained that, while inadequacy of price was not itself a ground for relief, it was evidence of a 'defect in consent': of fraud, mistake, duress, or a sort of moral constraint.[204] Still another approach was that of Glasson.

provided an exception for unemancipated minors, and Article 887 provided an exception for co-heirs in a division of property (*partage*). Some have wanted to count as an additional exception Article 1855, which provided that a partnership contract (*société*) is void if it gives one partner all the benefits. Others claim that such a contract is really void for lack of *cause*. (B. Starck, *Droit civil: Obligations* (Paris, 1972), §1592 n. 183.) In 1968 a further exception was created for persons of reduced capacity who have been put under 'the protection of justice'. (Article 491–2, as amended by Law no. 68–5 of 3 Jan. 1968.) Special statutes have also been enacted giving relief to buyers of fertilizer, seeds, and fodder, victims of sea or aviation accidents, and sellers of artistic and literary property; see Gordley, 'Equality in Exchange', *California Law Review*, 69 (1981), 1625–6.

[201] Locré, *supra* n. 198, xiv. 89, 90–1. The more traditional argument that the 'equity' of contracts requires a fair price had been made by Bigot-Préameneu on the drafting committee. (Ibid. xii. 195.)

[202] Demolombe, *supra* n. 2. xxiv, §194.

[203] Laurent, *supra* n. 2, xv, §485.

[204] Duranton, *supra* n. 2, x, §§200–1; Demante and Colmet de Santerre, *supra* n. 2, v, §28 *bis* (by Colmet de Santerre); V. Marcadé, *Explication théoretique et pratique du Code Napoleon* (Paris, 1859), 357–8. According to Colmet de Santerre,

Like Berlier, he thought that relief for *lésion* violated the 'principle of freedom of contract', by which 'one must accept responsibility for the consequences of one's actions'. Relief was justified as an exception to the normal rules of contract law for reasons of 'humanity'.[205]

German jurists also regarded their remedy for *laesio enormis* as an exception to the normal rules of contract law. Those who defended it generally explained, like Glasson, that it was an exception based on 'equity'. The basic principle of contract law was contained not in the Roman text that provided a remedy for those who sold land at less than half its just price,[206] but in another which said that in a sale 'it is permitted by nature for one party to buy for less and the other to sell for more, and thus each is allowed to outwit the other'.[207] This text must state the general principle, they said, because contracts are made by the will of the parties, and thus relief for an unjust price runs counter to the nature of a contract. According to Windscheid, this text stated a principle rooted 'in the nature of a contract of sale';[208] according to Vangerow, a principle 'lying in the nature of things'.[209] It must state the general principle, Holzschuher explained, because relief for a disparity in price interfered with 'the binding force of contracts'.[210] Nevertheless, there might be equitable reasons for an occasional exception to the principles of contract law. As Windscheid said, 'are there not limits to the advantage one contracting party can take of the other?'[211] Some pointed to the language of the text that provided a remedy to sellers of land: they should have a remedy because 'it is equitable' (*humanum est*).[212]

Equity, for these authors, seems to have been a vaguely conceived notion of fairness that sometimes justifies a departure from clear principle. They do not explain equity, much less invoke any definite concept of equality in exchange. The question that does concern

the victim of *lésion* acted 'under the dominion of an imperious necessity' and therefore was 'under a kind of moral constraint' (pp. 357–8). He seems to regard moral constraint are tantamount to duress, which in his view did vitiate consent. He may, however, have had the same view as Glasson.

205 E. Glasson, *Eléments du droit français* (Paris, 1884), 550, 553. Glasson denied that relief could be justified by 'purely legal arguments' (p. 559).

206 C. 4.44.2.

207 D. 19.2.22.3. See also D. 4.4.16.4.

208 Windscheid, *supra* n. 4, ii, §396 n. 2.

209 Vangerow, *supra* n. 34, iii, §611 n. 1.

210 R. von Holzschuher, *Theorie und Casuistik des gemeinen Civilrechts* (Leipzig, 1864), iii. 729–30.

211 Windscheid, *supra* n. 4, ii, §396 n. 2.

212 Vangerow, *supra* n. 34, iii, §611 n. 1 at 328–9 (describing the arguments of other authors); C. von Wächter, *Pandekten* (Leipzig, 1881), ii, §207 at 472–3.

them is how much of an exception for the sake of equity had been created. Some wished to limit relief to sellers of land because it was an exception;[213] others wished to extend relief to buyers of land and parties to other kinds of contracts because such relief would be equally equitable.[214] Everyone agreed, however, that they were dealing with an exceptional kind of relief that departed from the normal principles of contract law. In Germany, as in France, equality in exchange had ceased to belong among these normal principles.

Nineteenth-century English and American treatise writers reached similar conclusions although they presented them as an explanation of traditional English rules. According to one traditional rule, the common law does not examine the adequacy of consideration. As we have seen, this rule had not been developed to avoid judicial scrutiny of hard bargains. Nevertheless, according to the nineteenth-century jurists, the rule meant that a court would not give relief for disparities in price. They defended the rule thus interpreted with the same two arguments.

First, to give relief would raise imponderable questions about value. The rule was a good one, according to Joseph Story, because the value of a thing 'must be in its nature fluctuating and will depend upon ten thousand different circumstances. One man in the disposal of his property may sell it for less than another man would.'[215] Similarly, Chitty[216] and Metcalf[217] argued that there were 'no means' for determining whether consideration was 'adequate'. William Story[218] thought the enquiry would involve a 'psychological investigation into the motives of the parties', a view also held by Addison.[219] Pollock addressed the subject by quoting part of Hobbes's attack on the Aristotelian concept of justice: 'The value of all things contracted for is measured by the appetite of the contractors, and therefore the just value is that which they be contented to give.'[220]

213 Holzschuher, *supra* n. 210, iii. 729–30; Vangerow, *supra* n. 34, iii, §611; Wächter, *supra* n. 212, ii, §207. Some said the exception should be limited to sellers because it was meant to protect those in need, and sellers who accepted a low price would be more likely to be needy than buyers who paid a high one; e.g. Puchta, *supra* n. 4, §364; Keller, *supra* n. 30, 333.

214 e.g. J. Seuffert, *Praktisches Pandekten recht* (Wurzburg, 1852), ii, §272.

215 J. Story, *supra* n. 170, i. 339.

216 Chitty, *supra* n. 2, p. 7.

217 Metcalf, *supra* n. 66, p. 163.

218 W. W. Story, *supra* n. 66, p. 435.

219 C. Addison, *A Treatise on the Law of Contracts* (London, 1911), 12.

220 Pollock, *supra* n. 47, p. 172. For the quotation from Hobbes, see n. 47 above.

The second argument was that to give relief would be to interfere with the decision of the parties themselves. Joseph Story explained:

> [E]very person who is not from his peculiar condition under disability is entitled to dispose of his property in such a manner and upon such terms as he chooses; and whether his bargains are wise and discreet or profitable or unprofitable or otherwise, are considerations not for courts of justice but for the party himself to deliberate upon.[221]

A similar argument was made, in conjunction with the argument about value, by Chitty, Addison, Metcalf, and William Story.[222] It was also advanced in one form or another by Leake, Taylor, Bishop, Smith, Newland, and Hammon.[223]

This interpretation of the rule that adequacy of consideration would not be examined seemed to conflict with another rule the English and Americans had inherited. The rule was that courts of equity would not grant specific performance of an unconscionable bargain. If there was no such thing as a just price, and the determination of the price was a matter for the parties themselves, then it was hard to see why courts of equity refused to enforce all bargains. The treatise writers who faced this problem generally explained that a disparity in price was not in itself a ground for relief, but it was evidence that fraud had been committed.[224] While the fraud theory never swept the field,[225] it found its way into many treatises beginning with the early one by Powell in 1790.[226] Indeed, Joseph Story, William Story, and Metcalf[227] argued that the fraud theory must be correct since questions of value are imponderable.

[221] J. Story, *supra* n. 170, i. 337.

[222] J. Chitty, *Law of Contracts Not Under Seal* (London, 1826), 7; Addison, *supra* n. 219, p. 12; Metcalf, *supra* n. 66, p. 163; W. W. Story, *supra* n. 66, p. 435.

[223] Leake, *supra* n. 66, pp. 311–12; W. Taylor, *The Laws of England and Scotland Relating to Contracts* (London, 1849), 17; Bishop, *supra* n. 180, p. 18; J. Smith, *The Law of Contracts* (Philadelphia, 1847), *96; J. Newland, *Contracts Within the Jurisdiction of Courts of Equity* (1821), 357; Hammon, *supra* n. 18, p. 692.

[224] Occasionally, the disparity in price was said to be evidence not of fraud, but of a lack of freedom and reason that prevented genuine consent. Thus, according to one anonymous writer, relief was granted if 'the plaintiff was not a free agent, but was at the time under some urgent physical necessity—some overpowering terror—some superstitious idea that dominated over the mind'. ('Unconscionable Bargains', *The Law Times*, 49 (1870), 223 at 223.)

[225] See e.g. Parsons, *supra* n. 3, i. *362–3; J. Pomeroy, *Specific Performance of Contracts* (New York, 1897), 274–5.

[226] J. Powell, *Law of Contracts and Agreements* (London, 1790), ii. 157–8; Bishop, *supra* n. 180, pp. 18–19; Hammon, *supra* n. 18, pp. 694–5; Metcalf, *supra* n. 66, p. 163; Newland, *supra* n. 223, pp. 358–9; J. Story, *supra* n. 170, i. 341; W. W. Story, *supra* n. 66, pp. 437–8.

[227] J. Story, *supra* n. 170, i. 339; W. W. Story, *supra* n. 66, pp. 437–8; Metcalf, *supra* n. 66, p. 163.

According to some historians, the principle of equality was rejected by the nineteenth-century jurists because of the massive economic changes that were taking place at the time. The growth of large-scale markets undermined the belief that objects have a stable value. Moreover, a principle of equality would have thwarted the activities of rising commercial and industrial elites with whom the jurists sympathized.[228]

Since prices fluctuate the most wildly when markets are small or poorly organized, it is hard to see why the growth of large-scale markets is supposed to have made prices less stable. Even if it did, however, it is still harder to see how such an instability could have threatened the principle of equality in which the late scholastics and natural lawyers believed. As we have seen, their theory was not predicated on the belief that the value of objects was stable; they explained that the value of goods changes from day to day and from region to region.

Nor would the principle of equality, as the late scholastics and natural lawyers understood it, have presented much of an obstacle to nineteenth-century entrepreneurial activity. In the absence of government regulation, the just price was the market price. As we have seen, the principle of equality merely protected a person who had bought for more or sold for less than the market price because of ignorance or necessity. A nineteenth-century steel, railroad, or textile baron would not have found that principle overly confining. In addition, as we have already seen, American courts gave relief for one-sided bargains in practice even though they rejected the principle in theory. Although French courts were prohibited from doing so by the Code, German courts still gave relief for *laesio enormis* even though such relief was now said to be an equitable exception to the normal rules of contract.

The best evidence of why the jurists rejected the doctrine of equality in exchange is the statements of the jurists themselves. The doctrine seemed to them to involve mystical notions of value and disrespect for the will of the parties.

These arguments show not only why the nineteenth-century jurists rejected the doctrine, but the extent to which the earlier concept of equality in exchange had been forgotten. The late scholastics and the natural lawyers did not regard value as an intrinsic or stable property of things. They thought that value was determined by need, scarcity, and cost, and that the just price would fluctuate. They did not think they were imposing other people's

[228] M. Horwitz, *The Transformation of American Law 1780–1860* (Cambridge, Mass., 1977), 160–210.

judgments or notions of fairness on the contracting parties. In their theory, to require equality in exchange was not to disregard but to respect the will of the parties. Had one party wished to enrich the other at his own expense, he would have chosen not to exchange but to make a gift.

Had the nineteenth-century jurists been familiar with the earlier concept of equality in exchange, they could doubtless have devised arguments against it had they wished to do so. All one can know for certain is that they were not familiar with the concept. Once again an Aristotelian idea, used by older jurists, had dropped out of sight.

The significance of the change lay not in its practical consequences but in its theoretical result. The fairness of a contract could no longer be analysed. The older way of doing so had been rejected and no new way had been found. Moreover, an obstacle had been created to any attempt to find a new way. The will of the parties had been separated from, and indeed, opposed to, concern about the fairness of their contract. Through what they did not borrow, the nineteenth-century jurists thus changed the significance of what they did borrow: the concept of will itself. Will was now conceived as consent to the *ipsissima verba* of a contract, not as consent to a type of transaction with its own natural requirements, and not as the voluntary exercise of a particular virtue.

The Implied Terms of a Contract

In the Aristotelian and Thomistic tradition, the obligations of a contracting party followed from the type of contract he had entered into. Each contract had an essence or nature and an end or final cause in terms of which its essence was defined. One could move from the definition to a description of the obligations the contract entailed. They were means to the end of the contract or were included in the definition itself. The gap was thus bridged between the general principles of the law of contract and the obligations entailed by particular types of contract.

In the nineteenth century the Aristotelian concepts of essence and end were no longer available to bridge this gap. Some writers still spoke of the 'natural terms' of a contract, but to them, the phrase simply meant the terms that the law would read into a contract absent express provision by the parties.[229] Why the law should do so had become an open question.

Until the end of the nineteenth century, most jurists ignored that question. They defined contract in terms of the will of the parties

[229] Aubry and Rau, *supra* n. 11, iv, §43; Larombière, *supra* n. 2, i. 36–7; Puchta, *supra* n. 4, §58.

without explaining how the parties could will all the obligations the law attached to their contract. Sometimes, they spoke vaguely of the will of the parties as the source of all the parties' obligations.[230] Occasionally, they spoke as though the parties actually wished to assume these obligations, or would have wished to do so had they given the matter a little thought. For example, according to Laurent, the French Civil Code merely foresaw the terms the parties wanted when it provided rules for sales, leases, and other contracts. The Code did so 'to dispense the parties from writing them into their instruments . . .'.[231] His view, incidentally, was not that of the drafters of the Code, who believed, following Domat, that terms belonged to a certain type of contract naturally and as a matter of equity.[232]

Towards the end of the century, the will theorists were challenged by the proponents of an 'objective' theory of contract. The objectivists claimed that the parties did not will the legal consequences of their transaction, or at least that the law did not arrive at these consequences because the parties had willed them. One step in their argument was to claim that the parties could not have willed all the legal consequences of their transaction. Williston argued: 'To assume first that everybody knows the law, and, second, that everybody thereupon makes his contract with reference to it and adopts its provisions as terms of the agreement, is indeed to pile a fiction upon a fiction . . . .'[233] Similarly, the German objectivist Schlossmann observed that, 'in reality, many legal consequences arise which the person declaring his will did not foresee and could not foresee as possible consequences . . .'.[234] Moreover, it was

[230] e.g. Puchta, *supra* n. 4, §58.

[231] Laurent, *supra* n. 2, xvi, §182.

[232] The Code, paraphrasing Domat, said that the parties were bound to all the consequences that statute, equity, and custom attached to their agreement. (Code civil art. 1135; J. Domat, *Les Loix civiles* (Paris, 1713), I. i, pp. iii, I.) The drafters never suggested that they meant anything different than Domat. Indeed, Bigot-Préameneu said the provisions of the Code were based on features that were 'inherent to the contract, which differentiate its nature and effects'. (Fenet, *supra* n. 97, xiii. 239.) He evidently had in mind the view of the natural lawyers that different types of contracts had different sets of natural terms. A critic of the draft, Lacuée, objected that the Code might 'extend engagements well beyond the limits the contract debtor consented to give them' by 'imposing on this debtor obligations he could not have foreseen'. Tronchet, of the drafting committee, answered that 'the contract of sale, for example, admits obligations that are the natural result of the contract because they are drawn from its essence, and that have their effect although they are not expressed at all. Such is, among others, the guarantee.' (Fenet, *supra* n. 97, xiii. 54–5.) Again, there was no suggestion of a break with the past.

[233] Williston, *supra* n. 122, ii, §615. See Williston, 'Freedom of Contract', *Cornell Law Quarterly*, 6 (1921), 365 at 371.

[234] Schlossmann, review of E. Zitelmann, *Irrthum und Rechtsgeschäft*, in *Zeitschrift für das Privat- und öffentliche Recht der Gegenwart*, 7 (1980), 543 at 561.

circular to claim that the parties willed that their transaction be given whatever effects the law prescribed, even though they did not foresee what those effects might be: 'Question: what does the law will? Answer: what the parties will. What do the parties will? What the law wills!'[235]

For the objectivists, to show that some consequences of the parties' transaction were not willed was one step towards their ultimate conclusion that the will of the parties was not, in principle, the source of their obligations. Schlossmann argued: 'Accept that a transaction produces legal consequences because they are intended, and then this intention must extend to every single legal consequence produced under existing law by the transaction in question; and if any of these consequences did not fall within this intention, it cannot follow.'[236] Similarly, according to Kohler, since the parties did not will all the consequences of their transaction,one must conclude that they willed none of its consequences, or one must identify a certain minimum that the parties must will in order to contract. But no such minimum can be identified.[237]

The objectivists also had more general arguments why the will of the parties should not matter. In the United States, Holmes and Williston pointed out that a party was bound by the construction that the law and other parties placed upon his words whether he willed that construction or not.[238] Pollock answered this argument in the obvious way: the will mattered in principle, but for reasons of practicality 'men are taken to mean what they say'.[239]

The German objectivists went deeper by challenging the idea that the parties willed any legal consequences at all. According to Schlossmann, the will of a party was 'the consciousness of an urge advancing in realization'.[240] The party intends 'economic consequences', not legal consequences. He buys wine to fill his cellar, rents a house to have a place to live. He intends 'to have, to hold, to use, to consume', not to acquire a legal right to do so.[241] Similarly, Kohler claimed that the parties merely intend an 'economic result'. Once the parties have indicated their 'economic

[235] Schlossmann, *supra* n. 234, p. 562. [236] Ibid. 560–1.

[237] Kohler, 'Das Autorrecht, eine zivilistische Abhandlung, zugleich ein Beitrag zur Lehre vom Eigenthum, vom Miteigenthum, vom Rechtsgeschäft und vom Individualrecht', *Jahrbücher für die Dogmatik des heutigen römischen und deutschen Privatrechts*, ed. R. Ihering, 18 (1880), 129 at 149–50.

[238] Williston, *supra* n. 122, §§20, 605–8.

[239] Pollock, *supra* n. 47, pp. 456, 460. Thus, Williston himself noted that in practice he and Pollock arrived at the same results. (Williston, *supra* n. 122, §607, n. 20.)

[240] Schlossmann, *Vertrag* (Leipzig, 1876), 136–7.

[241] Schlossmann, *supra* n. 234, pp. 569–70.

object', the law determines the legal consequences of their transaction without regard to their intention.[242]

In the ensuing dialogue, the will theorists insisted that the law attaches consequences to the transaction because of the parties' intentions.[243] Jurists such as Enneccerus and Bruns conceded that the parties were not aware of all of the consequences of their transaction. They claimed that the parties tacitly or indistinctly willed legal consequences of which they were not consciously aware. Enneccerus said that the parties had a 'practical outlook' which was given clarity by the legal construction of the jurist.[244] Bruns admitted that the parties thought of their 'material and economic purposes', with no 'clear consciousness' of the legal consequences of their transaction. Nevertheless, these consequences were not imposed by the law; 'rather the law is immanent in the will of a person'.[245]

These jurists, in responding to the objectivists, gave will theory a strange twist. The parties did not will the full consequences of their act, but the full consequences followed in some way from what they did will.

Moderate objectivists, in responding to the will theorists, found themselves making a similar claim. Lenel and Bechmann agreed with Schlossmann that the parties did not will the legal consequences of their transaction. They had an 'economic intent',[246] an intent corresponding to the 'needs of life'.[247] Nevertheless, the will theorists were right that the law attached consequences to a transaction because of what the parties willed. According to Lenel, the law did so to serve the purposes the parties were pursuing.[248] According to Bechmann, the law enforced the explicit intentions of the parties, and when they had merely trusted each other to act in a decent fashion, the law filled the 'gaps' in their intentions by deciding what trust required and forcing the parties to live up to its demands.[249] Thus, for Lenel and Bechmann, the parties did not will the full consequences of their act, but these consequences followed from what they did will.

242 Kohler, *supra* n. 237, pp. 155–6.

243 e.g. Windscheid, *supra* n. 4, i, §75 n. 1a; L. Enneccerus, *Rechtsgeschäft, Bedingung und Anfangstermin* (Marburg, 1889), 17–19; Brus, *supra* n. 157, p. 453.

244 Enneccerus, *supra* n. 243, pp. 18–19.

245 Bruns, *supra* n. 157, p. 454.

246 Lenel, 'Parteiabsicht und Rechtserfolg', *Jahrbücher für die Dogmatik des heutigen römischen und deutschen Privatrechts* (1881), xix. 154 at 162–3.

247 Bechmann, *supra* n. 154, ii, §102.

248 Lenel, *supra* n. 246, pp. 163–4.

249 Bechmann, *supra* n. 154, ii, §120.

At this point, the distinction between will theory and objective theory began to blur. It became even less clear as the objectivists explained what the parties did will. While insisting that the parties did not will the legal consequences of their transaction, they conceived of the 'economic intent' of the parties in a normative way. Even for Schlossmann, a party did not intend simply to get wine or a house; he intended 'to have, to hold, to use, to consume'—words that denote distinct rights one can have to an object. Lenel went further. He claimed that one could not get from Schlossmann's economic intent to the idea of a binding contract. A party does not promise if he simply intends to do a thing; he must intend to bind himself to do it, even though he need not intend to be legally bound.[250] For Bechmann, parties not only intended to acquire rights that were not legal rights, as they did for Schlossmann, or obligations that were not legal obligations, as they did for Lenel: they intended to buy, to lease, and so forth. Thus, Bechmann claimed, words such as 'buy' and 'lease' have two meanings which, he said, we rarely distinguish: they refer to the 'empirical' intent of the parties, and to that intent coupled with a legal sanction.[251]

Will theorists and objectivists thus arrived at a similar position. The parties willed a certain normative relationship—which the will theorists called 'legal' and their opponents called 'empirical' or 'economic'. The legal consequences of that relationship were not explicitly willed but followed from the relationship.

This position, however, was like that of the late scholastics and natural lawyers. It consequently involved a paradox. Both will theorists and objectivists were speaking as though contracts had natures or essences. Indeed, it would be hard to explain the difference between saying that the parties willed a contract with a certain nature from which legal consequences followed and saying that they willed a certain normative relationship from which legal consequences followed. Yet if contracts had natures, it was hard to see the point of will theories or objective theories. These theories emerged only because jurists had ceased to speak of the nature or essence of a contract as the source of the parties' obligations. The source was identified as the will of the parties or the law, there being, supposedly, no other alternative. Moreover, if contracts had natures, the jurists should have continued to write like the late scholastics and natural lawyers. Instead of arguing about will theory and objective theory, they should have defined different types

[250] Lenel, *supra* n. 246, pp. 163–4, 199–200.
[251] Bechmann, *supra* n. 154, ii, §§104–5.

of contract and shown how legal consequences follow from the definitions.

Once again, the nineteenth-century jurists had tried to get along without an Aristotelian idea, used by earlier jurists, that was no longer clearly understood. Once again, they had failed to make their own theories work without that idea.

CONCLUSION

Writing in 1980, Valérie Ranouil listed the characteristics of the will theories that prevailed in nineteenth-century France. The binding force of a contract was not explained but was taken for granted. Contract was defined as the consent of the parties. That definition was then used to explain the need for an offer to be accepted. Defects in consent such as mistake, fraud, and duress were conceived in a 'façon exclusivement psychologique' as deviations from a 'volonté saine'. The content of the contract was determined by the will of the parties. For that reason *lésion* did not, in principle, invalidate a contract, and the effects of the contract were to be traced to the will of the parties.[252]

As we have seen, these features were characteristic of Anglo-American and German will theories as well, except that the German will theorists had a different approach to defects in consent. They generally maintained that, in principle, neither mistake nor fraud nor duress affected the validity of a contract.

As we have also seen, every feature on this list was an instance in which the nineteenth-century jurists modified the contract doctrine of the late scholastics and the natural lawyers by eliminating one or more Aristotelian philosophical concepts. In each case, the modification created difficulties which they recognized themselves and struggled to resolve.

It is a testimony to their failure to resolve these difficulties permanently that these features appear on Ranouil's list. In making the list, she was comparing the contract law of the nineteenth century not with earlier contract law, but with that of our own time. These features stand out because they seem odd to us today. The reason they seem odd is because we now regard the difficulties the nineteenth-century jurists wrestled with as insuperable. The concept of will, by itself, cannot do all that the will theorists claimed for it.

[252] Ranouil, *supra* n. 5, pp. 71–3.

8
LIBERALISM AND NINETEENTH-CENTURY CONTRACT LAW

ACCORDING to Williston, the will theories arose because '[a] gospel of freedom was preached by both metaphysical and political philosophers in the latter half of the eighteenth century'. Its 'classic expression . . . in the United States is found in the sweeping generalities of the Declaration of Independence'. 'In metaphysics, at the same time, philosophers were emphasizing the ego and the individual human will as the basic facts of life.' Similarly, economists such as Smith, Ricardo, Bentham, and J. S. Mill 'insisted on freedom of bargaining as the fundamental and indispensable requisite of progress'. '[I]t was a corollary of the philosophy of freedom and individualism that the law ought to extend the sphere and enforce the obligation of contract.' The law did so by requiring a meeting of the minds for the formation of a contract and by allowing the parties to contract on whatever terms they might choose.[1]

Williston was not an historian. Yet his hypothesis that the will theories were manifestations of a nineteenth-century philosophy of freedom and individualism has certainly appealed to historians. It is a thesis of Gilmore[2] and the theme of Atiyah's study, *The Rise and Fall of Freedom of Contract*.[3] According to Savatier, Tunc, and Ranouil, nineteenth-century French contract law was suited to an age of liberalism.[4] According to Ranouil, it was 'the masterpiece of

[1] Williston, 'Freedom of Contract', *Cornell Law Quarterly*, 6 (1921), 365 at 366–9.

[2] G. Gilmore, *The Ages of American Law* (New Haven, Conn., 1977), 65–6.

[3] P. S. Atiyah, *The Rise and Fall of Freedom of Contract* (Oxford, 1979).

[4] R. Savatier, *Les Métamorphoses économiques et sociales du droit privé d'aujourd'hui: l'Universalisme renouvelé des disciplines juridiques* (Paris, 1959), 6–8; A. Tunc, 'The Grand Outlines of the Code', in B. Schwartz (ed.), *The Code Napoleon and the Common-Law World* (New York, 1956), 19 at 40. Similarly, according to Duguit, 19th-c. contract law was 'a rigorous deduction' from the 'individualist system'. It was suited to 'an essentially individualist society, such as Roman society and those of Europe and America at the beginning of the 19th century'. (L. Duguit, *Les Transformations générales du Droit privé depuis le Code Napoléon*, 2nd edn. (Paris, 1920), 57–8.)

the philosophy of law that dominated the 19th century: that of legal individualism', a philosophy 'consecrated by the Declaration of 1789, and inspired by the doctrines of Rousseau and Kant'.[5] The leading German historian Franz Wieacker has said:

> Virtually every great age of technical legal studies has its background in generally recognized social and ethical doctrine: that of classical Rome in the philosophy of the Academy, the Peripatetics, and above all the Stoa; that of the Glossators, Canonists and Post-Glossators in the moral philosophy and social teachings of the medieval church; the *Pandektenwissenschaft* of the 19th century in Kant's ethic of freedom and duty.[6]

Wieacker's list, however, indicates a need for caution in drawing such connections. In the Roman texts and in the work of the Glossators, we have seen only a few poorly understood borrowings from the Greek philosophers Wieacker mentions. In that of the post-Glossators we have seen only discrete applications of Aristotelian and Thomistic philosophy to the interpretation of particular Roman texts. In none of the medieval civilians have we seen much if anything of the 'moral philosophy and social teachings' of the medieval church unless one counts the Thomistic philosophy just mentioned. The late scholastics did apply Aristotelian and Thomistic philosophy to legal problems self-consciously and consistently. But they did so not because this philosophy was generally accepted, but because they wished to revive it. As we have also seen, the connection between philosophy and legal doctrine snapped in the seventeenth and eighteenth centuries.

It is surely not an accident that the will theories shared the same century as intellectual and political movements that treated the will as an end in itself or as the indispensible engine of human progress. The historians must be right that there is some connection among them. The nature of this connection, however, is not obvious. As we have seen, the will theories emerged when the nineteenth-century jurists purged the doctrine they inherited of Aristotelian concepts they no longer understood. That process does not presuppose an allegiance to nineteenth-century liberal principles. Wolff did not subscribe to such principles and yet, as we have seen, he reached some of the same conclusions by the same process. In the writings of the nineteenth-century will theorists, moreover, we find little direct borrowing from philosophers, economists, or political theorists. Only rarely do we find any sign of a commitment to liberal

[5] V. Ranouil, *L'Autonomie de la volonté: naissance et évolution d'un concept* (Paris, 1980), 9. 10.

[6] K. Wieacker, *Privatrechtsgeschichte der Neuzeit under besonderer Berücksichtigung der deutschen Entwicklung*, 2nd edn. (Gottingen, 1967), 249.

values of freedom or individualism. We find almost the opposite: an insistence that the jurist can do his job without taking account of economics, philosophy, politics, or values such as freedom.[7]

In England and the United States, contract theory never became truly systematic until the time of Pollock. Jurists earlier in the century had groped towards system amidst a clutter of borrowed continental expressions and *ad hoc* modifications. They said almost nothing about any larger principles on which they were building. For that very reason, it is hard to believe they had any such principles in mind. If they did, moreover, one would expect to find the pattern we have already seen among the late scholastics: in the beginning, clear statements of philosophical principle loosely related to legal doctrine, and as time went on, a steadily better integration of principle and law. Instead, one finds a series of borrowings from older jurists in the beginning, modifications of these borrowings as time goes on, and hardly any statement of principle. The jurists write as though it were not their business to state their principles or examine them.

Although Pollock was the most systematic of the will theorists, he did not enlist larger philosophical, political, or economic principles in support of his theory. Instead, he explained that such principles were not the concern of jurists. 'Their business is to learn and know, so far as needful for their affairs, what rules the State does undertake to enforce and administer, whatever the real or professed reasons for those rules may be.'[8] When his contemporary Lorimer looked for such reasons in a book, *Institutes of Law*, Pollock objected that '[a]lmost the whole of it deals with topics which, according to the English view, may be philosophical, or ethical, or political, but are distinctly outside the province of jurisprudence'. Pollock said the book concerned '*Naturrecht* as the Germans call it', and his reaction was like that of a boy in a fairy tale who learned to shiver by being doused with a pail of cold water: 'Ugh! ugh! now I know what *Naturrecht* is.'[9] The 'morality of men living together in

[7] I once thought the will theories were an expression of 19th-c. liberalism. (A. T. von Mehren and J. Gordley, *The Civil Law System An Introduction to the Comparative Study of Law*, 2nd edn. (Boston, 1977), 859.) I now believe I was mistaken.

[8] F. Pollock, *A First Book of Jurisprudence for Students of the Common Law* (London, 1896), 26–7.

[9] Pollock, 'The Nature of Jurisprudence Considered in Relation to some Recent Contributions to Legal Science', in F. Pollock, *Essays in Jurisprudence and Ethics* (London, 1882), 1 at 19–20. It is interesting that less than a decade later, in 1900, Pollock wrote a very nice historical essay about the idea of natural law. (Pollock, 'The History of the Law of Nature', in F. Pollock, *Jurisprudence and Legal Essays* (New York, 1961), 124.) He described its foundations in Aristotelian philosophy and

settled societies', Pollock concluded, was 'an existing and sufficiently ascertained fact. It is for the moralist and the metaphysician to analyze it if they can; enough for us that it is there.'[10]

French historians have seen a commitment to liberalism not only in the work of the nineteenth-century jurists but in the Civil Code. According to Boistel, the Code enshrined the principle of the autonomy of the will.[11] According to Savatier, it was a 'bourgeois' code that rendered 'magnificent homage' to 'the will of the contracting parties'.[12] Tunc understood perfectly well that, in a field such as contracts, 'the law was left untouched by the Revolution' and '[t]he drafters of the Code therefore had no important decision to make'. And yet even he felt compelled to say, 'The law of contracts is clearly designed for a period of liberalism.'[13]

In fact, however, the French Civil Code neither contained a will theory of contract nor was founded on a liberal or individualistic philosophy. Indeed, the nineteenth-century interpreters of the Code who developed a will theory did not subscribe to such a philosophy either.

That the Code did not contain a will theory should be plain from the fact that virtually all its provisions on contracts were lifted, usually verbatim, from the works of Pothier and Domat. We have already seen that, in building their theories, the nineteenth-century jurists almost invariably had to read new meaning into a traditional formulation preserved by the Code. Modern scholars in looking for evidence of a will theory in the Code have generally pointed to article 1134, which says that contracts take the place of law between the parties.[14] That statement, however, had been made by Domat

its influence in medieval and modern times without any of the scorn he had expressed in his review of Lorimer's book. Apparently, jurists who wrote about universal principles long ago were in a different class from those who still wished to do so.

[10] Pollock, 'The Nature of Jurisprudence', *supra* n. 9, pp. 25–6. Similarly, in another essay he distinguished 'the theory of legislation', which 'shows us how we may know what laws are best in themselves' from 'jurisprudence', which deals with what the law actually is. (Pollock, 'The Science of Case-Law', in F. Pollock, *Essays in Jurisprudence and Ethics* (London, 1882), 237 at 262.) He admits that questions of what the law should be and what it is often run into each other when judges decide cases, but he seems to mean only that the law usually reflects what people think it ought to be, so that 'actual conflict . . . cannot be found on a large scale, or as a persistent state of things' (pp. 283–4). Certainly, he does not suggest that one must know what the law should be to decide what it is.

[11] A. Boistel, 'Le Code civil et la Philosophie du Droit', in *Le Code Civil 1804–1904 Livre du Centenaire* (Paris, 1904), i. 45 at 47–8.

[12] Savatier, *supra* n. 4, pp. 6–8. Similarly, A.-J. Arnaud, *Les Origines doctrinales du Code civil français* (Paris, 1969), 7–8, 172–4.

[13] Tunc, *supra* n. 4, p. 20.

[14] e.g. Savatier, *supra* n. 4, p. 6; Boistel, *supra* n. 11, p. 48; Arnaud, *supra* n. 12, pp. 199–202, 213–14. Tunc, *supra* n. 4, p. 40, tried to reconcile this claim with the

in a very traditional passage quoted earlier in which he explains that there are natural types of contracts. Domat had taken it from a collection of decretals of Pope Bonifacius VIII[15] who had taken it in turn from the *Digest*.[16] Neither the ancient Romans nor the Pope nor Domat had subscribed to a will theory of contract. Indeed, the drafters' one significant break with the past was that they curtailed the doctrine of *lésion* to the extent that Bonaparte permitted them to do so. Here, however, they were following Thomasius and the drafters of the Prussian *Allgemeineslandrecht* who, as we have seen, did not have a new theory of contract but found traditional ideas about equality unintelligible.[17]

This conservatism was not surprising given the attitude of the drafting committee. Portalis, the chairman, explained 'that instead of changing the laws it was almost always more useful to offer the citizens new reasons for loving them', since 'history shows us hardly two or three good laws promulgated in the space of several centuries'.[18] 'Modern theories are the systems of a few individuals, but ancient principle is the spirit of the centuries.'[19] The Code, therefore, was not to be a 'bold novelty' or 'grand conception'; if it were, it

Canon law origins of the text by saying the Code endorsed principles of freedom of contract that the canonists had developed. In that event, however, the drafters endorsed neither a will theory nor liberal philosophical principles. Similarly, Batiffol finds in article 1156 the idea that 'there is only an obligation to the extent that the parties so willed', an idea 'in perfect accord with the conception affirmed by the doctrine of the period'. (Batiffol, 'La "crise du contrat" et sa portée', *Archives de philosophie du droit*, 18 (1968), 13, 17.) Article 1156, however, merely provides that agreements should be interpreted not literally, but according to the 'common intention of the contracting parties', an ancient idea that the drafters took from Domat and Pothier. (J. Domat, *Les Loix civiles*, (Paris, 1713), I. i, pp. viii, 2; R. Pothier, *Traité des Obligations* (Paris, 1861), §91.)

[15] Liber Sextus V. 13.85.

[16] D. 50.17.23.

[17] It is hard to believe they were influenced by the supposedly bourgeois or liberal spirit of the French Revolution. The revolutionaries did temporarily suspend the remedy. (Décret qui abolit l'action en rescision des contrats de vente, 14 fructidor An III, *Collection générale des décrets rendus par la Convention nationale: lois civiles (intermédiares)* (Paris, 1794) xxxviii. 160; J. Domat, *Les Lois civiles (intermédiares)* (Paris, 1806), ii. 319–20.) The suspension was prompted, however, by a depreciation of the French currency, which had supposedly caused an 'infinity of lawsuits' by sellers of land who found themselves with now worthless paper money. (Décret qui renvoie au comité de législation un projet de décret relatif aux ventes attaquées pour cause de lésion, 9 fructidor An III, *Collection générale* (Paris, 1794). xxxviii. 122–3. See the proceedings of 4 Feb. 1973, noted in *Collection générale*, xxiii. 162. The remedy was soon reinstated on the ground that the difficulties with the currency had abated. (Loi qui lève la suspension en rescision des contrats de vente, 3 germinal An V, *Collection générale*, xlv. 11–12.) Instructions were given on how to deal with sales made during the period of depreciation. (Loi relative a l'action en rescision, 19 floréal An VI, 48, *Collection générale*, (Paris, 1797), xlviii. 214–16.)

[18] P. Fenet, *Recueil complet des travaux préparatoires du Code civil* (Paris, 1827), i. 467.

[19] Ibid. vi. 40.

would be merely another 'shining error' of those who, having 'discovered the system of the physical world', have 'the ambition to reconstruct the moral and political world' as well.[20]

The 'ancient principles' on which the Code was to be based were to be, in so far as consonant with 'present circumstances', 'principles of general equity', in effect, of natural law.[21] In enacting these principles, '[t]he legislator exercises less an authority than a priesthood'.[22] The judge is to interpret the Code in the light of these same principles, 'by a return to the natural law'.[23] The judge was to apply 'equity',[24] 'natural equity',[25] 'general equity',[26] 'universal equity',[27] 'natural reason',[28] 'legal science',[29] 'general principles',[30] 'principles',[31] 'doctrine',[32] and 'the natural light of justice and good sense'[33]—in short, he was to apply that 'equity' which was 'a return to the natural law in the silence, obscurity, or insufficiency of the texts'.[34] In doing so, the judge did not simply consult his conscience. The return to the natural law 'presupposes compendia, digests, treatises, and studies and dissertations in numerous volumes'.[35] In Turkey the magistrate can 'declare whatever he wishes' because 'legal studies are not an art'. In France, 'it is only too fortunate that legal studies form a science' to which '[a]n entire class of men devotes itself', and this class 'becomes a sort of seminary of magistrates'.[36] The judge would be forced to apply this learning in virtually every case before him, for, Portalis noted, 'no one pleads against a clear statutory text'.[37] 'Few cases', he said, 'are susceptible of being decided by a statute, by a clear text. It has always been by general principles, by doctrine, by legal science, that most disputes have been decided. The Civil Code does not dispense with this learning but, on the contrary, presupposes it.'[38]

Portalis could not have made his allegiance to the traditions of the natural law school any clearer. The brief remarks of his colleagues on the drafting committee indicate a general agreement. The Code had to be interpreted, according to Bigot-Préameneu, by 'principles of natural equity',[39] according to Tronchet, by 'general principles'.[40] The provisions of the Code governing contracts, according to Bigot-Préameneu, were intended to form a 'body of elementary doctrine' based on the 'great works' which 'in the last century, the most famous scholars of different parts of Europe . . .

[20] Ibid. 37–8. [21] Ibid. 41. [22] Ibid. i. 466.
[23] Ibid. 474. [24] Ibid. vi. 359; i. 474; vi. 51. [25] Ibid. vi. 21.
[26] Ibid. 41. [27] Ibid. i. 475. [28] Ibid. vi. 359; i. 469.
[29] Ibid. vi. 23. [30] Ibid. 23. [31] Ibid. 360.
[32] Ibid. 360; i. 474; vi. 23. [33] Ibid. vi. 359. [34] Ibid. 360.
[35] Ibid. i. 471. [36] Ibid. 471. [37] Ibid. vi. 269.
[38] Ibid. 23. [39] Ibid. 23–4. [40] Ibid. 23.

had prepared'. Among the 'most perfect' of these works were those of Pothier and Domat.[41] The view that the Code would regulate contracts in conformity with the principles of traditional legal science was echoed by the Tribunes charged with defending the draft.[42]

The break with the past was made not by the drafters of the Code, but by the nineteenth-century jurists who claimed to be interpreting it. They did not do so, however, in the name of new philosophical principles, liberal or otherwise. While disregarding the works of the natural law school, they unanimously affirmed that there was a natural law. Only, jurists should not try to determine what it was. They should confine themselves as far as possible to exegetical interpretation of the texts of the Code.

The natural law, according to Duranton, was promulgated by God and known by man through the light of natural reason.[43] According to Demante, it was given by God, engraved on our hearts, inseparable from our reason, and invariably attached to our nature.[44] Demolombe acknowledged its divine origin, its universality, and its immutability.[45] To deny that such a law exists, said Laurent, would be to deny God and to deny that man is a spiritual being, thereby reducing man to a brute and law to a chain.[46] To deny that the Creator engraved such a law on our hearts would be false and degrading, said Troplong.[47] Valette claimed that all nations recognize such a higher law and that the only people who do not are certain metaphysicians whose systems need not be considered.[48] Aubry and Rau defined the natural law as the ensemble of rules which would legitimate restraining a citizen by force.[49]

These professions of faith in a natural law, however, were sentimental introductions to exegetical commentaries on the French Civil Code. These commentaries were innocent of any real attempt to determine what the natural law was or to interpret the Code in its light. Demante said that the Code had to be interpreted in light of

[41] P. Fenet, *Recueil complet des travaux préparatoires du Code civil* (Paris, 1827), xiii. 217.

[42] Ibid. 414; xiii. 313.

[43] M. Duranton, *Cours de droit français suivant le code civil* (Paris, 1834–7), i, §§15–16.

[44] A. M. Demante and E. Colmet de Santerre, *Cours analytique de Code Civil* (Paris, 1883), i, §4 (by Demante).

[45] C. Demolombe, *Cours de Code Napoleon* (Paris, 1854–82), i, §§6, 8.

[46] F. Laurent, *Principes de droit civil français* (Paris, 1869–78), i, §4.

[47] R. Troplong, *De la vente* (Paris, 1837), i, preface, p. xvii, n. 1.

[48] A. Valette, *Cours de Code Civil* (Paris, 1872), i. 2.

[49] C. Aubry and C. Rau, *Cours de droit civil français* (Paris, 1869–71), i, §2.

the natural law,[50] but his works show an influence of the natural law tradition rather than an effort to explain and apply the natural law. Duranton said that recourse to natural reason and equity should be the last resource of the interpreter.[51] Demolombe took as his motto: 'The texts before all else.'[52] From the point of view of a jurist, he explained, there is only one true law, the positive law.[53] Troplong praised the jurist who measured his writings by the inflexible text of the Code.[54] Valette advised restraint in using principles of equity to interpret it.[55] Laurent claimed that the jurist should merely note defects in the Code, thus leaving to the legislator the task of bringing it into accord with natural law.[56] Aubry and Rau gave an account of interpretation which made no reference to natural reason or equity.[57]

They gave quite different reasons for reaching what was essentially the same conclusion. Duranton explained that, while natural law speaks to all men of virtue and intelligence, these men were simply too prone to make mistakes as to its secondary precepts.[58] Laurent thought that the natural law is revealed to the human conscience progressively as a people approaches perfection. The legislator, however, was supposed to keep pace with this progress; jurists were merely supposed to prepare for it by interpreting statutes and noting their defects.[59] Troplong[60] and Valette[61] contented themselves with general remarks about how perfect and complete the French Civil Code was. Demolombe agreed that, with a Code so complete, humane, and equitable, a case could scarcely arise in which natural law would be any different from positive law. Moreover, while there was a pre-existent, universal, and immutable

[50] Demante and Colmet de Santerre, *supra* n. 44, i, §23 (by Demante). On the other hand, he seems to have thought that recourse should be had to general principles of law or natural equity only in the rare instance in which a case is not covered by the letter or spirit of the statute or the statutory text is so obscure as to have no true sense. (Ibid. i. §28.)

[51] Duranton, *supra* n. 43, i, §96.

[52] Demolombe, *supra* n. 45, i, 1st preface, p. vi.

[53] Ibid. i, §8.53.

[54] Troplong, *supra* n. 47, i, preface, p. viii.

[55] Valette, *supra* n. 48, i. 4. While acknowledging that the judge must consult general principles of law to find a solution when statutory provisions are absent, Valette maintained that it would be astonishing to find a case in which these provisions were wholly lacking given the legislation enacted in the previous 70 years (i. 34–5).

[56] Laurent, *supra* n. 46, i, §§5, 30. For a judge to decide a case by natural law is permissible only when the texts are insufficient, and then it is a necessary evil (§§256–7.)

[57] Aubry and Rau, *supra* n. 49, i, §§40–1.

[58] Duranton, *supra* n. 43, i, §96.

[59] Laurent, *supra* n. 46, i, §5.

[60] Troplong, *supra* n. 47, i, preface, p. xii.

[61] Valette, *supra* n. 48, i. 34–5.

natural law, to think about such a law was more appropriate to a philosopher or a moralist than a jurist. For a jurist writing about the Code, the one true law was the positive law.[62] Aubry and Rau claimed that, while there were absolute and immutable principles such as the personality of man, the right of property, the constitution of the family, and the liberty and obligatory force of contracts, one could not determine *a priori* the rules by which these principles should be developed. While the principles were immutable, the rules were contingent and variable.[63] The only point on which the French did agree, then, was that their task was to interpret the Code exegetically and in so far as possible without recourse to the natural law in which they claimed to believe.[64]

Nor does one find among the French jurists much of a commitment to liberal values. Some of them speak of the respect for liberty enshrined in the Code, but some do not, and those who do speak of liberty in the most diverse ways. Duranton remarked that the original laws of the first human societies must have left each person the greatest possible liberty.[65] He also said that the law should promote virtue, lead men to happiness, promote the general good even at the cost of injustice to the individual, be founded on justice, natural reason, and equity, and conform to the sentiment God placed in our hearts.[66] Duranton collected platitudes the way some collect seashells, and seems to have wanted the most varied collection possible. Aubry and Rau said that the spirit of the Code was the protection of liberty and equality. They follow this remark with another that would not have appealed to a 'bourgeois liberal': it might still be legitimate to place restrictions on contracts in order to prevent permanent inequalities in wealth.[67] Both of these remarks, however, appeared in the first edition of their work, which was a mere translation of the commentary on the French Code of the German jurist Zacharia.[68] In subsequent editions they added their own observations to those of Zacharia, without, however, further elaborating on the liberty which was supposedly the foundation of the Code. Troplong believed that the Code crowned the long struggle of the third estate for liberty.[69] For Troplong, however, the

[62] Demolombe, *supra* n. 45, i, §§8–10.

[63] Aubry and Rau, *supra* n. 49, i, §2, n. 2.

[64] See. A.-J. Arnaud, *Les Juristes face à la sociétè du XIXe siècle à nos jours* (Paris, 1975), 53–60.

[65] Duranton, *supra* n. 43, i, §2.

[66] Ibid. i, §§11, 12, 16.

[67] Aubry and Rau, *supra* n. 49, i, §16.

[68] Ibid. (1st edn.), §16. The remark about the desirability of preventing permanent inequalities in wealth also derives from this edition (§16).

[69] R. Troplong, *Des Donations* (Paris, 1855), i, preface, pp. iii–iv. See also Troplong, *supra* n. 47, i, preface, p. xvii.

Code also represented the triumph of Christian morality over 'stoicism'[70] and of equity over the 'materialism of form'.[71] A few French jurists, then, would mention liberty, but they mentioned much else besides.

Perhaps the only leading commentator on the French Code who consistently wrote like a nineteenth-century liberal was the Belgian Laurent. He believed that, at the moment Bonaparte gave France a code, he gave it liberty.[72] Feudalism was abolished, the liberty of person and land was proclaimed, and for the first time since the world existed men were free and equal.[73] One consequence of their liberty, according to Laurent, was the full and entire liberty of the parties to a contract to arrange as they see fit their private interests, of which they are the best judges.[74] Certainly it would be surprising if an age of political liberals had not produced one leading liberal commentator on the Code. One must avoid, however, thinking that even Laurent believed all that we are accustomed to thinking that nineteenth-century liberals believed. Laurent also thought that the legislator ought to place social interests ahead of individual interest.[75] Although sceptical of the doctrine of *lésion*, which allowed a court to review the price of a sale of land, he believed the doctrine was justified to the extent that it rested on considerations of general interest, equity, or humanity.[76] Indeed, according to Laurent,

> There is a law that God has engraved on our hearts, and it is that of our moral development, the supreme end of our life. It is to assist men in their work of perfecting themselves that the legislator gave them full liberty to contract. But this liberty has some limits by reason of the very end for which it was established. If the legislator left men free to contract it is so that they perfect themselves. Are contracts, instruments of moral progress, able to become themselves means of corruption? Conscience answers that immoral agreements must be voided absolutely, radically, *de plein droit*, and by virtue of statute.[77]

Thus, even Laurent did not regard liberty as an absolute good or the foundation of an unqualified right to contract.

Moreover, it would be a mistake to think that the respect of the jurists for the French Civil Code arose from a liberal respect for the will of the people or for their representatives. In fact, they had no common view as to why the Code, which they all extolled, mattered

[70] Troplong, *supra* n. 47, i, preface, pp. xiii–xvii.
[71] Troplong, *supra* n. 69, i, preface, pp. v, lxiii.
[72] Laurent, *supra* n. 46, i, §1. [73] Ibid. i, §8. [74] Ibid. i, §37.
[75] Ibid. i, §§35, 39. He adds, however, that in so doing the legislator cannot invade the rights of citizens (i, §35).
[76] Ibid. i, §38. [77] Ibid. xv, §456.

so very much. Demante gave a traditional natural law account of why the will of the legislator was important. Each society needed an authority to punish violations of law, to promulgate the law so all can understand it, and to adapt universal justice to the character of particular peoples.[78] Duranton, paraphrasing a text of Gration, wrote a sort of historical tone poem in which legislators successively appear to simplify and regularize the law: initially, Bacchus on the Ganges, Saturn in Latium, Mercury Trismegisthus in Egypt, and Minos in Crete; later, Lycurgus in Sparta and Solon in Athens; still later, Justinian; and finally, the legislators of France.[79] Demolombe confined himself to a few remarks about how the legislator must reconcile respect for individual liberty with good order and the moral harmony of society.[80] Laurent wrote the ode to liberty just described, adding that the French Code attempted to reconcile Roman strictness and calculation with German sentiment and equity.[81] Aubry and Rau regarded customary law and legislation as alternate ways of translating the principles of natural law into fixed rules.[82]

Among the French jurists, then, instead of finding the philosophy of legal individualism of which Ranouil has spoken, we find that she herself, quoting Gounot, has called an 'instinctive distrust (*défiance*) of all that is called philosophy, metaphysics, natural law, the general theory of law'.[83] Although she believes the jurists were inspired by the teaching of Kant, she herself notes that they did not describe the will as Kant did; indeed, they never seem to have read Kant.[84] 'Autonomy of the will' is a Kantian expression, but, she notes,[85] aside from a thesis in 1891,[86] that expression was first used in private law in 1899 by Gény, a critic of nineteenth-century doctrine.[87] There were radical affirmations of the autonomy of the will by nineteenth-century writers such as Jourdan and Fouillée,[88] but, she notes, the will theorists themselves do not make such

[78] Demante and Colmet de Santerre, *supra* n. 44, i, §5 (written by Demante).
[79] Duranton, *supra* n. 43, i, §§1–7, paraphrasing *Decretum* D.7, c.1.
[80] Demolombe, *supra* n. 45, i, §4.
[81] Laurent, *supra* n. 46, i, §§1–7.
[82] Aubry and Rau, *supra* n. 49, i, §2.
[83] Ranouil, *supra* n. 5, p. 79 n. 59, quoting E. Gounot, *Le Principe de l'autonomie de la volonté en droit privé: contribution a l'étude critique de l'individualisme juridique* (thesis, Paris, 1912), 8.
[84] Ibid. 9, 53–5.
[85] Ibid. 17.
[86] R. Worms, *De la volonté unilatérale considerée comme source d'obligations* (thesis, Paris, 1891), 191.
[87] F. Gény, *Méthodes d'interprétation et sources en droit privé positif* (Paris, 1899), 144, 173.
[88] A. Jourdan, *Le Droit français, ses règles fondamentales, ses rapports avec les principes de la morale, avec l'économie politique et avec l'utilité générale* (Paris, 1875); A. Jourdan, *Cours analytique d'Economie politique* (Paris, 1882), 88–9; also by A. Fouillée, *La Science sociale contemporaine* (Paris, 1880), 89–90.

statements. Ranouil concludes that they made use of the conception of the autonomy of the will 'as Monsieur Jourdain used prose: without perceiving it'.[89] But unlike Monsieur Jourdain, who did speak prose, all the French writers say is that contracts are the will of the parties and that, as a matter of contract law, the parties can contract on whatever terms they choose. It is difficult to believe that they thought these propositions rested on some more basic conception of the autonomy of the will or legal individualism which they do not mention.

Germany, at first sight, seems to be an exception to the pattern we have seen in England, the United States, and France. Among the German jurists there was a widely shared philosophical account of law. This account owed much to Kant and Hegel. It gave a central place to the concept of freedom. Paradoxically, however, it was an account that left the German jurists in much the same position as the French and Anglo-Americans. The jurist was not to concern himself with the philosophical meaning of concepts such as freedom. His task was the exegesis of authoritative legal texts, and he was to undertake that task without the assistance of philosophy.

The account was first developed by Savigny. Savigny did not believe there were principles of natural law applicable in all societies and sufficiently definite to be of use to a jurist.[90] He was also sceptical of attempts to explain law as a 'a reasoned agreement in which everyone gives up a portion of his freedom in order to preserve the rest more securely'.[91] He recognized that freedom was necessary for man, and law was necessary to secure freedom. Indeed,

> For free beings to exist together in contact, helping each other and unobstructed in their development, is possible only by recognition of an invisible boundary within which secure free room is won for individual existence and effectiveness. The rule which defines these boundaries and this free room is law.[92]

One could not begin with the concept of freedom, however, and arrive at these boundaries by a process of deduction or by a reasoned agreement. The law had a quite different source.

[89] Ranouil, *supra* n. 5, p. 70.

[90] F. C. von Savigny, *System des heutigen Römischen Rechts* (Berlin, 1840–8), i, §8, 20–1. For that reason, the drafters of the French Civil Code were wrong to think that the Code could be interpreted in the light of natural equity. (F. C. von Savigny, *Vom Beruf unsrer Zeit für Gesetzgebung und Rechtswissenschaft* (Heidelberg, 1840), 74–6.)

[91] Savigny, *System*, *supra* n. 90, i, §52, 332–3.

[92] Ibid. 331–2.

This source was 'the common conviction of the people, the kindred consciousness of an inward necessity, excluding all notion of an accidental and arbitrary origin'.[93] This 'consciousness of an inward necessity' belongs to a particular people simply because it is a particular people sufficiently 'strong' and 'national' to have such a common conviction.[94] It belongs to the *Volksgeist*, the unconscious mind or spirit of that people.[95] It developed by 'internal silently-operating powers'.[96] As the people's 'national tendency' and level of civilization advances, law is elaborated in immense detail scientifically or systematically. This elaboration is made possible by the emergence of a class of jurists who represent the community and give formal expression to its consciousness of law. Savigny called the connection of law with the consciousness of a people its 'political element' and the elaboration of law by the jurists its 'technical element'.[97] The German jurists performed this task by interpreting the Roman texts that had been in force for over three centuries. The *Geist* of the German people had embraced and accepted these texts which were to be expounded in a distinctly German manner.[98]

The task of the German jurist, then, was to interpret Roman legal texts by a 'technical' method, one that brought to light values already in the legal sources. As Wieacker described this method, the law was to be found 'exclusively in the system, concepts and doctrinal propositions of legal science, without ascribing power to produce or alter law to extra-legal values or ends be they religious, social or scientific'. He quoted Windscheid: 'Ethical, political or economic considerations are not the business of the jurist as such.'[99]

Savigny had thus explained philosophically why the jurists should confine themselves to exegesis and ignore philosophy. He had borrowed from the philosophers only to make philosophy irrelevant to the jurists' task. He borrowed the concept of a *Geist* from Hegel. For Savigny, however, one could not begin with the concept and arrive at conclusions of help to the jurist. The German *Geist* produced the law it did because it was the *Geist* it was, and not

[93] Savigny, *Vom Beruf*, *supra* n. 90, p. 8.

[94] Ibid. 11.

[95] Savigny, *System*, *supra* n. 90, i, §8, p. 19.

[96] Savigny, *Vom Beruf*, *supra* n. 90, p. 14.

[97] Ibid. 12.

[98] See J. Whitman, *The Legacy of Roman Law in the German Romantic Era: Historical Vision and Legal Change* (Princeton, 1990), 125–31.

[99] Wieacker, *supra* n. 6, p. 431, quoting Windscheid, 'Die Aufgabe der Rechtswissenschaft', in B. Windscheid, *Gesamte Reden und Abhandlungen* (Leipzig, 1904), 101. Technical legal method was thus separated from these considerations, even though, as Paulo Cappellini has noted, Savigny's theory of the *Volksgeist* was a movement from 'the pure plane of a doctrinal system' to 'the level of a real system, of a genuine and proper *Lebenssystem*'. (P. Cappellini, *Systema iuris* (Milan, 1985), ii. 338.)

because of some reason or principle that philosophical analysis would lay bare. As Wieacker notes, Savigny took his concept of freedom and its relation to the legal order from Kant.[100] Unlike Kant, however, he did not try to derive conclusions from an analysis of that concept. Indeed, he explained that such an analysis lay beyond the province of a jurist when he discussed the effect of mistake, fraud, and duress on a declaration of will:

> We in the area of law are not at all occupied with the speculative difficulties of the concept of freedom. For us, freedom is based simply on the appearance (*Erscheinung*), that is, on the capacity, of making a choice among several alternatives.[101]

He then developed the central tenets of German will theory in a discussion that owed nothing to Kant or Hegel and in which the importance of human freedom never figured.

The Anglo-American, French, and German jurists, then, did not ground their legal doctrines on any definite philosophical or political principles, liberal or otherwise. They wished to escape philosophical or political commitments. The views of Pollock or of the French jurists required only the most minimal political commitment: an acknowledgement that the authoritative sources of law, whatever they might be, were authoritative. To regard these sources as self-sufficient was to avoid commitment to any philosophical principles for interpreting them. The German view of law did require one to believe that there was a *Geist* and that it was German. There, however, the jurists' political and philosophical commitment ended. Politically, he was not committed to liberalism or monarchy or political unification or to any definite views on economics. Philosophically, he was committed only to the proposition that the *Volksgeist* produced law. Philosophy had nothing to tell him about what law it produced. Nineteenth-century ideologies, whether liberal or socialist or Marxist, have been called secular religions. The jurists, however, found a sort of secular agnosticism.

Paradoxically, however, this very refusal to make political and philosophical commitments itself entailed political and philosophical commitments. It was not politically neutral to discuss contract law without regard to commutative justice, and consequently without regard to distributive justice or the fairness of a political or economic regime. To do so implied that, while contract law could be discussed objectively by jurists, these other matters could not. That conclusion had political consequences, although different ones for liberals than

[100] Wieacker, *supra* n. 6, pp. 353, 397, 431.
[101] Savigny, *System*, *supra* n. 90, iii, §114, p. 102.

for conservatives. For liberals, the idea that problems of distributive justice were irrelevant to contract law was one more reason to believe that government should leave economic decisions to the market-place and should not concern itself with these problems. Indeed, will theories were so useful to economic liberals that it is no wonder historians have thought they were inspired by liberalism. For conservatives, particularly in Germany, the idea that the fairness of a political regime was beyond the concern of the jurists was appealing because it protected ruling groups from criticism.

The will theories entailed philosophical commitments as well. Most obviously, they presupposed that one could build on the concept of will without using the metaphysical and moral principles relied on by the late scholastics.

That presupposition was almost the only one to which both the will theorists and the philosophers of the late eighteenth and early nineteenth centuries were committed. The philosophers believed that the attempt of Aristotelian and Thomistic philosophy to discover a moral order in nature had failed. They attempted to find the source of morality not in nature, but in freedom or human choice, although they thought of human choice in very different ways. Bentham spoke of a calculus of pleasure and pain, Kant of a truly free will giving laws to itself, and Hegel of a *Geist* working for a progressive realization of freedom.

Historians have thought the jurists were inspired by the philosophers because of this common commitment to building a theory around the idea of human choice. Actually, they were all responding to a common problem. The collapse of the Aristotelian philosophical tradition in the seventeenth and eighteenth centuries had left no other way to explain law and morality. One could no longer say that man, through reason, can choose those actions that move him to an end that belongs to him by nature. If the source of law and morality cannot be found in reason, then, it seemed, the source must be the will.

The philosophers responded to this problem, however, in a different way than the jurists. The philosophers tried to explain what it meant to choose or to will. They tried to account for the possibility of morality in a world in which no intelligible moral order could be discovered outside the human will. The jurists did not concern themselves with these problems. They borrowed little from the philosophers. Instead, as we have seen, they arrived at their will theories by starting with the doctrines of the natural lawyers and purging them of older Aristotelian concepts they did not understand. Will was the most important single concept that remained.

In this way, the jurists hoped to avoid philosophical commitments. Yet that very attempt committed them, like the philosophers, to the enterprise of building their theories on the idea of will alone. As we have seen, that enterprise entangled them in difficulties they were never able to resolve.

9
CONCLUSION

Twice, philosophy has transformed the work of jurists. In the sixteenth century, the late scholastics reorganized Roman law around concepts taken from Aristotle and Thomas Aquinas. Contract law acquired a systematic doctrinal organization for the first time. In the seventeenth century, the founders of modern critical philosophy called into question the concepts on which the late scholastics had built. For a long time, jurists preserved their doctrines while distancing themselves from the Aristotelian and Thomistic philosophy that had inspired them. Eventually they reworked these doctrines by eliminating the concepts of which modern philosophers had disapproved. The results were the will theories of contract.

If a will theory could make sense of any field of law, that field would be the law of contract. Yet the will theorists did not succeed. They never managed to make their doctrines work without the older Aristotelian concepts they had thrown away. Irresolvable controversies broke out at every point at which one of these older concepts had been excised.

Adversaries of the will theories discredited them by pointing to these difficulties. Partisans of 'objective theories' pointed out that the concept of will had not resolved the problems of offer and acceptance, mistake, fraud, duress, or implied terms. Indeed, every application of the concept resulted in paradox. Later critics observed that the will theories could not explain the numerous instances in which the law does and should concern itself with the fairness of a contract.

Today, we have no generally recognized theory of contract. The objective theories have lost even the limited support among jurists they once enjoyed. It is not helpful to define contract as a series of consequences the law attaches to the outward conduct of the parties if one cannot explain why the law attaches some consequences rather than others. There is widespread agreement that any viable theory of contract will have to take the fairness of a contract into account, yet there is no agreement as to how to do so.

Many jurists are now pessimistic about the very possibility of discovering general principles or doctrines that can explain the rules of positive law or the results most people regard as fair. Their pessimism is understandable. The attempt to build coherent doctrine seems to have ended in failure.

This study offers a diagnosis rather than a cure. The historical diagnosis is that the very points at which the will theories were weak were the points at which the will theorists tried to manage without the older Aristotelian concepts. We have rejected the will theories because of these weaknesses. Yet we do not have concepts of our own to do the intellectual work that these older concepts were once thought to handle.

Those who agree with this diagnosis may have very different suggestions as to a cure. To some, the very enterprise of constructing a general theory of contract and a set of coherent doctrines may seem a mistake. The enterprise was inspired by a now discredited philosophy. Perhaps we have finally learned that the task is impossible.

Curiously enough, this suggestion may appeal to two seemingly opposite types of people: traditionalists and radicals. The traditionalist is quite happy to dispense with general theory. He is most comfortable when he is reaching conclusions by a pragmatic and non-doctrinaire use of precedent and statute. He is least comfortable when he is asked for an account of the method by which he reached his conclusions or the intellectual assumptions on which they are based. The apparently futile search for a general theory of contract will confirm his conviction that law can get along quite well without a theory. Roman law had no theory until the late scholastics; the common law had none until the nineteenth century. Moreover, in each case, the search for theory had little influence on the rules actually in force. The mistake, the traditionalist may conclude, was for philosophers ever to intrude into the business of lawyers or for lawyers to dabble in philosophy. Let us read our cases.

The radical may agree that the task the late scholastics and the nineteenth-century jurists set themselves is impossible. He may draw a different conclusion. The lesson to be learned is that law is inherently incoherent. It cannot be based on neutral principles. Consequently, it cannot be more than a smokescreen concealing the efforts of the stronger to prey on the weaker. It is not enough for the traditionalist to claim he can reach conclusions without a general theory. The very point at issue is whether those conclusions rest upon neutral and coherent principles. The cure is not simply to abandon the search for general theories, but to abandon the notion that law and legal analysis should govern so much of our lives. Some members of the Critical Legal Studies movement in the United States might well draw this conclusion.[1]

Others might agree with the thesis of this article and propose a different remedy. The cure for our difficulties is to continue our efforts until we arrive at a new and correct theory of contracts. Such a theory, however, cannot rest upon a discredited Aristotelianism but must be grounded in some tenable modern philosophy—on the principles of Kantianism, for example, or utilitarianism. The mistake of the will theorists was that they ignored modern philosophy. This is the route taken by such scholars as John Rawls[2] and Charles Fried,[3] who are trying to found the law of contract on Kantian principles. It is the method, too, of adherents of the law and economics movement, who try to ground contract law on what seems to be a streamlined version of utilitarianism. One of the most comprehensive of such attempts has been made by Richard Posner.[4]

My own view is different. We can have a theory of contract, but to do so we need the very concepts that the nineteenth-century jurists threw out. If we consider our diagnosis carefully, we can see that this is the direction in which a cure must lie.

I know that we could not resurrect these concepts without major changes in the way we understand the world. I am also aware that it would take a good deal of hard thought to see how these concepts should be applied. Although we can learn from the late scholastics, we cannot simply copy them. There were issues that they did not resolve successfully. There are modern concerns and techniques of analysis that are valuable and should be integrated into a larger approach to contract.

Nevertheless, I do not see how that larger approach would be possible without using these older concepts. We can see the need for them if we reflect on the difficulties the will theorists confronted. These difficulties cannot be resolved by a Kantian or a utilitarian approach. They seem to be inherent in any theory that seeks the ultimate source of law or morality in human choice.

[1] Nevertheless, I do not think this conclusion must be drawn by people who are sympathetic to the Critical Legal Studies movement or opposed to the 19th-c. will theories. Much of Hugh Collins's critique of 19th-c. contract law would have been congenial from the older natural law perspective—e.g. the need to take into account fairness and trust between the parties and distributive justice among citizens; the need for general standards of fairness rather than precise technical rules. (H. Collins, *The Law of Contract* (London, 1986).

[2] J. Rawls, *A Theory of Justice* (Cambridge, Mass., 1971; Oxford paperback edn. 1973).

[3] C. Fried, *Contract as Promise: A Theory of Contractual Obligation* (Cambridge, Mass., 1981).

[4] R. Posner, *Economic Analysis of Law*, 2nd edn. (Boston, 1977).

As we have seen, one difficulty was the failure of the will theorists to explain why contracts are binding. They simply defined a binding contract in terms of the will of the parties. The absence of an explanation hampered them in analysing what the rules of contract should be. They could not, for example, analyse whether an offer had to be accepted or when it had to be accepted. Instead, they packed the need for an acceptance into their definition of contract and tried to extract from it a conclusion as to when a contract was formed.

This problem cannot be solved without giving a reason why promises are binding other than the mere fact that the promisor willed to be bound. So he did, but a promise is not merely a commitment or choice, but a commitment to do something for a promisee. No legal system we have examined enforces every commitment or choice, nor would we wish it to. To explain why the law treats promises differently, one must identify a result that promises enable the promisor to achieve. Thomas Aquinas did so: they enable the promisor to direct his actions in advance to the benefit of another person. Having identified that result, Thomas and the late scholastics asked whether, to achieve it, a promise must be communicated to the promisee, whether it must be accepted by him, whether and when his acceptance must be communicated to the promisor, and so forth.

In contrast, it is hard to see how Kantian or utilitarian philosophy could give a reason why promises are binding other than the fact that the promisor has chosen to commit himself. According to Kant, to act morally one must act in obedience to the law that a rational being would freely choose as the measure of its own actions. Thus, Kant arrived at the 'categorical imperative' to which all moral action must conform: one must act only by those rules that one could will to be universal law.[5] Promises are binding, he said, because one could not will, as a universal law, that promises should be broken. Promises would then be idle words.[6] Thus, the categorical imperative brings us right back to where we were with the will theorists, and before them with Wolff, and before him with Hobbes and Locke: promises are binding because they have been defined to be. No reason is given why one could not define all voluntary commitments to be binding.

In a later work in which he described the 'transcendental deduction of the concept of acquisition through contract', Kant went further: for a contract to be binding, there must be not only a promisee but

[5] I. Kant, *Grundlegung* (Leipzig, 1947), 44.
[6] Ibid. 46.

also an offer and an acceptance that have been outwardly declared. The reason is that the loss of a right by one party and its acquisition by the other are a single act that can be performed only by consent outwardly declared. Since one party's declaration of his consent must necessarily follow the other party's in time, there will be an interval during which the single act has not yet been performed and an offer can be revoked.[7] Again, as with the will theorists and with Wolff, the need for an offer and an acceptance have been packed into the definition of contract. It is never explained why one cannot conceive of an offer in some other way, for example as a commitment binding unless and until rejected by the other party.

In sharp contrast, and despite his admiration for Kant, Rawls does 'not regard promising as a practice which is just by definition'.[8] He does not try to infer the rules that should govern promising from higher principles of moral philosophy. 'Promising is an action defined by a public system of rules', by 'a set of constitutive conventions' like 'the rules of games'.[9] The most moral philosophy can explain is why a promisor is obliged to follow any 'fair' set of rules that prevail in his society. The reason is the 'principle of fairness', according to which one must abide by the rules of an institution if the institution is fair and if one has voluntarily taken advantage of its benefits.[10] The principle of fairness is thus like a clothes hanger on which one can hang a system of contract law after someone else makes it. It does not explain what the rules should be.

Fried explains the binding force of promises in the same way as Rawls: 'An individual is morally bound to keep his promises because he has intentionally invoked a convention whose function it is to give grounds—moral grounds—for another to expect the promised performance.'[11] When he tries to explain the rules of contract law—for example the need for a promisee and an acceptance—he begins to sound much more like Kant. Our intuitions about promising show that 'a promise is something essentially communicated to someone' and that 'the moral relation of promising' is 'voluntary on both sides'.[12] Fried should explain, however, why in a Kantian world one ought to have precisely these intuitions, why people cannot bind themselves by simply willing to do so. If he cannot give a reason, then, again, he is packing his conclusions into the definition of contract.

[7] I. Kant, *Metaphysik der Sitten* (Hamburg, 1986), §§18–19, pp. 78–81.

[8] Rawls, *supra* n. 2, p. 345.

[9] Ibid. 344.

[10] Ibid. 111–12, 342–5.

[11] Fried, *supra* n. 3, p. 16.

[12] Ibid. 42, 43.

The same difficulty arises for a utilitarian such as Bentham or a partisan of the law and economics movement such as Posner. They aim at increasing human welfare, and they take the choices people make as the best or only guide to welfare. Bentham thought that, in principle, human welfare could be measured in units of pleasure and pain called 'utility'.[13] One cannot know for certain what will contribute how much to another's utility since 'differences of character are inscrutable and there are no two individuals whose circumstances are alike'.[14] One will generally maximize human welfare, however, by allowing people to make choices for themselves. 'For no man can be so good a judge as the man himself, what it is gives him pleasure or displeasure.'[15] Modern economists build on this insight when they speak of efficiency. By its strict definition, an outcome is efficient if one person can be made better off without making anyone else worse off. By 'better off', the economists mean that the person can move to a position that he chooses in preference to another. Thus they speak of efficiency without committing themselves to whether, as Bentham thought, it is possible to measure the pleasure people experience in comparable units.

If the choices people make are the best or only guide to their welfare, however, it seems impossible to explain why the law treats some choices or commitments differently from others. As Posner notes, it is 'puzzling from an economic standpoint' that a husband cannot contract to burn himself to death on his wife's funeral pyre, that Shylock cannot enforce his contract with Antonio, or that a person cannot sell himself into slavery.[16] It should be at least as puzzling, to put it mildly, that the law enforces promises more readily than other commitments.

Just as the will theorists could not explain why promises should be treated differently from other commitments, so they could not explain why different promises should be treated differently. Yet every legal system we have examined enforces promises to give less readily than promises to exchange, and enforces some gifts, and some exchanges, more or less readily than others. Lacking a reason why the legal system should do so, the will theorists had difficulty even defining the difference between gift and exchange.

They did not define gifts positively, in terms of some good result that the donor wishes to achieve and that the law will respect. They

[13] J. Bentham, *Principles of Morals and Legislation* (London, 1970), I. i–iv. 11–12; IV. i–vi. 38–40.

[14] J. Bentham, *Principles of the Civil Code* (Edinburgh, 1859), I. vi, in *Works*, i. 305.

[15] Bentham, *supra* n. 13, XIII. iv. 159.

[16] Posner, *supra* n. 4, p. 187.

tried to do so negatively: in France and Germany, by the fact that nothing was sought in return; in England and the United States, by the absence of a bargain. As we have seen, these definitions produce paradoxes. It is really difficult to define an intentional action negatively, and in the case of gifts, the attempt to do so produces a collison with the law of unjust enrichment. Moreover, a negative definition cannot explain the ways in which the law treats gifts differently. Informal executory promises of gift have usually not been enforced even in periods when the jurists claimed that all promises were enforceable in principle. Executory informal promises of gifts to charities and to close relatives have been enforced by German, French, and Anglo-American courts despite the rules supposedly in force. It has mattered, then, whether the donor's promise is likely to be well considered and whether the donee is deserving. Thomas and the late scholastics had a fairly simple explanation of why it should matter: as Aristotle said, one should give 'to the right people, the right amounts, and at the right time'. When the will theorists gave up the older concept of liberality, an explanation became all but impossible.

Similarly, the will theorists tried to define exchange without regard to commutative justice or equality in exchange. They therefore found it difficult to distinguish exchange from gift. Moreover, they produced definitions that did not explain the relief the law gave, even in their own century, when a contract is unfair. Since the nineteenth century, French courts have extended the remedy for *lésion* by finding fraud, mistake, or duress to be present in a transaction when the only real flaw is a disparity in the values exchanged. German courts have given relief under the most general clauses of their Code: section 138, which prohibits immoral and oppressive contracts, and section 242, which requires good faith. In the United States, section 2–302 of the Uniform Commercial Code and section 208 of the Second Restatement of Contracts provide a general remedy for 'unconscionability'.[17] I have argued elsewhere that one cannot explain relief when a price is unfair without coming back to the concepts of a fair price, equality in exchange, and commutative justice.[18]

In contrast, it seems impossible to explain what promises the law will enforce by Kantian or utilitarian principles. If, as Kant said, promises are binding because one cannot will the violation of a

[17] On the French, German, and American remedies for one-sided bargains, see Gordley, 'Equality in Exchange', *California Law Review*, 69 (1981), 1587 at 1645–55.

[18] Ibid.

promise as universal law, then it would seem that all promises should be treated the same way. Kant himself defined a gratuitous contract in the same negative way as the German and French jurists: one party does not acquire a right, whereas in an exchange each party does.[19] He did not deal with the difficulties which, as we have seen, are entailed in this definition. His only explanation of why a gratuitous promise should be treated differently is that a court should not presume that the promisor willed that the promisee should have the right to enforce it.[20]

Indeed, Fried concludes on Kantian principles that there should not be a doctrine of consideration. The doctrine, he says, is built on two contradictory ideas: that a promise requires consideration to be enforceable, and that the adequacy of consideration does not matter. The second proposition 'affirms the liberal principle that the free arrangements of rational persons should be respected'. Therefore it contradicts the first, which 'holds that individual self-determination is not a sufficient ground of legal obligation'.[21] A late scholastic would have agreed there was a contradiction. In principle, however, he would not want to enforce the foolish gift or the unfair exchange. Fried says the law should enforce all acts of 'individual self-determination'.

Would Fried really enforce extravagant and foolish gifts or oppressive exchanges? As it happens, he would probably not, despite his Kantian principles. Gifts, he notes, must be made 'rationally, deliberately', and should not frustrate the 'legitimate interests of third parties'. Paraphrasing Lon Fuller with approval, he suggests that one good effect of the doctrine of consideration is to 'exclude the more dubious and meretricious kinds of gift in which strangers are promised the moon, to the prejudice of a spouse or children'.[22] The complaints of the spouse and children become legitimate, it seems, when, to paraphrase Aristotle, the promisor gives to the wrong people the wrong amount at the wrong time. Moreover, according to Fried, 'some bargains, though they meet all the tests I have set out so far, seem just too hard to enforce'.[23] For example, a rescuer should not be allowed to charge an excessive price to save the cargo of a disabled ship. That is because a random event has caused a breakdown of what Fried calls a 'functioning social system', a 'political system of social redistribution', within which exchange normally takes place.[24] Might one call it a system of commutative and distributive justice? Instead of announcing the

[19] Kant, *supra* n. 7, §21a, p. 85.
[20] Ibid. §37, pp. 110–11.
[21] Fried, *supra* n. 3, p. 35.
[22] Ibid. 38.
[23] Ibid. 109.
[24] Ibid. 109, 110.

Kantian principle that all acts of individual self-determination should be enforced and then finding exceptions, it would be easier to say that promise-keeping is a virtue but liberality and commutative justice are virtues as well. But then we seem to have left the Kantian world.

It is equally difficult for a utilitarian or a partisan of the law and economics movement to explain why the law does not treat all promises the same way. Posner, however, does not want the law to do so any more than Fried. Consequently, like Fried, he tries to find a way around what seem to be the plain consequences of his principles. At one point, he suggests that a gift is usually not enforced because it 'is not part of the process by which resources are moved, through a series of exchanges, to successively more valuable uses'.[25] On Posner's premises, however, any disposition of property should be deemed valuable simply because the owner has chosen it, whether he chooses to use the property himself, to give it away, or to destroy it.[26]

He develops an alternative and inconsistent account to explain why the law does enforce some gifts, for example a promise to reward a person who has saved one's life. This time he starts with a principle that seems more compatible with his premises: ideally, all promises should be enforced. Promises to give, however, are not enforced for an 'evidentiary reason': since such promises are rare, it is often hard to prove they were made. Nevertheless, the promise to reward the rescuer is enforceable because the circumstances show that the promisor might well have made such a promise.[27] We are not told, *inter alia*, why even a promise to make a rare sort of exchange is enforced, why an executed gift cannot be reclaimed even when the donee's possession does not tend to show he received the property as a gift, why a promise of gift is often not enforced even when the promisor admits he made the promise, why the promise to the rescuer could be enforced even if the occurrence of a

[25] Posner, *supra* n. 4, p. 69.

[26] Thus, as Posner recognizes elsewhere, a gratuitous promise 'would not be made unless it conferred utility on the promisor'. (Posner, 'Gratuitous Promises in Economics and Law', *Journal of Legal Studies*, 6 (1977), 411.) In that article, he considers why a donor would obtain more utility by making a binding promise to give than by simply giving without binding himself to do so. He finds the answer in the increased certainty that a binding promise affords the donee that the donor will actually make the gift. Since this certainty has a value to the donee, if the donor could not make a binding promise, he would have to promise a larger gift to make the donee as well off at the moment the promise is made. I am not sure how helpful this analysis is since it seems merely to say, in economic jargon, that promisors may want to reassure promisees, which is not too surprising. In any event, it does not explain why the law treats gratuitious promises differently.

[27] Posner, *supra* n. 4, pp. 188–9.

rescue were as much in dispute as the giving of a promise, or why gratuitous promises that are obviously foolish or extravagant but at least as common as promises to reward rescuers are not enforced.

He develops another explanation of why some one-sided exchanges are not enforced, for example a rescue at sea in which the captain of the only ship able to complete the rescue demanded and received a promise of a wholly exorbitant price. By enforcing the contract only at a reasonable price, the courts prevent an over-investment by shipowners in safety and rescue devices. They thus arrive at the economic result that a competitive market would have reached were there a competitive market. Posner acknowledges that the courts have not had this goal consciously in mind. They arrived at it 'unwitting[ly]'.[28]

Explanations like these are not derived from the central insight on which economic theory is supposedly built: that choices actually made by the parties are the best or the only guide to their welfare. They are constructed by fudging the notion of efficiency, as when a gift is said to be a less valuable use of resources; by discovering practical considerations that allow a result to be reached despite principle, as when evidentiary considerations are said to prevent gifts from being enforced except to deserving people such as rescuers; and by identifying flaws in the contracting process that prevent the parties from choosing for themselves and so justify a court in choosing for them, as when the rescuer charges too much. Yet these explanations are presented as the fruits of an economic analysis of contract in which respect for the choices the parties actually make is the central principle.

Any theory, of course, must acknowledge that its central principles often cannot be directly applied for pragmatic reasons. By itself, moreover, any one of these 'economic explanations' might be made to seem plausible. One loses confidence, however, when one encounters such an explanation at every turn, when the explanations are not obvious consequences of economic principles, when these subtle explanations are said to have subconsciously motivated law-makers, when the detection of a flaw in one such explanation promptly leads economists to search for another which is then said to have been the subconscious motivation of law-makers.

[28] Landes and Posner, 'Salvors, Finders, Good Samaritans and Other Rescuers: An Economic Study of Law and Altruism', *Journal of Legal Studies*, 7 (1973), 83 at 128. In his book on economic analysis, in contrast, he said: 'Economic analysis, at least, reveals no grounds other than fraud, incapacity and duress (the last narrowly defined) for allowing a party to repudiate the bargain that he made in entering into the contract.' (Posner, *supra* n. 4, p. 87.)

Fried and Posner have devised these explanations to show that one can believe in Kantian or 'economic' principles and still reach the results most people find sensible. To most people, however, their explanations would sound rather strange. Most people, I think, would find it far less strange to say that the law does not enforce 'the more dubious and meretricious kinds of gift in which strangers are promised the moon' because such a promise is foolish and the stranger has done nothing to deserve it. The law enforces the promise to reward the rescuer because the promisor ought to show his gratitude and, moreover, has received a service for which it may be unjust not to pay. The law does not enforce the promise of the exorbitant price because it is unfair. These explanations are much like the ones Aristotle or Thomas or the late scholastics gave. They do not sit easily with the principles of Fried and Posner, who consequently exert themselves to find Kantian or economic reasons for reaching the very results of which, according to the older thinkers, virtuous people would approve. To me, it seems far more likely that Fried and Posner are moved by an unacknowledged love of virtue than that these older thinkers were moved 'unwittingly' by the explanations they invent.

Centring as it did around the concept of will, the contract theory of the nineteenth-century jurists could not explain these differences among promises and among commitments. Yet, in applying the concept of will, they encountered the greatest difficulties of all. As they acknowledged, a contract is void for mistake unless the parties agree to a certain minimum. If they do, then they are bound not only to the terms they agreed on, but to many others as well. Yet the jurists gave no coherent account either of what constituted that minimum or of how these additional obligations were related to it.

To explain these matters, Thomas and the late scholastics said that, as in the case of other human actions, the essence of a contract is defined by its end. Strange as these terms may seem, I do not see how the problem of the will theorists can be avoided without returning to them. Once we say that certain features of a transaction are so critical that a party does not consent if he fails to understand them, we are talking about the essence of a transaction whether we use that expression or not. Presumably, these features are critically important because of their relation to the ends of the parties; yet, a party has many ends and will not get relief simply because one of them is not attained. It seems, then, that we must single out a particular end of the parties in terms of which these critical features can be defined. This end must be distinguished from others that a party to such a transaction may or may not have.

If a party enters into the transaction to acquire a certain object, we must therefore single out an end that defines that object for purposes of that transaction, and we must distinguish this end from the party's other ends. If we can do so, an error in the features that define the object will be, at once, an error in its identity, an error in the type of object it is defined to be, and an error in features that are critical to an end of the parties to such a transaction. We can therefore pay attention to all the considerations that the nineteenth-century jurists perceived to be important without the problems they experienced when they took these considerations singly.

Moreover, if terms are not read into an agreement arbitrarily, there must be some relationship between these terms and the features that define a certain type of transaction and on which the parties must actually agree. Indeed, as we have seen, both will theorists and moderate objectivists came to this position in the end. The parties willed a certain normative relationship which the will theorists called 'legal' and their opponents called 'empirical' or 'economic'. The terms that governed their contract were not explicitly willed but followed from the relationship. It is hard to see how the terms could follow from that relationship, however, unless they are means to an end that defines the relationship and for the sake of which the parties enter into it.

In contrast, it seems hopeless to try to solve these problems on Kantian principles. Indeed, they touch Kantian ethics at one of its most vulnerable points: the manner in which the duties prescribed by the categorical imperative relate to the empirical situation of the persons bound by them. That a promise should be kept is, for Kant, a matter of universal law, but that a promise with a particular content should even happen to be made is not. That a party should contract for a particular object is therefore 'wholly empirical', 'conventional', and foreign to 'metaphysical legal doctrine'.[29] Consequently, in cases of mistake, where the question is what the parties were supposed to give or get, there seems to be no standard that could clarify the content of their promises. The categorical imperative, presumably, does not say whether a cow can be pregnant or a ring can be copper and still be the very object promised in a particular transaction. Conventional usage is not helpful since, as noted in our discussion of the will theories, conventions are not established to settle mistake cases. Neither is it helpful to look to the beliefs or the will of the parties themselves. In any mistake case, a party will have had some false belief about what he was giving and

[29] Kant, *supra* n. 7, §21a, pp. 86–7.

getting, and, by hypothesis, the parties reached no agreement about what should happen then.

The terms that bind the parties when they have not otherwise agreed raise an analogous difficulty. It is hard to see how these terms could be deduced from the concept of universal law. Kant's occasional attempts to do so involve the same technique of packing conclusions into definitions that was described earlier. For example, he deduced from concepts of personal and real rights that someone who had merely been promised a thing as yet did not own it and therefore did not bear the risk of its destruction.[30] Presumably, not all terms are supposed to be derivable even in this way. For Kant, 'metaphysical legal doctrine' proceeding 'a priori' could identify a few 'simple and pure types of contracts' by making a 'logical and rational classification'. 'Empirically, however', the number of types was 'innumerable' and their content 'statutory' and 'conventional'.[31] Even when contractual terms are unambiguously fixed by statute or convention, however, a jurist building a theory of contract needs a reason why these terms are appropriate. Presumably, the categorical imperative does not provide a reason. Neither does the will of the particular parties who, by hypothesis, did not reach agreement on these terms.

Fried's approach again illustrates these difficulties. For Fried, the content of the promise is only what the parties consciously had in mind. There is no way to clarify this content when there are differences or ambiguities in what they had in mind, or when a term is needed that they did not provide themselves. In these cases, since the parties did not agree, a court must, in effect, impose an agreement on them. It does so by asking what the parties 'in all probability would have agreed but did not', or 'what somebody else, say, the ordinary person would have intended by such words of agreement', or what is required by 'extrinsic standards of fairness'. A court must ask these questions since it must find some solution, but no one should make the 'futile attempt to bring these cases under the promise principle'.[32]

If Fried is right, the 'promise principle', which seems to be the one contribution Kantian philosophy can make to contract law, is unable to explain most of the doctrines of contract law. The purpose of most of these doctrines is to determine, in doubtful cases, whether the parties have reached agreement and what the consequences of the agreement are to be. Indeed, if Fried is right, one

[30] Kant, *supra* n. 7, §21, pp. 82–4.
[31] Ibid., §21a, pp. 84–5.
[32] Fried, *supra* n. 3, pp. 60, 61, 63, 69.

wonders if there can be any cases that the 'promise principle' could resolve. It is hard to imagine a case in which a performance exactly matched a party's conscious thoughts and expectations.

In contrast, I think members of the law and economics movement have developed a method of analysis that contributes to a solution. The problem is that the solution is incomplete.

Like many of the will theorists, they approach problems of mistake and of reading terms into an agreement by asking what the parties would have done had they considered the matter. Unlike the will theorists, they have a method for analysing not what the parties actually would have done, which would depend on their imagination, educational level, and so forth, but what they should have done. They should have allocated the costs and the risks of a transaction to the party that could bear them most cheaply. They could then have adjusted the price to compensate each party for the risks and costs he was bearing so that they both would be happier with that allocation than with any other. Posner uses this approach to analyse problems of mutual mistake, liability for defects, and impossibility.[33]

The late scholastics, I believe, could have used this approach fruitfully. They thought that a transaction was defined by its end, and that the terms read into a contract absent express consent were those that best served this end. Yet often, as we have seen, they found themselves unable to decide which term was most appropriate. Often, they simply adopted the Roman rule and devised an explanation for it that was plausible but not decisive. Here, the techniques of modern economics could have helped them find the set of terms that would accomplish the parties' end at the lowest cost and at a price that they themselves would regard as fair.

The use of this approach, however, supposes that there is an end sought by both parties that, as the late scholastics would say, defines the essence of the transaction. Terms are read into a contract when they are the lowest-cost means to attain that end but not when they are the lowest-cost means to attain any other ends a party may happen to be pursuing. Posner, for example, would place the risk that goods are defective on the seller because he has the best access to information about the goods.[34] He would not allocate risks to the seller that were unrelated to the transaction but which the seller just happened to be best able to bear. Before terms can be read into an agreement, then, the parties must have made an agreement to which the terms are instrumental. The nature of the

[33] Posner, *supra* n. 4, pp. 73–9.
[34] Ibid. 74.

parties' agreement is therefore not something one can determine by simply knowing who can better bear risks and costs.

This point can be illustrated by Posner's analysis of *Sherwood* v. *Walker*,[35] a case in which the court voided a contract for mistake when a prize breeding cow, presumed to be sterile, was pregnant at the time it was sold. Posner wants to ask whether the buyer or seller could best bear the risk that the cow was pregnant. As he notes, 'this approach decomposes the contract into two distinct agreements: an agreement respecting the basic performance (the transfer of the cow) and an agreement respecting a risk associated with the transfer (that the cow will turn out to be different from what the parties believed)'.[36] That is quite right. Indeed, whenever one applies this method of analysis, one must identify such a 'basic transaction' before one can allocate the risks and costs associated with accomplishing it. What constitutes the 'basic transaction' cannot be determined by the economic techniques themselves. If we consider what does constitute a 'basic transaction', I think we will have returned to the idea that transactions have natures or essences defined in terms of ends common to the parties.

The Kantian and utilitarian or economic approaches to contract law thus seem to raise the same difficulties as the will theories. Ultimately, these difficulties have a common source. One cannot build contract doctrine around the single idea of choice or commitment. One has to explain why the law does not place the same value on all commitments or treat them all in the same way. This was the task once performed by the Aristotelian virtues of fidelity, liberality, and commutative justice. Moreover, one has to explain what it is to which the parties are committed and what that commitment entails. One cannot do so by simply looking to the thoughts or expectations of the parties themselves, which are ambiguous and usually different. This was the task once performed by the idea that the essence of an action can be defined in terms of its end.

That one cannot arrive at coherent contract doctrine after leaving the Aristotelian philosophical world would not have surprised David Hume. Indeed, in his criticism of Hobbes and Locke, he raised difficulties like those we have just examined. Hobbes and Locke said that one could frame definitions of general moral concepts such as contract and then extract conclusions from them by deductive logic. The duty to perform contracts followed from the definition of contract; the rights and obligations of a citizen from the definition of the social contract. Hume pointed out that the

[35] 66 Mich. 568, 33 NW 919 (1887).
[36] Posner, *supra* n. 4, pp. 73–4.

conclusions will be arbitrary if the definitions themselves are arbitrary. The definitions will be arbitrary unless there is some pre-existing relationship, independent of the will of the definer, that links together the elements of the definition and the consequences extracted from it.[37] This argument could equally well be directed against Kant. One cannot derive rules from the categorical imperative unless there is a pre-existing relationship between the particular rule and the concept of universal law. In a Kantian world, it is difficult to see what pre-existing relationship there could be. Thus, as Kant's critics perennially observe, there seems to be no way to move from this concept of universal law to particular rules of conduct.

Moreover, according to Hobbes and Locke, because one cannot speak of an ultimate end of man, one must speak instead about the preferences of individuals, about appetite and aversion, the pursuit of pleasure and the avoidance of pain. Hume noted, anticipating Bentham, that one can then define a 'public interest' in terms of these preferences. Hume was sceptical, however, about how much of contract law could be explained by considerations of 'public interest'. In a world without essences, contract was an 'infinitely complicated' idea that a 'hundred volumes of laws, and a thousand volumes of commentators have not been found sufficient' to define. Quite possibly, most of the law was based on fancy and imagination.[38]

In the Aristotelian tradition, these problems did not arise because one could speak of an ultimate end of man. Virtues and moral actions were defined by relation to man's ultimate end. Thus, the definition of a moral action did not depend on the arbitrary choice of the person framing the definition. One could speak not only of preferences, but of the exercise of virtues.

For that reason, it is hard to see how one could resolve these problems or resurrect the older concepts on which contract law was built without returning to an Aristotelian philosophical world in which it makes sense to speak of an ultimate end of man. Certainly, modern philosophers have raised serious questions about whether that older philosophical world exists. They have raised equally difficult questions, however, about whether any world outside of oneself exists, and indeed, about whether one exists oneself. Important as these questions may be, no sane person would suspend belief in his own existence or in that of other people until they are resolved. It would be equally foolish for a jurist to stop working until they are resolved. If he did, moreover, he might be waiting a

[37] See Ch. 5, pp. 118–19.
[38] See Ch. 5, pp. 120–1.

long time. For three and a half centuries, modern philosophers have been living in a world in which jurists are unable to work.

Many jurists have become sceptical about the possibility of coherent legal doctrine. Very few have become sceptical, however, because of philosophical arguments about the possibility of knowledge like those of Hume. Most of them are responding to their historical experience as jurists which has been one of failure. For a long time, jurists have been unable to win playing with the cards that modern philosophers have dealt them. They have begun to think it is in the nature of card games that it is impossible to win. The American cowboy would have reached a quite different conclusion a lot more quickly.

Their scepticism is reinforced, moreover, by the ways in which they have interpreted this historical experience. For some jurists, scepticism about what theory can achieve is reinforced by an exaggerated respect for what a pragmatic and non-doctrinaire approach to law has achieved. At the time Maitland wrote, this respect seemed warranted. The 'great elementary conceptions, ownership, possession, contract, tort and the like', seemed to have emerged without benefit of theory from an English legal tradition that stressed the practical and particular. But as we have seen, it did not happen that way. The great elementary conceptions of contract law came out of a Greek philosophical tradition grafted on to Roman law by moral philosophers. There is no way to understand those conceptions or to make use of them today without abstract thought. A traditionally minded jurist would do better to think in terms of a partnership in which both theoretical and pragmatic methods co-operate.

Some jurists are sceptical about both theoretical and pragmatic methods. Their scepticism is reinforced by another interpretation of our historical experience. They tend to explain doctrinal change by the influence of economics or of ideology. Indeed, a person who is completely sceptical about the value of both theoretical and pragmatic methods has almost nowhere else to turn. Since these methods are bound to fail, he cannot write a history about what they have achieved. Doctrines and principles must therefore flourish for reasons unconnected with what they explain. One reason is that they serve someone's material interests. Another is that they fit into some larger pattern of ideas which influenced jurists for reasons unconnected with its explanatory power. Radical critics like to put these two kinds of explanation together: material interests foster an ideology which causes doctrinal change.

Again, however, it did not happen that way. As we have seen, the major doctrinal changes in the law of contract were not responses to economic needs or the interests of economic classes. They had little economic effect. The late scholastics transformed the intellectual structure of contract law but changed very few rules. Their theories may have prompted some changes—most significantly, in the rule against enforcing executory innominate contracts. Yet, as Bartolus noted in the fourteenth century and Molina in the sixteenth, even that rule had little practical importance. Again, when the nineteenth-century jurists reformulated contract doctrine, few economically important changes occurred, even in England and the United States, where systematic doctrine was an innovation. Entrepreneurs did not significantly benefit when jurists rejected the doctrine of equality in exchange. Lawrence Friedman is one of the most sensitive of legal historians to the social and economic significance of legal rules. Yet, as he has said, in the nineteenth century,

> the concrete body of law *called* contract . . . hardly seemed worthy of the fuss. The law of contracts was essentially negative. Its doctrines gave more or less free play to individual choice. What people voluntarily agreed on, courts would enforce.[39]

That is what courts would have done, by and large, had they been applying the law of the Justianian as glossed by Accursius or the natural law as expounded by Grotius.[40]

Nor can one explain doctrinal change by ideologies or constellations of ideas that supposedly influenced jurists for reasons independent of their explanatory power. We have seen only one case in which a school of jurists systematically shaped doctrine to make it accord with ideas drawn from elsewhere: the late scholastics did so when they built their doctrines around the principles of Thomas Aquinas. Their work was atypical because their project was atypical: it was a self-conscious attempt to revive a particular philosophy and work out its implications. Other jurists borrowed only what contributed to their own quite different projects. Bartolus

[39] L. Friedman, *A History of American Law*, 2nd edn. (New York, 1985), 532–3.

[40] This is not to say that the jurists responsible for doctrinal changes were unconcerned about their economic consequences. Of course, they wished to arrive at results that seemed economically sensible. Thus, as noted, Accursius developed the doctrine of just price in the way he did, in part, because he had no wish to overturn thousands of seemingly normal market transactions. The natural lawyers, despite their belief that all promises were binding, did not insist on enforcing all informal promises of gifts. The 19th-c. lawyers strained their theories to find a doctrine of offer and acceptance that would protect the offeree. Rarely, however, were the jurists formulating doctrines in order to arrive at some new economic result. Nearly always, they were trying to understand economic results which seemed to nearly everyone to be correct.

and Baldus subscribed to the same Aristotelian and Thomistic principles as the late scholastics. They applied them in a different way since their project was to explain the meaning of Roman texts. The project of the natural lawyers was the moral enlightenment of mankind through humane learning. They borrowed from the late scholastics, and from the modern philosophers, only what seemed useful for that task. The nineteenth-century jurists wished to explain the doctrines they had inherited without resort to philosophy and without the use of the Aristotelian terminology in which these doctrines had been cast. They produced will theories by borrowing selectively from traditional doctrine, not by drawing on contemporary philosophy or ideology.

One cannot understand the way these ideas were borrowed and used without appreciating their contribution to the projects in which these jurists were engaged. This contribution cannot be understood by a complete sceptic who believes that all projects are equally impossible regardless of how they are approached. To understand our historical experience we must therefore be able to appreciate degrees of success and to see how success or failure depends upon the inherent difficulties of a project and the explanatory power of the ideas with which it is approached. If we can do so, however, we will not only be able to understand what others have built but to build ourselves.

SOURCES

REFERENCES to Aristotle are in a form that can be found in any modern edition. Quotations are from *The Basic Works of Aristotle*, ed. R. McKeon (1941). Unless otherwise noted, references to treatises on law, philosophy, and theology (other than those by contemporaries) are to the following editions.

MEDIEVAL PHILOSOPHERS AND THEOLOGIANS

Albertus Magnus, *Commentarii in quattuor libros sententiarum Petri Lombardi*, in *Opera omnia*, xxv, ed. A. Borgnet (Paris, 1890).

—— , *Ethica*, in *Opera omnia*, vii, ed. A. Borgnet (Paris, 1890).

Angelus Clavasius (Angelo Carletti), *Summa angelica de casibus conscientialibus* (Venice, 1525).

Antoninus of Florence, *Summa theologica* (Verona, 1740; repr. Graz, 1959).

Baptista Trovamala de Salis (Baptiste de Sale), *Summa roselle de casibus conscientiae* (Strassburg, 1516).

Bartholomaeus de Pisis (Bartolommeo da San Concordio, Pisano), *Summa pisana* (Venice, 1481).

Gabriel Biel, *Epitoma pariter et collectorium circa quattuor sententiarum libros* (Lyons, 1514).

John Duns Scotus, *Quaestiones in quattuor libros sententiarum (Opus oxoniense)*, in *Opera omnia*, viii–xxi, 2nd edn., ed. L. Wadding (Paris, 1893–4).

—— , *Reportata parisiensia in quattuor libros sententiarum*, in *Opera omnia*, xxii–xxiii, 2nd edn., ed. L. Wadding (Paris, 1894).

John of Freiburg, *Summa confessorum* (Augsburg, 1476).

Jean Gerson, *De contractibus*, in *Oeuvres complètes*, ix. 385 (Paris, 1973).

—— , *Summa theologica et canonica* (Venice, 1587).

Sylvester Prierias (Sylvestro Mazzolini da Prierio), *Summa sylvestrina, quae summa summarum, merito nuncupatur* (Venice, 1591).

Thomas Aquinas, *De malo*, in *Opera omnia*, ed. P. Fiaccadori, viii. 219 (Parma, 1852–73).

—— , *In decem libros ethicorum Aristotelis ad Nicomachum expositio*, ed. A. Pirotta (Turin, 1934).

—— , *In duodecim libros metaphysicorum Aristotelis expositio*, ed. M.-R. Cathala and R. M. Spiazzi (Turin, 1950).

—— , *Scriptum super libris magistri sententiarum* (Parma, 1868; repr. New York, 1950).

—— , *Summa theologica* (Biblioteca de autores cristianos, 3rd edn. (Madrid, 1963) (Leonine text).

William of Ockham, *Expositio super primum librum Perihermenias*, cap 1, in *Traditio*, iv. 320–35, ed. P. Boehner (1946).

——, *Quaestiones in librum secundum sententiarum (Reportatio)*, in G. Gal and R. Wood (eds.), *Opera philosophica et theologica: Opera theologica*, v (St Bonaventure, NY, 1981).

——, *Quaestiones variae*, in G. Etzkorn, F. Kelley, and J. Wey (eds.), *Opera philosophica et theologica: Opera theologica*, viii (St Bonaventure, NY, 1984).

——, *Quodlibeta septem*, in J. Wey (ed.), *Opera philosophica et theologica: Opera theologica*, ix (St Bonaventure, NY, 1980).

——, *Scriptum in librum primum sententiarum ordinatio*, in G. Gal, S. Brown, G. Etzkorn and F. Kelley (eds.), *Opera philosophica et theologica: Opera theologica*, i–iv (St Bonaventure, NY, 1970–9).

——, *Summa logicae*, in P. Boehner, G. Gal and S. Brown (eds.), *Opera philosophica et theologica: Opera philosophica*, i (St Bonaventure, NY, 1974).

MEDIEVAL JURISTS

Accursius, *Glossa ordinaria* (Venice, 1581).

Albericus de Rosate, *Commentaria in primam Digesti veteris partem* (Venice, 1585; repr. *Opera iuridica rariora*, xxi, Bologna, 1974).

Anonymous, *Brachylogus* (Frankfurt-on-Main, 1743).

Anonymous, *Distinctiones, Collectio Senesis*, in *Scripta anecdota glossatorum*, ii. 152; in A. Gaudentius (ed.), *Bibliotheca iuridica medii aevi* (Bologna, 1913).

Azo Portius, *Summa Codicis*, in Azo Portius, *Summa aurea* (Lyons, 1557; repr. Frankfurt-on-Main, 1968), fo. 2r.

——, *Summa Institutionum*, in Azo Portius, *Summa aurea* (Lyons, 1557; repr. Frankfurt-on-Main, 1968), fo. 267v.

Baldus de Ubaldis, *Commentaria Corpus iuris civilis* (Venice, 1577).

——, *In Decretalium volumen commentaria* (Venice, 1595; repr. Turin, 1971).

——, *Tractatus de pactis*, printed at the end of the *Commentaria in Digestum Novum* of the *Commentaria Corpus iuris civilis* (Venice, 1577).

Bartolus de Saxoferrato, *Commentaria Corpus iuris civilis* in *Omnia quae extant opera* i–ix (Venice, 1615).

——, *Tractatus de alveo*, in *Omnia quae extant opera*, x (Venice, 1615), fo. 141r.

Cinus de Pistoia, *In Codicem commentaria* (Frankfurt-on-Main, 1578; repr. Turin, 1964).

Hostiensis (Henricus de Segusio), *Summa aurea* (Venice, 1574).

Hugolinus de Presbyteris, *Diversitates sive dissensiones dominorum super toto corpore iure civilis*, ed. G. Haenel (Leipzig, 1834).

Iacobus Butrigarius, *Lectura super Codice* (Paris, 1516; repr. *Opera iuridica rariora*, xiii, Bologna, 1973).

Iacobus de Ravanis, *Lectura super Codice* (publ. under the name of Petrus de Bellapertica) (Paris, 1519; repr. *Opera iuridica rariora*, i, Bologna, 1967). (On the authorship, see E. M. Meijers, *Etudes d'histoire du droit*, iii, *Le Droit romain au moyen âge* (Leiden, 1959), 72–7.)

——, *Super Institutionibus commentaria* (publ. under the name of Bartolus de Saxoferrato in *Omnia quae extant opera* (Venice, 1615). (On the authorship see E. M. Meijers, *Etudes d'histoire du droit*, iii, *Le Droit romain au moyen âge* (Leiden, 1959), 68–9.)

Odofredus, *Lectura super Codice* (Lyons, 1552; repr. *Opera iuridica rariora*, vi, Bologna, 1968).

Petrus de Bellapertica, *Commentaria in Digestum novum Repetitiones variae* (Frankfurt-on-Main, 1571; repr. *Opera iuridica rariora*, x, Bologna, 1968).

——, *In aliquot Digesti veteris leges commentaria* (Frankfurt-on-Main, 1571; repr. in Petrus de Bellapertica, *Digestum Novum Repetitiones variae*, *Opera iuridica rariora*, x, Bologna, 1968).

——, *Lectura Institutionum* (Lyons, 1536; repr. *Opera iuridica rariora*, vii, Bologna, 1972).

——, *Quaestiones vel distinctiones* (Lyons, 1517; repr. *Opera iuridica rariora*, xi, Bologna, 1970).

Raymond of Penafort, *Summa de poenitentia, et matrimonio* (Rome, 1603; repr. Farnborough, Hants., 1967).

Rogerius, *Summa Codicis*, in *Scripta anecdota glossatorum*, in A. Gaudentius (ed.), *Bibliotheca iuridica medii aevi*, i. 47 (Bologna, 1913).

Summa trecensis, publ. as *Summa Codicis des Irnerius*, ed. H. Fitting (Berlin, 1894).

Vacarius, *Liber pauperum*, ed. F. Zulueta (London, 1927).

LATE SCHOLASTICS AND THEIR CONTEMPORARIES

Cajetan (Tomasso de Vio), *Commentaria* to Thomas Aquinas, *Summa theologica* (Padua, 1698).

F. Connanus, *Commentariorum juris civilis libri X* (Naples, 1724).

Conradus Summenhart, *De contractibus licitis atque illicitis tractatus, compendium* (Venice, 1580).

D. Covarruvias, *Variarum ex iure pontificio, regio et caesareo Resolutionum* (Lyons, 1568).

P. Decius, *Consilia* (Venice, 1570).

L. Lessius, *De iustitia et iure, ceterisque virtutibus cardinalis libri quatuor* (Paris, 1628).

I. Medina, *De poenitentia, restitutione, et contractibus* (Ingolstadt, 1581).

L. Molina, *De iustitia et iure tractatus* (Venice, 1614).

P. Parisius, *Consilia* (Venice, 1543).

J. Rubeus, *Consilia* (Lyons, 1540).

D. Soto, *De iustitia et iure libri decem* (Salamanca, 1553).

MODERN PHILOSOPHERS

J. Bentham, *An Introduction to the Principles of Morals and Legislation*, ed. J. H. Burns and H. L. A. Hart (London, 1970).

——. *Principles of the Civil Code*, in *The Works of Jeremy Bentham*, ed. J. Bowring, i. 297 (Edinburgh, 1859).

R. Descartes, *Méditations touchant la première philosophie*, in *Oeuvres philosophiques de Descartes*, ed. F. Alquié ii. 375 (Paris, 1967).

T. Hobbes, *Leviathan or the Matter, Forme and Power of a Commonwealth, Ecclesiaticall and Civill*, ed. A. R. Waller (Cambridge, 1935).

D. Hume, *An Enquiry Concerning the Principles of Morals*, in D. Hume, *Essays Moral, Political, and Literary*, ed. T. H. Green and T. H. Grose, ii. 167 (London, 1882; repr. Aalen, 1964).

——, *A Treatise of Human Nature Being an Attempt to Introduce the Experimental Method of Reasoning into Moral Subjects*, ed. T. H. Green and T. H. Grose (London, 1886; repr. Aalen, 1964).

I. Kant, *Grundlegung zur Metaphysik der Sitten*, ed. K. Vorländer (Leipzig, 1947).

——, *Metaphysische Anfangsgründe der Rechtslehre Erster Teil Metaphysik der Sitten*, ed. B. Ludwig (Hamburg, 1986).

J. Locke, *Essay on Human Understanding*, in *The Works of John Locke* i–iii (London, 1823; repr. Aalen, 1963).

——, *Two Treatises of Government*, in *The Works of John Locke*, v. 207 (London, 1823; repr. Aalen, 1963).

NORTHERN NATURAL LAWYERS AND THEIR CONTEMPORARIES

J. Barbeyrac, *Le Droit de la guerre et de la paix par Hugues Grotius: Nouvelle traduction par Jean Barbeyrac . . . avec les notes de l'auteur même . . . et de nouvelles notes du traducteur* (Amsterdam, 1729).

——, *Le Droit de la nature et des gens, ou système général des principes les plus importants de la morale, de la jurisprudence, et de la politique par le baron de Pufendorf, traduit du latin par Jean Barbeyrac, . . . avec des notes du traducteur; et une préface, qui sert d'introduction à tout l'ouvrage*, 5th edn. (Amsterdam, 1734).

J. Domat, *Les Loix civiles dans leur ordre naturel*, in J. Domat, *Les Loix civiles dans leur ordre naturel: Le droit public, et Legum delectus*, 2nd edn. (Paris, 1713). (The treatise proper begins on p. 1, and is cited, Les Loix civiles'. Preceding it and beginning on p. i is an introduction. 'Traité des loix', cited by that title.)

H. Grotius, *De iure belli ac pacis libri tres*, ed. B. J. A. de Kanter-van Hetting Tromp (Leiden, 1939).

——, *Inleiding tot de Hollandsche Rechts-geleertheyd*, ed. and trans. by R. W. Lee as *The Jurisprudence of Holland* (Oxford, 1926).

R. Pothier, *Traité des obligations*, in *Oeuvres de Pothier annotée et mises en*

corrélation avec le Code civil et la législation actuelle par M. Bugnet, ii. 1, 2nd edn. (Paris, 1861).
—— , *Traité du contrat de vente*, in *Oeuvres de Pothier annotée et mises en corrélation avec le Code civil et la législation actuelle par M. Bugnet*, iii. 1, 2nd edn. (Paris, 1861).
S. Pufendorf, *De iure naturae et gentium libri octo* (Amsterdam, 1688).
C. Thomasius, *Dissertationum academicorum varii inprimis iuridici argumenti* (Halle-on-Saale, 1777).
C. Wolff, *Ius naturae methodo scientifica pertractatum* (Frankfurt-on-Main, 1764).

THE NINETEENTH AND EARLY TWENTIETH CENTURIES

French Jurists

C. Aubry and C. Rau, *Cours de droit civil français d'après la méthode de Zachariae*, 4th edn. (Paris, 1869–71).
A. M. Demante and E. Colmet de Santerre, *Cours analytique de Code Civil*, 2nd edn. (Paris, 1883).
C. Demolombe, *Cours de Code Napoléon* (Paris, 1854–82).
M. Duranton, *Cours de droit français suivant le Code civil*, 3rd edn. (Paris, 1834–7).
E. Glasson, *Eléments du droit français considéré dans ses rapports avec le droit naturel et l'economie politique*, 2nd edn. (Paris, 1884).
M. L. Larombière, *Théorie et pratique des obligations ou commentaire des titres III & IV, livre III, du Code Napoléon art. 1101 à 1386* (Paris, 1857).
F. Laurent, *Principes de droit civil français*, 3rd edn. (Paris, 1869–78).
V. Marcadé, *Explication théorique et pratique du code Napoléon*, 5th edn (Paris, 1859).
C. B. M. Toullier, *Le Droit civil français suivant l'ordre du Code*, 4th edn. (Paris, 1824–37).
R. Troplong, *De la vente ou Commentaire du Titre VI du Livre III du Code Napoléon* (Paris, 1837).
—— , *Des donations entre-vifs et des testaments ou Commentaire du Titre II du Livre III du Code Napoléon* (Paris, 1855).
A. Valette, *Cours de Code Civil* (Paris, 1872).

German Jurists

A. Bechmann, *Der Kauf nach gemeinem Recht* (Erlangen, 1884).
A. Brinz and P. Lotmar, *Lehrbuch der Pandekten*, 2nd edn. (Erlangen, 1892).
C. Bruns, *Kleinere Schriften* (Weimar, 1882).
H. Dernburg, *Pandekten*, 4th edn. (Berlin, 1894).
W. Endemann, *Handbuch des deutschen Handels-, See-, und Wechselrechts* (Leipzig, 1882).
L. Enneccerus, *Rechtsgeschäft, Bedingung und Anfangstermin* (Marburg, 1889).

R. von Holzschuher, *Theorie und Casuistik des gemeinen Civilrechts* (Leipzig, 1864).

F. von Keller, *Pandekten* (Leipzig, 1861).

G. F. Puchta, *Pandekten*, 2nd edn. (Leipzig, 1844).

F. Regelsberger, *Pandekten* (Leipzig, 1893).

——, *Die Vorverhandlungen bei Verträgen* (Weimar, 1868).

F. C. von Savigny, *System des heutigen Römischen Rechts* (Berlin, 1840–8).

S. Schlossmann, *Der Irrtum über wesentliche Eigenschaften der Person und der Sache nach dem Bürgerlichen Gesetzbuch Zugleich in Beitrag zur Theorie der Gesetzesauslegung* (Jena, 1903).

——, *Der Vertrag* (Leipzig, 1876).

J. Seuffert, *Praktisches Pandektenrecht*, 3rd edn. (Wurzburg, 1852).

J. Unger, *System des osterreichischen allgemeinen Privatrechts*, 5th edn. (Leipzig, 1892).

K. von Vangerow, *Leitfaden für Pandekten-Vorlesungen* (Marburg, 1847).

C. von Wächter, *Pandekten* (Leipzig, 1881).

B. Windscheid, *Lehrbuch des Pandektenrechts*, 7th edn. (Frankfurt-on-Main, 1891).

E. Zitelmann, *Irrtum und Rechtgeschaft: Eine psychologisch-juristische Untersuchung* (Leipzig, 1879).

English and American Jurists

C. Addison, *A Treatise on the Law of Contracts*, 11th edn. (London, 1911).

W. Anson, *Principles of the English Law of Contract and of Agency in its Relation to Contract*, 8th edn. (London, 1898).

C. Ashley, *The Law of Contracts* (Boston, 1911).

E. Batten, *A Practical Treatise on the Law relating to the Specific Performance of Contracts* (London, 1849).

J. Bishop, *Commentaries on the Law of Contracts*, 2nd edn. (Chicago, 1907).

W. Blackstone, *Commentaries on the Laws of England* (London, 1766; repr. Chicago, 1979).

J. Chitty, *A Practical Treatise on the Law of Contracts Not under Seal and Upon the Usual Defences to Actions Thereon* (London, 1826).

S. Comyn, *A Treatise on the Law Relative to Contracts and Agreements Not Under Seal* (Flatbush, 1809).

A. Corbin, *Contracts* (St. Paul, Minn., 1963).

E. Fry, *A Treatise on the Specific Performance of Contracts*, 3rd edn. (London, 1892).

L. Hammon, *The General Principles of the Law of Contract* (St Paul, 1912).

O. W. Holmes, Jun., *The Common Law* (Boston, 1881).

J. Kent, *Commentaries on American Law*, 13th edn. (Boston, 1884).

C. C. Langell, *A Summary of the Law of Contracts*, 2nd edn. (Boston, 1880).

S. Leake, *The Elements of the Law of Contracts* (London, 1867).

T. Metcalf, *Principles of the Law of Contracts As Applied by Courts of Law* (New York, 1878).

J. Newland, *A Treatise on Contracts Within the Jurisdiction of Courts of Equity* (Philadelphia, 1821).

T. Parsons, *The Law of Contracts*, 4th edn. (Boston, 1860).

F. Pollock, *Principles of Contract: Being a Treatise on the General Principles concerning the Validity of Agreements in the Law of England*, 4th edn. (London, 1885).

J. Pomeroy, *A Treatise on the Specific Performance of Contracts as it is Enforced by Courts of Equitable Jurisdiction in the United States of America*, 2nd edn. (New York, 1897).

J. Powell, *Essay upon the Law of Contracts and Agreements* (London, 1790).

J. Smith, *The Law of Contracts in a Course of Lectures Delivered at the Law Institution* (Philadelphia, 1847).

J. Story, *Commentaries on Equity Jurisprudence as Administered in England and America*, 14th edn. (Boston, 1918).

W. W. Story, *A Treatise on the Law of Contracts Not Under Seal*, 3rd edn. (Boston, 1851).

W. Taylor, *A Treatise on the Differences Between the Laws of England and Scotland Relating to Contracts* (London, 1849).

S. Williston, *The Law of Contracts* (New York, 1920).

INDEX